Also Available from McGraw-Hill

Schaum's Outline Series in Computers

Each outline includes basic theory, definitions, and hundreds of solved problems and supplementary problems with answers.

Current List Includes:

Boolean Algebra
Computer Graphics
Computers and Business
Computers and Programming
Data Processing
Data Structures
Digital Principles, 2d edition
Discrete Mathematics
Essential Computer Mathematics
Introduction to Computer Science
Microprocessor Fundamentals
Programming with Advanced Structured Cobol
Programming with Basic, 3d edition
Programming with Fortran
Programming with Pascal
Programming with Structured Cobol

Available at Your College Bookstore

COMMON LISP

Wade L. Hennessey

McGraw-Hill Book Company

New York   St. Louis   San Francisco   Auckland   Bogotá   Caracas
Colorado Springs   Hamburg   Lisbon   London   Madrid   Mexico   Milan
Montreal   New Delhi   Oklahoma City   Panama   Paris   San Juan
São Paulo   Singapore   Sydney   Tokyo   Toronto

This book was set in Times Roman by Publication Services.
The editor was David Shapiro;
The production supervisor was F. W. Schulte.
The cover was designed by Joan E. O'Connor.
Cover illustration was done by Anne Green.
Project supervision was done by Publication Services.
R. R. Donnelley & Sons Company was printer and binder.

COMMON LISP

Copyright © 1989 by McGraw-Hill, Inc. All rights reserved. Printed in the United States of America. Except as permitted under the United States Copyright Act of 1976, no part of this publication may be reproduced or distributed in any form or by any means, or stored in a data base or retrieval system, without the prior written permission of the publisher.

2 3 4 5 6 7 8 9 0 DOC DOC 8 9 4 3 2 1 0 9

ISBN 0-07-028177-7

Library of Congress Cataloging-in-Publication Data

Hennessey, Wade L.
    COMMON LISP.
    Includes index.
    Bibliography: p.
    1. COMMON LISP (computer program language)
I. Title.
QA76.73.L23H48   1989   005.13'3   88-27301
ISBN 0-07-028177-7

ABOUT THE AUTHOR

Wade Hennessey received his Bachelor's degree in Mathematical and Computational Science, and his Master's degree in Computer Science, from Stanford University. He has taught Lisp at Stanford University several times, and has worked at the Stanford Artificial Intelligence Laboratory on an implementation of Common Lisp. Wade has also spent several years at Stanford working on a mobile robot to assist severely disabled people, and has worked as a consultant for Lucid, a major Common Lisp vendor. He is currently working on an optimizing compiler for Common Lisp.

To Olga

CONTENTS

	Preface	xv
1	**Introduction**	**1**
1.1	Lisp Usage	1
1.2	A Quick Overview of Lisp's Most Distinguishing Features	3
1.3	Lisp Quasimyths	4
1.4	The Joy of Clueless Programming	5
1.5	Lisp History	6
1.6	Overview of This Book	7
2	**Getting Started**	**9**
2.1	Playing with Lisp	9
	2.1.1 Evaluation	9
2.2	Symbols, Special Forms and Errors	13
2.3	Lists	16
2.4	Equality and Predicates	21
3	**Functions and Recursion**	**27**
3.1	Defining Our Own Functions	27
	3.1.1 The Substitution Model of Function Calls	29
	3.1.2 Side Effects and the Black Box Model of a Function	29
3.2	`IF`	30
3.3	`TRACE`	31
3.4	Recursion	32
	3.4.1 The Photocopier Model of Function Calling	32
	3.4.2 Numeric Recursion	33
	3.4.3 List Recursion	35
	3.4.4 Defining `APPEND` and `REVERSE`	39
4	**A Simple Lisp Program**	**45**
4.1	Program Development	45
4.2	Example: Peano Arithmetic	47
	4.2.1 Adding Integers	48
	4.2.2 Multiplying Integers	50

4.3		Giant-Ints	52
	4.3.1	**LET** Can Name Values	53
	4.3.2	**MEMBER**	55
	4.3.3	Writing **SUCCESSOR** for Giant-Ints	56

5 The Versatility of Lists — 60

5.1		List Equality	60
5.2		Pattern Matching	66
	5.2.1	Association Lists	67
	5.2.2	Implementing **MATCH**	68
	5.2.3	An Application of **MATCH**: Program Rewriting	70
5.3		Lists as Stacks	71
5.4		Lists as Sets	73

6 Data Abstraction and Structures — 75

6.1		Using Lists to Represent Abstract Data Types	75
6.2		**ERROR** and Backtrace	78
6.3		**DEFSTRUCT**	80
	6.3.1	**SETF** Is a Generalized Updating Function	82

7 Destructive Operations — 84

7.1		Memory Organization and Pointers	84
	7.1.1	Building Lists from Cons Cells	86
7.2		Destructive Operations	90
	7.2.1	Modifying Cons Cells	90
	7.2.2	Defining **NREVERSE**	92
	7.2.3	Sequencing and Side-Effects	95

8 Programs = Data — 99

8.1		The Advantage of Having Programs = Data	99
	8.1.1	**EVAL**: Interpreting a Piece of Data as a Program	100
8.2		Taking Derivatives with **DERIV**	101
	8.2.1	Improving **DERIV** with **CASE**	104
	8.2.2	Improving Derivative Specialists with Backquote	106
8.3		Data Driven Programming and **FUNCALL**	108
	8.3.1	Common Lisp Has Separate Function and Value Namespaces	110
	8.3.2	Passing Functions as Arguments	112
8.4		Evaluating Equations	113
	8.4.1	Using **SUBST** and **EVAL**	113
	8.4.2	Evaluating Equations with Bindings	114

9 Consequences of Lexical Scoping — 116

9.1		Mapping Functions	116
	9.1.1	**MAPCAR** Is a Collector	117
	9.1.2	**MAPCAN** Is a Filter	117
9.2		Lambda List Keywords	118
	9.2.1	**&REST** Arguments	118
	9.2.2	**&OPTIONAL** Arguments	121
	9.2.3	**&KEY** Arguments	122

9.3		Lexical Scoping and Anonymous Functions	124
	9.3.1	`LAMBDA`: A Name Is a Terrible Thing to Waste	124
	9.3.2	Lexical Scoping and Functional Objects Interact	127
9.4		Lexical Closures	130
	9.4.1	Capturing Local State with Lexical Closures	131
	9.4.2	Delaying Evaluation with Lexical Closures	133
9.5		`LABELS` and `FLET` Introduce Lexical Function Definitions	134
9.6		Some Other Consequences of Lexical Scoping	135
	9.6.1	Using Lexical Functions Correctly	135
	9.6.2	`EVAL` and the Null Lexical Environment	137
9.7		Dynamic Scoping	138

10 Syntactic Sugar Makes Lisp Taste Better 143

10.1		Iteration	143
	10.1.1	Tail-Recursion: Iteration by Any Other Name	144
	10.1.2	Iteration Viewed as Syntactic Sugar for Tail-Recursion	147
	10.1.3	Tail-Recursion Removal Can Hinder Debugging	147
	10.1.4	Frame Walking and Inspection	149
	10.1.5	`DO`: Yet Another Syntax	151
10.2		`BLOCK` and `RETURN-FROM` Provide Local Control Transfer	154
	10.2.1	Object Lifetimes: `BLOCK` Names Have Dynamic Extent	158
10.3		`CATCH` and `THROW` Provide Dynamic Control Transfer	159
10.4		Multiple Values	161

11 Macros 164

11.1		Program Rewriting With Macros	164
11.2		Macro Examples	166
	11.2.1	`LET` Can Be Written as a Macro	167
	11.2.2	The `ITERATE` Macro	169
	11.2.3	`PROG`: Lisp History	170
	11.2.4	`SELECT: CASE` with Evaluation	171
11.3		Macro Producing Macros	175
	11.3.1	Nested Backquotes	179
11.4		Advanced Macro Issues	181
	11.4.1	Argument Destructuring	181
	11.4.2	`MACROLET`	182
	11.4.3	Macro Restrictions and Problems	184

12 Arrays, Characters, Strings, and Sequences 185

12.1		Simple Arrays	185
	12.1.1	Problems with Linked Lists	185
	12.1.2	Using Arrays	186
12.2		Example: Generating Prime Numbers	187
12.3		Advanced Array Features	189
	12.3.1	Bit Arrays	189
	12.3.2	Multi-dimensional Arrays	189
	12.3.3	Example: Matrix Multiplication	192
	12.3.4	Array Displacement	194
	12.3.5	Fill Pointers and Adjustable Arrays	194

12.4	Characters and Strings	197
	12.4.1 Characters Are Objects	198
	12.4.2 Strings Are Vectors of Characters	198
12.5	Sequence Functions Operate on Lists, Vectors, and Strings	199

13 Input/Output and Tables 202

13.1	Input and Output Streams	202
	13.1.1 `OPEN` and Pathnames	202
13.2	Example: Reading an Index File	204
	13.2.1 `UNWIND-PROTECT`	206
13.3	Example: A Binary File Encoder	208
	13.3.1 `BYTE` Specifiers	211
13.4	Tables	212
	13.4.1 Hash Tables	213
	13.4.2 Lisp History: Property Lists	218

14 Games and Search 221

14.1	Tic-Tac-Toe and Minimax	221
	14.1.1 Trees	221
	14.1.2 Game Trees and Board Ranking	222
	14.1.3 Minimax	224
14.2	Implementing a Tic-Tac-Toe Game Using Minimax	227
	14.2.1 Declarations	227
	14.2.2 A Heuristic Tic-Tac-Toe Board Ranker	229
	14.2.3 Generating and Searching the Game Tree	233
	14.2.4 Putting It All Together	236

15 Missionaries and Cannibals, Backtracking Search 241

15.1	The Problem: Missionaries and Cannibals	241
15.2	A Solution to the Problem	241
	15.2.1 A Backtracking Search Algorithm	241
	15.2.2 Data Structures and Declarations	244
	15.2.3 State Manipulation Functions	245
	15.2.4 A Backtracking Search	248
15.3	Streams	250
	15.3.1 We Can Think of Lists as Eager Streams	250
	15.3.2 Changing Our Implementation to Use Streams	251
	15.3.3 Lazy Streams	252

16 Data Types and Object-Oriented Programming 256

16.1	The Common Lisp Type Hierarchy	256
	16.1.1 Contagion and Coercion	259
	16.1.2 Extending the Type System	261
16.2	Generic Functions	263
	16.2.1 N-ary Functions	265
16.3	Object-Oriented Programming	266
	16.3.1 Using `DEFMETHOD` to Define Generic Functions	267
	16.3.2 Generic Function Examples	268
	16.3.3 Message Passing	269

16.4	Implementing Our Object-Oriented System	270
	16.4.1 Representing and Applying Methods	271
	16.4.2 Representing Generic Functions	272
	16.4.3 Defining Methods	274
16.5	Inheritance	276
	16.5.1 Single Inheritance	276
	16.5.2 Multiple Inheritance	278

17 Logic Programming 281

17.1	Imperative versus Declarative Programming	281
17.2	Prolog in Lisp	283
	17.2.1 Facts	283
	17.2.2 Rules	284
	17.2.3 A Declarative Definition of `APPEND`	287
17.3	Implementing Prolog in Lisp	289
	17.3.1 Unification is Similar to Pattern Matching	289
	17.3.2 Maintaining the Database	292
	17.3.3 Rules and Backtracking	293
	17.3.4 The Inference Engine	297
17.4	Logic Programming Examples	302
	17.4.1 A Simple Natural Language Parser	302
	17.4.2 Prolog Implements Resolution	305
17.5	Advanced Logic Programming Topics	308
	17.5.1 Procedural Attachment	308
	17.5.2 Search and Efficiency	308

18 A Lisp Interpreter 310

18.1	Example: An Evaluator with Implicit Control Flow	310
	18.1.1 Environment Manipulation	316
	18.1.2 Problems with Implicit Control	317
18.2	Continuation Passing Makes Control Flow Explicit	317
	18.2.1 A CPS Version of Factorial	319
	18.2.2 Using CPS to Express Abnormal Control Transfer	320
	18.2.3 Upward Continuations	322

19 Lisp Implementation 325

19.1	Compiling Lisp Code	325
19.2	Storing Type Information	327
	19.2.1 Storing the Type in the Object	328
	19.2.2 Tagged Pointers	328
	19.2.3 Big Bag of Pages (BIBOP)	330
19.3	Dividing Memory into Storage Areas	331
19.4	Function Call Conventions	332
19.5	Dynamic Scoping	333
	19.5.1 Shallow Binding	333
	19.5.2 Deep Binding	335
19.6	Garbage Collection	335
	19.6.1 Stop and Copy	335
	19.6.2 Incremental Stop and Copy	341

		19.6.3 Generation Scavenging	342
		19.6.4 Mark and Sweep	344
		19.6.5 Reference Counting	346

20 Lisp Compilation — 348

- 20.1 Reducing Common Lisp to the Essentials — 348
- 20.2 Source Code Rewriting and Alphatizing — 349
  - 20.2.1 Single versus Multiple Namespaces — 350
  - 20.2.2 Alpha and Beta Conversion — 351
- 20.3 Using Continuation Passing Style as an Intermediate Language — 353
  - 20.3.1 CPS Makes All Temporary Quantities Explicit — 354
  - 20.3.2 Reordering Argument Evaluation — 354
  - 20.3.3 Function Calls and Tail-Recursion Removal — 355
  - 20.3.4 CPS Makes Multiple Values Simple — 355
- 20.4 Meta-Evaluation and Analysis — 356
  - 20.4.1 Meta-Evaluation — 356
  - 20.4.2 Analysis — 357
- 20.5 Register Allocation and Code Generation — 358
  - 20.5.1 Primitive Operations — 358
  - 20.5.2 Register Allocation — 359
  - 20.5.3 Code Generation — 359
- 20.6 Sample Compilation of **FACT** — 360

21 Efficiency and Large Systems — 365

- 21.1 **DECLARE** and Efficiency — 365
  - 21.1.1 Example: Matrix Multiplication — 365
  - 21.1.2 Declaring Variable Types — 366
  - 21.1.3 Speed versus Safety and Time over Space — 368
  - 21.1.4 Adding Declarations to **MATRIX-MULTIPLY** — 369
  - 21.1.5 Additional Declarations — 370
- 21.2 Garbage Avoidance — 371
  - 21.2.1 Taking Advantage of Dynamic Extent—Stack Allocation — 371
  - 21.2.2 Explicit Resource Allocation and Deallocation — 372
- 21.3 Packages — 372
- 21.4 Extensions to Common Lisp — 374
  - 21.4.1 Foreign Function Calls — 375
  - 21.4.2 Error Handling — 375
  - 21.4.3 **LOOP** — 375
  - 21.4.4 Interrupt Handling — 376
  - 21.4.5 Multiprocessing — 377
  - 21.4.6 Parallel Processing — 378
  - 21.4.7 Object-Oriented Programming — 378
  - 21.4.8 Environment Issues — 378
- 21.5 Delivering Applications — 379
- 21.6 Conclusion — 379

Bibliography — 381
Index — 383

PREFACE

This book is about the programming language Lisp. I don't have much to say in the preface, because I've said it in the introductory chapter.

However, I would like to thank David Shapiro, Ingrid Reslmaier and the rest of the editorial staff at McGraw-Hill for their help. I would also like to thank the following people for taking the time to read and comment on portions of this book: Eric Benson, Al Curran, Ron Goldman, Tom Hayse, Fred Lakin, Bill Lewis, Scott Minneman, Eric Schoen, Stefan Michalowski, Mr. Toad (who read it more often than anyone else), John Wambaugh, Wombat, and the following reviewers whose comments were solicited by McGraw-Hill: Michael Lebowitz, Morgan Stanley & Company; Peter Norvig, University of California at Berkeley; John Peterson, University of Arizona; Elaine Rich, Microelectronics and Computer Technology Corp.; and Paul D. Scott, University of Michigan. Finally, I would like to thank Olga for helping with the cover.

Wade L. Hennessey

COMMON LISP

CHAPTER 1

INTRODUCTION

The goal of this book is to introduce modern and practical ideas about writing Lisp programs. Over the last 30 years Lisp has evolved into a language suitable for building a wide range of complex applications. However, almost everyone who starts reading this book wants to learn about Lisp because they think they want to learn about Artificial Intelligence. This is certainly the reason that I first learned Lisp. However, I hope that when you are done with the book you will want to use Lisp for everyday applications as well as for "AI," whatever that is. AI is just the bait.

Lisp is *not* an AI language; rather, AI's primary language is Lisp. Lisp is a general purpose language which in many ways is similar to languages such as C, Fortran, and Pascal, although you would never guess this from the first implementations of Lisp.

1.1 LISP USAGE

Because Lisp takes care of many mundane details that other languages force upon programmers, its primary use is for rapidly developing new programs and solving problems that people do not understand completely. It has been said that solving a problem really amounts to writing a new language in which the solution to that problem can be trivially expressed. Thus, Lisp is often used to build new languages which are useful for describing the solutions to specific kinds of problems. Here are some typical Lisp applications:

- Vision—Trying to emulate human vision is extremely difficult and computationally expensive. High-quality Lisp implementations which can perform numeric computations with efficiency equal to Fortran or C have allowed vision researchers to use the flexibility and rapid program development offered by Lisp.
- Symbolic algebra—Lisp is good at manipulating symbolic data, including other Lisp programs. Symbolic algebra systems such as Macsyma and Reduce are some of the most useful Lisp applications ever written.
- Languages to express programming paradigms—Lisp's simple syntax and ability to manipulate other Lisp programs make it ideal for implementing other language systems. Object-oriented programming and logic programming are two areas in which dozens of special purpose languages have been developed in Lisp.
- Natural language—Understanding English or other natural languages is difficult and not well understood. Lisp's flexible data structures and extensive development environment have made it popular among people building natural language systems.
- Theorem proving—Lisp was originally invented to help prove that programs were correct with respect to a rigorous specification, and to this day it is used by researchers in this area.
- Planners—Programs which try to plan actions such as the path of a robot arm or a mobile robot require a good deal of knowledge about geometry and the real world. Once again Lisp is the premier language for writing such complex programs.
- Text editors—The ease with which Lisp programs may be incrementally extended and tested has made Lisp a popular language for implementing text editors. Gnuemacs is one of the most popular Lisp-based text editors ever written.
- Systems programming—Special purpose Lisp machines implement primitive Lisp operations in hardware. All the system software, from the device drivers to the window system, is written in Lisp. Virtually all Lisp compilers as well as compilers for languages such as ADA have also been written in Lisp.
- Computer-aided design—Lisp has been used to build complex mechanical and VLSI design systems, which require a high level of integration with other tools such as simulators and intelligent design aids.
- Education—Lisp has become a popular introductory programming language. Lisp's simple syntax and interactive nature make it easy to start writing and testing programs. At the same time, Lisp's powerful ability to deal with functions makes it useful for introducing programming ideas which are difficult to implement in other languages.

Lisp tends to be most often used in applications which are not fully understood or in situations in which flexibility and extensibility are especially important.

1.2 A QUICK OVERVIEW OF LISP'S MOST DISTINGUISHING FEATURES

This section summarizes some of Lisp's most distinctive features.

- *Functions*—The function is the hallmark of Lisp. A function accepts some data as *arguments*, performs a computation with the data, and passes the result of that computation (some new data) to another function which needs the information to continue computing. Functions themselves may be created and passed around just like numbers or strings.
- *Recursion*—Lisp naturally supports and encourages the definition of a function or data structure in terms of itself, just as the definition of factorial can be expressed in terms of itself. Recursive functions and recursive data structures such as linked lists are exploited to great benefit.
- *Automatic storage allocation*—Lisp automatically creates data such as numbers, functions, or lists as they are needed. When a piece of data is no longer needed, its machine resources are automatically recovered so that they can be used to create new pieces of data. By comparison, a language such as C requires that you explicitly allocate and deallocate resources for data, which is a burden on the programmer and leads to obscure bugs.
- *Programs equal data*—The list is the primary data structure in Lisp, and all Lisp programs are written as lists. Hence, Lisp programs are Lisp data! This is an extremely useful feature because it allows one Lisp program to easily analyze, create, and execute other Lisp programs. Lisp itself takes advantage of this capability by providing an extremely powerful macro facility which allows us to extend the syntax of the language.
- *Data types*—Each piece of data in Lisp also has *data type* information associated with it. This type can always be determined at any point during the data's lifetime, allowing Lisp to perform *runtime type checking*. It also eliminates the need for the programmer to declare what type of data a variable will hold, since data is typed, not variables. Contrast this with a language such as C. If we pass an integer to a C function, that function has no way of knowing at runtime whether it was passed an integer, a floating point number, or a string, because C data does not have type information associated with it. Instead, the function must rely on declarations about the data type of each argument and hope that callers of the function pass only the appropriate types of data.[1]
- *Generic functions*—Associating type information with data also leads to a uniform way of implementing *generic functions* and *object-oriented* programs, which determine at runtime how to perform a computation, based upon the type

---

[1] Later we will see that Lisp also relies on declarations to execute as quickly as possible on standard hardware.

of data they are passed. For example, a function such as + is generic because it can add many different kinds of numbers. If we introduce a new kind of numeric data type and tell + how to handle that data type, then we can expect all of our existing numeric code to work correctly without any changes.

- *Debugging and programming environment*—The dynamic nature of Lisp leads to an environment in which small changes can easily be tried, tested, and examined. The data type and function call information which Lisp maintains at runtime help in debugging. The current generation of special purpose Lisp machines provides perhaps the most sophisticated programming environment available anywhere.

1.3 LISP QUASIMYTHS

There are many quasimyths about Lisp. I'll call them quasimyths because they are much truer than many Lisp fanatics would like you to believe, but they are nevertheless false.

The most common myth is that Lisp is intrinsically slow. Unfortunately, the vast majority of the Lisp implementations in the world are slow in comparison to more conventional languages, and thus they are not attractive for writing programs for widespread use. However, that slowness is generally due to a lack of effort, interest, or knowledge on the part of a Lisp implementor, and there are several high-quality Lisp implementations today. There are only a few language features, such as automatic storage allocation and runtime type checking, which make it difficult to run Lisp quickly on standard hardware.

Another misconception is that Lisp can deal only with lists, integers, and symbols. Lisp provides a wide variety of data types, including hash tables, complex numbers, ratios, and complicated arrays. The extensibility of Lisp makes it easy to create new data types which integrate well with other data types and operations in Lisp.

Lisp also has a reputation for being slow at numeric computations. However, applications such as symbolic algebra, computer graphics, and vision have caused Lisp implementors to pay special attention to making Lisp as efficient as C or Fortran at numerically intensive applications. Lisp's ability to easily manipulate functions and compose new programs makes it exceptionally good at building libraries of complex numerical algorithms.

Although Lisp can run efficiently on standard hardware, it is often justly accused of being a memory hog. Lisp does not have to use much more memory than any other programming systems, but many Lisp implementors have taken the view that memory is "cheap, and getting cheaper all the time." Hence, some Lisps have been built without much attention being paid to memory requirements. The truth is that most machines in the world today do not have nearly the amount of memory some Lisp implementors wish they had, so Lisp's memory needs are sometimes an obstacle to its usage. Fortunately, this situation is changing.

1.4 THE JOY OF CLUELESS PROGRAMMING

The most interesting programs are the ones we do not know how to write. The combined effect of Lisp's features is a programming environment conducive to building large, complicated solutions to problems which are only partially understood. When trying to solve difficult problems, we need all the help we can get from our computer so that we can concentrate on solving the problem at hand.

It is commonly acknowledged that structured programming is a useful tool for building complex programs. Unfortunately, most languages require that you tediously specify all aspects of the problem you are trying to solve before you can write a working program. For example, a language such as Pascal requires that you declare the data type of every variable your program will use. Once this is done, it can be cumbersome to successively refine or make major improvements to the original program. For example, imagine writing a large program and then trying to add a new kind of numeric data type to allow infinite precision integer arithmetic. Such an addition would probably require massive changes to your original program even though what you have done is conceptually simple. Many languages are nice for building large, rigid structures, but changing and maintaining those structures is often like chiseling stone.

Lisp is different. Lisp has been compared to a ball of mud or to a living organism. Indeed, Lisp is a very fluid medium for expressing ideas. We can try to state the solution to a problem with little fuss about what type of variable SNARK will always be, or exactly how many arguments the function PLAN-PATH must always take. Most Lisp development systems allow us to write, test, debug, and change programs incrementally at *any* time — even while the program is running! This makes program development much faster than a system which requires that we recompile and link entire files of functions and declarations whenever we want to test the effect of a tiny change in our program.

Building complex programs requires more than simply decomposing a problem into many smaller pieces. It is more important to imagine a more general problem of which our problem is a specific instance. If we can discover a more general problem which encompasses our particular problem as a subcase, then we are on our way to building reusable, elegant programs. For example, if we want to sort an array of 57 test scores, we could write a special function which took precisely such an array and then proceeded to sort the integers in that array from lowest to highest. However, if we later discover that we also need to sort an array of 1456 records by the LAST-NAME field in each record, should we have to write a whole new sorting procedure? Of course not. Details such as the length of the array, how we access the sorting key, or what test we should use to compare keys are parameters which control the more general problem of sorting. In fact, whether we want to sort a linked list or an array shouldn't really matter, although that may affect the actual algorithm we use. Some languages make the creation of a general sorting function nearly impossible because they insist that we declare too many parameters of the problem ahead of time. The need to make decisions *statically* rather than *dynamically* has hurt us. Lisp, however, is quite conducive to writing such a general sorting function. In fact, Lisp already contains one.

Generalizing a problem is easier said than done, and we often will not realize how to generalize it until we have worked with it for a while. Thus, the ability to go back and rework what we have already written into a more general solution for a problem is extremely important. Trying to learn more about a problem by writing a program is sometimes called *exploratory programming*.[2]

1.5 LISP HISTORY

Lisp 1.5 was the first popular dialect of Lisp. It was invented around 1960 by John McCarthy at MIT. Various other dialects of Lisp sprouted from Lisp 1.5, and by the mid-70s Maclisp [Pit83] and Interlisp [Tei78] had become the two most important Lisp dialects. Unfortunately, the two dialects differed in a multitude of ways, and so it was difficult to port a program from one dialect to another. At around the same time, a very simple and elegant dialect of Lisp called Scheme [RC86] was invented by Guy Lewis Steele and Gerald Sussman. This dialect of Lisp was a cross between Lisp and Algol, and its most distinguishing features were its use of lexical scoping and its simplicity.

Unfortunately, each time a new kind of processor came out, a different kind of Lisp dialect was usually invented to run on it. An attempt was made at the University of Utah to produce a portable dialect of Lisp known as Portable Standard Lisp (PSL) [GB82], but it was incompatible with both Maclisp and Interlisp. As new processors and operating systems were developed, new dialects of Lisp such as Franz Lisp and NIL, the New Implementation of Lisp [BCE84], were developed. These new dialects were fairly compatible with Maclisp, but they also introduced a slew of new features. Scheme inspired another dialect of Lisp known as T, while people at MIT built special purpose Lisp hardware and their own dialect of Lisp known as Zetalisp.

By the early 80s, Lisp was exploding in a dozen incompatible directions, ensuring that it would never enter the computing mainstream. If Lisp was ever to grow beyond its niche as an AI research language, then some common dialect of Lisp had to be agreed upon by the supporters of the major dialects of Lisp. After about two years of discussion, almost all of which was by electronic mail, *Common Lisp the Language* [Ste84] was published.[3] It describes Common Lisp, a dialect which most of the major Lisp wizards in the world agreed upon. However, Common Lisp is more like the union of all known Lisp dialects rather than the intersection. It seems to be much easier to add a new feature than it is to remove one when trying to compromise on a language design.

---

[2] Also known as hacking.
[3] The design of Common Lisp and the resulting language would make an interesting book in itself.

This book describes Common Lisp, and the terms *Lisp* and *Common Lisp* are used interchangeably. Scheme and its relatives are the only other significant dialects of Lisp used today, and Scheme had a significant influence on the design of Common Lisp—notably on the decision to make Common Lisp lexically scoped. We will examine Common Lisp in this book not because it is better or worse than Scheme, but because it embodies most of the good Lisp features developed over the last three decades and is available on more different kinds of hardware than any other Lisp in the world.

1.6 OVERVIEW OF THIS BOOK

The term *Lisp* really refers to a family of languages united by a small core of features. For example, all dialects of Lisp are good at dealing with lists, functions, and recursion. This core provides a foundation upon which one can construct sophisticated and complex systems. Lisp is a simple, easy-to-learn language; Common Lisp is not.

Because Common Lisp tries to standardize upon so many extensions to the core of Lisp, it is a huge language which contains around 700 functions. There is no reason why we could not have written most of Common Lisp ourselves in terms of the core of Lisp, but to become proficient Common Lisp programmers we must learn what facilities have been standardized. In this book we will examine important examples of all the major parts of Common Lisp, but we will not exhaustively describe every single function and nuance. That need is best served by the Common Lisp manual [Ste84] itself. Instead we will concentrate on effectively using the features provided by Common Lisp to implement useful programming paradigms.

This book can be roughly divided into two major sections. The first section extends approximately from Chapter 1 through the end of Chapter 10. By the end of Chapter 10, most of the essential aspects of Lisp have been covered. The second section discusses more advanced ideas and introduces paradigms such as object-oriented programming and logic programming. The efficient use and implementation of Lisp are also discussed.

The discussions in this book generally assume that you are familiar with another computer language such as C or Pascal. While it is not absolutely essential that you know another language, you should at least be familiar with the overall structure and operation of your computer and a text editor.

Replacing variable assignment by variable binding is emphasized throughout the book. This tends to be one of the hardest ideas for programmers experienced in more traditional languages to get used to, but it is also one of the most important. In this case, knowing another computer language is actually a detriment, since people with fewer preconceptions seem to have an easier time accepting the functional style of Lisp programs.

When a new feature is introduced in this book, I will often lie about it. By this I mean that the whole truth may not be revealed immediately for the sake of explanation. Do not be alarmed if you read something which you know is somewhat incorrect. We may just be skipping over some features which cloud the issues we are discussing at the moment.

This book also tries to concentrate on introducing features as we need them to solve problems rather than grouping all related features together as a manual would. It is in no way an attempt to replace *Common Lisp the Language*, the definitive reference manual for Common Lisp. In fact it is expected that any serious Lisp user will also have that manual. The book instead concentrates on giving you an appropriate background for understanding everything in the manual, and more importantly for understanding when and how to properly use the distinctive features of Lisp.

CHAPTER 2

GETTING STARTED

2.1 PLAYING WITH LISP

The only way to really learn about Lisp is to write lots of Lisp programs. You should head directly to your computer and start a Common Lisp session:

```
my-favorite-computer-prompt> Lisp
;;; Common Lisp by Grandiose System Building
;;; Version 2.781

Lisp>
```

The exact command used to invoke Common Lisp varies from system to system. Once Lisp has started, you will usually be greeted with some sort of banner announcing what version of Lisp you are running and who wrote it. After that you may or may not see a prompt indicating that Lisp is ready for you to type something. The imaginary Lisp system used in this book will always present us with the prompt `Lisp>` when it is waiting for input.

2.1.1 Evaluation

The program we are now talking to is a Lisp *interpreter*. We can type an *expression* to the interpreter, and it will *evaluate* the expression according to the rules of Lisp and print out the result. An expression is sometimes called a *form* and is the name we use to describe a program which Lisp can evaluate. For example, here is how we can use Lisp to do arithmetic:

9

```
Lisp> (- 49 2.781)
46.219

Lisp> (+ 1 4 9)
14

Lisp> (* 121 7)
847

Lisp>
```

Most Lisp systems also have a *compiler* which can translate Lisp code into a lower level form, such as machine language, which can be directly executed by a computer. Compiling our programs will make them run faster and should not change their meaning. However, compiling programs takes time and may make them harder to debug, so we will usually use the interpreter to test and debug our programs. Most Lisp systems also provide convenient ways to edit and incrementally redefine functions. We will discuss these issues in more detail later.

Notice that a new Lisp prompt comes back after Lisp has evaluated the expression we just entered. Lisp is actually in an infinite loop called a *read-eval-print loop*. The loop is so named because it reads a single Lisp expression, evaluates that expression, and then prints the result of the evaluation. The loop then repeats until we exit Lisp.

The most interesting part of the read-eval-print loop is the evaluator. In order to ask Lisp to multiply two numbers, we enter a *list* consisting of three things: an operation which we want to perform and the two things we want to perform that operation on. We denote the start of a list with an open parenthesis, and the end of the list with a closing parenthesis. Between the parentheses we put the individual elements of the list, separating the elements with *whitespace*. Typically whitespace is just a regular space, but it could be a tab, a carriage return, or one of several other characters.

The Lisp interpreter evaluates the list according to the following rules:

1. Treat the first element of the list as a *function* which expects zero or more *arguments*. In our example, the function is *, which can take any number of arguments (even zero arguments). The interpreter doesn't actually do anything with the function yet.

2. Ask the Lisp interpreter to recursively evaluate each of the remaining elements of the list from left to right. An argument is evaluated exactly as if we had typed that argument directly to the Lisp prompt from our terminal. However, instead of printing the result of each argument evaluation, each individual result is saved until all of the arguments have been evaluated.

3. Once all the arguments have been evaluated, *call* the function we found as the first element of the list with all the results we obtained by evaluating the

arguments. The function will take the evaluated arguments and perform some sort of operation on them, eventually returning a result.

In our multiplication example, the Lisp interpreter examines the first element of the list (* 121 7) to be sure that it is the name of a function.[1] After that it recursively asks the Lisp interpreter to evaluate the number 121, since 121 is the first argument to the function *.

In Lisp, any number evaluates to itself. In order to convince ourselves of this, we can type numbers directly into Lisp and look at the results:

```
Lisp> 121
121

Lisp> 7
7
```

When the Lisp interpreter evaluates the number 121 during the evaluation of (* 121 7) it gets back the result 121. However, rather than printing the result out, it saves it away and proceeds to evaluate the next argument. Evaluating the next argument returns a 7 which Lisp also saves away.

At this point there are no more arguments to evaluate, so both of the evaluated arguments which have been saved away are handed off to the function *. The function * then multiplies the two numbers together and returns the number 847. The read-eval-print loop now has now finished evaluating the list (* 121 7), so it prints out the result 847 and prompts the user for another expression to read.

The function * will multiply any number of arguments together and return the result. For example, suppose that we want to determine the volume of a cylinder. The formula for finding the volume of a cylinder is $\pi r^2 h$, where r is the radius of the cylinder and h is the height of the cylinder. Thus, we can compute the volume of a cylinder with radius 11 and height 7:

```
Lisp> (expt 11 2)        ; radius squared
121

Lisp> (* 3.1415927 121 7)  ; pi * radius squared * height
2660.929
```

Notice that we can leave a *comment* on any line by preceding the comment with a semicolon. Lisp will ignore any input from the semicolon until the end

---

[1] Sometimes Common Lisp may not examine the function until *after* all the arguments have been evaluated. This often happens when code is compiled.

of the line, since that part of the line is intended for human, not computer, consumption.

EXPT is a function which expects exactly two numbers and uses the second number as an exponent for the first. Thus, (**EXPT 11 2**) squares the radius of our cylinder. We can then multiply π times the radius squared times the height of the cylinder to determine its volume. However, we can also do the following:

```
Lisp> (* 3.1415927 (expt 11 2) 7)
2660.929
```

Each argument to a function can be *any* other Lisp expression. Looking back at the second step of our rules for evaluation, this makes sense. In the case of *, the only requirement is that each form we pass as an argument must evaluate to a number, since the function * can only multiply numbers together.

Here are some other examples of numeric functions:

```
Lisp> (- 2 5)
-3

Lisp> (- 3)
-3

Lisp> (- 10 2 7)
1
```

Subtracting 1 from a number is so common that a shorthand function called 1- exists. This function expects a single numeric argument and returns that number minus 1. Notice that it does not subtract the number *from* 1. A similar function called 1+ adds one to its argument:

```
Lisp> (- 10 1)
9

Lisp> (1- 10)
9

Lisp> (+ 10 1)
11

Lisp> (1+ 10)
11
```

Some people find the use of 1- and 1+ to be stylistically objectionable, preferring to explicitly use + or - instead.

We can also perform more complicated numeric operations:

```
Lisp> (sqrt pi)
1.7724539

Lisp> (cos 1)
0.5403023

Lisp> (atan 4)
1.3258177
```

Problem. Translate the following Lisp expressions into regular algebraic notation:

```
(+ 97 34)
(* (- 27 (sin x)) (+ 4 (/ 3.14 16)))
(/ 75 21 9 (+ 8 11))
```

Problem. Translate the following polynomials into Lisp:

1. $xyz + 3(u+v)^{-3}$
2. $(xy - yx)/(xy + yx)$
3. $\pi + 7.77$

2.2 SYMBOLS, SPECIAL FORMS, AND ERRORS

Lisp allows us to give symbolic names to data, and some constants are already defined by Common Lisp. For example, rather than typing the value of π in every time we need it, we can refer to it by entering the symbol PI:

```
Lisp> pi
3.1415927

Lisp> (* pi (expt 11 2) 7)
2660.929
```

A Lisp symbol can include almost all the characters on your keyboard, including the character -. Thus, JUST-A-JUMP-TO-THE-LEFT is *one* symbol.

When Lisp evaluates a symbol it returns that symbol's *value*. Symbols such as PI and CALL-ARGUMENTS-LIMIT are constants which can never be changed. When a constant symbol is evaluated we will always get back the same value.

Sometimes we want to be able to enter a symbol and *not* have it evaluated. For example, we may want the interpreter to print out the symbol PI rather than the *value* of the symbol:

```
Lisp> (quote pi)
PI
```

When the interpreter tries to evaluate the list (QUOTE PI) it does not obey the rules of evaluation it followed when evaluating (* 121 7). The reason is that QUOTE is actually a *special form*. There are a moderate number of special forms in Lisp which do not obey the normal function calling rules which were presented above.

When the evaluator examines the first element of a list, it checks to see if that symbol names one of the special forms the evaluator knows about. If the symbol is not a special form, then it must be a function like *, so the left-to-right argument evaluation rule applies; however, if the first element of a list is a special form, then the remaining arguments are treated in a different way which is dependent upon the purpose of the special form.

The special form QUOTE expects a single argument. All QUOTE does is return that argument *without* evaluating it. Rather than evaluating PI and calling a function called QUOTE with the number 3.1415927, the symbol PI is immediately returned. Thus, QUOTE allows us to inhibit evaluation.

Notice that although we typed the symbol in lower case, the symbol we got back from the interpreter is printed in upper case. Lisp converts all symbols into upper case as soon as they are read. Thus, the symbols Gravitational-Constant and GRAVITATIONAL-CONSTANT and gravitational-constant all get turned into the symbol GRAVITATIONAL-CONSTANT as soon as they are read into Lisp. All Lisp expressions which are referenced from the text of this book will be written entirely in upper case to make them more readable.

If we want to find out the value of GRAVITATIONAL-CONSTANT, then we can type GRAVITATIONAL-CONSTANT directly to the interpreter:

```
Lisp> gravitational-constant
>>Error: GRAVITATIONAL-CONSTANT has no global value

SYMBOL-VALUE:
   Required arg 0 (S): GRAVITATIONAL-CONSTANT

:A    Abort to Lisp Top Level
:C    Try evaluating GRAVITATIONAL-CONSTANT again
->
```

The interpreter tried to look up the value of the symbol GRAVITATIONAL-CONSTANT and print it. However, since we never gave the symbol GRAVITATIONAL-CONSTANT a value, and GRAVITATIONAL-CONSTANT does not have a predefined value in Lisp, the interpreter signaled an error. Whenever the interpreter runs into a problem, it will enter the *debugger* with a message describing the problem. The debugger provides special commands to help us determine the reason for the error.

Common Lisp does not specify how the debugger should work or what error message should be printed when the Lisp system runs into a problem. However, the debugger is an important part of the Lisp system which we'll have to use.

In this book we will use a typical Lisp debugger, but you will have to refer to the manual for your Lisp to determine the exact commands understood by your debugger.

Now we are talking to a new read-eval-print loop, and the prompt has changed from `Lisp>` to `->` to remind us that we are in the middle of a *broken computation*. We entered the debugger because the interpreter had trouble evaluating the form we gave it. Rather than just giving up, the interpreter told us about the problem and has given us two choices to resolve it. We can tell the interpreter to just forget the whole thing by typing `:A`, causing us to exit the debugger and return to the top-level read-eval-print loop. We can also try to fix the problem in the debugger and then type `:C` to try to *continue* the broken computation.

In order to continue from our current error we have to give `GRAVITATIONAL-CONSTANT` a value. We can give a symbol a value with the special form `SETF`:

```
-> (setf gravitational-constant 9.8)
9.8

-> gravitational-constant
9.8
```

`SETF` is a special form which expects two arguments: a symbol and any Lisp expression. The symbol is *not* evaluated, but the Lisp expression is. The symbol is then given the value returned by the evaluation of the second argument, and that value is also returned as the result of the call to `SETF`.

At this point we have corrected the error which caused us to enter the debugger. The computation which signaled an error has been suspended for the entire time that we've been in the debugger, but now we can continue that computation:

```
-> :C
Will try to evaluate GRAVITATIONAL-CONSTANT again
9.8

Lisp>
```

The special debugger command `:C` causes the debugger to print out the message `Will try to evaluate GRAVITATIONAL-CONSTANT again` to indicate what it will to continue from the error. Now we have given `GRAVITATIONAL-CONSTANT` a value, so the evaluation succeeds and returns `9.8`. Notice that the `9.8` which is printed is the result of our original attempt to evaluate `GRAVITATIONAL-CONSTANT` and we are now back at the top-level `Lisp>` prompt.

Problem. Try evaluating the following forms:

```
(* 7 (/ 10 2) 9.8)
(quote 7)
'7
7
(quote g)
'g
g
(setf g 9.8)
(* 7 (/ 10 2) g)
(/ g 0)
```

2.3 LISTS

So far we've given commands to the Lisp interpreter as lists of symbols and numbers; however, we can also use lists as pieces of data, just as numbers are pieces of data. For example, we can maintain a list of colors:

```
Lisp> (setf colors (red green blue))
>>Error: RED has no global function definition

SYMBOL-FUNCTION:
   Required arg 0 (S): RED

:A     Abort to Lisp Top Level
:C     Try evaluating #'RED again
->
```

This call to **SETF** has resulted in an error. Since **SETF** always evaluated its second argument, it treated the list (RED GREEN BLUE) as though it were a call to the function RED with the arguments GREEN and BLUE, rather than treating it as a piece of data. Hence, we end up in the debugger with an error telling us that RED is not a function. To fix this problem, we need to use QUOTE to prevent Lisp from evaluating our list:

```
Lisp> (setf colors (quote (red green blue)))
(RED GREEN BLUE)
```

QUOTE is used to determine whether or not we want to use a Lisp expression as a piece of data or as a program, where the word *program* refers to an expression Lisp can evaluate. Consider the following:

```
Lisp> (setf quark (* 121 7))
847

Lisp> quark
847
```

```
Lisp> (setf quark (quote (* 121 11)))
(* 121 11)

Lisp> quark
(* 121 11)
```

In the first call to SETF, the list (* 121 7) is treated as a program, so it is evaluated according to the rules we learned earlier. However, in the second call to SETF, the list is quoted. QUOTE stopped the evaluation of the list (* 121 11), and thus it was treated as a piece of data. QUOTE is frequently used in Lisp programs, and it has a more compact notation:

```
Lisp> (quote quark)
QUARK

Lisp> 'quark
QUARK
```

Preceding any Lisp expression by the character '[2] is exactly equivalent to wrapping the expression in a call to QUOTE. We will usually use this shorthand notation.

Now that we can treat lists as pieces of data, we need to be able to take them apart, examine them, compare them to other lists, and build new lists. Lisp has many functions which can manipulate lists. We can examine the first element of a list with the function CAR:

```
Lisp> (setf quark '(drongo wombat ocelot))
(DRONGO WOMBAT OCELOT)

Lisp> (car quark)
DRONGO

Lisp> quark
(DRONGO WOMBAT OCELOT)
```

CAR is a function which expects a single list as an argument. CAR returns the first element of that list as the value of the call to CAR. Notice that the original list is not altered in any way.

The function CDR is closely related to CAR. CDR also expects a single list as an argument, but it returns a list consisting of all but the first element of the list it is given:

---

[2]Otherwise known as a quote, single quote, or an apostrophe

```
Lisp> (cdr quark)
(WOMBAT OCELOT)

Lisp> quark
(DRONGO WOMBAT OCELOT)
```

Notice that the original list is once again unchanged. `CDR` is pronounced *could-er*.

Now that we can take lists apart, we need to be able to build new lists. The most primitive function in Lisp for putting lists together is `CONS`:

```
Lisp> (setf temp '(OCELOT))
(OCELOT)

Lisp> (cons 'wombat temp)
(WOMBAT OCELOT)

Lisp> temp
(OCELOT)
```

`CONS` expects two arguments. The second argument should evaluate to a list, while the first argument may evaluate to anything.[3] `CONS` returns a new list which is built by adding the first argument to the front of the list passed as the second argument. Notice that the original list is not altered in any way.

`CAR`, `CDR`, and `CONS` are the most primitive ways to manipulate lists in Lisp. Figure 2.1 indicates the relationship of these three functions. `CONS` is a *constructor* function which can be used to build new lists, while `CAR` and `CDR` are *accessing* functions which allow us to pull lists apart:

```
Lisp> (setf temp '(first second))
(FIRST SECOND)
```

---

[3]When we learn about dotted pairs we will see that this restriction is not necessary.

```
(CAR '(FIRST SECOND)) → FIRST
                                    ⟩— (CONS 'FIRST' (SECOND)) → (FIRST SECOND)
(CDR '(FIRST SECOND)) → (SECOND)
```

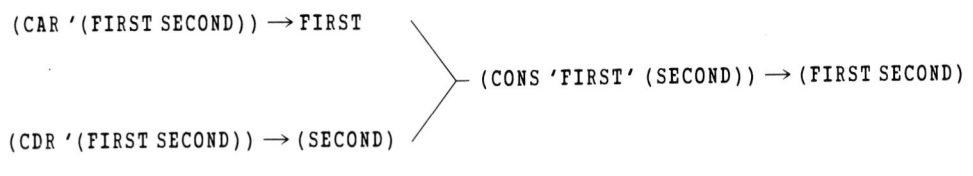

FIGURE 2.1
The relationship of `CAR`, `CDR`, and `CONS`.

```
Lisp> (car temp)
FIRST

Lisp> (cdr temp)
(SECOND)

Lisp> (cons (car temp) (cdr temp))
(FIRST SECOND)

Lisp> (car '((first) second))
(FIRST)
```

Notice that `CDR` always returns a list, while `CAR` may or may not return a list. Using combinations of `CAR` and `CDR` we can dissect a list in various ways:

```
Lisp> quark
(DRONGO WOMBAT OCELOT)

Lisp> (car (cdr quark))
WOMBAT

Lisp> (car (cdr (cdr quark)))
OCELOT
```

The names `CAR` and `CDR` may seem a bit strange. They actually come from the original implementation of Lisp on the IBM 704 computer, where `CAR` meant Contents of Address Register, while `CDR` meant Contents of Decrement Register. Common Lisp has a function called `FIRST` which is identical to `CAR`, and a function called `REST` which is identical to `CDR`. So why keep the old names around?

One reason is the historical significance of `CAR` and `CDR` in Lisp code. Another reason is that nested combinations of `CAR` and `CDR` sometimes occur in Lisp programs, and some specially named functions can be used to replace these combinations:

```
Lisp> (car (cdr quark))
WOMBAT

Lisp> (cadr quark)
WOMBAT

Lisp> (car (cdr (cdr quark)))
OCELOT

Lisp> (caddr quark)
OCELOT
```

The letters A and D may be inserted between a C and an R to represent various nested combinations of CAR and CDR, where each A stands for a call to CAR, while each D stands for a call to CDR. All combinations of CAR and CDR up to four nested calls are predefined in this way. If we need more than four nested calls to CAR and CDR, our program is probably a loser and should be rewritten.

Lisp also provides the functions FIRST through TENTH for accessing list elements, and the function REST for returning all but the first element of a list:

```
;;; FIRST is identical to CAR
Lisp> (first '(drongo wombat ocelot))
DRONGO

;;; REST is identical to CDR
Lisp> (rest '(drongo wombat ocelot))
(WOMBAT OCELOT)

Lisp> (second '(drongo wombat ocelot))
WOMBAT

Lisp> (third '(drongo wombat ocelot))
OCELOT
```

It is clearer to use a function such as THIRD rather than a function such as CADDR in our programs, so we will not frequently need nested combinations of CAR and CDR.

Problem. Try evaluating the following forms:

```
(setf colors '(red orange (yellow green ((blue) indigo)
            violet)))
(car 'colors)
(car colors)
(cdr 'colors)
(cdr colors)
(caaddr colors)
(caaddr (caddr colors))

(setf animals '(cat dog))
(cons 'rat animals)
animals
(cons '(horse cow) animals)
```

Problem. Write Lisp expressions to extract each color from the list (RED ORANGE (YELLOW GREEN ((BLUE) INDIGO) VIOLET)). For this exercise, use only combinations of CAR and CDR to be sure that you understand how they work.

2.4 EQUALITY AND PREDICATES

It is often necessary to determine when two pieces of data are equal to each other. The concept of equality is not quite as simple as it seems at first glance. For example, two separate copies of this book are equal to each other in the sense that the picture on the cover is the same, they each have the same number of pages, the same text, etc. However, two separate copies of this book are *not* equal in the sense that they are two distinct objects in the world. The book you are holding is equal to itself not only in the above sense (same cover, text, etc.), but also in the sense that there is exactly *one* instance of the book you are holding in the entire world.

At this point we need to clearly understand the difference between an *object* and an *object reference*. All types of data and programs in Lisp are known as *objects*. For example, when we enter the list (MEAN GRINCH), some computer memory is set aside to represent a list object. When a function wants to return a list like (MEAN GRINCH), it must return an *object reference*. An object reference is often called a *value* or a *pointer*, and it describes the chunk of computer memory which holds the object itself. Thus, it is possible to have many distinct references to a single object.

Now consider what happens when we enter the symbol SNARK twice:

```
Lisp> 'snark
SNARK

Lisp> 'snark
SNARK
```

Lisp could create two distinct objects which represent the symbol SNARK and return object references to different objects. However, only one copy of a symbol exists in Lisp. Every time we enter the symbol SNARK, Lisp looks inside its memory to see if a symbol with that name already exists. If so, then an object reference to the existing symbol is returned. If not, then a new symbol with the name SNARK is created and a reference to it is returned. Thereafter, every time we enter SNARK that symbol will be found. Thus, every symbol in Lisp is unique. The function EQ tests to see if two object references refer to the same object:

```
Lisp> (eq 'snark 'snark)
T

Lisp> (eq 'snark 'no-way)
NIL

Lisp> (setf s1 'snark)
SNARK
```

```
Lisp> (setf s2 'snark)
SNARK

Lisp> (eq s1 s2)
T
```

EQ expects exactly two arguments. If the two arguments both evaluate to the same object inside our computer, then EQ will return the symbol T. If the two arguments do not reference exactly the same object, then the symbol NIL will be returned. Thus, EQ will return T only if two objects are *identical* in the sense that this book is identical only to itself.

T and NIL are special symbols in Lisp because they are used to represent the boolean values *true* and *false* respectively. EQ is one of many *predicates* which returns a boolean value. T and NIL are also special because they have predefined, constant values just like PI. The value of T is T and the value of NIL is NIL:

```
Lisp> t
T

Lisp> nil
NIL
```

Lisp actually has a very loose idea of true and false. T is not the only way to indicate the concept of truth. Instead, any value other than NIL represents true, while *only* the symbol NIL represents the boolean value false. This scheme has various practical benefits, although some people object to it. Thus, EQ could have returned 7892 or (THIS IS NEVER FALSE) to indicate that two objects are identical.

Unlike symbols, similar lists inside of Lisp are usually not EQ:

```
Lisp> (setf list-1 '(wombat is not drongo))
(WOMBAT IS NOT DRONGO)

Lisp> (setf list-2 '(wombat is not drongo))
(WOMBAT IS NOT DRONGO)

Lisp> (eq list-1 list-2)
NIL

Lisp> (eq list-1 list-1)
T
```

Each time Lisp reads the textual representation of a list, a new list object is created inside of the computer without ever checking to see if a similar list has been created before. Thus, if we type in the same list twice, we get two unique object inside of Lisp, and thus they are not EQ. However, each list, just like every object in Lisp, is EQ to itself.

It is often useful to see if two objects are equal in the same sense that two copies of this book are equal. We can test for this looser definition of equality using the function EQUAL:

```
Lisp> (equal list-1 list-2)
T

Lisp> (equal list-1 list-1)
T

Lisp> (equal 3 3)
T
```

EQUAL expects two arguments, and it will return true if each argument has an identical structure. Thus, two objects which are EQ are always EQUAL.

Numbers in Lisp may not be unique either. Consider:

```
Lisp> (+ 3 3 -3)
3
```

This example will create four distinct numbers, each being represented by a different chunk of memory.[4] There is a third type of equality test called EQL which is slightly looser than EQ. EQL will return true if its two arguments are EQ or if they are the same number. In many Lisps, some numbers can be tested for equality with EQ, but Common Lisp does not guarantee this. EQL really only exists as a concession to efficiency, since using EQUAL would work, but may be slower than EQL when comparing objects.

Don't worry if all these types of equality seem confusing; they are at first.

Problem. Try evaluating the following forms:

```
(eq 3.0 3.0)
(eq 3 3.0)
(eq 'turtle 'turtle)
(eq '(mutant turtle) '(mutant turtle))

(eql 3.0 3.0)
```

---

[4]It may seem that arithmetic will be hopelessly slow in Lisp. However, we will see later that it can be efficiently implemented.

```
(eql 3 3.0)
(eql 'turtle 'turtle)
(eql '(mutant turtle) '(mutant turtle))

(equal 3.0 3.0)
(equal 3 3.0)
(equal 'turtle 'turtle)
(equal '(mutant turtle) '(mutant turtle))
```

The predicate > expects one or more numeric arguments, and returns T if each argument is greater than the argument that follows it:

```
Lisp> (> 2 -3)
T

Lisp> (> 2)
T

Lisp> (> 5 7.9)
NIL

Lisp> (> 100 50 10)
T

Lisp> (= 3 4)
NIL

Lisp> (= 3 3)
T
```

The predicates <, <=, >=, and = are all similar to >, although each uses the test that its name suggests. Notice that we've sneaked in *another* equality test called =. This equality test works only with numeric arguments, unlike the equality predicates we saw earlier.

Another frequently used Lisp predicate is **ZEROP**:

```
Lisp> (zerop 0)
T

Lisp> (zerop 3.14)
NIL
```

```
Lisp> (zerop 4)
NIL

Lisp> (zerop 0.0)
T
```

ZEROP expects exactly one numeric argument and it returns T if that argument is equal to 0. We can easily duplicate the functionality of ZEROP with =:

```
Lisp> (= 0 0)
T

Lisp> (= 3.14 0)
NIL

Lisp> (= 4 0)
NIL

Lisp> (= 0.0 0)
T
```

This may seem a bit confusing. Why do we need a function named ZEROP if we can always replace it with an even shorter call to =? Common Lisp frequently offers many ways to accomplish the same goal. Sometimes this redundancy is provided to make our programs clearer, but it stems largely from the fact that Common Lisp tries to maintain compatibility with older dialects of Lisp such as Maclisp and Zetalisp. These dialects were actively used to build large programs and to experiment with new ideas in Lisp, so they did not always have the benefit of being carefully designed and refined ahead of time. In order to maintain some degree of compatibility with older dialects of Lisp, functions such as ZEROP still exist.

The name ZEROP is an example of a general rule for naming predicates in Lisp. Many predicates end in the letter P if there are no dashes in the name of the predicate, or in -P if there are dashes in the predicate name. Thus, there are predicate names such as NUMBERP and SIMPLE-STRING-P.

Problem. Try evaluating the following forms:

```
(= 3.0 3.0)
(= 'turtle 'turtle)
(= '(mutant turtle) '(mutant turtle))
```

```
(> 3 2 1)
(> 'turtle 3)

(zerop 'zero)
(zerop 0 3)

(+)
(*)
```

CHAPTER 3

FUNCTIONS AND RECURSION

3.1 DEFINING OUR OWN FUNCTIONS

In the last chapter we learned about a few kinds of Lisp objects and some simple functions which can manipulate those objects. Now we will use some of those simple functions to build new functions of our own design.

The special form `DEFUN` allows us to define a new function. In the last chapter we were able to compute the volume of a cylinder of radius 11 and height 7 with the Lisp expression `(* PI (EXPT 11 2) 7)`. However, this is just a specific application of the formula `(* PI (EXPT RADIUS 2) HEIGHT)`. We can create a function to capture this formula:

```
;;; Define a function named CYLINDER-VOLUME which accepts
;;; arguments named RADIUS and HEIGHT
Lisp> (defun cylinder-volume (radius height)
        (* pi (expt radius 2) height))
CYLINDER-VOLUME
```

The first argument to `DEFUN` must be a symbol. The symbol is not evaluated; it is the name we want to give to our new function. The next argument to `DEFUN` is a list of symbols. Each symbol is the name of a *formal parameter* to the function. These parameters are used to name the actual arguments which will be passed to the function when it is called. The whole list of symbols is sometimes called the *argument list* of the function. The final argument to `DEFUN` is called the *body* of the function, and it may be any Lisp expression. Thus, `CYLINDER-VOLUME` expects exactly two arguments, which can be referred to by the names `RADIUS` and `HEIGHT` in the body of our function. The body contains the formula for actually computing the volume of a cylinder. `DEFUN` returns the name of the function we defined.

Now we can call our new function just like any other function in Lisp:

```
Lisp> (cylinder-volume 11 7)
2660.929
```

The function we have just defined is like any other Lisp function, and when we call it from the interpreter the arguments in the call are evaluated from left to right. Next, Lisp evaluates the body of our function, and the result of that evaluation is returned as the result of the call to `CYLINDER-VOLUME`. However, the body of the function is evaluated in such a way that each of the evaluated arguments can be referred to by the name of its corresponding formal parameter. Thus, a call to `CYLINDER-VOLUME` results in the evaluation of of the body `(* PI (EXPT RADIUS 2) HEIGHT)`. If we try this at the top level, we get an unbound variable error:

```
Lisp> (* pi (expt radius 2) height)
>>Error: RADIUS has no global value

SYMBOL-VALUE:
   Required arg 0 (S): RADIUS

:A    Abort to Lisp Top Level
:C    Try evaluating RADIUS again
->
```

At top level, we get an error because the symbol `RADIUS` was never associated with a value. We would also have gotten an error saying that `HEIGHT` has no value, but Lisp never got far enough to find that out, since arguments are evaluated from left to right. However, when `CYLINDER-VOLUME` is called, Lisp *temporarily* associates the symbols `RADIUS` and `HEIGHT` with the values of the arguments given in the call. Each of these temporary symbol-value associations is called a *binding*, and they last for the duration of the function call. So, when the expression `(* PI (EXPT RADIUS 2) HEIGHT)` is evaluated during the call to `CYLINDER-VOLUME`, we do not get an error because `RADIUS` and `HEIGHT` have been temporarily bound to the values 11 and 7 respectively. When the call is complete, the bindings are undone, and `RADIUS` and `HEIGHT` each revert to whatever value they had before the call. In this case, each symbol reverts to having no value at all.

Problem. Define a function named `CUBE-VOLUME` which computes the volume of a cube given the length of a side.

3.1.1 The Substitution Model of Function Calling

The parameter list in a function defined by `DEFUN` is needed to associate names with argument values so that those values can be referenced in the body of the function. This means that we can rewrite a function call by substituting the actual *value* of a parameter for every *reference* to that parameter in the function body. Thus, every time we see the function call `(CYLINDER-VOLUME 11 7)` we can replace it by the function body `(* PI (EXPT RADIUS 2) HEIGHT)` if we replace every reference to `RADIUS` or `HEIGHT` with the values 7 and 11 respectively, producing the equivalent expression `(* PI (EXPT 7 2) 11)`. We call this the *substitution* model of function calling, since we can trivially rewrite all calls to functions whose bodies are known by substituting actual arguments in place of formal parameter references. This leads to the view that formal parameters are nothing more than names for values.

3.1.2 Side Effects and the Black Box Model of a Function

Now we can formulate a slightly more abstract notion of what a function is. We can view any function as a "black box" into which we can push some arguments, wait a little while, and get back a new value. Figure 3.1 depicts this idea.

We've already seen that the formal parameters in a function's argument list are used to name the actual arguments. What happens in between the time we put the arguments into the box and the time we get a value back is completely unknown to the caller of the function. Furthermore, the function cannot alter the world that the caller of the function sees; that is, the *only* effect of calling a function is to generate a return value. When the call is done, no variables have changed value, no data structures have been changed, etc.

Unfortunately, it is very easy, and sometimes necessary, to violate the black box model in our Lisp programs. For example, consider the following function:

```
Lisp> (setf quief 0)
0

Lisp> (defun produce-a-side-effect (x)
        (setf quief x))
PRODUCE-A-SIDE-EFFECT

Lisp> (produce-a-side-effect 7)
7
```

FIGURE 3.1
The black box model of a three-argument function.

```
Lisp> quief
7
```

Although the call to **PRODUCE-A-SIDE-EFFECT** involved passing one argument and returning one value, the value of the global variable **QUIEF** has also changed value. Hence, the world that the caller of **PRODUCE-A-SIDE-EFFECT** sees has been changed by the call. We call any such change to the caller's world a *side effect*. The black box model of a function call says that the only reason to ever call a function is to receive its value; however, a function with side effects may be called not because we are interested in its value, but because we are interested in the changes the function will make to the state of our Lisp environment. For example, we call the function **DEFUN** because it will add a new function to our top-level Lisp environment, not because we are interested in the symbol which **DEFUN** will return.

An even more obvious example of a function which we usually call only for its side effect is **PRINT**:

```
Lisp> (print 'foobar)

FOOBAR
FOOBAR
```

PRINT simply prints its argument on our terminal and then returns its argument as a result. Notice that in our example, **FOOBAR** has been printed twice. The first **FOOBAR** was printed by our explicit call to **PRINT**. However, **PRINT** then returned **FOOBAR** as a value to the read-eval-print loop, which then printed the result out *again*.

3.2 IF

Suppose we want to write a function called **CLASSIFY-CYLINDER** to classify a cylinder as **HUMUNGOUS** if the cylinder has a volume greater than 1000, or **PUNY** if the volume is less then or equal to 1000:

```
Lisp> (classify-cylinder 11 7)
HUMUNGOUS

Lisp> (classify-cylinder 1 2)
PUNY
```

We can use the special form **IF** to write **CLASSIFY-CYLINDER**:

```
Lisp> (defun classify-cylinder (radius height)
        (if (> (cylinder-volume radius height) 1000)
            'humungous
            'puny))
CLASSIFY-CYLINDER
```

IF expects three arguments. The first argument, called the *test*, is always evaluated. The result of evaluating the test is used to decide which of the other two arguments should be evaluated. If the test value is equal to **NIL**, then the third argument (called the *else* expression) is evaluated. If the test value is anything other than **NIL** (i.e., represents the boolean idea of truth in Lisp), then the second argument (called the *then* expression) is evaluated. **IF** returns the value of whichever expression it chooses to evaluate after the test. Thus, *either* the then expression or the else expression will be selected for evaluation, but never both.

If the volume of the cylinder with the given radius and volume is greater than 1000, then the call to the predicate > will return **T**, and thus the **IF** will chose to evaluate the expression **'HUMUNGOUS** and return the symbol **HUMUNGOUS**. If > returns **NIL**, then **IF** will choose to evaluate **'PUNY** and return the symbol **PUNY**.

3.3 TRACE

Lisp provides a useful debugging tool called **TRACE** which allows us to actually "see" a function call occurring. **TRACE** is a special form which expects one or more function names as arguments. The function names are *not* evaluated, and **TRACE** returns a list of the function names which were passed to it. As a side effect, **TRACE** alters each function it is passed so that a message will be printed each time that function is called:

```
Lisp> (trace classify-cylinder cylinder-volume)
(CLASSIFY-CYLINDER CYLINDER-VOLUME)

Lisp> (classify-cylinder 11 7)
1 Enter CLASSIFY-CYLINDER 11 7
| 2 Enter CYLINDER-VOLUME 11 7
| 2 Exit CYLINDER-VOLUME 2660.929
1 Exit CLASSIFY-CYLINDER HUMUNGOUS
HUMUNGOUS

Lisp> (classify-cylinder 1 2)
1 Enter CLASSIFY-CYLINDER 1 2
| 2 Enter CYLINDER-VOLUME 1 2
| 2 Exit CYLINDER-VOLUME 6.28
1 Exit CLASSIFY-CYLINDER PUNY
PUNY
```

The exact format of the information that **TRACE** prints is implementation dependent, but most implementations provide output similar to what is shown. Whenever a function being traced is called, Lisp prints the name of that function followed by the arguments which are being passed to the function. When a function call occurs within another function call, then the output of **TRACE** is indented a bit to indicate that we are in the middle of one or more other function calls. The greater the indentation, the greater the function call nesting.

Every time a function exits, the name of the function is printed along with the value that is being returned. The exit message is indented the same amount as the matching entry message. Hence, we can use `TRACE` to watch parts of our program execute. For example, we can see the call to `CYLINDER-VOLUME` which occurs within a call to `CLASSIFY-CYLINDER`. Selectively tracing functions whose operation is in question is a powerful debugging tool.

Trace output can soon become overwhelming and annoying. We can stop tracing a function by calling `UNTRACE`:

```
Lisp> (untrace classify-cylinder cylinder-volume)
(CLASSIFY-CYLINDER CYLINDER-VOLUME)

Lisp> (classify-cylinder 11 7)
HUMUNGOUS
```

`UNTRACE` is similar to `TRACE`, except that it causes a function to stop being watched. Calling `UNTRACE` with no arguments stops all functions from being traced. Thus, we could have simply used `(UNTRACE)` to stop watching the execution of `CLASSIFY-CYLINDER` and `CYLINDER-VOLUME`.

3.4 RECURSION

In this section we will examine an important class of functions which are defined in terms of themselves. Defining a concept in terms of itself is known as *recursion*. In order to understand recursion, we should have a better understanding of how function calls work.

3.4.1 The Photocopier Model of Function Calling

The operation of `TRACE` suggests an interesting mental model for how function calling works. Imagine that every time we define a function with `DEFUN`, that definition is written on a piece of paper and saved in a filing box. When we later wish to call a function, we look for the piece of paper with the definition of that function on it, just as we might look for a recipe in a filing box. If we find a piece of paper with the definition, we then make a *photocopy* of it and put the original piece of paper back in the box in case anyone else wants to use it.

Now that we have a photocopy of the original function, we can write things on it without altering the original in any way. The first thing we'll do is write down the actual arguments which are being passed on the sheet of paper we just got out of the photocopier.

For example, the call `(CLASSIFY-CYLINDER 11 7)` which we traced earlier is achieved by photocopying the master copy of the definition of `CLASSIFY-CYLINDER` as shown in Figure 3.2. We can use the scratch area of the photocopy to write down the values of the arguments passed to

```
                Master copy in filing box                    Scratch area

  (defun classify-cylinder (radius height)        args: ____ ____
     (if (> (cylinder-volume radius height)       (>
            1000)                                       1000)
         'humungous
         'puny))

                    Photocopy        ↓            Scratch area

  (defun classify-cylinder (radius height)        args: 11 7
     (if (> (cylinder-volume radius height)       (> 2660.929
            1000)                                    1000)
         'humungous
         'puny))
```

FIGURE 3.2
The photocopier model of function calling.

the function and any intermediate results such as the value returned by the call to **CYLINDER-VOLUME**. When we are all done with the function call, we can throw the piece of scratch paper away, knowing that the master copy is safely stored in the filing box.

TRACE helps us to visualize the photocopying process. Every time we photocopy a function definition and write the initial arguments in the scratch area of the copy, **TRACE** prints out an entry message to let us know that a copy has been made. When we exit the function and discard the photocopy, **TRACE** prints an exit message to tell us the value of the function call.

Now we can use the photocopier model of function to help us understand how functions defined in terms of themselves work.

3.4.2 Numeric Recursion

Suppose that we want to find the factorial of a number. The definition of factorial is as follows:

$$0! = 1$$
$$n! = n \times (n - 1)!$$

We can translate this into pseudo-Lisp as:

```
(FACT 0) = 1
(FACT N) = (* N (FACT (- N 1)))
```

which leads to a definition of **FACT** in Lisp:

```
Lisp> (defun fact (n)
        (if (= n 0)
            1
            (* n (fact (- n 1)))))
FACT
```

If the number passed to **FACT** is equal to 0, then we return the number 1. However, if the number is greater than 0 (we will assume only positive integers are passed), then we need to compute the factorial of one less than N and multiply the answer by N.

Trying to compute the factorial of (- N 1) while in the middle of computing the factorial of N bothers some people. However, we've already seen that calling a function just involves photocopying the master definition of that function, as this trace of **FACT** shows:

```
Lisp> (trace fact)
(FACT)

Lisp> (fact 0)
1 Enter FACT 0
1 Exit FACT 1
1

Lisp> (fact 3)
1 Enter FACT 3
|  2 Enter FACT 2
|  |  3 Enter FACT 1
|  |  |  4 Enter FACT 0
|  |  |  4 Exit FACT 1
|  |  3 Exit FACT 1
|  2 Exit FACT 2
1 Exit FACT 6
6

Lisp> (untrace fact)
(FACT)

;;; Lisp can easily handle large integers
Lisp> (fact 100)
93326215443944152681699238856266700490715968264381621468592963895217599993229915608941463976156518286253697920827223758251185210916864000000000000000000000000
```

When trying to compute (`FACT 3`), we make a photocopy of `FACT` and write `3` in the scratch area. However, to complete the call we need to find the value of (`FACT 2`). Thus, we make *another* photocopy of the master definition of `FACT` and we write `2` in the scratch area of the photocopy. This in turn results in us making more photocopies to compute (`FACT 1`) and (`FACT 0`). Thus, at one point we have four pieces of paper, each of which is a photocopy of the master definition of `FACT` but with different numbers written in the scratch area.

We know how to compute (`FACT 0`) immediately, so we can throw out the fourth photocopy and write the answer to (`FACT 0`) in the scratch area of the third copy. We can then finish computing (`FACT 1`) and discard the third photocopy we made, writing the answer down on the piece of paper we are using to compute (`FACT 2`). This process continues until we have finally computed the value of (`FACT 3`). When we are all done we have created and subsequently thrown away four photocopies of the definition of `FACT`. The trace of `FACT` helps make the photocopying process clear. Notice that we can make a copy of a function we are in the middle of, and we can have as many copies of it around as we need.

`FACT` is an example of a *recursive* function because it is defined in terms of itself. Recursion is quite natural and pervasive in Lisp programming, and we'll see many examples of it throughout this book. The photocopying model of function calling is actually not unlike the way in which a computer really executes our Lisp code.

`FACT` is an example of a numeric recursion. Recursion works by dividing a problem into two parts: a *base case* and a *recursive case*. The base case is a part of the problem which we can solve immediately. Thus, (`FACT 0`) is our base case because we immediately know that the answer is `1` without any further computation. The recursive case is (`* N (FACT (- N 1))`). The whole function works because the recursive case has made the problem we are trying to solve a little bit easier than the original problem, since (`- N 1`) is a bit smaller than `N`. In other words, the recursive case invariably pushes our problem a bit closer to the base case, and so we eventually must end up trying to compute the base case. Without a base case, though, we could end up with an *infinite* recursion, which never ends. Likewise, if our recursive call was (`FACT N`) or (`FACT (1+ N)`) instead of (`FACT (1- N)`), then we would once again end up with an infinite recursion, since our recursive call has not made the subproblem any easier than the original problem.

3.4.3 List Recursion

The Lisp function `LENGTH` computes the length of a list:

```
Lisp> (length '(a bikini whale))
3

Lisp> (length '(lobsters eat (bikini whales) and (narwhals)))
5
```

`LENGTH` will return the number of elements in the list. Notice that `(BIKINI WHALES)` and `(NARWHALS)` count as single elements in the list.

We can determine the number of elements in a list by seeing how many times we can take the `CDR` of it before we reach the end. This raises an interesting question, though: What is at the end of a list?

```
Lisp> (cdr '(a bikini whale))
(BIKINI WHALE)

Lisp> (cdr '(bikini whale))
(WHALE)
```

Each time we take the `CDR` of list, we throw out the first element of the list and are left with only the remaining element. Thus, we expect that when we `CDR` down a list with only one element, we will be left with a list containing no elements:

```
Lisp> (cdr '(whale))
()
```

The result `( )` is called the *empty list*. However, most Lisp implementation will do the following instead:

```
Lisp> (cdr '(whale))
NIL

Lisp> '()
NIL

Lisp> ()
NIL

Lisp> (eq '() nil)
T
```

The empty list `( )` and the symbol `NIL` are just two different printed representations of the *same* object inside of Lisp. Many Lisp printers prefer to always print this object as `NIL`, although Lisp knows that both `( )` and `NIL` mean the same thing. From now on we will use the terms empty list, `( )`, and `NIL` interchangeably. We do not have to quote `( )` because it already evaluates to `NIL`, but as a matter of style we will usually `QUOTE` it just as we would `QUOTE` any other list. Here is a summary of the three important roles that `NIL` plays:

- The boolean value "false"
- The empty list `( )`
- The symbol named `NIL`

We can build lists from scratch using `CONS`:

```
Lisp> (cons 'whale '())
(WHALE)

Lisp> (cons 'whale nil)
(WHALE)

Lisp> (cons 'bikini (cons 'whale nil))
(BIKINI WHALE)
```

All lists are built up starting with the empty list, and if we diligently take a list apart by `CDR`ing down it, we *must* eventually end up with the empty list.

Now that we know how a list ends, we can write a function called `OUR-LENGTH` which will do what the built in function `LENGTH` does. We will often define our own version of functions which are predefined in Lisp, but they will begin with `OUR-` to avoid redefining the corresponding Lisp functions:

```
Lisp> (defun our-length (l)
        (if (eq l '())
            0
            (+ 1 (our-length (cdr l)))))
OUR-LENGTH

Lisp> (our-length '())
0

Lisp> (our-length nil)
0

Lisp> (trace our-length)
(OUR-LENGTH)

Lisp> (our-length '(a bikini whale))
1 Enter OUR-LENGTH (A BIKINI WHALE)
| 2 Enter OUR-LENGTH (BIKINI WHALE)
|   3 Enter OUR-LENGTH (WHALE)
|   | 4 Enter OUR-LENGTH NIL
|   | 4 Exit OUR-LENGTH 0
|   3 Exit OUR-LENGTH 1
| 2 Exit OUR-LENGTH 2
1 Exit OUR-LENGTH 3
3

Lisp> (untrace)
(OUR-LENGTH)
```

```
Lisp> (our-length '(lobsters eat (bikini whales) and (narwhals)))
5
```

`OUR-LENGTH` takes advantage of two facts:

1. The length of the empty list is 0. This is the base case which we can solve immediately.
2. Every time we take the `CDR` of a list, we have discarded exactly one element. Thus, the length of a list is equal to one plus the length of the `CDR` of the list. This is our recursive case.

Infinite recursion could be a problem in `OUR-LENGTH` if we make an error and forget the base case or if our recursive case is not making our problem closer to the base case. For example, if we forget to `CDR` down the list `L` in our recursive call, then we will always be trying to find the length of the same list:

```
Lisp> (defun our-length (l)
        (if (eq l '())
            0
            (+ 1 (our-length l))))  ; This is missing a CDR
OUR-LENGTH

Lisp> (our-length '(a bikini whale))
>>Error: Stack Overflow

OUR-LENGTH:
   Required arg 0 (L): (A BIKINI WHALE)

:A    Abort to Lisp Top Level
:C    Attempt to grow the stack and continue
->
```

Most implementations of Lisp will eventually signal an error such as `Stack Overflow` when this happens, although it may take a while for this situation to occur. The error `Stack Overflow` means that the photocopier inside of Lisp ran out of paper, and thus no more calls, recursive or otherwise, can occur. At this point we should simply abort the entire computation and correct our error. However, we can sometimes legitimately run of of paper in the middle of a very long computation, such as `(FACT 100000)`. In that case, we can try to add more paper to the photocopier by "growing the stack." However, if you ever see a stack overflow error, it is most likely that you have an infinite recursion in your program.

Testing for the empty list is so common that Lisp even provides a special predicate called `NULL`. `NULL` returns `T` if its single argument is `NIL`, and returns `NIL` if its argument is anything other than `NIL`:

```
Lisp> (null nil)
T

Lisp> (null '())
T

Lisp> (null t)
NIL

Lisp> (null 'no-soap-radio)
NIL
```

Thus, rather than using `(EQ L '())` in `OUR-LENGTH`, we could simply have said `(NULL L)` and achieved the same effect.

3.4.4 Defining APPEND and REVERSE

Now we are ready to look at the recursive definition of two other simple Lisp functions. `APPEND` expects two lists and returns the concatenation of those lists:

```
Lisp> (append '(subject mongos) '(verb eat))
(SUBJECT MONGOS VERB EAT)

Lisp> (setf subject '((subject mongos)))
((SUBJECT MONGOS))

Lisp> (setf verb '((verb eat)))
((VERB EAT))

Lisp> (append subject verb))
((SUBJECT MONGOS) (VERB EAT))

Lisp> subject
((SUBJECT MONGOS))

Lisp> verb
((VERB EAT))
```

The easiest way to think of how `APPEND` works is to imagine that it removes the closing parenthesis of the first list and the opening parenthesis of the second list and then joins the two lists together. Of course, this is simply a syntactic explanation involving the printed representation of lists. It explains nothing about how the actual list objects inside the machine are being manipulated. Notice that just as `CAR` and `CDR` do not alter their arguments in any way, `APPEND` does not alter the values of `SENTENCE` or `VERB`. Here is a recursive definition of our own version of `APPEND`:

```
Lisp> (defun our-append (head tail)
        (if (null head)
            tail
            (cons (car head) (our-append (cdr head) tail))))
OUR-APPEND

Lisp> (trace our-append)
OUR-APPEND

Lisp> (our-append '(do mongos) '(eat booms ?))
1 Enter OUR-APPEND (DO MONGOS) (EAT BOOMS ?)
| 2 Enter OUR-APPEND (MONGOS) (EAT BOOMS ?)
|  3 Enter OUR-APPEND NIL (EAT BOOMS ?)
|  3 Exit OUR-APPEND (EAT BOOMS ?)
| 2 Exit OUR-APPEND (MONGOS EAT BOOMS ?)
1 Exit OUR-APPEND (DO MONGOS EAT BOOMS ?)
(DO MONGOS EAT BOOMS ?)
```

OUR-APPEND is a bit harder to write than the other functions we have seen so far. When confronting a new problem, it is often easiest to first identify a base case we can solve immediately. If we think about OUR-APPEND, we notice that we can APPEND the empty list to any other list and the result will simply be that other list:

```
Lisp> (append '(eat booms) nil)
(EAT BOOMS)

Lisp> (append nil '(eat booms))
(EAT BOOMS)
```

Thus, testing to see if one of the lists is equal to NIL seems like a good base case. But which list should we test? At this point we need to consider the recursive case.

We can formulate a recursive case by noticing that we can OUR-APPEND two lists by CONSing the first element of the first list onto the result of OUR-APPENDing the CDR of the first list to the second list:

```
Lisp> (our-append '(mongos) '(eat booms))
(MONGOS EAT BOOMS)

;;; The above call to APPEND can be solved by our recursive
;;; case:
Lisp> (cons 'mongos (our-append '() '(eat booms)))
(MONGOS EAT BOOMS)
```

Notice that our recursive case `CDR`s down `HEAD`, and thus `HEAD` must eventually become the empty list. This suggests that `(NULL HEAD)` is a good base case. Choosing `(NULL TAIL)` as a base case would lead to an infinite recursion because `TAIL` is not changing on each recursive call.

There is no cookbook method for writing functions. However, it often helps to write down everything we know about a problem and then start playing around. The worst we can do is produce an incorrect program, and that is generally much more instructive than not writing anything down at all.

Next we can use `APPEND` to define `REVERSE`. `REVERSE` expects a list as an argument and returns the reverse of that list:

```
Lisp> (reverse '(do mongos eat booms ?))
(? BOOMS EAT MONGOS DO)

Lisp> (setf sentence '((subject mongos) (verb eat)
                       (object booms)))
((SUBJECT MONGOS) (VERB EAT) (OBJECT BOOMS)))

Lisp> (reverse sentence)
((OBJECT BOOMS) (VERB EAT) (SUBJECT MONGOS))

Lisp> sentence
((SUBJECT MONGOS) (VERB EAT) (OBJECT BOOMS)))
```

Just as `LENGTH` did not count the elements of sublists, `REVERSE` does not reverse the sublists of `SENTENCE`. The reason is that `REVERSE` and `LENGTH` only operate on the outermost level of the list they are passed. By this, we mean that the order of any sublist is left untouched. Notice that a completely new list is returned by `REVERSE`, and the original `SENTENCE` is unchanged.

Reversing the empty list is the easy case of `REVERSE`:

```
Lisp> (reverse '())
NIL
```

In order to reverse a longer list, it helps to know how to make a single-element list:

```
Lisp> (cons 'mongos '())
(MONGOS)

Lisp> (list 'booms 'eat 'mongos)
(BOOMS EAT MONGOS)

Lisp> (list (car '(mongos eat booms)))
(MONGOS)
```

We can produce a single-element list by CONSing that element onto the empty list, or we can use the function LIST, which accepts zero or more arguments and returns a list of those arguments.

Now we are ready to try to reverse longer lists by noting the following relationship:

```
Lisp> (reverse '(mongos eat booms))
(BOOMS EAT MONGOS)

Lisp> (append (reverse (cdr '(mongos eat booms))
          (list (car '(mongos eat booms))
(BOOMS EAT MONGOS)

Lisp> (append '(booms eat) '(mongos))
(BOOMS EAT MONGOS)
```

We can use LIST to make a single-element list out of the first element of the list we want to reverse, and then APPEND this new list onto the *end* of the reverse of the CDR of the original list:

```
Lisp> (defun our-reverse (l)
        (if (null l)
            nil
            (append (our-reverse (cdr l)) (list (car l)))))
OUR-REVERSE

Lisp> (trace our-reverse)
OUR-REVERSE

Lisp> (our-reverse '(mongos eat booms))
1 Enter OUR-REVERSE (MONGOS EAT BOOMS)
| 2 Enter OUR-REVERSE (EAT BOOMS)
|   3 Enter OUR-REVERSE (BOOMS)
|   | 4 Enter OUR-REVERSE NIL
|   | 4 Exit OUR-REVERSE NIL
|   3 Exit OUR-REVERSE (BOOMS)
| 2 Exit OUR-REVERSE (BOOMS EAT)
1 Exit OUR-REVERSE (BOOMS EAT MONGOS)
(BOOMS EAT MONGOS)
```

These functions may be a bit confusing. The best way to really understand them is to play with them and observe their operation using TRACE. Common Lisp also provides a special form called STEP which allows us to proceed through the evaluation of a form step by step. You might find the stepper useful if you are having a difficult time understanding or debugging a program. Refer to the manual for your Lisp implementation for details about how your particular stepper works. Take advantage of the interactive nature of Lisp by using the interpreter to see how pieces of the functions you write will work on specific examples.

> Note: You should not use global variables or **SETF** to solve any of the following problems.

Problem. Write a function called **SAME-LENGTH-P** which expects two lists as arguments, and returns T if both lists contain the same number of elements, or **NIL** if they are of differing length:

```
Lisp> (same-length-p '(recombinant dna) '(apple pie))
T

Lisp> (same-length-p '(((((((x))))))) y) '(3))
NIL

Lisp> (same-length-p '(((((((x))))))) y) '(3 4))
T
```

You may not use the function **LENGTH** in your definition of **SAME-LENGTH-P**.

Problem. Write a function named **COUNT-OCCURRENCES** which counts the number of times an atom appears in a list:

```
Lisp> (count-occurrences 'dog '(a dog is a dog is a dog))
3
```

Problem. Write a function called **COMMON-TAIL** which expects two lists of any length and returns the longest common sublist which comes at the end of both lists:

```
Lisp> (common-tail '(move from r1 to r3)
                   '(move from r7 to r3))
(TO R3)

Lisp> (common-tail '(move from r1 to r7)
                   '(move from r1 to r8))
NIL
```

Problem. Write a function to merge two ordered lists of numbers. Each list may be of any length, but the numbers in each list must already appear in ascending order:

```
Lisp> (merge-lists '(1 3) '(2 4 6))
(1 2 3 4 6)

Lisp> (merge-lists '(1 3 3 5) '(3 4 6 10 34 67 98))
(1 3 3 3 4 5 6 10 34 67 98)
```

Problem. Write a function which returns the position of an atom within in a list, or NIL if the atom does not appear in the list:

```
Lisp> (position-in-list 'c '(a b c d e))
2

Lisp> (position-in-list 'a '(a b c d e))
0

Lisp> (position-in-list 'z '(a b c e e))
NIL
```

Notice that the first element in a list is numbered 0 rather than 1. You might find it helpful to solve this problem by defining two functions.

Problem. Write a function named ENUMERATE which accepts a starting number, an increment, and a count as arguments and returns the corresponding list of enumerated numbers:

```
Lisp> (enumerate 1 1 5)
(1 2 3 4 5)

Lisp> (enumerate 0 2 5)
(0 2 4 6 8)

Lisp> (enumerate 0 10 7)
(0 10 20 30 40 50 60)
```

CHAPTER 4

A SIMPLE LISP PROGRAM

In this chapter we will write several functions which work together to solve a simple problem.

4.1 PROGRAM DEVELOPMENT

At this point you might be getting tired of typing functions directly into a read-eval-print loop, since once you have entered an expression, you cannot make even a minor change without typing the whole thing again.[1] One solution to this problem is to enter your functions into a file using your favorite text editor. You can then use the Lisp function `LOAD` to read and evaluate the contents of the file. Thus, we could create a file called `PLAYING.LISP` (or `PLAYING.LSP` if your computer only allows three-character file extensions) with the definitions of `FACT` and `OUR-LENGTH`:

```
(defun fact (n)
  (if (zerop n)
      1
      (* n (fact (- n 1))))))
```

---

[1]Some Lisp systems provide a convenient way to recall and edit previous input lines.

```
(defun our-length (l)
  (if (null l)
      0
      (+ 1 (our-length (cdr l)))))
```

From now on we will present most function definitions as though they have been typed into a file rather than typing each one into the read-eval-print loop. Once we have a file of definitions, we can load it:

```
Lisp> (load "playing.lisp")
#P"$DISK1:[WADE]playing.lisp"
```

LOAD expects the name of a file as an argument and it returns the name of the file it loads. We pass the file name as a *string* and receive a *pathname* back from LOAD. These are two new data types in Lisp, which we will discuss later.

After loading our file of definitions, we can try them out. If we find that they do not work correctly, then we can go back into the editor, fix the functions, save the file, and then LOAD the file again.

We can also use the function COMPILE-FILE to convert our Lisp code into a machine code which will run more quickly than interpreted code:

```
Lisp> (compile-file "playing.lisp")
"playing.bin"
```

The Lisp compiler not only compiles code but it also checks for obvious errors and reports them. It is a good idea to compile code immediately after it is written in order to detect and correct simple errors. For example, most compilers will warn us about variables which are bound but never used, since this usually indicates that we mistyped a variable name somewhere. Once our program is free of the simple errors which the compiler can detect, we can proceed to debug our program in the interpreter in order to take advantage of the better debugging facilities usually provided for interpreted code. We will discuss compilation in greater detail in Chapter 20.

The Lisp environment in which we develop programs is an important part of Lisp as a whole. However, nobody can agree on exactly what a good environment looks like, so Common Lisp does very little to specify the details of the programming environment. For example, Common Lisp specifies that the function ED will invoke a system-dependent editor, but says nothing more about the subject.

A good editor, such as EMACS [Sta87], is essential to using Lisp. Many Lisp systems can communicate directly with an editor and allow us to redefine a function with only a few keystrokes. Another important feature of a Lisp editor is parenthesis balancing and automatic indentation. These features are crucial to writing large Lisp programs since Lisp code is unfathomable to humans unless it is correctly indented (Lisp does not care at all).

The indentation of the examples in this book is not accidental but is intended to clearly represent the structure and meaning of our programs. You should learn how to indent by copying the indentation style presented in this book or by letting your text editor perform all of your indentation.

We already know that we can insert a comment into a program with a semicolon. However, there are some conventions for how comments should look:

```
;;; Comments for an entire function or group of functions
;;; should start at the left margin and begin with three
;;; semicolons.
(defun too-many-comments-in-this-example-p (x)
  ;; Comments which are indented to the same column as a
  ;; form in the body should begin with two semicolons.
  (and (brain-dead-p x)         ; Use a single semicolon
                                ; for comments
       (random-lossage-p x)))   ; that start on the same
                                ; line as a form
```

We have already seen these commenting conventions used in earlier examples, and we will continue to use them throughout the book.

Individual Lisp users have very different ideas about what constitutes the best way to edit and incrementally build programs. For now we will leave this subject alone, noting only that possibilities other than what is discussed here exist. However, it is *extremely* worthwhile for you to take a bit of time now to learn how to use a few of the program development features provided by your system. These features will make playing with Lisp and the examples in this book much easier and more enjoyable.

4.2   EXAMPLE: PEANO ARITHMETIC

Even the most complicated Lisp programs are ultimately created by building upon a very small foundation of *primitives*. We combine primitives by defining new functions, which in turn can be joined together to build even larger functions.

One interesting example of how powerful composing primitives can be is an arithmetic system which is based only on very simple arithmetic primitives:

```
(defun zero ()
  0)

(defun successor (n)
  (1+ n))

(defun predecessor (n)
  (1- n))

(defun our-zero-p (n)
  (= n (zero)))
```

The function `ZERO` simply returns the number 0 so that we do not have to hardwire the value of zero into the functions we write. `SUCCESSOR` increments a number, while `PREDECESSOR` decrements a number, and the predicate `OUR-ZERO-P` tests whether or not a number is equal to zero. The simple system we have just described is known as *Peano arithmetic*. Of course, Lisp does not really perform arithmetic this way, but we can build an amazing library of functions from these primitives.

4.2.1 Adding Integers

The first higher level function we will write is an adder. The problem seems fairly simple. If we want to add 5 and 3, then we can simply add 1 to 5 exactly 3 times. Likewise, if we want to add 5 to -3, then we can simply subtract 1 from 5 exactly 3 times. Of course, this supposes that we can figure out whether a number is positive or negative, but we will pretend that we already have such a function for now. The code for `ADD` could look something like this:

```
(defun add (x y)
  (if (positivep y)
      (add-positive x y)
      (add-negative x y)))

(defun add-positive (x y)
  (if (our-zero-p y)
      x
      (add-positive (successor x) (predecessor y))))

(defun add-negative (x y)
  (if (our-zero-p y)
      x
      (add-negative (predecessor x) (successor y))))
```

The function `ADD` examines the sign of its second argument and passes off the real work of addition to either `ADD-POSITIVE` or `ADD-NEGATIVE`. This is called *dispatching* on the sign of `Y`, since we are selecting which of several paths is needed to continue. `ADD-POSITIVE` and `ADD-NEGATIVE` are quite similar, so we will only examine `ADD-POSITIVE`.

`ADD-POSITIVE` first checks to see if we are trying to add `X` to 0. If so, then we are done. Thus, we have a base case. If `Y` is not zero, then we call `ADD-POSITIVE` again, but first we increment `X` and decrement `Y`. This is the recursive part of the function. It is important to notice that this recursion must terminate at some point, since if we subtract 1 from a positive number enough times, we must reach zero. However, if we had made a mistake and started adding one to `Y` on each recursive call, then our function would never terminate. Once again, dividing a function into a base case and a recursive case is not enough.

We must also be sure that the recursive case is slowly pushing us towards the base case.

Now we have to write **POSITIVEP**. If we are given a positive number, then if we subtract 1 from it enough times, we will eventually reach 0. Likewise, if we are given a negative number, then if we add 1 to it enough times, we will again reach 0. The only trouble is that each of these statements presupposes that we already know what we are trying to find: whether or not the number is positive! If we just guess, and start subtracting one from a negative number, our program isn't going to work. Since we do not know the sign of the number, we must search in both directions at once:

```
(defun positivep (x)
  (positivep-1 x x))

(defun positivep-1 (down up)
   (if (our-zero-p down)       ; consider 0 to be "positive"
       t
       (if (our-zero-p up)
           nil
           (positivep-1 (predecessor down) (successor up)))))
```

POSITIVE-P just starts off **POSITIVEP-1** with **DOWN** and **UP** being equal to the number we are testing the sign of. Since we test for **DOWN** being 0 first, we will consider anything greater than or equal to 0 to be positive. Next we check if **UP** has reached 0; if so, then the original number must have been negative, so **POSITIVEP** should return **NIL**. If both of these tests fail, then we execute our catch-all case, which simply calls **POSITIVEP-1** again, decrementing and incrementing **DOWN** and **UP** respectively; sooner or later one of the two **OUR-ZERO-P** tests must be true.

Nested **IF** expressions often appear in computer programs, and Lisp provides a simpler way to express the nested **IF**s in **POSITIVEP-1**:

```
(defun positivep-1 (down up)
  (cond ((our-zero-p down) t)         ; consider 0 be positive

        ((our-zero-p up) nil)
        (t (positivep-1 (predecessor down)(successor up)))))
```

COND is a special form with the general form:

```
(cond (test-expression-
      (test-expression-2  result-expression-2)
       .
       .
       .
      (test-expression-n result-expression-n))
```

The test expressions in the `COND` are evaluated sequentially. If the value of a test expression is not `NIL` (boolean true), then the `COND` immediately returns the result of evaluating the corresponding result expression. Thus, the first true test "short circuits" the `COND`. In `POSITIVEP-1`, the `COND` first evaluates the test expression `(OUR-ZERO-P DOWN)`. If the result is not `NIL`, then the `COND` immediately returns the value of the expression `T`. However, if `(OUR-ZERO-P DOWN)` is `NIL`, then the `COND` evaluates `(OUR-ZERO-P UP)` in a similar fashion. Notice that the last test in the `COND` is `T` and thus the last test always succeeds. `T` is used as the last test in virtually all `COND`s in order to provide a "catch all" or "fall through" case. If the result of every test is `NIL`, then `COND` will return `NIL`; however, this is considered bad practice, since the failure of all tests often indicates an unanticipated case, and thus a bug in our program.

`POSITIVEP-1` is called a *helping* or *auxiliary* function because it does the real work of the main function `POSITIVEP`. This idiom is often used in Lisp. If we cannot think of a good name for a helping function, then it will be named by the function it helps followed by `-N`, where `N` is 1, 2, 3, etc. For example, we have only one auxiliary function to help `POSITIVEP`, and we have called that function `POSITIVEP-1`. If we had needed another helping function we would have called it `POSITIVEP-2`. Some people also use the convention of naming an auxiliary function by adding `-AUX` to the end of the main function. We won't use this approach primarily because it does not easily generalize to more than one auxiliary function. Often the helping function does all the real work, with the main function simply setting up an initial call to the helping function. `POSITIVEP` is an example of this.

Problem. Write a function called `SUBTRACT` which will subtract two integers in a manner similar to the way `ADD` works.

4.2.2 Multiplying Integers

Next we would like to write a function called `TIMES` which multiplies two numbers. However, we can still ultimately use only `SUCCESSOR` and `PREDECESSOR`. To multiply 5 times 3, we could cumulatively add 1 to 0 fifteen times. However, it is much easier to use the `ADD` function we just wrote to cumulatively add 5 to 0 three times. Likewise, if we want to multiply 5 times −3, then we can cumulatively subtract 5 from 0 three times using `SUBTRACT`.

```
(defun times (x y)
  (if (positivep y)
      (times-positive (zero) x y)
      (times-negative (zero) x y)))

(defun times-positive (product multiplicand times)
  (if (our-zero-p times)
      product
      (times-positive (add product multiplicand)
```

```
              multiplicand
              (predecessor times))))

(defun times-negative (product multiplicand times)
  (if (our-zero-p times)
      product
      (times-negative (subtract product multiplicand)
                      multiplicand
                      (successor times))))
```

The structure of `TIMES` is similar to the structure of `ADD`, with `TIMES` dispatching to a more specific multiplication routine, depending on the sign of `Y`. In `TIMES-POSITIVE`, rather than adding 1 on each recursive call, as in `ADD-POSITIVE`, we add the `MULTIPLICAND` to the current product. We stop adding to the product after we have done `TIMES` adds.

It is interesting to note that we can rename the argument `MULTIPLICAND` in `TIMES-POSITIVE` to `ADD`, and `TIMES-POSITIVE` will still work correctly:

```
(defun times-positive (product add times)
  (if (our-zero-p times)
      product
      ;; ADD will have two meanings below!
      (times-positive (add product add)
                      add
                      (predecessor times))))
```

We are able to call the *function* `ADD` with an argument named `ADD`. A symbol may be treated as both a variable and a function at the same time in Common Lisp, although this isn't true in all other Lisps. In the expression `(ADD PRODUCT ADD)`, the first occurrence of `ADD` refers to the functional value of `ADD`, since it is in the functional position of the list. This is the definition that we gave to `ADD` via `DEFUN`. The second occurrence of `ADD` refers to the value of `ADD` as a variable. As we have already seen, variables can be given values via `SETF`, or by appearing as the formal parameter in a function definition. Although it is possible to take advantage of this property in our programs, it is poor style and should usually be avoided.

At this point we will stop, although we could continue to write other numeric functions. The important point is that we have built multiplication on top of addition, and addition on top of `SUCCESSOR`, and `TIMES` has no knowledge of how `ADD` is implemented. Thus, if we were to one day find that our machine really did have an addition instruction in it, then we could rewrite our original `ADD` to be more efficient, without changing any of our code which already uses `ADD`.

Problem. Write a `DIVIDE` function which is similar to `TIMES`. You may ignore any remainder.

Problem. Add an `EXPONENT` function which accepts two integers x and n and returns x^n.

4.3 GIANT-INTS

One day we might need to deal with extremely large integers, only to find that the integers on our machine are limited to a certain range. In the last chapter we saw that Lisp can already deal with large integers such as the factorial of 100.[2] We will call such large integers *giant-ints*. However, rather than using Lisp's built-in representation of integers, we can represent any integer as a list of digits. For example, the integer 125 would be represented by the list `(ONE TWO FIVE)`. Of course, now that we have an entirely new representation for integers, we will need to rewrite all of our functions which deal with integers. Or will we?

A close look at the numeric functions we just wrote (and many others we could have written) shows that all we have to do is define `ZERO`, `SUCCESSOR`, `PREDECESSOR`, and `OUR-ZERO-P` to work correctly for a given representation of integers. If we can make those work for our giant-ints, then we can reuse all the higher level code we've written to do useful things with integers. This is an important consequence of relying only upon what operation a function performs, and not how it performs that operation. This idea is the essence of abstraction and the black box model of functions.

Unfortunately, it is not always easy to see exactly how to generalize a problem. For example, normally we deal only in base 10 arithmetic. However, why should we limit ourselves to just base 10? What if we want to use binary or hexadecimal arithmetic? Does that really change any of our algorithms? Of course not. The base only affects the number of digits in our numeric language, and how we arrange those digits to represent a number. Having noticed this, we will allow our new implementation of giant-ints to automatically switch to whatever base we wish to use. To accomplish this, we will maintain a global variable called `*DIGITS*`, which will always be set to the list of the digits in our numeric system. The list should be written in ascending order. Thus, we will need a list of 10 digits to work in decimal:

```
(defvar *digits*
  '(zero one two three four five six seven eight nine)
  "A list of the digits in the current number system")
```

We have used a new special form named `DEFVAR` to define `*DIGITS*`. `DEFVAR` expects three arguments: the name of a variable, the initial value of that variable, and a *documentation string*. If the variable already has a value, then the `DEFVAR` is essentially ignored. However, if the variable does not already have a value, then the initial-value argument is evaluated and the variable is `SETF`ed to

---

[2]Such large integers are called *Bignums* in Lisp.

the result of that evaluation. The documentation string may or may not be saved away by Lisp for future reference. We will discuss the use of DEFVAR in more detail when we learn about *dynamic scoping*. For now it provides a convenient way to initialize and document global variables.

Notice that we chose the name *DIGITS* rather than DIGITS for our global variable. By convention, global variables in Common Lisp should begin and end with the character *. This is only a convention to let readers of our program know that a symbol is being used as a global variable—Lisp does not care that the symbol name contains asterisks.

We must also change the functions which deal with zero:

```
(defun zero ()
  (first *digits*))

(defun our-zero-p (giant-int)
  (if (null (cdr giant-int))      ; only 1 digit?
      (eq (car giant-int (zero)))  ; and that digit is zero?
      nil))
```

Because the list of *DIGITS* is always written in ascending order starting from zero, the first element of the list must represent zero. The predicate OUR-ZERO-P will only return T if it is given a one-element list containing the symbol which represents zero.

Now we need to rewrite SUCCESSOR to work with giant-ints. Before we go on, though, we will introduce two new Lisp features which will make writing SUCCESSOR easier.

4.3.1 LET Can Name Values

Sometimes we would like to use the value returned by a function more than once. We could repeat the same function call each time we need its value, but that is often inefficient. Sometimes we cannot even repeat a function call and expect to see the same result if the function we are calling has side effects. Consider the following example:

```
Lisp> (defvar *global-counter* 1 "A random global variable")
1

Lisp> (defun side-effecty (n)
        (setf *global-counter* (* *global-counter* n)))
SIDE-EFFECTY

Lisp> (side-effecty 2)
2

Lisp> (side-effecty 2)
4
```

```
Lisp> (side-effecty 2)
8
```

Calling **SIDE-EFFECTY** repeatedly with the same argument does not produce the same result each time since the arguments to **SIDE-EFFECTY** are not the only pieces of data involved in computing its value. **SIDE-EFFECTY** also alters the global state of our program by changing the value of the symbol *GLOBAL-COUNTER*.

Sometimes we really do need to give names to results which we may need to use more than once. We can already do this by defining a function and passing the value we want to name as an argument to that function. However, rather than defining a new function every time we want to name a value, we can use the special form **LET**. **LET** has the general form

```
(let ((name-1 expression-1)
      (name-2 expression-2)
       .
       .
       .
      (name-n expression-n))
  body-forms)
```

The first argument to **LET** should be a list of sublists. The second element of each sublist should be an expression. The expressions are evaluated from top to bottom, and the result of each evaluation is saved away. This is identical to the way in which the arguments in a function call are evaluated from left to right and the results are written down in the scratch area of a piece of paper. Once all of the expressions have been evaluated, then each name is bound to the result of evaluating the corresponding expression. After these bindings have been made, the body of the **LET** is evaluated and may refer to the new bindings introduced:

```
Lisp> (defun simple (x y)
        (let ((result (* x y)))
          (* result result)))
SIMPLE

Lisp> (simple 3 4)
144

Lisp> (defun simple (x y)
        (simple-1 (* x y)))
SIMPLE

Lisp> (defun simple-1 (result)
        (* result result))
SIMPLE-1
```

```
Lisp> (simple 3 4)
144
```

Note that the results of using **LET** to bind variables are absolutely *identical* to what occurs during a function call such as (**SIMPLE-1** (* X Y)). The only difference is that we have avoided defining an extra function just so that we could name some values. Beware of the following problem when using **LET**:

```
Lisp> (let ((x 3)
            (y x))
        (* x y))
>>Error: X has no global value

SYMBOL-VALUE:
   Required arg 0 (S): X

:A      Abort to Lisp Top Level
:C      Try evaluating X again
->
```

Since **LET** has the same semantics as a function call, no initial value expression in the **LET** can refer to any of the bindings which the **LET** creates, since the bindings do not occur until *after* all of the expressions have been evaluated. Thus, we could solve our problem by rewriting the form:

```
Lisp> (let ((x 3))
        (let ((y x))
          (* x y)))
9
```

By nesting **LET**s, we can allow Y to refer to the binding of X. However, this nesting is a bit verbose and can quickly cause our code to run off the right-hand side of the page. Instead, we can use the special form **LET***:

```
Lisp> (let* ((x 3)
             (y x))
        (* x y))
9
```

This time we do not get an error, because each name is bound to the value of the corresponding expression *immediately* after the evaluation rather than waiting for all the expressions to be evaluated first. Thus, **LET*** allows us to create bindings sequentially, while **LET** will only allow us to create bindings in parallel, just as a function call does. Notice that we can always rewrite a **LET*** as a sequence of nested **LET**s.

4.3.2 MEMBER

The other function we will need in order to write SUCCESSOR for giant-ints is called MEMBER, and it expects two arguments. The first argument may be anything, while the second argument must be a list. MEMBER will check to see if the first argument is a member of the second argument. The function EQL is used to see if the first argument is actually equal to some element in the second argument. If the first argument is a member of the second argument, then MEMBER will return true; if not, member will return NIL:

```
lisp> (member 'b '(a b c))
(B C)

lisp> (member 'd '(a b c))
NIL
```

You may notice that the results are a bit odd; In the first example, MEMBER had an unusual way of returning true. Instead of just returning T, it returned a part of the list in which we were checking for membership. MEMBER will always return the rest of the list starting with the element we were searching for. Since we were searching for B in (A B C), member returned the rest of (A B C), starting with B, giving us (B C).

Why didn't MEMBER just return T, since that would be sufficient to tell us that B was indeed a member of the list (A B C)? The answer lies in the flexibility of truth in Lisp, and the natural definition of MEMBER. Recall that anything which is *not* NIL is true. Thus, rather than just returning T, which only answers a yes or no question, we can instead return something more useful. In this case, it turns out that the natural definition of MEMBER will make the rest of the list, starting with the element we are looking for, readily available. Thus, why not make MEMBER useful in two ways: as a boolean test of membership, and as a way to throw away everything in a list up to a particular element? Since the remaining list is always going to be considered true by Lisp, we can satisfy both meanings of MEMBER at once. In fact, we are going to be relying on the second property of MEMBER when we write SUCCESSOR.

Problem. Write your own version of MEMBER called OUR-MEMBER.

4.3.3 Writing SUCCESSOR for Giant-ints

Now we can use the new features we have learned to write SUCCESSOR for giant-ints:

```
(defun successor (giant-int)
  (reverse (successor-1 (reverse giant-int))))

(defun successor-1 (rev-giant-int)
  (if (null rev-giant-int)
```

```
;; Tried to carry "one" past the end of the number,
;; so extend the number.
(list (second *digits*)))
(let ((next-digit (second (member (first rev-giant-int)
                                      *digits*))))
    (if (null next-digit)       ; wrap to zero?
        (cons (zero)
              ;; carry "one"
              (successor-1 (rest rev-giant-int)))
        (cons next-digit (rest rev-giant-int)))))))
```

The operation of these functions is a bit complicated, so it may take some time and playing with **TRACE** to understand them. The following examples demonstrate the use of **SUCCESSOR**:

```
lisp> (successor '(three nine nine))
(FOUR ZERO ZERO)

lisp> (successor '(one one one one))
(ONE ONE ONE TWO)
```

The real work is done by the helping function **SUCCESSOR-1**. **SUCCESSOR** reverses the giant-int so that **SUCCESSOR-1** can easily perform addition starting with the least significant digit. **SUCCESSOR-1** uses the "remaining list" property of **MEMBER** to add 1 to the least significant digit, producing **NEXT-DIGIT**. If adding 1 results in the **NEXT-DIGIT** being 0, then we must carry 1 to the next significant digit by calling **SUCCESSOR-1** again to compute the result of adding the carry to the rest of the number; if no carry is needed, then the rest of the number is unchanged and we have a base case.

Eventually we might end up adding one to the most significant digit of the number and still have to carry. In this case, there are no more digits left in the giant-int, so our recursive call to **SUCCESSOR-1** will try to add 1 to **NIL**. In order to accommodate this case, **SUCCESSOR-1** returns the giant-int which represents 1. This constitutes a second base.

You may find this recursion difficult to follow explicitly. It is often easier to read or write a recursive function by simply *believing* that it works. This may sound like wishful thinking to hide confusion, but it is in fact quite sound.[3] If we believe that a function call does what it is advertised to do, then we need not think any further about what that call will return. We can instead concentrate on making sure that we have a valid base case and that our recursive calls are indeed making the original problem simpler in some sense, moving us a little closer to the base case. In the above example, adding 1 without a carry is a base case, as

---

[3] Does this remind you of induction?

is adding 1 to `NIL`, while adding 1 to the rest of the number as the result of a carry is the recursive case. Note that we must reach the base case eventually, since no list, and hence no giant-int, is infinite.

We can now switch bases simply by changing `*DIGITS*`:

```
lisp> (setf *digits* '(zero one))
(ZERO ONE)

lisp> (successor '(one one one one))
(ONE ZERO ZERO ZERO ZERO)
```

We have succeeded in adding one to the binary number 1111 (decimal 15) without changing any of our code, hence generalizing our original problem along a new dimension. Of course, there are still other ways to generalize our giant-int system. For example, how do we deal with negative numbers? For now we cannot, because there is no concept of a sign being associated with a number. Likewise, we could also try to handle rational and complex numbers in a general way, building up from a foundation of primitives like `SUCCESSOR`, `PREDECESSOR`, and `OUR-ZERO-P`.

Notice that in many other languages, we would have to explicitly maintain our lists of digits as a linked list of dynamically allocated storage. This would require that we explicitly allocate and deallocate storage blocks and that we use explicit pointer operations to manipulate those blocks. The entire system is clearly more cumbersome and prone to error than the simple giant-int system we just wrote in Lisp. Of course, for such a small program, the detail is not hard to manage; however, imagine a program 50 times larger. The ensuing problem of correctly managing such details becomes burdensome.

Much of Lisp's power is derived from the simplicity and the power of lists, and the natural way that they implement a recursive structure. The simplicity of our code owes much to the ease with which lists can be pulled apart and put back together again. We need not worry about where our next cons cell is coming from, or what will happen to it when we are done. Allocating storage is busy work for the system. Whenever we first write a program, we should strive to think about the general concepts we are trying to understand and implement.

Problem. Rewrite `SUCCESSOR` for giant-ints without calling `REVERSE` twice. What are the advantages and disadvantages of doing this?

Problem. Extend our giant-int system to allow both positive and negative integers. How much code did you have to change?

Problem. We can represent a ratio as a list of the form `(RATIO numerator denominator)`. For example, `(RATIO 1 3)` represents the fraction 1/3. Write a function called `SIMPLIFY-RATIO` which can simplify ratios:

```
Lisp> (simplify-ratio '(ratio 8 12))
(RATIO 2 3)
```

You may find the Lisp function `GCD` useful. `GCD` expects any number of integers and returns their greatest common divisor:

```
Lisp> (gcd 24 16)
8

Lisp> (gcd 9 12 15)
3

Lisp> (gcd 8 9 12)
1
```

Problem. Now extend our numeric system to include the functions `RATIO-ADD` and `RATIO-TIMES`:

```
Lisp> (ratio-add '(ratio 1 3) '(ratio 1 6))
(RATIO 1 2)

Lisp> (ratio-times '(ratio 2 3) '(ratio 5 6))
(RATIO 5 9)
```

CHAPTER 5

THE VERSATILITY OF LISTS

One of the most powerful features of Lisp is the ease with which we can create and manipulate lists, and infinite-precision arithmetic is only one of their possible applications. In this chapter we will examine some others.

5.1 LIST EQUALITY

Many list applications require that we be able to determine when two lists have the same structure. In Chapter 2 we learned that the function EQUAL can be used for this purpose:

```
Lisp> (equal '(* pi (expt radius 2) height)
             '(* pi (expt radius 2) height))
T

Lisp> (equal '(* pi radius radius) '(* pi (expt radius 2)))
NIL

Lisp> (eq '(expt radius 2) '(expt radius 2))
NIL

Lisp> (eql '(expt radius 2) '(expt radius 2))
NIL
```

EQUAL is a less stringent test of equality than **EQ** or **EQL**, since these tests will return **T** only if the two values being compared refer to the same object.

In order to write our own simple version of **EQUAL** in terms of **EQL**, we need to recognize that each element of a list is either another list, which can be taken apart with **CAR** and **CDR**, or an *atom*, which cannot be decomposed further. The predicate **ATOM** (which violates the naming convention for predicates since it should be called **ATOMP**) returns **T** if its argument cannot be decomposed by **CAR** and **CDR**:

```
Lisp> (atom 'gelatinous-cube)
T

Lisp> (atom 3.14)
T

Lisp> (atom '(expt radius 2))
NIL
```

We can define a simple version of **EQUAL** called **OUR-EQUAL-P** with the following rules:

1. If either argument is an atom, then it cannot be decomposed by **CAR** or **CDR**, and thus both values must be **EQL** if **OUR-EQUAL-P** is to be true. This constitutes a base case for our function.
2. If neither argument is an atom, then both arguments must be lists. Two lists are **OUR-EQUAL-P** if the **CAR**s of each list are **OUR-EQUAL-P** and the **CDR**s of each list are **OUR-EQUAL-P**. This is the recursive case.

The definition of **OUR-EQUAL-P** given above requires that we be able to determine when one argument *or* the other is an atom. Similarly, we must also be able to determine when both the **CAR**s *and* the **CDR**s of two lists are **OUR-EQUAL-P**. Here is one possible way to write **OUR-EQUAL-P**:

```
(defun our-equal-p (x y)
  (if (if (atom x)                            ; OR
          t
          (atom y))
      (eql x y)
      (if (our-equal-p (car x) (car y))       ; AND
          (our-equal-p (cdr x) (cdr y))
          nil)))
```

The *test* part of the outer **IF** is another **IF** which returns **T** if either argument is an atom. If either argument is an atom, then **OUR-EQUAL-P** simply reduces to applying **EQL** to both arguments. However, if both arguments are lists, then the

IF in the *else* part of the outer **IF** will return **T** only if the **CAR**s and the **CDR**s of each list are **OUR-EQUAL-P**. **TRACE** can help us to see how a list is pulled apart and examined by **OUR-EQUAL-P**:

```
Lisp> (trace our-equal-p)
(OUR-EQUAL-P)

Lisp> (our-equal-p 'snark 'snark)
1 Enter OUR-EQUAL-P SNARK SNARK
1 Exit OUR-EQUAL-P T
T

Lisp> (our-equal-p '(snark sleeps) '(snark sleeps))
1 Enter OUR-EQUAL-P (SNARK SLEEPS) (SNARK SLEEPS)
| 2 Enter OUR-EQUAL-P SNARK SNARK
| 2 Exit OUR-EQUAL-P T
| 2 Enter OUR-EQUAL-P (SLEEPS) (SLEEPS)
|   3 Enter OUR-EQUAL-P SLEEPS SLEEPS
|   3 Exit OUR-EQUAL-P T
|   3 Enter OUR-EQUAL-P NIL NIL
|   3 Exit OUR-EQUAL-P T
| 2 Exit OUR-EQUAL-P T
1 Exit OUR-EQUAL-P T
T
```

We have used **IF** to simulate the effect of the boolean operations **OR** and **AND**, but this idiom is so frequently used that Lisp has built-in **OR** and **AND** predicates. These boolean operations are special forms which expect zero or more arguments:

```
Lisp> (and t nil)
NIL

Lisp> (or t nil)
T

Lisp> (and t t t t nil)
NIL

Lisp> (or t t t t nil)
T

Lisp> (or nil nil)
NIL
```

```
Lisp> (and t t)
T
```

OR works by evaluating each argument from left to right, returning the first result which is *not* NIL. All remaining arguments will not be evaluated. If the result of evaluating each argument is NIL, then OR will return NIL. Similarly, AND will evaluate each argument from left to right, returning the first result which is NIL. If none of the arguments evaluates to NIL, then the result of evaluating the last argument is returned:

```
Lisp> (or 'first-argument)
FIRST-ARGUMENT

Lisp> (or t 'second-argument)
T

Lisp> (and t 'second-argument)
SECOND-ARGUMENT

Lisp> (setf *flag* 'not-evaluated)
NOT-EVALUATED

Lisp> (and nil (setf *flag* 'evaluated))
NIL

Lisp> *flag*
NOT-EVALUATED

Lisp> (or t (setf *flag* 'evaluated))
T

Lisp> *flag*
NOT-EVALUATED
```

Since AND and OR return a result as soon as possible, they are *short circuiting*, just like COND, which will short circuit as soon as one of the tests it evaluates is true. In the example above, *FLAG* is never set to EVALUATED because the short-circuiting nature of AND and OR didn't allow the second argument to be evaluated in these cases. Many languages define AND and OR differently, always evaluating every argument before returning a result.

Problem. Can you write AND and OR as functions using DEFUN? Explain.

Problem. Explain why the following version of MEMBER does not go into an infinite loop:

```
(defun memq (e l)
  (and (not (null l))
       (or (and (eq e (car l)) l)
           (memq e (cdr l)))))
```

Now we are ready to rewrite `OUR-EQUAL-P` more clearly in terms of `OR` and `AND`:

```
(defun our-equal-p (x y)
  (if (or (atom x)
          (atom y))
      (eql x y)
      (and (our-equal-p (car x) (car y))
           (our-equal-p (cdr x) (cdr y)))))
```

The short-circuiting property of `AND` and `OR` is a direct consequence of the fact that these operations are defined in terms of `IF`, and this property has some practical benefits. For example, it prevents the function `OUR-EQUAL-P` from needlessly checking if the `CDR`s of a list are `OUR-EQUAL-P` if it already knows that the `CAR`s are not `OUR-EQUAL-P`.

A related boolean function is called `NOT`. `NOT` expects a single argument and returns the logical negation of that argument:

```
Lisp> (not nil)
T

Lisp> (not t)
NIL

Lisp> (not 'frumious)
NIL

Lisp> (not '(any old list))
NIL
```

If `NOT` looks like a familiar function, it is:

```
Lisp> (null nil)
T

Lisp> (null t)
NIL

Lisp> (null 'frumious)
NIL
```

```
Lisp> (null '(any old list))
NIL
```

NULL and **NOT** have *identical* functionality. Using one name instead of the other is purely a matter of style and clarity. **NULL** is used when we want to see if a value is equal to the empty list, and so it is often used to see if we have reached the end of a list in a recursive function call. On the other hand, **NOT** is a boolean function which is usually used to negate the result of a predicate, as in `(NOT (ZEROP NUMBER))`.

Problem. Write a function called **OUR-COPY-TREE** which returns a copy of a list and its sublists. Lisp already contains a function called **COPY-TREE**. Be sure that your function recursively copies each sublist of the list it is given:

```
Lisp> (setf *l* '(teenage mutant ninja turtles))
(TEENAGE MUTANT NINJA TURTLES)

Lisp> (setf *copy* (copy-tree *l*))
(TEENAGE MUTANT NINJA TURTLES)

Lisp> (equal *l* *copy*)
T

Lisp> (eq *l* *copy*)
NIL
```

Problem. Write a function named **MAXIMUM-HEIGHT** which returns the maximum height of a tree:

```
Lisp> (maximum-height '())
0

Lisp> (maximum-height '(a b c d))
1

Lisp> (maximum-height '(a (b) ((c)) d))
3
```

You will probably want to use the function **MAX** in your definition of **MAXIMUM-HEIGHT**:

```
Lisp> (max 3 4)
4

Lisp> (max 3 3)
3

Lisp> (max 4 3 9 7)
9
```

Problem. Write a function called **FLATTEN** which "flattens out" a tree so that the maximum height of the new tree is 1:

```
Lisp> (flatten nil)
NIL

Lisp> (flatten '((up down) (left right) (north south)))
(UP DOWN LEFT RIGHT NORTH SOUTH)

Lisp> (flatten '(nil (up down)))
(NIL UP DOWN)

Lisp> (flatten '(pirahnas love to dine out))
(PIRAHNAS LOVE TO DINE OUT)

Lisp> (flatten '(pirahnas ((love (to)) dine (((out))))))
(PIRAHNAS LOVE TO DINE OUT)
```

5.2 PATTERN MATCHING

EQUAL is able to compare two constant pieces of data, but it is unable to compare a piece of data to a *pattern* which contains some constant parts and some variable parts. For example, suppose we have a list containing lists of family relations such as ((FATHER WARD WALLY) (MOTHER JUNE BEAVER)). If we want to find all the children of WARD, then we could match each family relation list against the pattern (FATHER WARD $CHILD). We will use the convention that any symbol which begins with a dollar sign is a *pattern variable* which can match any other piece of data in the same position:

```
Lisp> (match '(father ward wally) '(father ward $child))
(($CHILD WALLY))

Lisp> (match '(mother june beaver) '(father ward $child))
FAIL

Lisp> (match '(father ward wally) '(father $parent $child))
(($PARENT WARD) ($CHILD WALLY))

Lisp> (match '(* pi radius radius) '(* pi (expt radius 2)))
NIL     ; match succeeded, no bindings needed
```

MATCH is a more versatile version of **EQUAL**. If the pattern does not match the data, then the symbol **FAIL** is returned. However, if the pattern matches the data, then the set of pattern variable bindings which allow the match to succeed is returned. Each binding is represented as a list consisting of a variable followed by its value, and a list of all such bindings is returned by **MATCH**. We call such a list an *association list*.

5.2.1 Association Lists

An association list, usually called an *a-list*, is a list whose elements are other lists. The `CAR` of each sublist is called a *key*, while the `CDR` of each sublist is called a *datum*. Thus, the a-list `(($PARENT WARD) ($CHILD WALLY))` associates the key `$PARENT` with the datum `(WARD)` and the key `$CHILD` with the datum `(WALLY)`.[1]

We can look up the value of a key using the function `ASSOC`.[2] `ASSOC` expects a key and an a-list as arguments and it returns the entire sublist (not just the datum) associated with the key, or `NIL` if no sublist starting with the key is found. If there is more than one sublist associated with a key, then the first such sublist is returned.

```
Lisp> (assoc '$parent '(($parent ward) ($child wally)))
($PARENT WARD)

Lisp> (assoc '$child '(($parent ward) ($child wally)))
($CHILD WALLY)

Lisp> (assoc '$grandparent '(($parent ward) ($child wally)))
NIL

Lisp> (second (assoc '$child '(($parent ward)
                                ($child wally))))
WALLY

Lisp> (assoc '(adverb quickly) '(((adjective small) large)
                                  ((adverb quickly) slowly)))
NIL
```

We can use `SECOND` to extract the datum from the result of `ASSOC`. Notice that if we try to use a list as a key, `ASSOC` does not find the corresponding sublist. The reason is that `ASSOC` uses `EQL` to compare sublist keys to the key we are looking for, and we have already seen that lists are usually not `EQL`.

Problem. Write your own version of `ASSOC`.

---

[1] Later we will introduce *dotted pairs* which are more commonly used to build a-lists.
[2] Pronounced either *uh-sosh* or *uh-soak*.

5.2.2 Implementing `MATCH`

Now we are ready to implement `MATCH`. However, our version of `MATCH` will accept an a-list as a third argument which specifies any existing pattern variable bindings. If `MATCH` succeeds in matching the pattern to the data, then the third argument is extended to include any new bindings which were needed to satisfy the match. Because `NIL` is an a-list, we return the symbol `FAIL`, which is not an a-list, if the match fails:

```
Lisp> (match '(father ward wally) '(father ward $child) nil)
(($CHILD WALLY))

Lisp> (match '(mother june beaver)
             '(father ward $child)
             nil)

FAIL

Lisp> (match '(father ward wally)
             '(father $parent $child)
             '(($child wally)))
(($PARENT WARD) ($CHILD WALLY))

Lisp> (match '(father ward wally)
             '(father $parent $child)
             '(($child beaver)))
FAIL
```

Notice that the last call to `MATCH` fails because `$CHILD` is already constrained to have the value `BEAVER` when `MATCH` is called, and yet it needs to have the value `WALLY` in order to succeed.

We can view `MATCH` as a modification of `OUR-EQUAL-P`:

```
(defun our-equal-p (x y)
  (if (or (atom x)        ; expand this single base case into
          (atom y))       ; 2 base cases
      (eql x y)
      (and (our-equal-p (car x) (car y))   ; remember result
           (our-equal-p (cdr x) (cdr y)))))
```

The single base case in `OUR-EQUAL-P` must expand into two base cases: one for handling a pattern variable and another for handling a constant atomic pattern. We must also modify the recursive case to pass along to the second recursive call any pattern variable bindings established by the first recursive call:

```
(defun match (pattern data bindings)
  (cond ((atom pattern)
         (if (variablep pattern)
             (maybe-extend-bindings pattern data bindings)
```

```
            (if (equal pattern data)
                bindings
                'fail)))
       ((atom data) 'fail)
       (t (let ((car-bindings (match (car pattern)
                                     (car data)
                                     bindings)))
            (if (eq car-bindings 'fail)
                'fail
                (match (cdr pattern)
                       (cdr data)
                       car-bindings))))))
```

MATCH is the most complex function we have yet encountered, and you may have to play with it for a while using **TRACE** to fully understand how it works.

If the **PATTERN** is an atom, then it cannot be decomposed any further, so we have a base case. However, rather than immediately calling **EQL** to see if the **PATTERN** equals the data, we first check to see if the pattern is a variable. If so, we try to return an extension of the current set of bindings. If the pattern is not a variable, then it is an atom which must be equal to the data in order for **MATCH** to succeed and return the current set of bindings unchanged. If the pattern and the data are not equal, then the atom **FAIL** is returned.

If the pattern is not atomic, then we check to see whether the data is atomic. If so, then we immediately return **FAIL**, since an atomic piece of data can never match a non-atomic pattern. This constitutes the second base case for **MATCH**.

The third arm of the **COND** is the recursive case of **MATCH**. We reach this case if both the pattern and the data are lists. In order to match two lists, the **CAR** and the **CDR** of each list must match, just as the **CAR** and the **CDR** of two lists must be the same in order for the lists to be equal. However, unlike **OUR-EQUAL-P**, we need to remember the pattern variable bindings which allow the **CAR** of each list to match in order to continue and match the **CDR** of each list.

If the **CAR** of the pattern fails to match the **CAR** of the data, then the entire match must also fail. However, if the **CAR**s do match, then we attempt to extend the bindings which allowed the **CAR**s to match by matching the **CDR** of each list.

Now we can turn our attention to some smaller functions which are needed by **MATCH**. **MAYBE-EXTEND-BINDINGS** expects a pattern variable, a constant piece of data, and a binding a-list:

```
(defun maybe-extend-bindings (var data bindings)
  (let ((existing-binding (assoc var bindings)))
    (if (null existing-binding)
        ;; add a new binding
        (cons (list var data) bindings)
        (if (equal (binding-value existing-binding) data)
            bindings
            'fail))))
```

We first use `ASSOC` to check if `VAR` has already been given a binding in `BINDINGS`. If the result of the `ASSOC` is the empty list, then there was no previous binding for `VAR`, so we are free to return an extended version of `BINDINGS` in which `VAR` is bound to `DATA`. However, if a binding already exists for `VAR`, then `DATA` must be equal to the value already assigned to `VAR` in order to succeed. `BINDING-VALUE` is an *accessing* function which returns the second element of the binding list returned by `ASSOC`:

```
(defun binding-value (var-val-list)
  (second var-val-list))
```

The final function we need is the predicate `VARIABLEP`, and it returns `T` when given a pattern variable. We are not ready to fully understand how this definition works yet, so we'll gloss over it for the time being. The basic idea is to be sure that `V` is really a symbol, and if so return `T` if the first element in the symbol's name is the character `$`:

```
(defun variablep (v)
  (and (symbolp v)
       (char= (char (symbol-name v) 0) #\$)))
```

We will be able to fully understand this definition after talking about strings and character objects in Chapter 12.

Problem. Rewrite `MATCH` to allow *kleene closures* to appear in patterns. A kleene closure is analogous to an ellipsis in English text because it allows a variable to be matched zero or more times:

```
;;; A variable which starts with $* can match a piece
;;; of data 0 or more times.
Lisp> (match '(progn $*form) '(progn 1 2 3) nil)
($*form (1 2 3))
```

5.2.3 An Application of `MATCH`: Program Rewriting

One interesting use of a pattern matcher is to implement *rewrite rules*. We have already seen that Lisp provides several different ways to accomplish the same thing, and a Lisp compiler might want to convert certain kinds of Lisp code into a simpler form. For example:

- `(1+ $x) => (+ 1 $x)`
- `(list $x) => (cons $x nil)`
- `(second $x) => (cadr $x)`
- `(cadr $x) => (car (cdr $x))`
- `(append $x nil) => $x`

- `(zerop $x) => (= $x 0)`
- `(if nil $then $else) => $else`
- `(if (not $test) $then $else) => (if $test $else $then)`

The left-hand side of each rule represents a Lisp expression which could occur in a program, while the right-hand side represents an equivalent expression. Thus, the Lisp expression `(SECOND *REGISTERS*)` will match the left-hand side of the rule `(SECOND $X) => (CADR $X)`, and can be rewritten as the expression `(CADR *REGISTERS*)` if we replace the variable `$X` by the symbol `*REGISTERS*`. Similarly, `(CADR *REGISTERS*)` could then be transformed into `(CAR (CDR *REGISTERS*))`.

After a match has succeeded, we need to replace each instance of a pattern variable on the right-hand side of a rule by the value that variable assumed on the left-hand side. We can use the function SUBST to perform such substitutions. SUBST expects three arguments, which we will call *new*, *old*, and *list*, and it returns a new version of *list* in which all occurrences of *old* have been replaced by *new*:

```
Lisp> (subst 4 '$x '(+ 1 $x))
(+ 1 4)

Lisp> (setf form '(car (cdr $x)))
(CAR (CDR $X))

Lisp> (subst '(father fred pebbles) '$x form)
(CAR (CDR (FATHER FRED PEBBLES)))

Lisp> form
(CAR (CDR $X))
```

SUBST uses the function EQL to compare *old* to each subpart of the given *list*, and if some part of *list* is EQL to *old*, then it is replaced by *new* in the new list which SUBST will return. Notice that SUBST builds a new list, leaving the original list unchanged.

Problem. Write your own version of SUBST called OUR-SUBST.

Problem. Complete the source code–rewriting system by writing a function called REWRITE. REWRITE should accept a list of rules and a program. It should repeatedly try to rewrite the program until no more rewrites are possible.

5.3 LISTS AS STACKS

Lists are often used as *stacks*. A stack is a simple data structure analogous to a pile of paper. We can stack sheets of paper on top of each other, and only the top sheet of paper is visible. In order to retrieve a specific sheet, we need to keep taking papers off of the top of the stack until we find the sheet we want. Putting paper on the stack is called *pushing* and taking paper off the stack is called *popping*.

The empty list corresponds to an empty stack. CONSing a new element onto the front of a stack is equivalent to a push, while CDRing down the list and returning the element we just discarded corresponds to a pop. The special forms PUSH and POP implement these operations:

```
Lisp> (setf *objects* '())
NIL

Lisp> (push 'cylinder *objects*)
(CYLINDER)

Lisp> (push 'cube *objects*)
(CUBE CYLINDER)

Lisp> *objects*
(CUBE CYLINDER)

Lisp> (pop *objects*)
CUBE

Lisp> *objects*
(CYLINDER)

Lisp> (pop *objects*)
CYLINDER

Lisp> *objects*
NIL
```

Of course, we do not need PUSH and POP to use stacks in our programs. We are always free to CONS a new element onto a list before passing it to another function, or to CDR down a list to pop elements off of a stack. PUSH and POP are usually only needed when we want to name a stack with a global variable.

Problem. Why do PUSH and POP have to be special forms?

Problem. We can use a stack to determine whether a given word (or sentence) is a *palindrome*. A word is a palindrome if it reads the same forwards and backwards. RADAR and MADAM are examples of palindromes. Write a function called PALINDROMEP which accepts a list, and returns true if the list is a palindrome. Of course, you could use (EQUAL LIST (REVERSE LIST)) to define PALINDROMEP, but try doing it with a stack. Here is an example of PALINDROMEP:

```
Lisp> (palindromep '(r a d a r))
T

Lisp> (palindromep '(p i r a h n a))
NIL
```

Problem. Mathematical expressions can be written in a number of different ways. For example, we can write the formula for the volume of a cylinder in three different ways:

1. Infix: $\pi * r^2 * h$
2. Prefix: `(* pi (* (expt r 2) h))`
3. Postfix: `(pi ((r 2 expt) h *) *)`

Mathematics is normally written using *infix* notation. The notation is called infix because operators such as * come in between the arguments to that operator (this convention does not apply to functions such as sine which accept only one argument). Lisp expresses all function calls in *prefix notation*. The name *prefix* is derived from the fact that the operator (function) always precedes all of the arguments. Languages such as C and Pascal use a mixture of infix and prefix notation. The third form shown is called *postfix* notation because the operator always comes after all of the arguments. A certain popular brand of calculators uses this convention which is also known as reverse Polish notation (RPN).

All three forms can be used to express the same idea. Write the following conversion functions (you may assume that all operations in the expressions accept exactly two arguments):

- `PREFIX->INFIX` expects a prefix expression and returns the equivalent infix expression.
- `INFIX->PREFIX` converts the infix expression it is given into a prefix expression. This is a difficult problem because you must obey the order of operations (multiplication before addition, etc.). You should correctly handle functions which contain `+`, `-`, `*`, `/`, `EXPT`. Hint: You might want to maintain two stacks to hold operands and operators which you are not ready to handle yet. Think about how you enter an infix expression into an RPN calculator.

5.4 LISTS AS SETS

Lists are also a convenient, although not especially efficient, way to implement *sets*. A set is a collection of objects, with no object being included more than once. A quick survey of some of the set operations provided by Lisp is given below. Refer to the Common Lisp manual for more details:

```
Lisp> (setf *people* '(ollie rambo garbanifar fawn))
(OLLIE RAMBO GARBANIFAR FAWN)

Lisp> (adjoin 'ronny *people*)
(RONNY OLLIE RAMBO GARBANIFAR FAWN)
```

```
Lisp> (adjoin 'terminator *people*)
(TERMINATOR OLLIE RAMBO GARBANIFAR FAWN)

Lisp> *people*
(OLLIE RAMBO GARBANIFAR FAWN)

Lisp> (union *people* '(ollie ronny terminator))
(FAWN GARBANIFAR RAMBO OLLIE RONNY TERMINATOR)

Lisp> (intersection *people* '(sylvester brigette))
NIL

Lisp> (intersection *people* '(ollie fawn))
(OLLIE FAWN)

Lisp> (subsetp '(ollie fawn) *people*)
T

Lisp> (set-difference *people* '(rambo garbarnifar))
(OLLIE FAWN)
```

Problem. Write your own versions of **UNION** and **INTERSECTION**. What is the difference in the performance of your algorithm on two lists of 10 elements versus two lists of 1000 elements? Can you think of a more efficient representation for sets?

Problem. Write a function named **LIST-ROTATE** which accepts two arguments: a list and a count. **LIST-ROTATE** should return a new list representing the result of rotating the elements of the original list the specified number of times. The list should be rotated to the left if the count is positive, and to the right if the count is negative:

```
Lisp> (list-rotate '(a b c d e) 1)
(B C D E A)

Lisp> (list-rotate '(a b c d e) 6)
(B C D E A)

Lisp> (list-rotate '(a b c d e) -1)
(E A B C D)

Lisp> (list-rotate '(a b c d e) -3)
(C D E A B)
```

CHAPTER 6

DATA ABSTRACTION AND STRUCTURES

6.1 USING LISTS TO REPRESENT ABSTRACT DATA TYPES

Whenever we write computer programs, we should strive to model the world we are working in as clearly as possible, and achieving this goal often involves grouping related pieces of information. For example, we earlier used the following function to compute the volume of a cylinder:

```
(defun cylinder-volume (radius height)
  (* pi (expt radius 2) height))
```

The problem with this function is that we have to pass the radius and the height of a cylinder as two separate arguments to `CYLINDER-VOLUME`, even though the two pieces of information are related. For example, we might be writing a program to control a robot arm which is mounted on a mobile base. A human could command the robot to run around a room, avoiding obstacles and moving things to do useful work. In order to accomplish this, the robot must have a complete model of all the objects in the room so that it can reason about them. Some objects may be shaped like cylinders, and any given cylinder may actually have the following properties:

75

- A radius
- A height
- A color

In order to model cylinders in the real world, we really want to create a new kind of object called a `CYLINDER` in our Lisp system. Thus, we should be able to make new cylinders, pull existing cylinders apart, and tell if two cylinders are equal. One simple way to accomplish this is to represent a cylinder as a list of four items: The atom `CYLINDER` followed by the radius, height, and color of a specific cylinder. Thus, a cylinder with radius 11, height 7, and color purple would be represented by the list `(CYLINDER 11 7 PURPLE)`.

Now that we've defined how a cylinder is represented, we need to define the following kinds of functions:

- A *constructor function* called `MAKE-CYLINDER` which can build new cylinders, just as `CONS` or `LIST` can build new lists
- *Accessing functions* such as `CYLINDER-HEIGHT` to allow us to extract the subcomponents of a cylinder, just as `CAR` and `CDR` allow us to access the subcomponents of a list
- A predicate called `CYLINDERP` which will return `T` if the object passed to it is a cylinder

Here are the definitions of these functions:

```
(defun make-cylinder (radius height color)
  (list 'cylinder radius height color))

(defun cylinder-radius (cylinder)
  (second cylinder))

(defun cylinder-height (cylinder)
  (third cylinder))

(defun cylinder-color (cylinder)
  (fourth cylinder))

(defun cylinderp (object)
  (eq (first object) 'cylinder))
```

These functions have very simple definitions, so why should we bother to even define them? One reason is that the name `CYLINDER-COLOR` is much more meaningful when reading a program than `(FOURTH CYLINDER)`, or worse yet `(CADDDR CYLINDER)`. Another reason is that these functions allow us to abstract out the interesting properties of a cylinder, considering them independently of the representation we use for cylinders. Thus, when we later learn about arrays in

Lisp, we can go back and change the definitions of our cylinder functions to use arrays without changing any of the code which uses cylinders. This is the essence of abstraction, and is related to the black box model of a function, since the caller of a function has no way of knowing what goes on inside of that function.

For example, the function CYLINDER-VOLUME can now be rewritten:

```
(defun cylinder-volume (cylinder)
  (* pi
     (expt (cylinder-radius cylinder) 2)
     (cylinder-height cylinder)))
```

We can use this new function to compute the volume of cylinders in our world:

```
Lisp> (setf *c1* (make-cylinder 11 7 'purple))
(CYLINDER 11 7 PURPLE)

Lisp> (setf *c2* (make-cylinder 11 7 'green))
(CYLINDER 11 7 GREEN)

Lisp> (cylinder-volume *c1*)
2660.929

Lisp> (cylinderp '(a completely bogus object))
NIL

Lisp> (cylinderp *c1*)
T
```

If we consider each cylinder to represent a cylinder in the real world, then it may sometimes be necessary to change one or more of the attributes of a cylinder. For example, one day someone might paint cylinder *C1* chartreuse. Now we would like to change *only* the color attribute of *C1*. In most languages this would be accomplished with an assignment statement which changes the value of the color field in a cylinder record or structure. However, so far we do not have any way to change only one element of a list, leaving all the other elements alone. We can create a completely new list, though, changing only the attribute we are interested in:

```
(defun set-cylinder-radius (cylinder new-radius)
  (make-cylinder new-radius
                 (cylinder-height cylinder)
                 (cylinder-color cylinder)))

(defun set-cylinder-height (cylinder new-height)
  (make-cylinder (cylinder-radius cylinder)
```

```
                    new-height
                    (cylinder-color cylinder))))

(defun set-cylinder-color (cylinder new-color)
  (make-cylinder (cylinder-radius cylinder)
                 (cylinder-height cylinder)
                 new-color))
```

These functions could be called *updating* functions because they update the value of a specific cylinder attribute. Unfortunately, they work by always creating new cylinders rather than reusing an existing cylinder. Thus, we get the following behavior:

```
Lisp> *cl*
(CYLINDER 11 7 PURPLE)

Lisp> (set-cylinder-color *cl* 'chartreuse)
(CYLINDER 11 7 CHARTREUSE)

Lisp> *cl*
(CYLINDER 11 7 PURPLE)

Lisp> (setf *cl* (set-cylinder-color *cl* 'chartreuse))
(CYLINDER 11 7 CHARTREUSE)

Lisp> *cl*
(CYLINDER 11 7 CHARTREUSE)
```

`SET-CYLINDER-COLOR` makes a copy of `*Cl*` with a new color. The original cylinder is unchanged; `SET-CYLINDER-COLOR` has no side effects.

Problem. Define a new object called a `POINT` which consists of x, y, and z coordinates.

Problem. Write a function named `DISTANCE` which accepts two points as arguments and returns the distance between them.

Problem. Write a function named `ADD-POINTS` which accepts two points and returns a new point representing their sum.

6.2 ERROR AND BACKTRACE

Consider what happens to `CYLINDER-VOLUME` when we accidentally pass it an object which is not a cylinder:

```
Lisp> (cylinder-volume '(a completely bogus object))
>>Error: non-numeric argument COMPLETELY
```

```
EXPT:
   Required arg 0 (X): COMPLETELY
   Required arg 1 (N): 2

:A    Abort to Lisp Top Level
->
```

Of course, we usually do not *intentionally* pass bad arguments to our functions, but we also do not intentionally put bugs in our programs, and yet they always seem to occur. Unfortunately, the error message we get does not tell us that (`A COMPLETELY BOGUS OBJECT`) is not a cylinder. Instead, it says that `COMPLETELY` is not a number. Why?

At this point it is useful to invoke a debugger tool called a *backtrace*. In our archetypal debugger, we can get a backtrace by typing `:B`:

```
-> :b
EXPT <- CYLINDER-VOLUME <- EVAL
```

The format of the backtrace output and the way it is invoked are implementation dependent. Thus, you'll have to read your Lisp system manual to find out about how to obtain similar functionality from your Lisp. Our backtrace prints out the names of functions separated by `<-`. Going back to the photocopier model of function calling, each function name represents a sheet of paper that is currently being used to compute the value of a function. The backtrace should be read from left to right, with the leftmost function being the most recently called. Hence, the example backtrace says that we are currently trying to compute a call to the function `EXPT`, and this function call was caused by a call to `CYLINDER-VOLUME`. The call to `CYLINDER-VOLUME` was in turn caused by someone calling the function `EVAL`. `EVAL` happens to be the *evaluation* part of the read-eval-print loop.

`EVAL` was trying to compute the value of the expression (`CYLINDER-VOLUME '(A COMPLETELY BOGUS OBJECT)`). The first thing that `CYLINDER-VOLUME` did was to compute (`CYLINDER-RADIUS '(A COMPLETELY BOGUS OBJECT)`). Unfortunately, `CYLINDER-RADIUS` just assumes that it was passed a cylinder, so it blindly returned the second element of the list it was passed, since this is where the radius is stored in a cylinder. However, in our object the symbol `COMPLETELY` was in the second position of the list. At this point the computation we are performing is wrong, but the Lisp code is unaware of this. Thus, `CYLINDER-VOLUME` next tries to square the radius it got from `CYLINDER-RADIUS` by calling `EXPT` with the arguments `COMPLETELY` and `2`. `EXPT` *does* check to be sure that it has been passed numeric arguments, and signals an error because `COMPLETELY` is not a number.

Backtrace is a useful tool for figuring out exactly how Lisp got to the current error. Without it, we would be forced to guess what chain of function calls have occurred. Many people learning Lisp ignore backtrace. However, it is one of the most powerful debugging tools available to you, and it behooves you to become familiar with it.

However, we are still left with the problem that the error message we receive from **EXPT** is not very helpful because it does not describe the real problem with our program. The trouble is that after the initial error—passing an object which was not a cylinder to **CYLINDER-VOLUME**—our computation should not have been allowed to continue. Instead, **CYLINDER-VOLUME** should have used **CYLINDERP** to be *sure* that it was given a cylinder before proceeding any further. If the object it is passed is not a cylinder, then **CYLINDER-VOLUME** should signal an error, just as **EXPT** did when it was not passed a number.

We can signal errors in Lisp by calling the function **ERROR** with a string describing the nature of the error. Thus, we can define a new, safer version of **CYLINDER-VOLUME**:

```
(defun cylinder-volume (cylinder)
  (if (cylinderp cylinder)
      (* pi
         (expt (cylinder-radius cylinder) 2)
         (cylinder-height cylinder))
      (error "Argument is not a cylinder")))
```

Our new version of **CYLINDER-VOLUME** will only compute the volume of **CYLINDER** if **CYLINDERP** says that **CYLINDER** really is a cylinder. If not, then **ERROR** is called with a meaningful error message:

```
Lisp> (cylinder-volume '(a completely bogus object))
>>Error: Argument is not a cylinder

CYLINDER-VOLUME:
   Required arg 0 (CYLINDER): (A COMPLETELY BOGUS OBJECT)

:A     Abort to Lisp Top Level
-> :b
CYLINDER-VOLUME <- EVAL
```

This time we never get as far as calling **EXPT**, because an invalid object was caught by the explicit error check in our code. Notice that the error signalled by a call to **ERROR** looks similar to the error signalled by the built-in functions in Lisp. The only thing the user can do now is abort the entire computation and try again.

Problem. Change the point functions you wrote earlier so that they signal an error if they are not given points as an argument.

6.3 DEFSTRUCT

We have succeeded in defining the equivalent of a `record` in Pascal or a `struct` in C by using lists. However, we had to do a lot of work writing little functions. Defining these functions is quite tedious and mechanical. Since structures are used so often in Lisp programs, the special form `DEFSTRUCT` exists to allow us to easily define new structures. Here is how we could define a cylinder structure using `DEFSTRUCT`:

```
Lisp> (defstruct cylinder radius height color)
CYLINDER
```

The first argument to `DEFSTRUCT` is the name of the structure we want to define, while the remaining arguments are the names of the fields which we want this structure to have. Fields in a structure are often called *slots* in Lisp, and we will use the two terms interchangeably from now on. `DEFSTRUCT` does not evaluate any of its arguments, and it simply returns the name of the structure we are defining.

`DEFSTRUCT` has many side effects, though. Our sample call has caused the following new functions to be defined:

1. A constructor function called `MAKE-CYLINDER`
2. The accessing functions `CYLINDER-RADIUS`, `CYLINDER-HEIGHT`, and `CYLINDER-COLOR`
3. The predicate `CYLINDER-P` which returns `T` if its argument is a cylinder. The predicate defined by `DEFSTRUCT` will always end in a `-P`, and thus it may sometimes violate the convention for only adding a dash before the `P` if there is at least one other dash in the symbol. Too bad.
4. A function called `COPY-CYLINDER` which will return a copy of the cylinder which it is passed. We did not write this function when implementing structures as lists, although we could have used `COPY-LIST` for this purpose.

Now we can make a new cylinder using `MAKE-CYLINDER`:

```
Lisp> (setf *cl* (make-cylinder))
#S(CYLINDER RADIUS NIL HEIGHT NIL COLOR NIL)
```

Notice that the funny printed representation of a cylinder starts with `#S`. All structures defined with `DEFSTRUCT` have a printed representation which looks like a list with `#S` in front of it.[1] The first element of the structure tells us this structure is a cylinder, while the rest of the printed representation lists the name of each field followed by the value of that field. Structures made by `MAKE-CYLINDER` initially have all of their slots set to `NIL`. However, we can initialize any slot by using a *keyword argument* which names a specific slot followed by the initial value for that slot:

---

[1] In order to make this example work, `*PRINT-STRUCTURE*` should be set to `T` if your system has it.

```
Lisp> (make-cylinder :radius 11 :height 7 :color 'green)
#S(CYLINDER RADIUS 11 HEIGHT 7 COLOR GREEN)

Lisp> (make-cylinder :color 'blue :height 7)
#S(CYLINDER RADIUS NIL HEIGHT 7 COLOR BLUE)
```

Any symbol which starts with a colon is called a *keyword*. The advantage of keyword arguments is that we may initialize any combination of slots in any order, rather than requiring that a fixed number of slots be initialized in a specific order every time a structure is created.

We can also create a new structure by entering the printed representation of that structure, just as we can create a new list by entering the printed representation of the list:

```
Lisp> (setf *c3* #S(cylinder radius 2
                             height 100
                             color fuchsia))
#S(CYLINDER RADIUS 2 HEIGHT 100 COLOR FUCHSIA)
```

Thus, there are a number of ways to create structures and initialize their fields. Once a structure is created, we can dissect it using the accessing functions which **DEFSTRUCT** defined for us:

```
Lisp> (cylinder-height *c3*)
100

Lisp> (cylinder-color *c3*)
FUCHSIA
```

We can explicitly use the function **CYLINDER-P** to test if an object is a cylinder, just as we did when trying to check for the correct argument type in the accessing functions we wrote by hand. However, one nice thing about the accessing functions defined by **DEFSTRUCT** is that they provide built-in error checking on the type of their arguments. Thus, the type check which we had to explicitly put into the accessing functions we wrote is automatically included in the accessors defined by **DEFSTRUCT**.[2]

6.3.1 SETF Is a Generalized Updating Function

SETF is actually a generalized *setting* or *updating* function which can *destructively modify* part of an object. The first argument to **SETF** must be an accessing form,

---

[2] The type check may not be performed if we compile our code and want it to run as fast as possible on standard hardware.

while the second argument is the new value we want the accessing form to retrieve. So far the only accessing form we have used with `SETF` is a symbol. Whenever we evaluate a symbol, we access the symbol's value. Therefore, when we `SETF` a symbol, we update its value. Similarly, `CYLINDER-HEIGHT` accesses the `HEIGHT` slot of a cylinder, and we can change the value of that slot with `SETF`:

```
Lisp> *c3*
#S(CYLINDER RADIUS 2 HEIGHT 100 COLOR FUCHSIA)

Lisp> (setf (cylinder-height *c3*) 25)
25

Lisp> *c3*
#S(CYLINDER RADIUS 2 HEIGHT 25 COLOR FUCHSIA)
```

Notice that a new copy of the cylinder was not created. Instead, the value of the `HEIGHT` slot was actually changed to a new number. `SETF` can also destructively modify objects other than structures. In order to understand more about destructive operations, we should understand how objects and object references can be represented in Lisp.

Problem. Reimplement the `POINT` problems given earlier, using structures.

Problem. Rewrite the ratio exercises at the end of Chapter 4 using a structure rather than a list to represent a ratio.

CHAPTER 7

DESTRUCTIVE OPERATIONS

7.1 MEMORY ORGANIZATION AND POINTERS

So far we have discussed objects inside of Lisp as though they were abstract entities whose inner compositions were unknown. In order to extend our understanding of Lisp, it helps to dive a bit deeper into one possible representation of these objects. A general familiarity with the organization of a computer is useful in understanding this discussion.

The mythical computer we have been running Lisp on contains a memory capable of holding 1000 megabytes of information, as shown in Figure 7.1. Each byte is a compartment that can hold eight bits of information, and each compartment has an *address* which is written next to the box representing that byte.

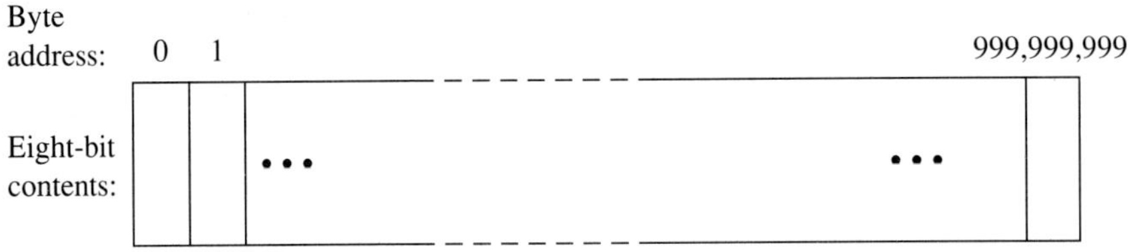

FIGURE 7.1
One thousand megabytes of memory.

The interpretation that we assign to each byte is completely up to us. We can build objects by grouping together sequential bytes of memory, interpreting the bits in a way specific to the kind of object we want to create. We may represent a number with 4 contiguous bytes of memory or a symbol with 24 bytes of memory by interpreting the bytes in a predefined way. We can reference an object with a *pointer*. Since objects are nothing more than chunks of memory, a pointer is just the address of the first byte of an object. This helps to explain how **EQ** might work. **EQ** expects two pointers as arguments and it simply compares them. If the pointers contain the same address, then **EQ** returns **T**, otherwise it returns **NIL**.

How many bytes of memory do we need to represent a pointer? Since an object will start at some byte, a pointer must be able to hold a number from 0 to 999,999,999. If we represent numbers in binary, then one byte can represent the numbers from 0 to 255, two bytes (16 bits) can represent the numbers from 0 to 65,535, and three bytes (24 bits) can represent the numbers from 0 to 16,777,215. However, we need to represent even larger addresses; thus we need four bytes (32 bits) per pointer so that we represent addresses up to 4,294,967,295. This is more than enough to hold the address of the first byte of any block of memory, and thus it is sufficient to "point" to any Lisp object we can create. Figure 7.2 shows two different close-up views of 16 bytes of memory.

Sixteen bytes of memory

Sixteen bytes viewed as four 32-bit pointers.
Pointer 1 points to the start of pointer 2.

Sixteen bytes viewed as two cons cells

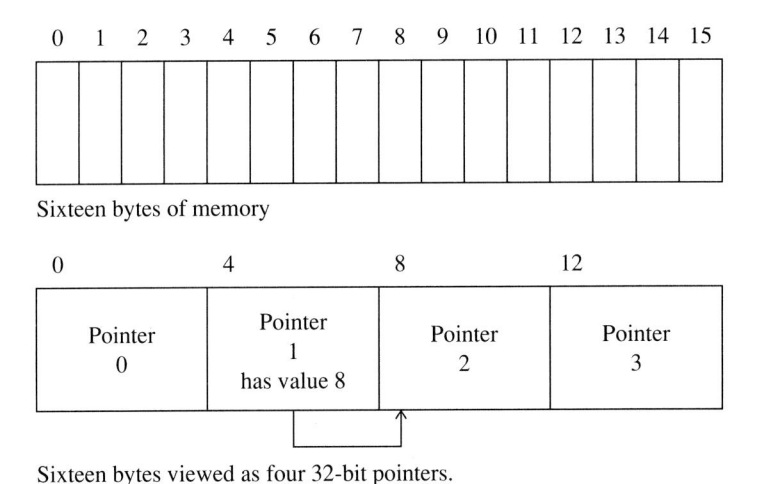

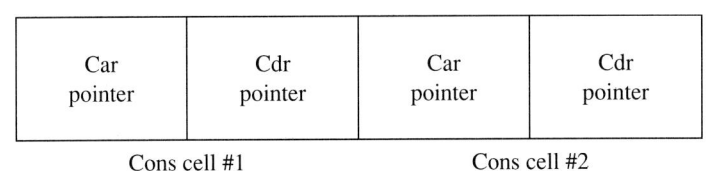

FIGURE 7.2
Three different views of 16 bytes of memory.

7.1.1 Building Lists from Cons Cells

One of the simplest objects in Lisp is called a *cons cell*. A cons cell is simply a pair of pointers, with the first pointer called the *car pointer* and the second pointer called the *cdr pointer*. Since each pointer is four bytes long, a cons cell must be an eight-byte long object. Thus, we can use 16 bytes of memory to represent two adjacent cons cells, as shown in Figure 7.2. The graphical convention we are using to describe the layout of objects in memory is called *box and pointer* notation.

Every time we call the function CONS, we are actually passing two pointers which reference two objects. CONS creates a *new* cons cell from eight bytes of free memory. The first pointer in the cons cell is initialized to the address specified by the first pointer we passed, while the second pointer in the cons cell is initialized to the address specified by the second pointer we passed. Figure 7.3 depicts the single cons cell which is created by the call (CONS '$X 'HUNT).

Graphically representing objects in memory as a sequence of bytes quickly becomes cumbersome and takes up a lot of space, so we will often use a mixed notation as in Figure 7.3. We represent the cons cell as a pair of pointers, but we represent the symbol objects being pointed to as simply $X and HUNT rather than as other blocks of memory.

In order to print the cons cell shown in Figure 7.3, Lisp uses a special notation which we have not seen before:

```
Lisp> (setf *cl* (cons '$x 'hunt))
($X . HUNT)

Lisp> (car *cl*)
$X

Lisp> (cdr *cl*)
HUNT
```

This notation is called *dotted pair* notation. The object before the dot is the object pointed to by the first pointer in the cons cell, while the object after the dot is the object pointed to by the second pointer. The accessing functions CAR and

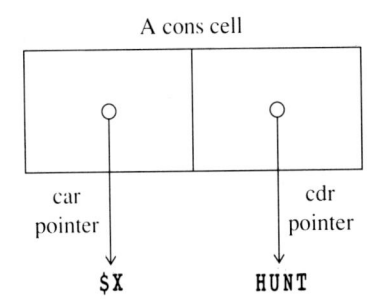

FIGURE 7.3
Graphic view of a cons cell representing ($X. HUNT) —a pair of pointers.

CDR expect a pointer to a cons cell, and they each return one of the pointers in that cell. Thus, we can pair two objects together using CONS and we can examine each half of the pair using CAR and CDR.

Now we can build *linked lists* out of the cons cells. The first pointer in a cons cell can point to any Lisp object which we want to be an element of the list, while the second pointer must point to another cons cell which is used to represent the remainder of the list (the recursive case). Of course, at some point we have to end the list, so by convention whenever the second pointer of a cons cell points to the symbol NIL (also known as the empty list), we consider the list to have ended. Thus, we can create a single-element list by consing together the element and the symbol NIL:

```
Lisp> '(hunt)
(HUNT)

Lisp> (cons 'hunt nil)
(HUNT)

Lisp> '(hunt . nil)
(HUNT)
```

Notice that we can CONS two elements together not only by calling the function CONS, but also by typing in the dot notation for that cons cell. However, Lisp prints out the list according to the notation we have been using for lists all along. The printer always tries to print lists without dots whenever possible, and a list whose last CDR points to NIL, and thus can be printed without dots, is sometimes called a *proper list*. Until now we have only been dealing with proper lists.

We can create a two-element list out of two cons cells:

```
Lisp> (list 'snark 'hunt)
(SNARK HUNT)

Lisp> (cons 'snark (cons 'hunt nil))
(SNARK HUNT)

Lisp> '(snark . (hunt . nil))
(SNARK HUNT)
```

In each case, we have created the list (SNARK HUNT), and Lisp always prints this list out in the same way, no matter how we enter it. Figure 7.4 graphically depicts the cons cells which constitute this list. The dot notation is the textual representation most suggestive of the way a list is built, but it is also the most verbose and cumbersome.

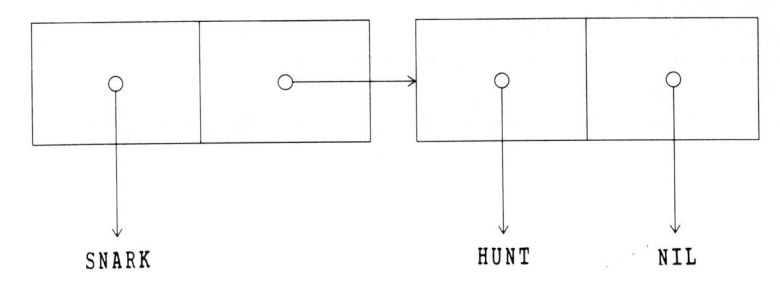

FIGURE 7.4
The list `(SNARK HUNT)` built from two cons cells.

Even if Lisp did not provide cons cells as a built-in data type, we could use `DEFSTRUCT` to define our own cons cells. For example, we could define the data type `PAIR`:

```
(defstruct pair
  castor
  pollux)
```

`MAKE-PAIR` would be the equivalent of `CONS`, and `PAIR-CASTOR` and `PAIR-POLLUX` would be the equivalents of `CAR` and `CDR` respectively. Unfortunately, our new data type would not be as convenient to use when building lists as cons cells are:

```
Lisp> (setf l (make-pair :castor 'first-element
                         :pollux nil))
#S(PAIR CASTOR FIRST-ELEMENT POLLUX NIL)

Lisp> (pair-castor l)
FIRST-ELEMENT

Lisp> (pair-pollux l)
NIL
```

Our new lists are not very pretty to look at since the list we would normally write as `(FIRST-ELEMENT)` prints out as a lengthy structure. Likewise, these lists would be difficult to type into the computer. However, Common Lisp allows us to specify exactly how structures will be printed, and thus with more effort we would force `PAIR`s to be printed out in a more readable format. Likewise, we can extend the part of Lisp which reads our input to construct `PAIR`s using our own notation.

Problem. Allow `PAIR`s to be entered and printed using braces rather that parentheses. You will need to read more about `DEFSTRUCT` and `READTABLES` in the Common Lisp manual in order to do this. This is a complicated exercise, and you might want to read further in this book before attempting it.

The important point to remember here is that there is nothing really special about cons cells or any of the other built-in data types and operations which Lisp provides, since we are free to define our own new types of objects and operations. The primary advantage of having certain types built in is convenience and efficiency.

Now that we know about dotted pairs we can improve our representation of a-lists. We previously represented each element of an a-list as a two-element list such as (`$X MR-POTATO-HEAD`). However, this is fairly wasteful, since we could get away with using only one cons cell by representing each a-list entry as a dotted pair such as (`$X . MR-POTATO-HEAD`). This representation also makes accessing the data portion of an a-list entry a bit faster since we can use `CDR` rather `CADR` to access it.

Most a-list entries are usually represented as single cons cells if there is only one data item associated with the key. In fact, the Lisp functions `ACONS` (A-list `CONS`) and `PAIRLIS` make creating such lists a bit easier. `ACONS` can be used to add a new key and data pair onto the front of an a-list, while `PAIRLIS` can be used to "zip together" two lists, appending the resulting list onto another a-list:

```
Lisp> (setf l '(($x . mr-potato-head)))
(($X . MR-POTATO-HEAD))

Lisp> (acons '$y 'egg-head l)
(($Y . EGG-HEAD) ($X . MR-POTATO-HEAD))

Lisp> (pairlis '($y $z) '(penguin joker))
(($Y . PENGUIN) ($Z . JOKER))

Lisp> (pairlis '($y $z) '(penguin joker) l)
(($Y . PENGUIN) ($Z . JOKER) ($X . MR-POTATO-HEAD))
```

The third argument to `PAIRLIS` should be an a-list, but if it is not provided it defaults to the empty list. The new representation of a-lists leads to a printed representation which is a bit more confusing than our old representation because of the rules for printing dotted pairs:

```
Lisp> (acons '$y '(a bunch of crooks) l)
(($Y A BUNCH OF CROOKS) ($X . MR-POTATO-HEAD))
```

Notice that even though we added the pair (`$Y . (A BUNCH OF CROOKS)`), it prints as (`$Y A BUNCH OF CROOKS`). This makes sense since the printer tries to avoid dot notation whenever possible, but it can be a bit confusing if we forget this fact.

7.2 DESTRUCTIVE OPERATIONS

In the last chapter we saw how SETF can alter the value of a structure slot. In this section we will see that SETF can modify other kinds of objects, such as cons cells.

7.2.1 Modifying Cons Cells

Recall that when we represented a structure as a list of slots, we had no way to change a single element in the structure because we had no way to change a single element in a list. However, just as Lisp gives us a way to "cons up" a pair of pointers, it will also allow us to assign new values to those pointers after the cons cell has been created. Updating the value of a pointer is called a *destructive operation* because it overwrites the pointer which used to be contained in a cell with a new address, thus destroying the old pointer.

We can update the pointers in a cons cell using SETF, just as we updated the slots in a structure created by DEFSTRUCT using SETF. Recall that the first argument to SETF must be an accessing form, while the second argument evaluates to the object which we want the accessing form to retrieve. In terms of pointers, the first argument describes the address of a particular pointer in memory, while the second argument to SETF is the new address we want that pointer to contain. Thus, we can pass accessing forms which contain calls to CAR or CDR to change the pointers those calls retrieve:

```
Lisp> (setf *c* '($X . HUNT))
($X . HUNT)

Lisp> (setf (car *c*) 'new-$x)
NEW-$X

Lisp> *c*
(NEW-$X . HUNT)

Lisp> (setf (cdr *c*) 'new-hunt)
NEW-HUNT

Lisp> *c*
(NEW-$X . NEW-HUNT)
```

In the example above we constructed a cons cell which initially pointed to $X and HUNT. We "smashed" the car of the cell to instead make it contain the address of the symbol NEW-$X rather than the address of the symbol $X. Similarly, we changed the address stored in the second pointer of the cons cell so that it now points to the starting address of the symbol NEW-HUNT.

We can also use destructive operations to split the two-element list in Figure 7.4 into two distinct lists of one element each:

```
Lisp> (setf *l* '(snark hunt))
(SNARK HUNT)

Lisp> (setf (car *l*) 'not)
NOT

Lisp> *l*
(NOT HUNT)

Lisp> (setf *cdr-l* (cdr *l*))
(HUNT)

Lisp> (setf (cdr *l*) nil)
NIL

Lisp> *l*
(NOT)

Lisp> *cdr-l*
(HUNT)
```

The two lists which result from the example above are depicted in Figure 7.5. Rearranging the cons cells in a list is sometimes called *list surgery*, and in older Lisps such destructive operations used to be accomplished with the functions `RPLACA` and `RPLACD`. `RPLACA` (RePLAce CAr) updates the car pointer of a cons cell, while `RPLACD` (RePLAce CDr) updates the cdr pointer of a cons cell. These functions are obsolete, but are retained in Common Lisp (like so many other constructs) for the sake of compatibility with older Lisps.

Function calls to accessing functions such as `(CAR L)` or `(CYLINDER-VOLUME C)` are sometimes called *generalized variables*. The idea is that a variable is *any* method we might use to name a storage location (i.e., a pointer) inside of our computer.

Updating the value of a pointer is called a *destructive operation* because it overwrites the address which used to be contained in the pointer with a new

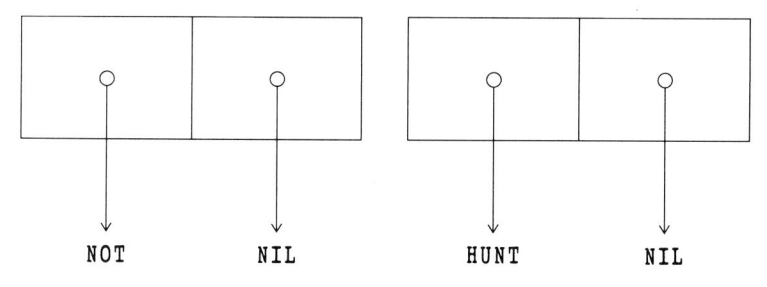

FIGURE 7.5
Two single-element lists.

address, thus destroying the old pointer. Notice that this only changes the *address* stored in a pointer—the object which was at that address is not touched.

> **Problem.** Rewrite the updating functions we wrote when representing a cylinder as a list of slots. The new updating functions should destructively modify the list rather than creating a new copy with the appropriate slot changed.

> **Problem.** Write a function called `OUR-CONS`. It should maintain a *free list* of cons cells joined together by their cdr pointers. When a new cons cell is needed, the free list should first be checked to see if any cells are available, and if so the next available cell should be removed from the list and returned with its car and cdr pointers set to the arguments to `OUR-CONS`. If no cells are available, then a new one should be created with `CONS`. Also write `FREE-CONS` so that we can explicitly return cons cells to the free list if we know that we are done with them.

7.2.2 Defining NREVERSE

Now that we know about how lists are actually represented inside of the machine, we can understand one of Lisp's greatest problems: memory usage. Every time we build a new cons cell, Lisp gives us a new chunk of memory. This seems fine until we consider what happens if we try the following:

```
Lisp> (setf *l* '(the snark *was* a boojum))
(THE SNARK *WAS* A BOOJUM)

Lisp> (setf *l* '(a new and improved object))
(A NEW AND IMPROVED OBJECT)
```

We can hang onto an object by making a global variable point to it. However, after the second call to `SETF`, we have no way of accessing the cons cells which were allocated to build the list (THE SNARK *WAS* A BOOJUM) because we destructively changed the only pointer we had to that list. Thus, we have allocated some memory which we can never use again. This may seem acceptable until we consider a example such as:

```
Lisp> (defun consume (i ignore)
        (if (zerop i)
            'burp
            (consume (1- i) (cons 'how 'cheap?))))
CONSUME

Lisp> (consume 1000000)
BURP
```

The call to `CONSUME` in this example will cause 1 million cons cells to be allocated. The only problem is that once the function call is over, *we can never use these cells again!* Once again, no object we can reference has any pointers to the cons cells we allocated. In general almost all Lisp programs generate objects (not just cons cells) which are used for a short period of time and then discarded. These short-lived objects usually represent the intermediate state of some computation, and when that computation is over, all pointers to the intermediate objects are lost.

Objects which are occupying memory but can no longer be used by any program are called *garbage*. If garbage were allowed to occupy memory forever, the entire address space of our Lisp would rather quickly become filled with it and our programs would have to stop running because we would be out of memory. In order to proceed, a *garbage collector*, often called a *gc*, must be called to recycle all the memory currently occupied by garbage objects. After the garbage collection, all the objects currently in use have been identified, and any remaining space has been given back to Lisp to be used for new objects.

A garbage collector is an essential part of virtually all Lisps,[1] since most programs would quickly exhaust all available memory without one. We will discuss garbage collection in much greater detail when we get to Lisp implementation issues. A second solution to the memory exhaustion problem is not to create garbage objects in the first place. For example, suppose that **L1** points to the list **(DOGO DOGERE PUPSI BITUM)**, and that we want the reverse the list. If we used the function **REVERSE**, then the list **(BITUM PUPSI DOGERE DOGO)** will be created from four *new* cons cells:

```
Lisp> (setf l1 '(dogo dogere pupsi bitum))
(DOGO DOGERE PUPSI BITUM)

Lisp> (setf l1 '(reverse l1))
(BITUM PUPSI DOGERE DOGO)
```

If **L1** was the only pointer we had to the original list as shown in Figure 7.6, then the four cons cells that were used to build that list will become garbage after the second call to **SETF**. However, we could *reuse* the cons cells in that list to create the reversed list, as shown in Figure 7.7; thus, no new cons cells would be allocated and no garbage would be left behind.

In order to reuse the existing cons cells to build the reversed list, we can use the function **NREVERSE**. **NREVERSE** expects a single list as an argument and it returns the reverse of that list as a result. However, it destructively modifies the cdr pointers in each cons cell of the original to create a reversed list:

---

[1] One notable exception is the Lisp implementation NIL which never had a gc. Early MIT Lisp machines did not have a gc either. When the machine ran out of memory, you had to reboot it and start over! Each of these Lisps used a large virtual address space, so you could do a lot of work before running out of memory.

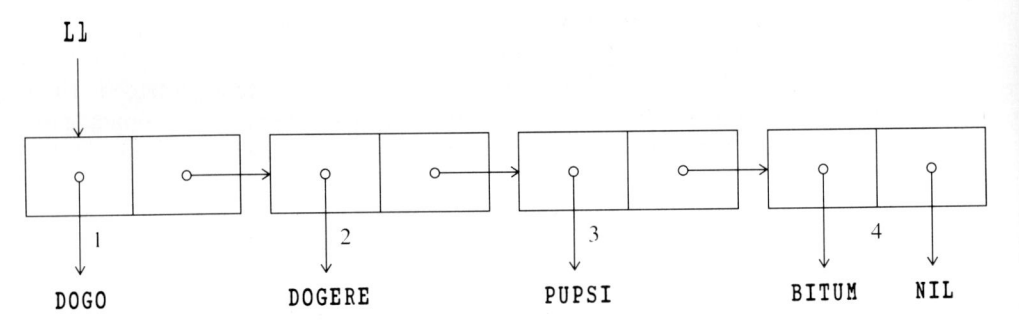

FIGURE 7.6
L1 points to the list (DOGO DOGERE PUPSI BITUM).

```
Lisp> (setf l1 '(dogo dogere pupsi bitum))
(DOGO DOGERE PUPSI BITUM)

Lisp> (setf old-l1 l1)
(DOGO DOGERE PUPSI BITUM)

Lisp> (setf l1 (nreverse old-l1))
(BITUM PUPSI DOGERE DOGO)

Lisp> l1
(BITUM PUPSI DOGERE DOGO)

Lisp> old-l1
(DOGO)
```

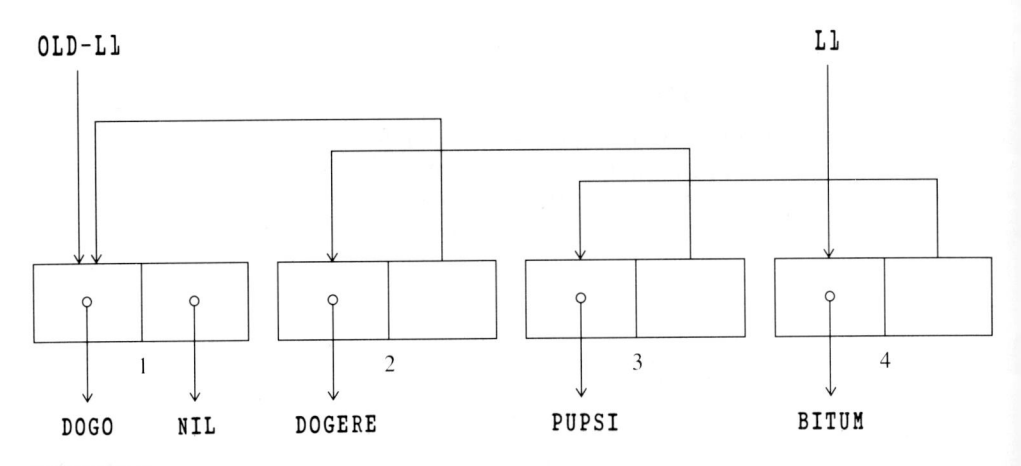

FIGURE 7.7
The result of destructively reversing L1.

Figure 7.7 depicts the pointer arrangement which results from the example above. Notice that `OLD-L1` prints as the list `(DOGO)`, which is actually the tail of the list pointed to by `L1`. Thus, `OLD-L1` points into a piece of the list pointed to by `L1` and the two lists share a common tail.

We can write our own version of `NREVERSE` using the destructive operations we have already learned:

```
(defun our-nreverse (l)
  (our-nreverse-1 nil l))

(defun our-nreverse-1 (head tail)
  (let ((rest (cdr tail)))
    ;; Notice explicit sequencing we perform by calling
    ;; OUR-NREVERSE-2
    (our-nreverse-2 (setf (cdr tail) head) rest tail)))

(defun our-nreverse-2 (ignore rest tail)
  (if (null rest)
      tail
      (our-nreverse-1 tail rest)))
```

The idea is to always keep a pointer to two consecutive cons cells in the list. We will call one pointer the `HEAD` and the other pointer the `TAIL`. Initially `HEAD` and `TAIL` will point to the first and the second cons cells in the list we want to reverse. In order to reverse the list we will destructively modify the cdr pointer of the `TAIL` cons cell to point to the `HEAD` cons cell. Then we will advance `HEAD` and `TAIL` so that `HEAD` points to `TAIL` and `TAIL` points to the cell that follows it. However, we can no longer find that cell since we just smashed the only pointer we had to it!

Thus, we need to maintain a third variable called `REST`, which will point to the cons cell which follows the cell pointed to by `TAIL`. Once `REST` points to the cons cell following `TAIL`, we can safely change the cdr of `TAIL` and still find the cell which follows. When `REST` becomes `NIL` we have reached the end of the original list and are done with the destructive reversal.

Problem. Try tracing the functions used by `OUR-NREVERSE` and watch how they work on some simple lists.

7.2.3 Sequencing and Side Effects

Notice that we had to define the function `OUR-NREVERSE-2`. However, the only reason we had to define this function was so that we could perform two operations in sequence. We had to `SETF` the cdr of `TAIL` before advancing the `HEAD` and `TAIL` pointers. However, in order to do this we had to label the result returned by `(SETF (CDR TAIL) HEAD)` as `IGNORE` even though we do not care about the *value* returned by `SETF`; instead, we are only concerned with the destructive *side effect* performed by `SETF`.

So far we have only been allowed to perform one function call in the body of a function we have defined. There was usually no reason to allow a *sequence* of function calls. For example, the following code makes no sense:

```
(defun silly (x)
  (cdr x)
  (car x))
```

What value should `SILLY` return? A function can only return a single value, so suppose that we return the value of `(CAR X)`. Then what point would there have been in calling `(CDR X)` before that? Nobody is interested in the value returned by that call, so instead it must be ignored or discarded. According to the black box model of function calling, we only call a function because we are interested in the value it returns. Since we are going to ignore the value returned by `CDR`, there is no point in calling it!

However, `SETF` has an important side effect. The only reason we call it in `OUR-NREVERSE-1` is because we are interested in that effect, not the value returned. We use the argument `IGNORE` in `OUR-NREVERSE-2` so that we can execute the call to `SETF` before the recursive call to `OUR-NREVERSE-1` occurs.

Lisp will actually allow us to write a sequence of function calls in many of the places we have been using only one call. For example, the body of a `DEFUN` and of a `LET` both allow us to write a sequence of forms to be executed, although only the value of the last form is returned as the value of the `DEFUN` or the `LET`. Other forms should be included only if they have interesting side effects. We can use this feature to rewrite `OUR-NREVERSE` more clearly:

```
(defun our-nreverse (l)
  (our-nreverse-1 nil l))

(defun our-nreverse-1 (head tail)
  (let ((rest (cdr tail)))
    (setf (cdr tail) head)
    (if (null rest)
        tail
        (our-nreverse-1 tail rest))))
```

We take advantage of the sequencing offered by `DEFUN` to eliminate the definition of `OUR-NREVERSE-2`. Lisp also provides an explicit sequencing function called `PROGN`. `PROGN` is similar to the `BEGIN` and `END` statements of Pascal or braces in C.

The bodies of `DEFUN` and `LET` are said to contain an *implicit* `PROGN` since they allow sequences of functions to occur without us explicitly wrapping them inside of a call to `PROGN`. Thus, the following two definitions of `SAMPLE` are identical:

```
Lisp> (defun sample ()
        (print 1)
        (print 2)
        (print 3))
SAMPLE

Lisp> (sample)

1
2
3
3

Lisp> (defun sample ()
        (progn (print 1)
               (print 2)
               (print 3)))
SAMPLE

Lisp> (sample)

1
2
3
3
```

Notice that the 3 is printed twice. As we saw much earlier, the first 3 was printed as a side effect of the call (PRINT 3), while the second 3 was printed because (SAMPLE) returned 3 and the read-eval-print loop prints whatever object (SAMPLE) returns.

PROGN does not give us any power that we did not have before. In fact, we have always been able to execute function calls sequentially because the arguments in a function call are guaranteed to be evaluated from left to right. Thus, PROGN is just like + in that it accepts an arbitrary number of arguments which are evaluated from left to right; however, rather than adding its arguments up, PROGN simply returns the last one.

If PROGN did not exist (implicitly or explicitly), then we could always have rewritten the above as:

```
(defun sample ()
  (temp-1 (print 1)))

(defun temp-1 (ignore)
  (temp-2 (print 2)))

(defun temp-2 (ignore)
  (print 3))
```

`PROGN` just gives us a cleaner way of doing something we could already do.

Problem. Lisp includes a destructive version of `APPEND` called `NCONC`:

```
Lisp> (setf l1 '(1))
(1)

Lisp> (setf l2 '(5))
(5)

Lisp> (nconc l1 l2)
(1 5)

Lisp> l1
(1 5)

Lisp> l2
(5)
```

Write a function called `OUR-NCONC` which joins two lists together by destructively making the cdr pointer of the last cons cell in the first list point to the first cons cell in the second list. Show the result of calling `NCONC` on two lists using box and pointer notation.

Problem. Common Lisp contains a destructive version of `SUBST` called `NSUBST`. Write your own version called `OUR-NSUBST`.

Problem. Consider the following Lisp function:

```
(defun circularize! (l)
  (if (null l)
      ;; The empty list is already
      ;; "circular" in a sense.
      l
      ;; LAST returns the last cons cell in a list
      (setf (cdr (last l)) l)))
```

Use box and pointer notation to describe the object returned by the call `(CIRCULARIZE! '(DIZZY))`. What happens if you try to print the result returned by `CIRCULARIZE!`? Try setting the variable `*PRINT-CIRCLE*` to `T` and calling `CIRCULARIZE!` again.

Problem. Create an "infinite" list of zeros using only one cons cell.

Problem. Rewrite the `LIST-ROTATE` function written as an exercise in Chapter 5 so that it destructively modifies the list it is passed rather that creating a new list.

CHAPTER 8

PROGRAMS = DATA

In the last chapter we got a closer look at how data structures in Lisp can be represented on a traditional computer. These data structures are also used to represent programs which Lisp can execute.

8.1 THE ADVANTAGES OF HAVING PROGRAMS = DATA

The pattern matcher in the source code rewriter that we discussed earlier made good use of the fact that programs can be pulled apart using `CAR` and `CDR` and examined with normal Lisp primitives. The ability to treat a list as a piece of data at one moment and as a program at another is quite powerful. Later we will learn about *macros* which take advantage of this fact by rewriting Lisp programs into other Lisp programs.

Lisp was originally invented by John McCarthy because he was interested in proving things about programs. When you write a program, how can you be *sure* that it has no bugs; that is, it lives up to its specifications? The equivalence of programs and data in Lisp is useful when writing programs which try to prove facts about other programs.

We are temporarily ignoring the fact that Lisp programs have more than one representation. Most Lisp implementations provide a *compiler* which transforms Lisp into a much simpler language—usually the machine language of a particular processor. In fact, without such compilers Lisp would be a mere toy. The price we pay for compilation is that programs may now have two different representations: interpreted and compiled code.[1]

One frequently touted advantage of the fact that programs equal data is that Lisp programs can easily modify themselves using destructive operations. Some people claim that this enables programs to "learn." In reality, making programs modify themselves is generally a terrible idea, since it leads to confusing programs which can never be compiled.

8.1.1 EVAL: Interpreting a Piece of Data as a Program

The function **EVAL** allows us to interpret a list as a program:

```
Lisp> (setf l '(* pi (expt 11 2) 7))
(* pi (expt 11 2) 7)

Lisp> (eval l)          ; treat l as a program
2660.929

Lisp> (car l)           ; treat l as data
*
```

EVAL expects a list as an argument, and it evaluates that list just as though we had typed it into the top-level read-*eval*-print loop. In fact, the read-*eval*-print loop calls **EVAL** itself. The fact that we can explicitly invoke the evaluator leads to some curious results, though:

```
Lisp> (setf l '(list l l))
(LIST L L)

Lisp> (trace eval list)
(EVAL LIST)

Lisp> (eval l)
1 Enter EVAL (EVAL L)         ; caused by read-EVAL-print loop
| 2 Enter EVAL (LIST L L)     ; our explicit call to EVAL
|   3 Enter LIST (LIST L L) (LIST L L)
|   3 Exit LIST ((LIST L L) (LIST L L))
| 2 Exit EVAL ((LIST L L) (LIST L L))
1 Exit EVAL ((LIST L L) (LIST L L))
((LIST L L) (LIST L L))
```

---

[1] Compiled code can be anything from microcode or machine instructions for a Reduced Instruction Set Computer (RISC) to byte codes for a simple stack machine.

Let us carefully consider what happens when we type (`EVAL L`) into the read-*eval*-print loop. First, Lisp reads the expression and creates the two-element list (`EVAL L`) out of two cons cells. Next, the function `EVAL` is called with that list as an argument; notice that this call to `EVAL` is caused by the *eval* portion of the read-*eval*-print loop. When the first call to `EVAL` tries to evaluate (`EVAL L`), it must first evaluate `L` and then call the function `EVAL` with the result. Thus, a *second* call to `EVAL` occurs with the argument (`LIST L L`).

The second call to `EVAL` calls the function `LIST` with the two arguments (`LIST L L`) and (`LIST L L`), each of which is the result of evaluating the symbol `L`. This call to `LIST` then returns the list ((`LIST L L`) (`LIST L L`)), which is then returned as the value of the second call to `EVAL`. But the result of the second call to `EVAL` is the value of the original call to `EVAL` done by the read-eval-print loop. Thus, our original expression ultimately evaluates to ((`LIST L L`) (`LIST L L`)), which is then printed out by the call to `PRINT` in the read-eval-*print* loop. Do not worry if this seems confusing at first; it is. The only way to really understand this is to play with some examples in front of Lisp.

8.2 TAKING DERIVATIVES WITH `DERIV`

In the late 1960s, project MAC at MIT started to developed a symbolic algebra program called Macsyma [Gro83]. Macsyma is probably the most famous and useful application ever written in Lisp, and its development had an enormous effect on the effort put into improving Maclisp. One reason that Lisp is such a good language for symbolic algebra is that formulas can be manipulated as pieces of data at one moment, and be evaluated to produce numeric results the next.

Symbolic differentiation is a small example of what Macsyma can do. In high school most people learn how to take the derivatives of equations. For example, here are some rules of differentiation:

$$\frac{d(c)}{dx} = 0$$

$$\frac{d(x)}{dx} = 1$$

$$\frac{d(u+v)}{dx} = \frac{du}{dx} + \frac{dv}{dx}$$

$$\frac{d(uv)}{dx} = u\frac{dv}{dx} + v\frac{du}{dx}$$

$$\frac{d(u/v)}{dx} = \frac{v(du/dx) - u(dv/dx)}{v^2}$$

$$\frac{d(u^n)}{dx} = nu^{n-1}\frac{du}{dx}$$

Rather than finding derivatives by hand, we can embed our knowledge about derivatives in a function called `DERIV`. `DERIV` should accept the name of a variable and an equation as arguments, and it should return the partial derivative of that equation with respect to the given variable. We will represent equations using Lisp's prefix notation rather than the standard infix notation given above:

```
Lisp> (deriv 'x 'x)
1

Lisp> (deriv 'y 'x)
0

Lisp> (deriv 'x '(expt x 3))
(* 3 (EXPT X 2))

Lisp> (deriv 'x '(+ (* 3 x) 7))
3

Lisp> (deriv 'x '(+ (* a (expt x 2)) (* b x)))
(+ (* 2 A X) B)
```

Do not worry if you cannot remember the actual rules for differentiation which are being used; that is the least interesting aspect of this problem. The most interesting fact is that we can easily manipulate equations, a class of programs specifying numeric computations, as pieces of data to be transformed.

Here is one possible definition of `DERIV`:

```
(defun deriv (var expr)
  (if (atom expr)
      (if (eq expr var)
          1
          0)
      (let ((operator (first expr))
            (arg1 (second expr))
            (arg2 (third expr)))
        (cond ((eq operator '+) (deriv-add var arg1 arg2))
              ((eq operator '*) (deriv-mult var arg1 arg2))
              ((eq operator '/) (deriv-div var arg1 arg2))
              ((eq operator 'expt)
               (deriv-expt var arg1 arg2))
              (t (error "Unknown operator"))))))
```

`DERIV` attempts to solve easy derivatives immediately in the base case where `EXPR` is an atom. If `EXPR` is a variable equal to the variable we are differentiating with respect to, then `DERIV` returns 1, otherwise `EXPR` is a numeric constant or a variable other than `VAR`, in which case `DERIV` returns 0.

If `EXPR` is not an atom, then it must be a list. `DERIV` then *dispatches* to the correct sub-function which knows a particular rule about differentiation. For example, if the `OPERATOR` in `EXPR` is +, then `DERIV` calls `DERIV-ADD` with `VAR` and the two arguments to +:

```
(defun deriv-add (var arg1 arg2)
  (list '+ (deriv var arg1) (deriv var arg2)))
```

`DERIV-ADD` has knowledge about how to take the derivative of a summation "hard-wired" into it. As shown earlier, the derivative of a sum of two operands is the sum of the derivatives. Thus, `DERIV-ADD` returns a new equation which is built by returning a list starting with + followed by the derivative of each operand.

Here are the definitions of the other functions which `DERIV` calls:

```
(defun deriv-mult (var arg1 arg2)
  (list '+
        (list '* (deriv var arg1) arg2)
        (list '* arg1 (deriv var arg2))))

(defun deriv-div (var arg1 arg2)
  (list '/
        (list '-
              (list '* arg2 (deriv var arg1))
              (list '* arg1 (deriv var arg2)))
        (list 'expt arg2 2)))

(defun deriv-expt (var arg1 arg2)
  (list '*
        (list '* arg2 (list 'expt arg1 (list '- arg2 1)))
        (deriv var arg1)))
```

We can think of each function as a derivative specialist which knows how to take a particular kind of derivative, and the only thing `DERIV` has to do is to refer us to the appropriate specialist. Here are some examples using this first version of `DERIV`:

```
Lisp> (deriv 'x 'x)
1

Lisp> (deriv 'y 'x)
0

Lisp> (deriv 'x '(expt x 3))
(* (* 3 (EXPT X (- 3 1)))
   1)
```

```
Lisp> (deriv 'x '(+ (* 3 x) 7))
(+ (+ (* 0 X)
      (* 3 1))
   0)

Lisp> (deriv 'x '(+ (* a (expt x 2)) (* b x)))
(+ (+ (* 0 (EXPT X 2))
      (* A (* (* 2 (EXPT X (- 2 1)))
              1)))
   (+ (* 0 X) (* B 1)))
```

Notice that although **DERIV**'s answers are correct, they are not nearly as simple as they could be. In order to make the output more pleasing to read, we need to perform various algebraic simplifications on it.

> **Problem.** Write an algebraic simplifier called **SIMPLIFY**. **SIMPLIFY** will accept an equation as input, possibly perform some algebraic simplifications, and return an equivalent equation as a result. It should perform at least the following simplifications:
>
> - Remove all 0s from sums and differences
> - Simplify multiplications or divisions involving 0 or 1
> - Simplify powers involving 0 or 1
> - Reduce all functions which have only constants as arguments to a constant. This is called *constant folding*.
>
> Here are some examples of **SIMPLIFY**:
>
> ```
> Lisp> (simplify '(+ x 0))
> X
>
> Lisp> (simplify '(* (expt x (+ 0 0))
>                    (expt y (+ 0 (- x 0)))))
> (expt y x)
> ```

8.2.1 Improving DERIV with CASE

Although our definition of `DERIV` works, there are a few new Lisp features which we can use to improve it. The `COND` in `DERIV` selects which derivative specialist knows how to handle `EXPR`, but the special form `CASE` is more expressive than `COND` in this instance:

```
(defun deriv (var expr)
  (if (atom expr)
      (if (eq expr var)
```

```
            1
            0)
    (let ((operator (first expr))
          (arg1 (second expr))
          (arg2 (third expr)))
      (case operator
        (+ (deriv-add var arg1 arg2))
        (* (deriv-mult var arg1 arg2))
        (/ (deriv-div var arg1 arg2))
        (expt (deriv-expt var arg1 arg2))
        (t (error "Unknown operator ~A" operator))))))
```

CASE has the general form

```
(case key
  (key-list-1 consequent-1)
  (key-list-2 consequent-2)
   .
   .
   .
  (key-list-n consequent-n))
```

CASE first evaluates the form *KEY* to produce a *key-object* and saves the result. Each *key-list* should be a list of literal objects; in other words, the objects in each key-list are not evaluated. If the key-object is a member (using EQL) of *KEY-LIST-1*, then *CONSEQUENT-1* is evaluated and returned as the result of the CASE. If the key-object is not a member of *KEY-LIST-1*, then CASE behaves like COND and checks to see if the key-object is a member of *KEY-LIST-2*, etc.

Some useful shortcuts are allowed in CASE. A key-list such as (EXPT) which consists of a single atom can be replaced by that atom. We took advantage of this feature when we rewrote DERIV. One notable exception is that the key-list (NIL) may not be replaced by () because it could be confused with the empty key-list.

If the last key-list is equal to the symbol T or the symbol OTHERWISE, then the corresponding consequent clause is always evaluated, no matter what the value of the key-object. This provides a useful catch-all case in case none of the other keys match the key-object. We use this feature in DERIV to signal an error when we encounter an unknown operator. Notice what happens when we try to take the derivative of a function which DERIV does not know about:

```
Lisp> (deriv 'x '(sin x))
>>Error: Unknown operator SIN

DERIV:
   Required arg 0 (VAR): X
```

```
    Required arg 1 (EXPR): (SIN X)

:A    Abort to Lisp Top Level
->
```

Rather than just saying `Unknown Operator`, `DERIV` tells us what operator is unknown. We accomplished this by putting ~A in the error string and passing `OPERATOR` as an argument to `ERROR` after the error string. In general, `ERROR` accepts a *format string* which may contain *formatting directives*. A format directive always starts with a tilde followed by a letter. In this case, the directive we used was ~A which tells `ERROR` to print the value of the next argument after the format string instead of printing ~A.

Format strings can be extremely complex and are also useful with a general output function called `FORMAT`:

```
Lisp> (format t "Hex: ~x ~%Cardinal: ~R  ~%Roman: ~@R"
              123 123 123)
Hex: 7B
Cardinal: one hundred twenty-three
Roman: CXXIII
NIL
```

The first argument to `FORMAT` is called a *stream* and describes where we want to send our output. Passing the symbol `T` says that we want to send output to the console. The remaining arguments to `FORMAT` are just like the arguments we pass to `ERROR`—a control string followed by more arguments which may be consumed by directives beginning with a tilde in the control string. As you can see from this simple example, `FORMAT` is quite powerful and sometimes cryptic. Refer to the Common Lisp manual for all the gory details about `FORMAT`.

8.2.2 Improving Derivative Specialists with Backquote

It is interesting to note that `SIMPLIFY` is similar in function to the source code rewriting system we saw earlier, since it rewrites its input equation into an equivalent output equation. Likewise, `DERIV` can also be formulated as a rewriter. Given an input equation, we know the *template* for an output equation which represents the derivative of our input.

Unfortunately, we have to build our output equation using function calls to `LIST` and `CONS`. Using this method to build a list actually obscures the structure of the equation we are trying to build. It is quite common to want to build a list which is mostly constant, but which has a few variable parts that need to be filled in when our program is run. In order to facilitate building such lists, Lisp provides a feature called *backquote*. Backquote is just like `QUOTE` in that it inhibits evaluation. However, backquote allows us to turn evaluation *back on* with a comma:

```
Lisp> (setf source 'table)
TABLE

Lisp> (setf destination 'floor)
FLOOR

Lisp> `(move from source to destination)
(MOVE FROM SOURCE TO DESTINATION)

Lisp> `(move from ,source to ,destination)
(MOVE FROM TABLE TO FLOOR)

Lisp> (list 'move 'from source 'to destination)
(MOVE FROM TABLE TO FLOOR)
```

A comma within a backquoted expression is analogous to the directive ~A within a format string, since it allows us to fill in a variable slot within a constant template. We can reproduce the results of using backquote by using LIST and QUOTE, but backquote is clearer when the expression we are building consists primarily of constants. We can use QUOTE to see that backquoted forms turn into the calls to LIST and QUOTE that we would have entered ourselves:[2]

```
Lisp> (quote `(move from ,source to ,destination))
(LIST 'MOVE 'FROM SOURCE 'TO DESTINATION)
```

Now we can use backquote to rewrite our derivative specialist functions:

```
(defun deriv-add (var arg1 arg2)
  `(+ ,(deriv var arg1) ,(deriv var arg2)))

(defun deriv-mult (var arg1 arg2)
  `(+ (* ,(deriv var arg1) ,arg2)
      (* ,arg1 ,(deriv var arg2))))

(defun deriv-div (var arg1 arg2)
  `(/ (- (* ,arg2 ,(deriv var arg1))
```

---

[2] Many implementations of backquote turn into calls to a function such as BQ-LIST rather than LIST so that the printer can determine which expressions were produced by backquote and print them out as they were originally written.

```
            (* ,arg1 ,(deriv var arg2)))
       (expt ,arg2 2)))

(defun deriv-expt (var arg1 arg2)
  `(* (* ,arg2 (expt ,arg1 (- ,arg2 1)))
      ,(deriv var arg1)))
```

The use of backquote makes the rewrite rules that our derivative specialists are using much clearer. Later we will see that backquote is also extremely useful when we start rewriting Lisp source code using *macros*.

8.3 DATA-DRIVEN PROGRAMMING AND `FUNCALL`

Although we have improved the style and readability of `DERIV`, we have not increased its functionality. For example, there is no derivative specialist for `SIN`. Of course, it would be easy to add a new line to the `CASE` statement so that `DERIV` could call a specialist named `DERIV-SIN`. However, this change involves modifying existing code. Right now it is easy to modify our code; we just wrote it, are quite familiar with it, and know exactly where to look for the `CASE` statement to change.

However, if we were to trying to increase the functionality of a much larger program which someone else wrote a year ago, it would be more cumbersome and error-prone to try to modify that code. We would have to read it and understand how it works, being careful not to break any of its existing functionality when we add a new feature.

It would be much nicer if we could extend `DERIV`, or any program for that matter, by adding new code *without changing* any of our existing code. In order to do this, we can adopt an approach which we will call *data-driven programming*.[3] In data-driven programming, `DERIV` has no knowledge about what specialists exist in the world. Instead, it will "ask" the equation it is given what derivative specialist knows how to take the derivative of that equation. Then `DERIV` only has to call that derivative specialist. Our data-driven version of `DERIV` will look something like:

```
(defun deriv (var expr)
  (if (atom expr)
      (if (eq expr var)
          1
          0)
      (let ((deriv-func (lookup-deriv-func expr))
```

---
[3] Later we will see how this is essentially a form of *object-oriented programming*.

```
            (arg1 (second expr))
            (arg2 (third expr)))
        (if (null deriv-func)
            (error "unknown operator ~S" (car expr))
            ;; This line contains a bug!
            (deriv-func var arg1 arg2)))))
```

We "ask" **EXPR** what its derivative function is by calling **LOOKUP-DERIV-FUNC** with **EXPR** as an argument. If **NIL** is returned, then **EXPR** does not know of a derivative specialist, so we signal an error. Some people like to view this whole process as sending a message called **DERIV** to **EXPR**. We can implement **LOOKUP-DERIV-FUNCTION** using an a-list which maps operators onto the space of derivative functions:

```
(defvar *deriv-functions*
  '((+ . deriv-add)
    (* . deriv-mult)
    (/ . deriv-div)
    (expt . deriv-expt))
  "An a-list mapping math operators to deriv function names")

(defun lookup-deriv-func (equation)
  (let* ((operator (first equation))
         (entry (assoc operator *deriv-functions*)))
    (if (null entry)
        nil
        (symbol-function (cdr entry)))))
```

An a-list is used to record the mappings between operators and derivative specialists. **LOOKUP-DERIV-FUNC** merely checks to see if the **OPERATOR** in **EXPR** is associated with a derivative specialist in *DERIV-FUNCTIONS*. Notice that the following two forms are equivalent:

```
(if (null entry)
    nil
    (symbol-function (cdr entry)))

(if entry
    (symbol-function (cdr entry))
    nil)
```

We choose to use the first form rather than the second as a matter of style, even though the second is shorter. The reason is that we are asking the question "Is **ENTRY** the empty list?", and the first form reflects this question, while the second form takes advantage of the fact that anything which is not **NIL** represents truth in Lisp. This is a minor point, but consistent attention to such details will make your programs clearer with absolutely no loss in efficiency when compiled by a decent compiler. In fact, the source code rewriter presented in Chapter 5 could easily perform the rewrite shown above.

If a derivative specialist is not found by **LOOKUP-DERIV-FUNC**, then **DERIV** signals an error. If a derivative specialist is found, then **DERIV** tries to call it with **VAR**, **ARG1**, and **ARG2** as arguments. However, if we try out our new version of **DERIV** we will encounter a problem:

```
Lisp> (deriv 'x '(+ x y))
>>Error: DERIV-FUNC has no global function definition

SYMBOL-FUNCTION:
   Required arg 0 (S): DERIV-FUNC

:A    Abort to Lisp Top Level
:C    Try evaluating #'DERIV-FUNC again
->
```

8.3.1 Common Lisp Has Separate Function and Value Namespaces

(**DERIV-FUNC VAR ARG1 ARG2**) seems to be the most natural way to call the function which was returned by **LOOKUP-DERIV-FUNC**, but it will not work because a symbol in the function position of a list is treated differently than a symbol in the argument position of a list. We saw this in Chapter 4 when we were able to write (**ADD PRODUCT ADD**). The first **ADD** refers to the function **ADD** while the second **ADD** refers to the variable **ADD**. Since a symbol can name both a function and a variable value at the same time, we say that there are separate function and value *namespaces* in Common Lisp.

The problem with **DERIV** is that **DERIV-FUNC** is a variable, whose value is a function which we want to call. We need some way to bridge the gap between the function and value namespaces. Fortunately, we can use the function **FUNCALL** to do this. **FUNCALL** expects one or more arguments. The first argument must be a function, while the remaining arguments will be used as arguments in a function call to that function:

```
Lisp> (cons 'x (+ 1 2))
(X . 3)

Lisp> (funcall #'cons 'x (+ 1 2))
(X . 3)

Lisp> (let ((func #'cons))
        (funcall func 'x (+ 1 2)))
(X . 3)
```

```
Lisp> (funcall #'deriv-add 'x 'x 4)
(+ 1 0)
```

FUNCALL itself is a regular function which evaluates all of its arguments from left to right. Notice that we use the syntax #' to introduce the function CONS, just as we would use ' to introduce the symbol CONS as a piece of data. We need #' because there are separate function and value namespaces in Lisp, and we want to pass the functional value of CONS to FUNCALL rather than the symbol CONS or the value of the variable named CONS. #' is really just a shorthand notation for a call to the special form FUNCTION, just as ' is a shorthand notation for a call to the special form QUOTE. We will examine the need for FUNCTION in greater detail in the next chapter.

Of course, there is no reason to write an expression like (FUNCALL #'CONS 'X (+ 1 2)) because this is more clearly expressed as (CONS 'X (+ 1 2)). However, FUNCALL is useful when we actually perform a computation to determine the function to call. We can use this feature to rewrite DERIV to perform a *computed function call*:

```
(defun deriv (var expr)
  (if (atom expr)
      (if (eq expr var)
          1
          0)
      (let ((deriv-func (lookup-deriv-func expr))
            (arg1 (second expr))
            (arg2 (third expr)))
        (if (null deriv-func)
            (error "unknown operator ~A" (car expr))
            ;; call DERIV-FUNC correctly
            (funcall deriv-func var arg1 arg2)))))
```

Now the value of **DERIV-FUNC** will be looked up by **LOOKUP-DERIV-FUNC** in the value namespace, but that value will then be called as a function with the values of **VAR**, **ARG1**, and **ARG2** as arguments. Now **DERIV** dispatches to the correct specialist using **FUNCALL**.

It might seem that we do not really need **FUNCALL** since we could use **EVAL** to replace it. For example, we might try to rewrite (FUNCALL DERIV-FUNC VAR ARG1 ARG2) as (EVAL `(,DERIV-FUNC ',VAR ',ARG1 ',ARG2)). While this will work, it conses a list which we are going to throw away soon, thus needlessly creating garbage. In addition, it is extremely unlikely that a Lisp compiler will generate good code from the source code using **EVAL**. Be wary of misusing **EVAL** when you should be using **FUNCALL**.

Problem. Is it possible to **FUNCALL** the special form **IF**? What about **AND**? Explain.

Problem. Add the following differentiation rules to our new version of **DERIV**:

$$\frac{d(\sin u)}{dx} = \cos u \frac{du}{dx}$$

$$\frac{d(\cos u)}{dx} = -\sin u \frac{du}{dx}$$

$$\frac{d(\ln u)}{dx} = \frac{1}{u}\frac{du}{dx}$$

Problem. Here is a function to take the nth derivative of an equation:

```
(defun nth-deriv (n var expr)
  (if (= n 0)
      expr
      (nth-deriv (1- n) var (deriv var expr))))
```

Generalize this function so that it also accepts as an argument the function to be called n times.

Problem. Rewrite the `SIMPLIFY` function you wrote earlier to work in a data-driven style.

8.3.2 Passing Functions as Arguments

Just as `LOOKUP-DERIV-FUNC` can return a function, we can pass a function as an argument to another function. Common Lisp uses this ability to solve a problem that we encountered at various times in earlier chapters.

Recall that functions like `MEMBER`, `ASSOC`, and `SUBST` all use the function `EQL` to look for a specific element in a list. While this often works, it does not usually work if the element we are looking for is a list:

```
Lisp> (member '(verb run) '((verb walk)
                            (verb run)
                            (verb jump)))
NIL
```

Because lists are not usually `EQL`, our example fails. We would like to tell `MEMBER` that it should use the test `EQUAL` rather than `EQL` to search for `(VERB RUN)`.

Fortunately, `MEMBER`, `ASSOC`, and `SUBST` (as well as many other Lisp functions) accept a keyword argument named `:TEST`:

```
Lisp> (member '(verb run)
              '((verb walk) (verb run) (verb jump))
              :test #'equal)
((VERB RUN) (VERB JUMP))
```

Lisp's ability to pass functions as arguments and return them as values is extremely useful, although potentially a bit complicated, as we will see in the next chapter.

Problem. Rewrite the function `OUR-SUBST` presented in a problem in Chapter 5 so that it accepts a test function as a fourth argument.

8.4 EVALUATING EQUATIONS

Now that we can take the derivative of an equation, we might want to evaluate that derivative at one or more points. In this section we will examine two different ways to do this.

8.4.1 Using *SUBST* and *EVAL*

The simplified derivative of `(+ (expt x 2)) (* 7 x))` with respect to X is `(+ (* 2 X) 7)`. If we want to evaluate this derivative at X equal to 4, we could manually substitute 4 for X in the derivative and call `EVAL`. If we want to repeatedly perform such substitutions for values of X from 1 to 100, then we might like to use `SUBST`:

```
Lisp> (subst 4 'x '(+ (* 2 x) 7))
(+ (* 2 4) 7)
```

Now we can write a function to evaluate an equation over a range of values, returning an a-list of points and values:

```
(defun eval-over-range (low high var expr)
  (if (> low high)
      nil
      (acons low
             (evaluate-at-point low var expr)
             (eval-over-range (1+ low) high var expr))))

(defun evaluate-at-point (point var expr)
  (eval (subst point var expr)))
```

`EVAL-OVER-RANGE` evaluates `EXPR` at points from `LOW` to `HIGH` using `EVALUATE-AT-POINT`. `EVALUATE-AT-POINT` creates a new equation on the fly by substituting all occurrences of `VAR` in `EXPR` by `POINT`, and then it evaluates this new equation to produce a numeric result:

```
Lisp> (eval-over-range 1 5 'x '(expt x 2))
((1 . 1) (2 . 4) (3 . 9) (4 . 16) (5 . 25))
```

```
Lisp> (trace subst)
(SUBST)

Lisp> (eval-over-range 1 5 'expt '(expt 2 expt))
1 Enter SUBST 1 EXPT (EXPT 2 EXPT)
1 Exit SUBST (1 2 1)
>>Error: Unknown operator 1 in (FUNCTION 1)

EVAL:
   Required arg 0 (EXPRESSION): (1 2 1)

:A    Abort to Lisp Top Level
-> :b
EVAL <- EVALUATE-AT-POINT <- IF  <- EVAL-OVER-RANGE <- EVAL
```

Unfortunately, our approach is a bit too simple, since **SUBST** blindly substitutes the value of **POINT** for **VAR** without any knowledge that our Lisp programs have separate function and value namespaces. We only want the second reference to **EXPT** in the equation (**EXPT 2 EXPT**) to be replaced by **POINT**, since that reference is in the value namespace. If a program-manipulating program such as **EVALUATE-AT-POINT** is to work correctly, then it must know something about the semantics of Lisp.

8.4.2 Evaluating Equations with Bindings

Fortunately we can easily fix **EVALUATE-AT-POINT** by using the variable-binding mechanism of Lisp:

```
(defun evaluate-at-point (point var expr)
  (eval `(let ((,var ,point)) ,expr)))
```

Now we create a small Lisp program which binds the variable to the point, and then evaluates **EXPR** in an environment in which that binding is visible. Since **LET** can only bind names to values in the value namespace, we have not changed the value of **EXPR** in the function namespace as we did before:

```
Lisp> (trace eval)
(EVAL)

Lisp> (evaluate-at-point 5 'expt '(expt 2 expt))
1 Enter EVAL (EVALUATE-AT-POINT 5 'EXPT '(EXPT 2 EXPT))
| 2 Enter EVAL (LET ((EXPT 5)) (EXPT 2 EXPT))
| 2 Exit EVAL 32
1 Exit EVAL 32
32
```

```
Lisp> (eval-over-range 1 5 'x '(expt x 2))
((1 . 1) (2 . 4) (3 . 9) (4 . 16) (5 . 25))

Lisp> (eval-over-range 1 5 'expt '(expt 2 expt))
((1 . 2) (2 . 4) (3 . 8) (4 . 16) (5 . 32))
```

It is interesting to see how we can mix the usage of **DERIV** and **EVAL-OVER-RANGE**:

```
Lisp> (eval-over-range 1 5 'x (deriv 'x '(expt x 2)))
((1 . 2) (2 . 4) (3 . 6) (4 . 8) (5 . 10))
```

DERIV symbolically calculates that the derivative of (**EXPT X 2**) is (*** 2 X**), and **EVAL-OVER-RANGE** then evaluates that derivative at a number of points. Lisp's ability to easily mix symbolic computations such as **DERIV** with numeric computations such as **EVAL-OVER-RANGE** is a powerful feature.

CHAPTER 9

CONSEQUENCES OF LEXICAL SCOPING

9.1 MAPPING FUNCTIONS

By now it is clear that the ease with which Lisp manipulates lists and functions is one of its most distinguishing characteristics. For example, suppose that we have collected a list of data points from an experiment and we want a new list containing the squares of those points. Some simple Lisp functions can accomplish this:

```
(defun square (n) (expt n 2))

(defun square-iterate (list)
  (if (null list)
      nil
      (cons (square (car list))
            (square-iterate (cdr list)))))
```

SQUARE-ITERATE will call SQUARE on each element of LIST and return a list of the results:

```
Lisp> (square-iterate '(1 2 3))
(1 4 9)
```

Applying a function to each element of a list and returning a list of the results is such a common idiom that Lisp has a function called **MAPCAR** which makes it easier to express.

9.1.1 MAPCAR Is a Collector

MAPCAR expects at least two arguments—a function and a list—and it will apply the function to each element of the list, returning a list of the results:

```
Lisp> (mapcar #'square '(1 2 3))
(1 4 9)
```

MAPCAR is a more general form of **SQUARE-ITERATE**. It will not only accept any function as an argument, but it will also accept an arbitrary number of lists as arguments. For example, we can use **MAPCAR** to build an a-list of numbers and their squares:

```
Lisp> (mapcar #'cons '(1 2 3) '(1 4 9))
((1 . 1) (2 . 4) (3 . 9))
```

When **MAPCAR** receives more than one list as an argument, it will apply the given function to corresponding elements of each list, returning a list of the results when one of the argument lists runs out. Like most of the built-in functions which Lisp supplies, we can easily write our own version of **MAPCAR**:

```
(defun single-list-mapcar (func arg-list)
  (if (null arg-list)
      arg-list
      (cons (funcall func (car arg-list))
            (single-list-mapcar func (cdr arg-list)))))
```

SINGLE-LIST-MAPCAR looks just like **SQUARE-ITERATE** except that the function to be called is passed as the argument **FUNC** rather than being constant. Since we are passing the function as an argument, we now need to call it with **FUNCALL**. **SINGLE-LIST-MAPCAR** behaves like the **MAPCAR** built into Lisp, although we are not able to pass an arbitrary number of argument lists:

```
Lisp> (single-list-mapcar #'square '(1 2 3))
(1 4 9)
```

9.1.2 MAPCAN Is a Filter

Another popular mapping function is called **MAPCAN**. **MAPCAN** repeatedly applies a function to successive elements of one or more argument lists, but rather than creating a list of all the results, it destructively appends them all together using **NCONC**. Thus, the function we pass to **MAPCAN** must always return a list. For example, suppose that we want to filter out all of the negative numbers from our list of data points, producing a new list containing only positive numbers. Our mapping function will accept a number and return it wrapped inside a list if the number is positive, or return **NIL** if the number is negative:

```
Lisp> (defun list-if-greater-than-0 (N)
        (if (> n 0)
            (list n)
            nil))
GREATER-THAN-0

Lisp> (mapcan #'list-if-greater-than-0 '(1 -3 5 6 8 -2 9))
(1 5 6 8 9)
```

Just as **MAPCAR** is useful for collecting a list of results, **MAPCAN** is useful for filtering out specific elements of a list.

Problem. Write a function named **SINGLE-LIST-MAPCAN** which behaves like **MAPCAN** but can only accept a single argument list.

9.2 LAMBDA-LIST KEYWORDS

There are many functions which are predefined in Lisp but which we are not yet able to write by ourselves. For example, **MAPCAR** and **MAPCAN** accept a variable number of arguments, and the constructor functions created by **DEFSTRUCT** accept variable numbers of keyword arguments. Fortunately, Lisp provides ways for us to write these functions.

9.2.1 &REST Arguments

If we want to write our own version of **MAPCAR** or **MAPCAN** which can accept an arbitrary number of arguments, then we need to use **&REST** arguments. If the argument list of a function contains the symbol **&REST**, then the formal parameter which follows the **&REST** will be bound to a list of all the remaining arguments:

```
Lisp> (defun n-ary (x &rest l)
        (list x l))
N-ARY

Lisp> (n-ary 'a 'b 'c 'd 'e)
(A (B C D E))
```

X is bound to the first argument passed to **N-ARY**, while L is bound to a list consisting of all of the remaining arguments. Notice that all the arguments will still be evaluated before the call to **N-ARY** occurs. The symbol **&REST** is called a *lambda-list keyword*. A lambda-list keyword begins with & and signals that we want to receive some of the arguments in a special way. Thus, we could never have a formal parameter named &REST. Do not confuse lambda-list keywords such as &REST with keywords such as :TEST which begin with a colon.

Now we can write a function called OUR-MAPCAR which can receive an arbitrary number of argument lists. However, we still have a problem because we need to perform a computed function call to FUNC, but FUNCALL expects us to know when we write OUR-MAPCAR exactly how many arguments we are going to pass. Similarly, when we perform a recursive call to OUR-MAPCAR we do not know how many arguments we will be passing until OUR-MAPCAR is actually called. Fortunately we can use the function APPLY to call a function on an arbitrary list of arguments:

```
Lisp> (apply #'+ '(1 2 3))
6

Lisp> (apply #'list '(a b c))
(A B C)

Lisp> (apply #'append '((semper ubi) (sub ubi)))
(SEMPER UBI SUB UBI)

Lisp> (apply #'+ 1 2 '(3 4))
10
```

APPLY expects a function as its first argument. It will call that function on any remaining arguments, but the last argument must always be a list and each element of that list will be passed as an individual argument to the function being called. Thus, APPLY *spreads* a function call over a list of arguments.

Problem. Write a version of FUNCALL called OUR-FUNCALL using APPLY.

Problem. Write a version of OUR-APPEND which will accept an arbitrary number of lists as arguments.

APPLY is exactly what we need to complete our new version of OUR-MAPCAR:

```
(defun our-mapcar (func &rest arg-lists)
  (if (some-null-element-p arg-lists)
      nil
      (cons (apply func (single-list-mapcar
                          #'first arg-lists))
            (apply #'our-mapcar
                   func
                   (single-list-mapcar
                    #'rest
                    arg-lists)))))
```

```
(defun some-null-element-p (lists)
  (cond ((null lists) nil)
        ((null (car lists)) t)
        (t (some-null-element-p (cdr lists)))))
```

OUR-MAPCAR now accepts an arbitrary number of argument lists. First we check to see if any list is empty using the function SOME-NULL-ELEMENT-P:

```
Lisp> (some-null-element-p '((1 2) (3)))
NIL

Lisp> (some-null-element-p '((1) nil))
T
```

If all argument lists are not empty, then we need to call FUNC on the first argument in each list. Thus, we use SINGLE-LIST-MAPCAR to collect the FIRST element of each argument list and we APPLY FUNC to the resulting list of arguments. We also use APPLY to recursively call OUR-MAPCAR on the REST of each argument list. A TRACE of OUR-MAPCAR helps to see what is going on:

```
Lisp> (our-mapcar 'cons '(1 2) '(3 4))
1 Enter OUR-MAPCAR CONS (1 2) (3 4)
| 2 Enter OUR-MAPCAR CONS (2) (4)
|  3 Enter OUR-MAPCAR CONS NIL NIL
|  3 Exit OUR-MAPCAR NIL
| 2 Exit OUR-MAPCAR ((2 . 4))
1 Exit OUR-MAPCAR ((1 . 3) (2 . 4))
((1 . 3) (2 . 4))

Lisp> (our-mapcar 'cons '(1 2) '(3))
1 Enter OUR-MAPCAR CONS (1 2) (3)
| 2 Enter OUR-MAPCAR CONS (2) NIL
| 2 Exit OUR-MAPCAR NIL
1 Exit OUR-MAPCAR ((1 . 3))
((1 . 3))
```

In order to simplify OUR-MAPCAR a bit, we can replace the function SOME-NULL-ELEMENT-P with the built-in Lisp function SOME. SOME is a generalization of SOME-NULL-ELEMENT-P which expects a predicate and one or more lists as arguments. The predicate must take as many arguments as there are argument lists, and SOME applies the predicate to the first argument in each list. If the predicate returns NIL, then SOME applies the predicate to successive elements of each list, returning the first non-NIL result, or NIL if the predicate is never satisfied:

```
Lisp> (some #'numberp '(1 a b))
T
```

```
Lisp> (some #'null '((1 2) (3)))
NIL

Lisp> (some #'null '((1) nil))
T

Lisp> (some #'> '(1 2) '(3 4))
NIL

Lisp> (some #'> '(1 5) '(3 4))
T
```

SOME is like a short circuiting mapping function which returns the first non-NIL result it finds. Thus, we can replace the expression (SOME-NULL-ELEMENT-P ARG-LISTS) by (SOME #'NULL ARG-LISTS).

Problem. Write a function called OUR-MAPCAN which behaves like the MAPCAN built into Lisp.

9.2.2 &OPTIONAL Arguments

Sometimes we want to write a function which has a fixed number of required arguments followed by a fixed number of *optional arguments*. For example, suppose that we write our own version of MEMBER:

```
(defun our-member (x l)
  (if (or (null l) (eql x (car l)))
      l
      (our-member x (cdr l))))
```

This version is like the version of MEMBER which is built into Lisp; however the equality function EQL is hard-wired into our code, and thus certain uses of OUR-MEMBER will fail:

```
Lisp> (our-member 'next '(wombats next (5 km)))
(NEXT (5 KM))

;;; Lists are not usually EQL, so this call fails.
Lisp> (our-member '(5 km) '(wombats next (5 km)))
NIL
```

We could provide a third argument to OUR-MEMBER which allows the caller to specify which comparison test to use; however, we do not want callers who want the default test of EQL to always have to tediously specify this argument. We could achieve this functionality with an &REST argument, but a much cleaner way is to use the lambda-list keyword &OPTIONAL:

```
(defun our-member (x l &optional (test #'eql))
  (if (or (null l) (funcall test x (car l)))
      l
      (our-member x (cdr l) test)))
```

Our new lambda-list says that a third argument called **TEST** may optionally be supplied by the caller. If it is not supplied, then **TEST** is bound to a *default value*, which in this case is the function **EQL**. Notice that we have to pass the value of **TEST** as an argument in the recursive call to **OUR-MEMBER** to make sure that the test specified by the caller is always used. Now we can repeat our original example both with and without specifying the **TEST** argument:

```
Lisp> (our-member 'next '(wombats next (5 km)))
(NEXT (5 KM))

Lisp> (our-member '(5 km) '(wombats next (5 km)) #'equal)
((5 KM))
```

Here is a slightly more complex example of what can be done with optional arguments:

```
Lisp> (defun optional-demo (x &optional foo (baz 3)
                                       (bar (+ x baz)))
        (list x foo baz bar))
OPTIONAL-DEMO

Lisp> (optional-demo 5)
(5 NIL 3 8)
```

Notice that the argument names are bound to the actual argument values from left to right, so an initialization form can refer to the value of any variable which appears to the left of it. For more information about optional arguments, refer to the Common Lisp manual.

9.2.3 &KEY Arguments

While optional arguments are useful, they have some drawbacks. For example, suppose that we want to rewrite the function **MAKE-CYLINDER** that we wrote in Chapter 6 so that it now takes optional arguments:

```
(defun make-cylinder (&optional radius height color)
  (list 'cylinder radius height color))
```

Our function originally required that we pass all three arguments every time we called `MAKE-CYLINDER`, but now we are free to omit some or all of the arguments:

```
Lisp> (make-cylinder)
(CYLINDER NIL NIL NIL)

Lisp> (make-cylinder nil nil 'red)
(CYLINDER NIL NIL RED)
```

Unfortunately, there is no way to specify a value for `COLOR` while omitting values for `RADIUS` and `HEIGHT`. The reason is that arguments are implicitly named by their position in the argument list. This can be annoying if a function has a long argument list and we are interested in specifying only one of the last arguments, allowing the others to assume their default values. Additionally, it can be difficult to remember in what order a function takes its arguments. It would be easy to forget that `COLOR` is the last argument rather than the first if we had not dealt with the cylinder code in a while.

We have already seen that `DEFSTRUCT` solves these problems by creating constructor functions with *keyword arguments*. Similarly, we can write our own functions which accept keyword arguments. Keyword arguments let us explicitly match formal parameters with actual arguments, and thus keyword arguments may be passed in any order and in any possible combination:

```
Lisp> (defun make-cylinder (&key radius height color)
        (list 'cylinder radius height color))

Lisp> (make-cylinder :color 'red)
(CYLINDER NIL NIL RED)

Lisp> (make-cylinder :color 'blue :height 7)
(CYLINDER NIL 7 BLUE)
```

We can also make keyword arguments assume default values other than `NIL`:

```
Lisp> (defun demo (x &key (foo x) (baz 3) (bar (+ x 3)))
        (list x foo baz bar))

Lisp> (demo 4 :baz 7)
(4 4 7 7)

Lisp> (demo 5 :bar 0 :foo 'out-of-order)
(5 OUT-OF-ORDER 3 0)
```

The lambda-list keywords may all be used together in various combinations, and there are a few more features of lambda-lists that we have not discussed. Refer to the Common Lisp manual for more details.

9.3 LEXICAL SCOPING AND ANONYMOUS FUNCTIONS

One annoying aspect of the first example in this chapter is the need to define functions such as `LIST-IF-GREATER-THAN-0` and `SQUARE`. The code to implement `SQUARE` is extremely simple, and may not be needed anywhere else in our program, so it seems wasteful to have to give that code the name `SQUARE`. Instead we would like to introduce an *anonymous function* which will be used in only one place in our program.

Up until know we have been very sloppy about the distinction between a function and the *name* of a function. Many programming languages do not even make such a distinction. However, just as the list `(1 2 3)` is an object which we may or may not want to give the name `DATA`, a function which squares its argument is an object which we may or may not want to name `SQUARE`.

9.3.1 `LAMBDA`: A Name Is a Terrible Thing to Waste

In Lisp an anonymous function is denoted by a list which starts with the symbol `LAMBDA`[1] followed by a list of symbols called the argument list. The remaining elements of the list are forms which constitute the body of the function. However, just as we need the special form `QUOTE` to use a list as a piece of data, we need the special form `FUNCTION` to use a list starting with `LAMBDA` as a function. We can use an anonymous function to rewrite one of our earlier calls to `MAPCAR`:

```
Lisp> (mapcar (function (lambda (n)
                         (expt n 2))
              '(1 2 3))
(1 4 9)
```

In this example our anonymous function expects a single argument named `N` and it evaluates the body `(EXPT N 2)` when called. When we defined the function `SQUARE` with `DEFUN` we were globally associating the name `SQUARE` with the function `(LAMBDA (N) (EXPT N 2))` in the function namespace. We can use anonymous functions anywhere we would use a named function:

```
Lisp> ((lambda (n) (expt n 2)) 5)
25
```

---

[1] The name lambda comes from the lambda calculus of Alonzo Church [Chu41], upon which Lisp is based.

```
Lisp> (let ((square (function (lambda (n) (expt n 2)))))
        (funcall square 5))
25
```

Notice that when we put an anonymous function in the functional position of a list, we do not need to wrap it in a call to **FUNCTION** because Lisp knows the first element of a list is always a function. Also realize that **LAMBDA** is *not* a function or a special form. It is simply part of a convention we use to denote functions as lists.

9.3.2 Lexical Scoping

So far we have not explicitly talked about how we can determine the binding to which a variable reference refers. For example, in the function **(LAMBDA (N) (EXPT N 2))**, the variable **N** in the argument list **(N)** is bound to the argument passed to this function, while the variable reference to **N** in **(EXPT N 2)** obviously refers to this binding. However, we can easily write programs in which it is not so obvious what binding is referred to by a variable reference.

Consider the rather contrived program in Figure 9.1. The variable references in **CONTRIVED-SCOPE-EXAMPLE** could be interpreted in several different ways. In the expression **(LIST X Y)**, does **X** refer to the binding established by the enclosing **LET**, or does it refer to the binding established by a call to **CONTRIVED-SCOPE-EXAMPLE**? An even trickier problem is a reference to **Z**. Suppose we call **MAIN** with the argument **7**, thereby establishing a binding for **Z**. **MAIN** will in turn call **CONTRIVED-SCOPE-EXAMPLE** which contains a reference to **Z**. Does this reference refer to the binding for **Z** established by **MAIN**, or does it refer to a global variable? Perhaps it is an error.

We and the computer clearly need to agree upon a single set of *scoping* rules that can be used to unambiguously determine what binding is referred to by a variable reference. Common Lisp uses a set of rules known as *lexical scoping*. If you are familiar with the scoping rules for any of the Algol-based languages such as Pascal, C, Ada, Modula-2, etc., then you are already familiar with lexical scoping.

Each time a new set of variable bindings is introduced, a new *lexical block*[2] is created. We can graphically depict the scope of a block by drawing a box around the variables introduced by the block and the body of the form which introduced them. For example, we have drawn a scoping block around the argument list and the body of the function **MAIN**. The argument list introduces a set of variables which will be bound upon entry to that block, and these bindings are *lexically visible* anywhere inside the box we just drew. Thus, any reference to **Z** inside of that box refers to the binding of **Z** established by the argument list.

---

[2] A lexical block is often called a *lexical contour*.

```
(defun main (z)
  (contrived-scope-example z 3))
```

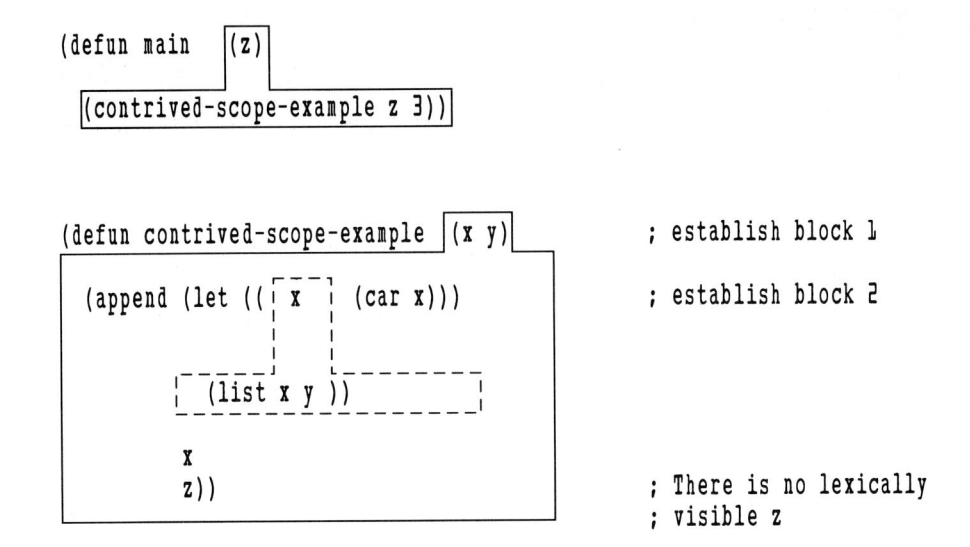

```
(defun contrived-scope-example (x y)     ; establish block 1
  (append (let ((x (car x)))              ; establish block 2
            (list x y))
          x
          z))                             ; There is no lexically
                                          ; visible z
```

FIGURE 9.1
Block structure and lexical scoping.

However, any reference to Z *outside* of this box cannot refer to this binding. This same idea can be applied to other forms, such as LET, which also introduce new variable bindings.

CONTRIVED-SCOPE-EXAMPLE is a bit complicated because it contains two scoping blocks. The first block is drawn around the argument list (X Y) and the body of the function. The second block is drawn around the X introduced by the LET expression and around the body of the LET. Notice that we do *not* include the initialization forms in the LET inside the scoping block. This is because all the initialization forms are evaluated before the new bindings are created, and therefore they cannot refer to these bindings.

The reference to X in (CAR X) refers to the binding for X established by block 1 since the reference is contained only inside of block 1. However, the reference to X in (LIST X Y) is inside of both block 1 and block 2, and each block introduces a binding for X. To which binding does the reference to X refer? According to the rules of lexical scoping, bindings in an inner block *shadow* bindings of the same name in any outer blocks. Thus, the binding for X established by block 2 obscures the binding for X established by block 1, so the X in (LIST X Y) refers to the inner binding. The Y in (LIST X Y) refers to the binding of Y established by block 1, though. It is generally a bad idea to shadow a variable binding because it makes your function harder to read.

In order to find the binding referred to by a variable reference, we search from the innermost to the outermost block. When we find a binding for the variable, we are done. As soon as the LET has returned a value, the bindings introduced by block 2 are undone, so the reference to X as the second argument to `APPEND` refers to the binding established by block 1. Notice that a reference can only refer to a binding established by a block which completely surrounds the reference. Thus, the reference to `Z` as the third argument to `APPEND` cannot refer to the binding for `Z` established by `MAIN`. However, block 1 does not introduce a binding for `Z`, and thus there are no lexically visible bindings. If no bindings are lexically visible, then we say that `Z` is a *free variable*.

In most lexically scoped languages, there is an outermost or root block which contains global variables, and thus `Z` would be referring to the value of `Z` in the root block. Similarly, in Lisp, if we say `(SETF Z 'DRAGON)`, then we are giving `Z` a global or top-level value. If `Z` does not have a global value in our example, then a call to `MAIN` will signal an error.

Trying to follow a textual discussion of scoping rules may make the whole matter seem much more confusing and complex than it really is. The beauty of lexical scoping is that it is textually local, making it easy to understand as soon as you can visualize the implicit boxes which we have been discussing.

9.3.3 Lexical Scoping and Functional Objects Interact

Functions seem like pretty simple objects now. We understand how to introduce anonymous functions, pass functions as arguments, and resolve variable references in function bodies. However, there is an interesting interaction between lexical scoping and passing functions as arguments. In order to understand these interactions, we will look at an example which tries to use `QUOTE` rather than `FUNCTION` to introduce an anonymous function. Although this sometimes works in Common Lisp, it is only allowed for compatibility with older dialects of Lisp. You should *never* do this in your programs. We are doing it here only to illustrate why it sometimes does not work and why we really do need `FUNCTION`.

Consider the definitions of `OUR-MAPCAR` and a generalization of `SQUARE-ITERATE` called `EXPT-ITERATE` shown in Figure 9.2. We *expect* `EXPT-ITERATE` to work as follows:

```
Wish-Lisp> (expt-iterate '(1 2 3) 3)
(1 8 27)                            ; This doesn't really happen!
```

However, if we actually run our code we will encounter an error:

```
Lisp> (expt-iterate '(1 2 3) 2)
>>Error: POWER has no global value

SYMBOL-VALUE:
   Required arg 0 (S): POWER

:A    Abort to Lisp Top Level
:C    Try evaluating POWER again
->
```

```
(defun our-mapcar (func list)
  (if (null list)
      list
      (cons (funcall func
                     (car list))
            (our-mapcar func
                        (cdr list)))))
```

```
(defun expt-iterate (numbers power)           ; block 1
  (our-mapcar (quote (lambda (n)              ; block 2
                       (expt n power)))
              numbers))
```

FIGURE 9.2
The interaction between lexical scoping and functional arguments.

If we draw scoping blocks around our functions, we can start to see what went wrong when evaluating (EXPT N POWER). We can resolve the variable references in the expression (EXPT N POWER) since N refers to the binding established by block 2 and POWER refers to a binding established by block 1. However, we are going to pass our anonymous squaring function into OUR-MAPCAR as an argument.

We can simulate the call to OUR-MAPCAR by replacing each reference to FUNC and LIST in its body with the function and the list of numbers that we are actually passing. Doing this produces the code shown in Figure 9.3.

Now we have a big problem. When our anonymous function gets called by FUNCALL, the binding for POWER is no longer lexically visible! In order to execute (EXPT N POWER) we need the binding of POWER which is established by block 1. However, we are no longer *lexically* inside of block 1 because we have transferred control to OUR-MAPCAR. The body of OUR-MAPCAR does not appear lexically within block 1, so the reference to POWER results in an unbound variable error.

To fix this problem we need to revise our notion of a function. So far we have considered a function to be simply a piece of code represented as a list; however, we also need the correct *environment* in which to run that code. An environment records the bindings of all variables which were lexically visible when we defined the function. Until now we have only needed the environment which is created when a function is *called*, which in this example is the environment created by block 2. However, now we also need to capture the environment

```
(if (null numbers)
    numbers
    (cons (funcall (quote (lambda (n)          ; block 2
                             (expt n power)))  ; no binding for POWER!
                   (car numbers))
          (our-mapcar (quote (lambda (n)       ; block 2
                               (expt n power))) ; no binding for POWER!
                      (cdr numbers)))))
```

FIGURE 9.3
Expanding the body of OUR-MAPCAR shows how the binding for POWER has escaped!

that existed when our function was *created*, which in this case is the environment created by block 1. A function which captures the environment in effect when it is created is called a *lexical closure*, since it "closes" over the creation environment and does not allow bindings like those established by block 1 to "escape."[3] Figure 9.4 shows how things would look if we passed a lexical closure to OUR-MAPCAR rather than just a piece of code without its creation environment.

---

[3]The problem we have just encountered is sometimes referred to as the *funarg problem* [Mos70]. The environment in which a function is created is sometimes called its *definition* environment.

```
(if (null numbers)
    numbers
    (cons (funcall (quote (lambda (n) +[POWER binding]   ; block 2
                             (expt n power)))
                   (car numbers))
          (our-mapcar (quote (lambda (n) +[POWER binding] ; block 2
                               (expt n power)))
                      (cdr numbers)))))
```

FIGURE 9.4
POWER must be captured by a lexical closure.

9.4 LEXICAL CLOSURES

The special form `QUOTE` exists so that we can introduce data into our programs. Thus, when we used `QUOTE` to introduce the functional object `(LAMBDA (N) (EXPT N POWER))`, we were only able to introduce the code portion of our anonymous function, and failed to capture the necessary environment information.

Now we can see why we need the special form `FUNCTION` to introduce complete functions which include both code and environment information. These complete functions are called *lexical closures* because they close over the environment in which they were created, thereby guaranteeing that all variables which are lexically visible at the time of function creation are available later on when the function is actually called. This creation environment is augmented at function call time when the formal arguments are bound to the actual arguments.

In our example, an anonymous function is not created until the function named `EXPT-ITERATE` is actually run and block 1 establishes an environment in which `POWER` is bound. When the anonymous function is created, the environment containing a binding for `POWER` is closed over. That environment is later augmented with a binding for the formal parameter `N` when the anonymous function is called from within `OUR-MAPCAR`. We need both of these pieces of environment information to correctly execute the body `(EXPT N POWER)`.

A lexical closure is a *first-class object*, just like any other object in Lisp. It can be passed around and manipulated by our programs. Our example will work if we use `FUNCTION` rather than `QUOTE` to introduce the anonymous function:

```
Lisp> (defun expt-iterate (list power)
        (our-mapcar (function (lambda (n)
                    (expt n power)))
                    list))
EXPT-ITERATE

Lisp> (expt-iterate '(1 2 3) 3)
(1 8 27)
```

Recall that `#'` is a shorthand notation for `FUNCTION`, just as `'` is a shorthand notation for `QUOTE`, so we can make `EXPT-ITERATE` syntactically a bit simpler:

```
Lisp> (defun expt-iterate (list power)
        (our-mapcar #'(lambda (n)
                    (expt n power))
                    list))
EXPT-ITERATE

Lisp> (expt-iterate '(1 2 3) 2)
(1 4 9)
```

Remember that we only used `QUOTE` to introduce a function so that we could understand why we need lexical closures. We would *never* really use `QUOTE` to introduce a function, and from now on we will always introduce them using `FUNCTION` or `#'`.

> **Problem.** Write a function called `OUR-SORT` which accepts a list and a two-argument predicate as arguments. `OUR-SORT` should return a new list which has been sorted according to the sorting predicate:
>
> ```
> Lisp> (our-sort '(3 4 1) #'>)
> (4 3 1)
> ```
>
> Lisp already contains a `SORT` function which will do this for you, but do not use it in your definition. Would `OUR-SORT` always work correctly if Lisp did not have lexical closures? If not, give an example that fails.

9.4.1 Capturing Local State with Lexical Closures

So far we have primarily passed functions *into* other functions. However, lexical closures allow us to safely return functions from other functions.[4] For example, earlier we wrote the function `LOOKUP-DERIV-FUNC` which returned a function as a value, although we did not need closures to do this. However, consider the following curious function:

```
(defun make-pair (castor pollux)
  #'(lambda (selector)
      (case selector
        (castor castor)
        (pollux pollux)
        (t (error "Unknown selector ~A" selector)))))
```

Here we have yet another possible implementation of `CONS` cells. `MAKE-PAIR` returns an anonymous function of one argument, and that function is defined in an environment in which the variables `CASTOR` and `POLLUX` are each bound. Without lexical closures our anonymous function could not refer to these bindings if it is later called. Thus, a Lisp without lexical closures cannot claim to treat functions as "first-class citizens" in the society of data types, since without closures we cannot pass functions around and always expect them to work correctly. `MAKE-PAIR` takes advantage of closures as a means to capture some *local state* information in the variables `CASTOR` and `POLLUX`, and we can retrieve this information with the following functions:

---

[4] A function which is passed into another function is sometimes called a *downward-funarg*, while a function which is returned from another function is sometimes called an *upward-funarg*.

```
(defun castor (closure)
  (funcall closure 'castor))

(defun pollux (closure)
  (funcall closure 'pollux))
```

The functions **CASTOR** and **POLLUX** expect a closure returned by **MAKE-PAIR** as an argument and they call that closure with the appropriate selector. The closure in turn examines the **SELECTOR** and returns the value of the corresponding variable:

```
Lisp> (setf c (make-pair 'gumby 'pokey))
#<Interpreted-Function (LAMBDA (SELECTOR)
                        (CASE SELECTOR
                          (CASTOR CASTOR)
                          (POLLUX POLLUX)
                          (T (ERROR
                              "Unknown selector ~A"))))
                        [closed over CASTOR = GUMBY,
                                     POLLUX = POKEY]
                        10B73D7>

Lisp> (castor c)
GUMBY

Lisp> (pollux c)
POKEY
```

We can view the closure returned by **MAKE-PAIR** as an object to which we can send a message asking for a particular component of the pair. Recall that earlier we implemented pairs using **DEFSTRUCT** and now we have implemented exactly the same functionality in a very different way using lexical closures. In fact, we can even build our own linked lists using closures as cons cells!

Notice that the printed representation of the function returned by **MAKE-PAIR** starts with #<. Any printed Lisp object which starts with #< cannot be read back into Lisp. Many complex Lisp data types are printed in the form #<*useful-information*>. In the above case, the useful information is the code for the interpreted function we created and the variable bindings which are closed over. The hexadecimal number is a pointer to the function object in memory. The useful-information portion of the #<*useful-information*> syntax is not standardized by Common Lisp, and each implementation of Lisp is free to print whatever it sees fit. Although our imaginary Lisp prints out what portions of the function creation environment are closed over, most Lisp systems do not.

Problem. Write the functions `SET-CASTOR` and `SET-POLLUX` which will destructively modify the `CASTOR` and `POLLUX` slots in one of our new cons cells.

Problem. Read the Common Lisp manual and figure out how to make `SETF` work properly with `CASTOR` and `POLLUX` so that we do not explicitly have to call `SET-CASTOR` and `SET-POLLUX`.

9.4.2 Delaying Evaluation with Lexical Closures

Another feature of closures is that they allow us to delay evaluation. For example, we already know that `IF` must be a special form because it only evaluates either its *then* argument or its *else* argument. However, consider the following function:

```
Lisp> (defun branch (test then else)
        (if test
            (funcall then)
            (funcall else)))
BRANCH

Lisp> (if (> 3 4)
          (print 'then)
          (print 'else))

ELSE
ELSE

Lisp> (branch (> 3 4)
              #'(lambda () (print 'then))
              #'(lambda () (print 'else)))

ELSE
ELSE
```

`BRANCH` has the same functionality as `IF`, but it is an ordinary function. The trick is to delay the evaluation of both the *then* and the *else* arguments by wrapping them inside of an argumentless anonymous function. Thus, when `BRANCH` is called with the result of evaluating `(> 3 4)`, two functions are used to capture all the information needed to evaluate both the *then* and the *else* arguments without actually evaluating them. `BRANCH` then *forces* the evaluation of one argument or the other using `FUNCALL`. In our example, since 3 is greater than 4, the *else* function was called, and so the symbol `ELSE` was printed and then returned (and printed again by the read-eval-print loop).

Both `MAKE-PAIR` and `BRANCH` may seem like neat but useless functions.

However, we will later see how the basic techniques demonstrated by these functions can be used to simplify certain kinds of programs.

9.5 LABELS AND FLET INTRODUCE LEXICAL FUNCTION DEFINITIONS

Now that we understand the rules of lexical scoping, we can clean up a problem we had earlier with helping functions. Recall the definition of **POSITIVEP**, which we examined in Chapter 4:

```
;;; Return T if X is greater than or equal to 0, else NIL.
(defun positivep (x)
  (positivep-1 x x))

(defun positivep-1 (down up)
  (cond ((is-zero-p down) t)        ; let 0 be positive
        ((is-zero-p up) nil)
        (t (positivep-1 (minus-one down) (plus-one up)))))
```

The only function in the world which cares about the helping function **POSITIVEP-1** is **POSITIVEP**, and yet **POSITIVEP-1** is visible to all the functions in Lisp because it is globally defined. It would be cleaner to somehow define **POSITIVEP-1** so that only **POSITIVEP** can call it. We can use the special form **LABELS** to introduce temporary function definitions local to a function:

```
(defun positivep (x)
  (labels ((positivep-1 (down up)
             (cond ((is-zero-p down) t) ; let 0 be positive
                   ((is-zero-p up) nil)
                   (t (positivep-1 (minus-one down)
                                   (plus-one up))))))
    (positivep-1 x x)))
```

LABELS has the general form:

```
(labels ((func-name-1 arg-list-1 body-1)
         (func-name-2 arg-list-2 body-2)
            .
            .
            .
         (func-name-n arg-list-n body-1))
  main-body)
```

LABELS introduces a new lexical block which temporarily defines new functions with a syntax similar to that used by **DEFUN**. When a **LABELS** is evaluated, the main body is evaluated in an environment in which these new function definitions are visible, and the value of the main body is the value of the **LABELS**. All the bodies in a **LABELS** are wrapped in an implicit **PROGN**.

The names of each local function defined by **LABELS** can be referenced from the bodies of those functions, and hence we are able to make the version of `POSITIVEP-1` defined by **LABELS** recursively call itself, just as the version defined by **DEFUN** could call itself. Since the name of each locally defined function can be referenced from the body of any of those functions, we can write mutually recursive functions using **LABELS**.

Sometimes we do *not* want the body of a local function to be able to call itself recursively. For example, suppose that we want to add a "wrapper" around a function such as `REVERSE` so that if we tried to reverse any object other than a list we could simply return that object rather than signalling an error. We can add such a wrapper using the special form **FLET**:

```
Lisp> (flet ((reverse (l)
              (if (listp l)
                  ;; This is a call to the GLOBAL
                  ;; definition of REVERSE.
                  (reverse l)
                  l)))
        ;; The next two calls to REVERSE refer to the local
        ;; definition, not the global definition.
        (list (reverse 3) (reverse '(I am the walrus))))
(3 (WALRUS THE AM I))
```

FLET is syntactically identical to **LABELS** except that the names of the local functions cannot be referenced by the bodies of those functions. **LABELS** would not have worked in this example, since the call to `REVERSE` in the local definition of `REVERSE` would have referred to itself, producing an infinite recursion.

FLET is analogous to **LET**, since **LET** introduces temporary variables, while **FLET** introduces temporary functions using the same scoping rules. However, **LABELS** is not directly analogous to anything in Common Lisp, although we can think of it as being similar to a special form which we might call **LET-RECURSIVE**. We only need **LABELS** and **FLET** because we have separate variable and function namespaces, and in general **FLET** is less useful than **LABELS**.

> **Problem.** Do **LABELS** and **FLET** give us any new power? If not (hint, hint), show how you can rewrite the examples in this section so that they still use local functions but do not use **LABELS** or **FLET**.

9.6 SOME OTHER CONSEQUENCES OF LEXICAL SCOPING

9.6.1 Using Lexical Functions Correctly

Now that we can shadow global function definitions with local definitions, we have a problem. Consider the following example:

```
(defun example (l)
```

```
(flet ((> (x y)
        (< x y)))
  (sort l '>)))       ; Passing '> is incorrect
```

We have shadowed the global definition of > with our own local definition. However, if we try to pass the *symbol* > in a call to `SORT`, things do not quite work as expected:

```
Lisp> (example '(1 5 9))
(9 5 1)
```

Our list of numbers was sorted from high to low using the global definition of > rather than from low to high using our local definition of >. Once again, the problem is that we tried to use `QUOTE` where we should have used `FUNCTION`. We only passed the *symbol* > to the function `SORT`, and when `SORT` called the function associated with the symbol >, our local definition was no longer lexically visible.

The solution to this problem is to actually pass the *function* named by >. We can also use the special form `FUNCTION` to look up the current functional value of a symbol. Notice that we only need to do this because we have separate function and value namespaces:

```
Lisp> (function >)
#<Compiled-Function > 444FAF>

Lisp> #'>
#<Compiled-Function > 444FAF>
```

Now we can rewrite our example to work correctly:

```
Lisp> (defun example (l)
        (flet ((> (x y)
                (< x y)))
          (sort l #'>)))
EXAMPLE

Lisp> (example '(1 5 9))
(1 5 9)
```

This is why we *always* pass functions using #' rather than passing the *names* of functions using '. We could easily rewrite our `FLET` example above as

```
Lisp> (defun example (l)
        (let ((> #'(lambda (x y)
                    (< x y))))
          (sort l >)))
EXAMPLE
```

Function namespace	Value namespace
FLET	LET
#'var-name	var-name
LABELS	No counterpart. We might call it LET-RECURSIVE if one existed.
DEFUN can only change global function definitions	SETF can change global or local bindings

FIGURE 9.5
Relationship between environment functions.

```
Lisp> (example '(1 5 9))
(1 5 9)
```

Now we do not need to use #' when referring to > because **LET** binds names in the value namespace. **FLET** binds names in the function namespace, so we need #' to reference a binding created by **FLET**. Figure 9.5 shows the parallels between forms which can alter or establish bindings in the function and value namespaces respectively.

Problem. Show how you can simulate the functionality of **LET-RECURSIVE** even though Lisp does not supply it as a primitive.

9.6.2 EVAL and the Null Lexical Environment

EVAL is not quite as powerful as it seems at first sight because it evaluates an expression in the *null lexical environment*. Thus, even though a binding *should* be lexically visible from a form we might pass to **EVAL**, it will not be seen:

```
Lisp> (defun dumb-square (x)
        (eval '(* x x)))
DUMB-SQUARE

Lisp> (dumb-square 4)
>>Error: X has no global value

SYMBOL-VALUE:
   Required arg 0 (S): X
```

```
:A     Abort to Lisp Top Level
:C     Try evaluating X again
-> :a
```

EVAL evaluates the expression (`* X X`) as though we entered it at the top level. However, at top level there are no local bindings, and thus the binding for **X** established by the call to **DUMB-SQUARE** is not visible.

9.7 DYNAMIC SCOPING

There is a drawback to lexical scoping which we have not yet seen. Suppose that we have a list of numbers which represent the intensity values of some pixels in a small graphic image we have computed, and we would like to print the value of each pixel, one to a line. We can do this by calling the function **PRINT** on each element of the list.

```
Lisp> (defun print-line-of-pixels (pixel-list)
        ;; MAPC is just like MAPCAR except that it discards
        ;; the result of each call to PRINT, returning
        ;; the value of PIXEL-LIST instead.
        (mapc #'print pixel-list))
PRINT-LINE-OF-PIXELS

Lisp> (print-line-of-pixels '(4 14))

4
14
(4 14)
```

But now suppose that we want to print out the pixel values in binary. We can print numbers in any base we like by calling the output function **WRITE** with the keyword argument **:BASE**:

```
Lisp> (defun print-line-of-pixels (pixel-list)
        (mapc #'(lambda (pixel-value)
                  ;; TERPRI prints out a
                  ;; newline (carriage return)
                  (terpri)
                  (write pixel-value :base 2))
              pixel-list))
PRINT-LINE-OF-PIXELS

Lisp> (print-line-of-pixels '(4 14))

100
1110
(4 14)
```

If a complete binary image is a list of many lines of pixels, then we can write `DUMP-IMAGE` to linearly print the value of every pixel in the image:

```
Lisp> (defun dump-image (image)
        (mapc #'print-line-of-pixels image))
DUMP-IMAGE
```

However, suppose we would like to control the base in which an entire image is printed. Now we must make `DUMP-IMAGE` and `PRINT-LINE-OF-PIXELS` accept another argument called `BASE` which will be passed on to `WRITE`. The general problem is that some high-level piece of code may want to communicate with a very low-level piece of code, and the only way we have to do this right now is to have every intermediate piece of code which connects the high- and low-level functions accept and pass on the information of interest.

We really do not want every intermediate function to have to deal with passing information, such as the print base, on to the low-level function. For example, there are many other aspects of printing which we might like to control. How can we possibly predict which options might be needed by some high-level piece of code when writing our intermediate functions?

We can solve our problem by passing the information through a global variable such as `*PRINT-BASE*`. Thus, `DUMP-IMAGE`, or a higher level piece of code, can simply `SETF *PRINT-BASE*` to the appropriate base, and `PRINT` and `WRITE` can use the value of `*PRINT-BASE*` to control printing. In fact, `PRINT` and `WRITE` actually do use the value of `*PRINT-BASE*` as the base in which to print:

```
Lisp> (defun print-line-of-pixels (pixel-list)
        ;; Calls to PRINT use the value of *PRINT-BASE* to
        ;; determine the default radix for printing numbers.
        (mapc #'print pixel-list))
PRINT-LINE-OF-PIXELS

Lisp> (defun dump-binary-image (image)
        (setf *print-base* 2)
        (dump-image image))
DUMP-BINARY-IMAGE

Lisp> (dump-binary-image '((4 14) (15 3)))
100
1110
1111
11
((100 1110) (1111 11))

Lisp> 10            ; numbers are read in base ten but now
1010                ; they are still printed in base two!
```

DUMP-BINARY-IMAGE controls printing by destructively modifying the value of *PRINT-BASE*. However, calling DUMP-BINARY-IMAGE has the undesirable side effect of losing our original value of *PRINT-BASE*, and thus numbers continue to be read in base 10 but printed in base 2 even after a call to DUMP-BINARY-IMAGE finishes! We can fix this by rewriting DUMP-BINARY-IMAGE:

```
(defun dump-binary-image (image)
  (let ((old-base *print-base*))
    (setf *print-base* 2)
    (dump-image image)
    (setf *print-base* old-base)))
```

Now the original value of *PRINT-BASE* is restored after the call to DUMP-IMAGE. However, this seems like a lot of code to accomplish such a simple task. Also, consider what happens here if DUMP-IMAGE contains an error and aborts to top level. The second call to SETF which restores OLD-BASE may never be executed if control does not return normally from DUMP-IMAGE.

We would really like to temporarily *bind* *PRINT-BASE* to 2 only during the call to DUMP-IMAGE. Thus, we would like to rewrite DUMP-BINARY-IMAGE as:

```
(defun dump-binary-image (image)
  (let ((*print-base* 2))
    (dump-image image)))
```

But by the rules of lexical scoping, the binding for *PRINT-IMAGE* is only visible within the body of the LET. It is not visible from within the definition of PRINT or WRITE, which is where we need to reference this binding. Thus, lexical scoping will not solve our problem.

However, *dynamic scoping* will solve this problem. The symbol *PRINT-BASE* is actually a *dynamic* or *special* variable in Lisp. All bindings of a special variable are called *special bindings*. References to special variables refer to the most recent binding in time, and thus PRINT or WRITE can refer to *PRINT-BASE* and see the value 2 in our example. The special binding lasts only for the duration of the LET, and when the LET exits *PRINT-BASE* is restored to whatever value it had before entering the LET. Thus, our new version of DUMP-BINARY-IMAGE works correctly:

```
Lisp> (dump-binary-image '((4 14) (15 3)))

100
1110
1111
11
((4 14) (15 3))
```

```
Lisp> 10
10
```

Special variables provide essentially the same functionality as our rewrite of `DUMP-BINARY-IMAGE` which explicitly saved and restored the original value of `*PRINT-BASE*`. However, even if the call to `DUMP-IMAGE` within `DUMP-BINARY-IMAGE` were to terminate abnormally, the special binding is guaranteed to be undone, no matter how the `LET` is exited.

We can define our own special variables using the special form `DEFVAR` which we saw in Chapter 4:

```
(defvar *digits*
  '(zero one two three four five six seven eight nine)
  "A list of the digits in the current number system")
```

`DEFVAR` not only provides a convenient way to initialize and document a global variable, but it also declares that the variable is special. Thus, all bindings of and references to `*DIGITS*` are dynamic rather than lexical in scope. Note that a *lexical* closure does not capture the value of any *special* variables; however we can look up the current dynamic value of a symbol using the function `SYMBOL-VALUE`. Thus, we could replace every special reference to `*DIGITS*` with the call `(SYMBOL-VALUE '*DIGITS*)`.

The form `DEFCONSTANT` is similar to `DEFVAR` except that it is used to declare variables whose value should never change. It is also possible to specify that a variable be special only at specific points in our program by using the special form `DECLARE`:

```
(setf *zerbina* 'meltdown)

;;; Create a special binding for *zerbina*
(defun special-binder (*zerbina*)
  (declare (special *zerbina*))
  (examine))

;;; Create a lexical binding for *zerbina*
(defun lex-binder (*zerbina*)
  (examine))

;;; Lookup the most recent special binding for *zerbina*
(defun examine ()
  (declare (special *zerbina*))
  *zerbina*)
```

Rather than using `DEFVAR` to proclaim that `*ZERBINA*` will always be special, we can locally decide in each of the above functions whether references to `*ZERBINA*` are lexical or special:

```
;;; The special binding of *ZERBINA*  shadows the global
;;; value of *ZERBINA*
Lisp> (special-binder 'fuelrod)
FUELROD

;;; The lexical binding of *ZERBINA*  does not shadow the
;;; global value of *ZERBINA*
Lisp> (lex-binder 'fuelrod)
MELTDOWN
```

The primary use of dynamic variables is to communicate between various functions without passing arguments all around, as we saw above.[5] Richard Stallman points out that dynamic scoping is better than lexical scoping for writing extensions to the EMACS [Sta81] editor. Local dynamic bindings should generally be avoided because they can lead to very confusing code, and excessive use of dynamic variables can make your programs quite opaque, so use them judiciously.[6]

---

[5]Unfortunately, Common Lisp does not support lexically scoped global variables, and thus any global variable *must* be dynamically scoped. In practice this can occasionally cause problems, and it is not consistent with other lexically scoped languages.

[6]For a long time all Lisps used only dynamic scoping in the interpreter while the compiler used a mixture of dynamic and lexical scoping. This meant that programs which ran fine under the interpreter would often break when compiled. To avoid this, the Common Lisp compiler and interpreter obey exactly the same scoping rules.

CHAPTER 10

SYNTACTIC SUGAR MAKES LISP TASTE BETTER

So far we have only used function calls and special forms such as `IF` to control the flow of execution in our programs. If you are used to a programming in a language other than Lisp, then you might be wondering why Lisp doesn't seem to have a `WHILE` or a `FOR` statement to perform iteration, or a `BREAK` statement to abnormally alter the flow of control.

It turns out that we can express *all* known control constructs using nothing more than function calls, and thus we do not really need these kind of statements. However, it may be a bit verbose or tedious to express all control constructs using function calls, so we sometimes prefer to express common idioms such as iteration using a compact and agreed-upon syntax. However, this syntax can always be translated into the appropriate set of functions and function calls. Therefore, we will view *all* control constructs as nothing more than *syntactic sugar*. Syntactic sugar adds absolutely no new power to our language; instead, it simply makes our programs shorter and easier to understand.

10.1 ITERATION

In this section we will examine some ways to express iteration in Lisp.

10.1.1 Tail-Recursion: Iteration by Any Other Name

In order to understand why we only need function calls to express idioms such as iteration, we need to examine more closely what happens during a function call. So far we have described all functions which call themselves as recursive functions. However, all recursive calls are not the same, and there is an important distinction which we can make to subdivide recursive calls into two classes. For example, consider the definition of OUR-REVERSE which we saw in Chapter 3:

```
(defun our-reverse (l)
  (if (null l)
      nil
      (append (our-reverse (cdr l)) (list (car l)))))
```

Recall the explanation of OUR-REVERSE in terms of the photocopier model of recursion, and how TRACE helped illuminate how it worked:

```
Lisp> (trace our-reverse)
(OUR-REVERSE)

Lisp> (our-reverse '(athos porthos aramis))
1 Enter OUR-REVERSE (ATHOS PORTHOS ARAMIS)
| 2 Enter OUR-REVERSE (PORTHOS ARAMIS)
|   3 Enter OUR-REVERSE (ARAMIS)
|   |   4 Enter OUR-REVERSE NIL
|   |   4 Exit OUR-REVERSE NIL
|   3 Exit OUR-REVERSE (ARAMIS)
| 2 Exit OUR-REVERSE (ARAMIS PORTHOS)
1 Exit OUR-REVERSE (ARAMIS PORTHOS ATHOS)
(ARAMIS PORTHOS ATHOS)
```

Each time OUR-REVERSE is called, a new photocopy of the master definition of OUR-REVERSE is made, and the values of the arguments and any local variables are written on that sheet of paper. TRACE indicates each time a new photocopy is made by printing an Enter message. When we have completed a call, the photocopy for that call is discarded and TRACE prints an Exit message displaying the value being returned.

When we call OUR-REVERSE on the list (ATHOS PORTHOS ARAMIS), we can watch the photocopying process occur. By the time we enter OUR-REVERSE for the fourth time, we have four photocopies of the master definition, each with a different argument. We are able to satisfy the fourth call immediately by returning NIL, and thus continue the computation on the third photocopy. In order to finish the third photocopy, we need to append the NIL returned by the fourth call onto the list (ARAMIS). Thus, we *must* keep the third photocopy around when we make the fourth call because we need to remember the value of L in the third call in order to complete the call to APPEND.

Similarly, we must retain each sheet of paper until the recursive call to OUR-REVERSE on that sheet is over because we need the information on that paper to complete the call. If we examine the TRACE of OUR-REVERSE, we can clearly see how the reversed list is slowly built up as we exit each recursive call, and we do not have the entire answer until the last call exits.

Now consider a different implementation of the function REVERSE. It achieves the same effect with a different approach:

```
(defun tail-reverse (l)
  (tail-reverse-1 l nil))

(defun tail-reverse-1 (old result)
  (if (null old)
      result
      (tail-reverse-1 (cdr old) (cons (car old) result))))
```

TAIL-REVERSE operates by passing all the work off to the helping function TAIL-REVERSE-1. TAIL-REVERSE-1 works by CDRing down the original list, called OLD, and building up a reversed list called RESULT. When we reach the end of OLD, we need only return the RESULT list we have been building up:

```
Lisp> (trace tail-reverse tail-reverse-1)
(TAIL-REVERSE TAIL-REVERSE-1)

Lisp> (tail-reverse '(athos porthos aramis))
1 Enter TAIL-REVERSE (ATHOS PORTHOS ARAMIS)
| 2 Enter TAIL-REVERSE-1 (ATHOS PORTHOS ARAMIS) NIL
|   3 Enter TAIL-REVERSE-1 (PORTHOS ARAMIS) (ATHOS)
|   | 4 Enter TAIL-REVERSE-1 (ARAMIS) (PORTHOS ATHOS)
|   |   5 Enter TAIL-REVERSE-1 NIL (ARAMIS PORTHOS ATHOS)
|   |   5 Exit TAIL-REVERSE-1 (ARAMIS PORTHOS ATHOS)
|   | 4 Exit TAIL-REVERSE-1 (ARAMIS PORTHOS ATHOS)
|   3 Exit TAIL-REVERSE-1 (ARAMIS PORTHOS ATHOS)
| 2 Exit TAIL-REVERSE-1 (ARAMIS PORTHOS ATHOS)
1 Exit TAIL-REVERSE (ARAMIS PORTHOS ATHOS)
(ARAMIS PORTHOS ATHOS)
```

We can also explain the operation of TAIL-REVERSE in terms of the photocopier model of function calling. When the fourth call to TAIL-REVERSE-1 (labeled as 5 Enter above) occurs, we have four photocopies of the function TAIL-REVERSE-1. We can complete the fourth call immediately, returning the value of RESULT to the third call. However, the third call has no more work to do, since the value of the third call is nothing more than the value of the fourth call. Similarly, each recursive call exits immediately with the same result. This time we are not building up a result as we exit each recursive call; instead, we know the correct answer as soon as we complete the final recursive call.

But what was the point of making four photocopies—one for each recursive call? This time we do *not need* the information on those photocopies to complete each recursive call. We know the answer to the original call to `TAIL-REVERSE-1` as soon as the last recursive call completes. After that we just waste our time exiting each recursive call, discarding photocopies which we needlessly saved.

We will call the recursive call to `TAIL-REVERSE-1` a *tail call* since it is the last or "tail" function call in the function `TAIL-REVERSE-1`. Our observations of tail-recursive calls suggests that we should modify the photocopier model of function calls to include the rule:

```
IF      we need the information on a photocopy to continue
        the current function after calling another function

THEN    make a photocopy for the call on a new sheet of
        paper

ELSE    reuse the current photocopy rather than wasting a
        new sheet of paper. By reuse we mean erase the
        current sheet and use it to make the new photocopy.
```

We can safely erase and reuse the current photocopy when we no longer need the information on it. The information on a photocopy is actually the lexical environment for a function call, and we are free to discard that environment as soon as we do not need it anymore. In fact, it does not even matter that we are making a recursive call. Any call which is the last call made in the execution of a function body is a tail call, and thus we can discard the current lexical environment since nobody else could possibly need it.[1]

The critical distinction between the two definitions of `REVERSE` we have just examined is that the former requires an amount of paper *proportional to the length* of the list we are trying to `REVERSE`, while the latter requires only a *constant* amount of paper. This distinction is critical because our photocopier has a limited amount of paper. We might one day give `OUR-REVERSE` a long list which would exhaust the supply of paper in the photocopier, and thus we would never get an answer. However, `TAIL-REVERSE-1` can reverse *any* list we might give it without any danger of running out of paper. Put in more conventional terms, `TAIL-REVERSE-1` is an *iterative* definition of `REVERSE` even though it is written as a recursion.

---

[1] Except a person trying to debug a program. Sigh.

Problem. Write a tail-recursive version of factorial named **TAIL-FACT**. Trace both **TAIL-FACT** and the definition of factorial given in Chapter 3 and compute the factorial of 5 using each definition. How do the traces differ?

Problem. Rewrite the definition of **OUR-MAPCAR** given in Chapter 9 so that it is tail-recursive.

10.1.2 Iteration Viewed as Syntactic Sugar for Tail-Recursion

At this point we need to make an important point about Common Lisp. **TAIL-REVERSE-1** worked just fine with our original wasteful rule for function calls which said "always make a fresh photocopy." However, if we use this old rule then **TAIL-REVERSE-1** cannot be considered iterative because we might run out of paper. Common Lisp does not specify which photocopying rule must be used, and thus we are not guaranteed that a tail-recursive call will not use a new sheet of paper. We will call an implementation of Lisp which invariably avoids wasting paper during tail-recursive calls a *properly tail-recursive* implementation. The act of reusing a photocopy to perform a tail-recursive call is called *tail-recursion removal*.

Common Lisp views the removal of tail-recursion as an optimization which can increase the speed of our programs, while we will view it as an essential part of the *semantics* of Lisp which allows us to faithfully perform iteration. This is a useful way of unifying various syntactically different forms of iteration, but we must remember that completely portable Common Lisp programs cannot rely on tail-recursion removal to accomplish iteration.[2]

10.1.3 Tail-Recursion Removal Can Hinder Debugging

There is an important drawback to tail-recursion removal that we have not encountered yet. Suppose that we accidentally wrote **TAIL-REVERSE-1** as follows:

```
(defun tail-reverse-1 (old result)
  (if (null old)
      reslt              ; typographic error
      (tail-reverse-1 (cdr old) (cons (car old) result))))
```

We will encounter an error when we try to test our function:

---

[2] Most Common Lisp implementations can perform tail-recursion removal when compiling code.

```
Lisp> (tail-reverse '(aramis porthos athos))
>>Error: RESLT has no global value

SYMBOL-VALUE:
   Required arg 0 (S): RESLT

:A    Abort to Lisp Top Level
:C    Try evaluating RESLT again
->  ;;; backtrace of the example run
->  ;;; without tail-recursion removal
->  :b
SYMBOL-VALUE <- TAIL-REVERSE-1 <- TAIL-REVERSE-1
<- TAIL-REVERSE-1 <- TAIL-REVERSE-1 <- TAIL-REVERSE <- EVAL
```

The backtrace clearly shows that we were in the middle of our fourth call to **TAIL-REVERSE-1** when trouble occurred.

However, if tail-recursion is removed, the backtrace is less helpful:

```
SYMBOL-VALUE <- TAIL-REVERSE-1  <- TAIL-REVERSE <- EVAL
```

Even though four calls to **TAIL-REVERSE-1** have occurred, we see only a single call since any record of the previous three calls has been lost when we erased their photocopies. Similarly, if we have a set of functions such as:

```
Lisp> (defun a (x) (b x))
A

Lisp> (defun b (x) die)
B

Lisp> (a 3)
>>Error: DIE has no global value

SYMBOL-VALUE:
   Required arg 0 (S): DIE

:A    Abort to Lisp Top Level
:C    Try evaluating DIE again
->  ;;; backtrace of the example run
->  ;;; without tail-recursion removal
->  :b
SYMBOL-VALUE <- B <- A <- EVAL
```

We get a nice backtrace as long is tail-recursion is not removed. However, if tail-recursion is removed, we get the backtrace

```
SYMBOL-VALUE <- B <- EVAL
```

Tail-recursion removal means that any record of the original call to **A** is gone. Thus, tail-recursion removal can hinder debugging because it eagerly discards information as soon as possible.

10.1.4 Frame Walking and Inspection

Each sheet of paper Lisp uses to record the lexical environment for a function call is usually called a *frame*. When we ask for a backtrace in the debugger, Lisp actually prints the name of each function which currently has an active frame. However, most debuggers allow us to move back and forth between frames, examining their contents. For example, when testing our buggy version of **TAIL-REVERSE-1**, we got the following backtrace:

```
Lisp> (tail-reverse '(aramis porthos athos))
>>Error: RESLT has no global value

SYMBOL-VALUE:
   Required arg 0 (S): RESLT

:A    Abort to Lisp Top Level
:C    Try evaluating RESLT again
-> :b
SYMBOL-VALUE <- TAIL-REVERSE-1 <- TAIL-REVERSE-1
<- TAIL-REVERSE-1 <- TAIL-REVERSE-1 <- TAIL-REVERSE <- EVAL
```

If we wanted to find out more about why Lisp called **SYMBOL-VALUE**, we can move to the next frame, which is waiting for **SYMBOL-VALUE** to return:

```
-> :n    ; Examine next frame
TAIL-REVERSE-1:
   Required arg 0 (OLD): NIL
   Required arg 1 (RESULT): (ATHOS PORTHOS ARAMIS)
```

The debugger command **:N** moves to the "next" frame and displays its contents. Since **OLD** is bound to **NIL**, we have obviously reached the base case of our function, causing the evaluation of the symbol **RESLT**. We can also examine other frames with the **:N** command:

```
-> :n
TAIL-REVERSE-1:
   Required arg 0 (OLD): (ATHOS)
   Required arg 1 (RESULT): (PORTHOS ARAMIS)
```

```
-> :n
TAIL-REVERSE-1:
   Required arg 0 (OLD): (PORTHOS ATHOS)
   Required arg 1 (RESULT): (ARAMIS)

-> :n
TAIL-REVERSE-1:
   Required arg 0 (OLD): (ARAMIS PORTHOS ATHOS)
   Required arg 1 (RESULT): NIL

-> :n
TAIL-REVERSE:
   Required arg 0 (L): (ARAMIS PORTHOS ATHOS)

-> :p              ; Examine previous frame
TAIL-REVERSE-1:
   Required arg 0 (OLD): (ARAMIS PORTHOS ATHOS)
   Required arg 1 (RESULT): NIL
```

We can examine successive frames until we finally reach a call to **TAIL-REVERSE**. At that point, we can start moving in the other direction using the command **:P**.

Examining the lexical environment stored in each frame is a useful debugging aid, and most Lisp debuggers have many more useful features. For example, we can usually alter the contents of a frame or force a frame to return a specific value in order to continue a computation. In this case we might want to force the call to **SYMBOL-VALUE** to return **NIL** in order to complete our original call to **TAIL-REVERSE**.

Sometimes our programs may run for a long time or enter an infinite loop. Most Lisps allow us to pause a computation with an interrupt character such as *control-c*. Typing the interrupt character will place us in the debugger so that we will have all of our normal debugging tools available for inspecting the state of the interrupted computation. After examining Lisp, and possibly making some changes, we can then resume the interrupted computation as though nothing happened. The constant availability of a powerful debugger is one of Lisp's most distinguishing features.

Problem. The following tail-recursive version of **LENGTH** contains a bug:

```
(defun tail-length (l)
  (tail-length-1 l 0))

(defun tail-length-1 (rest i)
  (if (null rest)
      i
      (tail-length-1 rest (1+ i))))
```

Calling **TAIL-LENGTH** on any list should eventually throw you into the debugger. Try using the debugging tools available in your Lisp to examine the stack to see what is wrong with **TAIL-LENGTH**.

10.1.5 DO: Yet Another Syntax

We can improve our tail-recursive definition of **TAIL-REVERSE** by using **LABELS** to make **TAIL-REVERSE-1** a local function:

```
(defun tail-reverse (l)
  (labels ((tail-reverse-1 (old result)
             (if (null old)
                 result
                 (tail-reverse-1 (cdr old)
                                 (cons (car old) result)))))
    (tail-reverse-1 l nil)))
```

This definition of **TAIL-REVERSE** is cleaner since we do not needlessly make our helping function visible to the world. However, a disadvantage of defining **TAIL-REVERSE-1** via **LABELS** is that we cannot **TRACE** it because most Lisps only allow us to **TRACE** top-level function definitions. There is nothing in the Common Lisp specification which prevents tracing local functions, but most Lisp implementations do not provide this facility.

Unfortunately, we still cannot always rely on this definition of **TAIL-REVERSE** to be properly tail-recursive in all Common Lisps, and some people find the verbosity and syntax unpleasant. To solve these problems, we can rewrite **TAIL-REVERSE** using the special form **DO**:

```
(defun tail-reverse (l)
  (do ((old l (cdr old))
       (new nil (cons (car old) new)))
      ((null old) new)))
```

We can view this new definition as a purely syntactic transformation of our version using **LABELS**.[3] Thus, **DO** is an iteration construct which is essentially equivalent to our use of **LABELS** in a Lisp which can remove tail-recursion. **DO** has the general form

```
(do ((iteration-var-1 init-form-1 stepping-form-1)
```

---

[3]Technically we cannot transform a **DO** loop into the equivalent **LABELS** form because the Common Lisp manual says that iteration variables in a **DO** are updated using assignment rather than binding. However, this distinction is visible only in rare circumstances involving closure over the stepping variables.

```
          (iteration-var-2 init-form-2 stepping-form-2)
           •
           •
           •
          (iteration-var-n init-form-n stepping-form-n))
         (termination-test result-form)
  body-form-1
  body-form-2
   •
   •
   •
  body-form-n)
```

Each iteration variable introduced by DO corresponds to an argument to a tail-recursive function, while the corresponding initialization forms are the arguments in an initial call to that function. Thus, OLD and RESULT are the iteration variables in TAIL-REVERSE-1, and L and NIL are the initial arguments passed to it.

After the iteration variables are bound to the initial values, the termination test, (NULL OLD) in this case, is evaluated. If the test returns true, then the value of the result form is returned as the value of the entire DO loop. Thus, when our example terminates, the value of RESULT is returned.

If the termination test returns NIL, then the DO loop continues by sequentially executing the body forms. We have no body forms in our example, and in fact many DO loops are like this. Only body forms which have side effects make sense, since there is no structured way for the body forms to affect the state of the iteration variables.

After the body forms have been executed, each stepping form is evaluated and the iteration variables are bound in parallel to the results. Stepping the iteration variables corresponds to the tail-recursive call to the iteration function represented by the DO. Notice that the previous values of the iteration variables are lost when we erase the current photocopy which contains them. This erasure is what allows the iteration to proceed without consuming more paper.

Thus, DO is essentially an alternate syntax for iteration via tail-recursion. One advantage of explicit top-level tail-recursion over DO loops is that we can usually use TRACE to observe a tail-recursive iteration as it progresses, while we are unable to TRACE the action of a DO loop.

Problem. Rewrite your definition of TAIL-FACT so that it uses a DO loop rather than tail-recursion.

Problem. Rewrite your tail-recursive version of OUR-MAPCAR so that it uses a DO loop.

Problem. Rewrite the TAIL-LENGTH function given earlier so that it uses a DO loop, but do not remove the bug from the program. What happens when you call your function on a short list? Does it fail in the same way that the tail-recursive version failed?

Defining local functions is useful even if we are not going to be using tail-recursion. For example, recall our earlier definition of the function EVAL-OVER-RANGE:

```
;;; Evaluate EXPR as VAR ranges from LOW to HIGH.
;;; Return an a-list of the results.
(defun eval-over-range (low high var expr)
  (if (> low high)
      nil
      (acons low
             (evaluate-at-point low var expr)
             (eval-over-range (1+ low) high var expr))))
```

As we iterate, only the value of LOW is changing, and yet we must also pass the values HIGH, VAR, and EXPR around on each iteration. However, we can rewrite EVAL-OVER-RANGE to include a local function which performs the actual iteration:

```
(defun eval-over-range (low high var expr)
  (labels ((loopy (i)
             (if (> i high)
                 nil
                 (acons i
                        (evaluate-at-point i var expr)
                        (loopy (1+ i))))))
    (loopy low)))
```

Now EVAL-OVER-RANGE only passes one argument on each iteration. Although a clever compiler might perform this transformation automatically, we might want to do it ourselves in order to emphasize the iteration variable in a complex computation. It is interesting to compare this definition of EVAL-OVER-RANGE to a tail-recursive definition:

```
(defun eval-over-range (low high var expr)
  (labels ((loopy (i result)
             (if (> i high)
                 ;; notice we have to reverse RESULT!
                 (reverse result)
                 (loopy (1+ i)
                        (acons
                         i
                         (evaluate-at-point i var expr)
                         result)))))
    (loopy low nil)))
```

As usual, our tail-recursive version requires an extra argument called RESULT to carry the a-list we are building up. Once again, we can mechanically translate our usage of LABELS into a DO loop:

```
(defun eval-over-range (low high var expr)
  (do ((i low (1+ i))
       (result nil (acons i
                          (evaluate-at-point i var expr)
                          result)))
      ;; notice we have to reverse RESULT!
      ((> i high) (nreverse result))))
```

Notice that a list is naturally built up in reverse using iteration, and our tail-recursive version of REVERSE relied on this fact; however, often we do not want our result list to be reversed, so we must explicitly undo the reversal brought about by iteration by explicitly calling REVERSE on RESULT. Unfortunately, there are two drawbacks associated with performing an extra REVERSE. The first is that we must examine every element in the list again, thus slowing down our algorithm. The second problem is that we needlessly cons up a new list out of fresh cons cells when we call REVERSE, even though we just consed up our RESULT list, thus wasting half the cons cells we have used. As we saw earlier, these cells will eventually have to be reclaimed by a garbage collector. While a good garbage collector will efficiently recover the cons cells we have wasted, we can avoid wasting any cons cells by using NREVERSE rather than REVERSE.

Recall that NREVERSE is the destructive version of REVERSE. We can safely call it on RESULT because RESULT is the *only* variable in the world which has a pointer to the list which we have just built, and thus we will not inadvertently destroy a list which is used by other parts of our program. Destructive functions must be used judiciously, since we can easily destroy shared structures, causing obscure bugs in our program. However, applying NREVERSE to a list which has been created by an iterative function is a common and generally safe use of a destructive operation.

Problem. Can you rewrite the tail-recursive version of EVAL-OVER-RANGE so that it is does not require any list reversal and yet is still tail-recursive?

10.2 BLOCK AND RETURN-FROM PROVIDE LOCAL CONTROL TRANSFER

In Chapter 8 we wrote an iterating function which would evaluate a function at a number of points and return an a-list of points and function values:

```
Lisp> (eval-over-range 1 5 'x '(- (* 2 x) 2))
((1 . 0) (2 . 2) (3 . 4) (4 . 6) (5 . 8))
```

Functions such as $f(x) = 2x - 2$ have *fixed points* at which x equals $f(x)$. Clearly $f(x) = 2x - 2$ has a fixed point at $x = 2$. If we want to determine whether an a-list of points and values contains a fixed point, we can linearly search the a-list, returning the first pair whose elements are equal, or NIL if no such pair exists:

```
Lisp> (defun find-fixed-point (pairs)
        (labels ((iterate (rest)
                   (cond ((null rest) nil)
                         ((= (caar rest) (cdar rest))
                          (car rest))
                         (t (iterate (cdr rest))))))
          (iterate pairs)))
FIND-FIXED-POINT

Lisp> (find-fixed-point '((1 . 0) (2 . 2) (3 . 4) (4 . 6)
                          (5 . 8)))
(2 . 2)
```

There are actually two termination tests (base cases) in our iteration: one if REST is NIL, and a second if we have found a fixed point. However, if we try to perform this iteration using DO we run into some trouble:

```
(defun find-fixed-point (pairs)
  (do ((rest pairs (cdr rest)))
      ((or (null rest)
           (= (caar rest) (cdar rest)))
       ;; Fold together the return forms NIL and (CAR REST).
       ;; This relies on the fact that (CAR NIL) ==> NIL.
       (car rest))))
```

LABELS allows as many termination test/return pairs as we want, while DO only allows a single test/return pair. We can combine both termination tests using an OR, and luckily we can fold together the return form NIL and (CAR REST) because the CAR of NIL is NIL. However, in general we would need to repeat the termination tests to see which one caused us to exit.

To avoid this, we can rewrite the DO loop to separate the termination tests, prematurely exiting the DO loop if one of the termination conditions is true:

```
(defun find-fixed-point (pairs)
  (block exit-do
    (do ((rest pairs (cdr rest)))
        ((null rest) nil)
      (if (= (caar rest) (cdar rest))
          ;; abnormally terminate the DO
          (return-from exit-do (car rest))
          nil))))
```

Now the `DO` loop will exit normally with the value `NIL` if there are no fixed points. However, we perform the second termination test in the body of the `DO`, prematurely exiting the entire `DO` loop if we find a fixed point. We are able to exit the `DO` using the special forms `BLOCK` and `RETURN-FROM`:

(BLOCK *block-name* &rest *body*)

(RETURN-FROM *block-name* *result-form*)

The *block-name* must always be a symbol, and we use `&REST` to indicate that *body* may consist of a sequence of forms. The *block-name* is not evaluated, and thus it does not need to be quoted. `BLOCK` simply executes its body as though it were wrapped in a `PROGN`. However, if one of the body forms is a call to `RETURN-FROM` with the same *block-name* as the enclosing block, then the block is abnormally exited with the result of evaluating *result-form*.

Here are some examples of these two constructs:

```
Lisp> (block whale
        (print 'help)
        (return-from whale 'ok)
        (print 'too-late))

HELP
OK
```

When the form `(RETURN-FROM WHALE 'OK)` is evaluated the enclosing `BLOCK` immediately returns with the value `OK`. Similarly, if a fixed point is found in our latest version of `FIND-FIXED-POINT`, the block named `EXIT-DO` will prematurely exit, thus exiting from the `DO` itself. Notice that we only evaluate the `RETURN-FROM` because of its *control* side effect, just as we only use `SETF` for its data side effect.

Every `DO` is implicitly surrounded by a block named `NIL`, and thus we do not need to explicitly establish a block around the `DO`. The special form `RETURN` performs a `RETURN-FROM` from the block named `NIL`:

```
Lisp> (block nil
        (print 'help)
        (return 'ok)
        (print 'too-late))

HELP
OK
```

Thus, we can rewrite `FIND-FIXED-POINT` as:

`(defun find-fixed-point (pairs)`

```
    (do ((rest pairs (cdr rest)))
        ((null rest) nil)
      (when (= (caar rest) (cdar rest))
        ;; Return-from the implicit block named NIL
        ;; which surrounds the DO.
        (return (car rest))))))
```

Notice that our call to **IF** has been replaced by a call to the special form **WHEN**. **WHEN** is like an **IF** whose else form is always **NIL**:

```
Lisp> (when t 'nihil)
NIHIL

Lisp> (when nil 'veritas)
NIL
```

We will use **WHEN** to replace an **IF** whose *else* value is ignored. The only reason to call **IF** and ignore the *else* value as we did in **FIND-FIXED-POINT** is because the *then* form has a side effect, in which case **WHEN** makes our intention clearer.

DO still requires like a lot of effort from us just to iterate over a list, so there is a simplified version of **DO** called **DOLIST** which makes list iteration simpler:

```
Lisp> (dolist (x '(a b c))
        (print x))

A
B
C
NIL
```

This example binds the variable **X** to successive elements of the list '(A B C), evaluating the body (**PRINT X**) once for each binding of **X**. When the end of the list is reached, the **DOLIST** terminates and returns the value **NIL**.

We can use **DOLIST** to make **FIND-FIXED-POINT** even simpler:

```
(defun find-fixed-point (pairs)
  (dolist (next-entry pairs)
    (when (= (car next-entry) (cdr next-entry))
      (return next-entry))))
```

Notice that **DOLIST** is useful only if its body contains side effects, since there is no way to collect results in other variables as there is in a **DO**.

Common Lisp provides many different ways to express a single idea. However, remember that all the different iteration forms we have seen are just *syntactic* variants of a single method for performing iteration. When properly used, Lisp's ability to capture common idioms and make them simple to express without specifying many tiny details can make our programs easier to understand and debug. In the next chapter we will see how we can automate the transformation of new syntactic forms into simpler constructs using *macros*.

> **Problem.** Write a version of ASSOC which uses BLOCK and RETURN-FROM to exit as soon as it finds an a-list entry that begins with the given key.

10.2.1 Object Lifetimes: BLOCK Names Have Dynamic Extent

There is an unfortunate restriction on when we may actually return from a named block in Common Lisp. In order to understand this restriction, consider the following unusual (and rather ugly) definition of FIND-FIXED-POINT:

```
(defvar *escape-procedure* nil "An escape procedure")

(defun find-fixed-point (pairs)
  (setf *escape-procedure* #'(lambda (value)
                               (return-from find-fixed-point
                                            value)))
  (dolist (entry pairs)
    (escape-if-fixed-point-entry entry)))

(defun escape-if-fixed-point-entry (next-entry)
  (when (= (car next-entry) (cdr next-entry))
    (funcall *escape-procedure* next-entry)))
```

Rather than exiting from FIND-FIXED-POINT with a call to RETURN, we go out of our way and set *ESCAPE-PROCEDURE* to a function which can return from FIND-FIXED-POINT. This escape procedure is then called from within ESCAPE-IF-FIXED-POINT-ENTRY when a fixed point is found. Our convoluted version of FIND-FIXED-POINT is functionally equivalent to our earlier versions:

```
Lisp> (find-fixed-point '((1 . 0) (2 . 2) (3 . 4) (4 . 6)
                          (5 . 8)))
(2 . 2)

Lisp> *escape-procedure*
#<Interpreted-Function (LAMBDA (VALUE)
                         (RETURN-FROM FIND-FIXED-POINT
                                      VALUE))
                       [closed over block FIND-FIXED-POINT]
                       109E967>
```

Notice that we can still reference the escape procedure even after `FIND-FIXED-POINT` exits because we set the global value of the symbol `*ESCAPE-PROCEDURE*` to the procedure. Since we can still reference the function, it should still be legal to call it:

```
Lisp> (funcall *escape-procedure* '(2 . 2))
>>Error: Attempt to RETURN-FROM block
        FIND-FIXED-POINT occurred from within
        a closure which no longer exists!

unnamed function:
   Required arg 0 (VALUE): (2 . 2)

:A    Abort to Lisp Top Level

->
```

To successfully call the escape procedure we need to exit from the block named `FIND-FIXED-POINT` which implicitly surrounds the body of the function `FIND-FIXED-POINT`. This block *should* still exist, since our escape procedure would now like to reference it, but it is gone because block names have *dynamic extent*. An object which has dynamic extent only exists, and therefore may only be legally referenced, as long as the construct which established it is executing. Thus, a block established by a call to `BLOCK` is destroyed as soon as that call exits.

Until now we have not talked about the *lifetime* of an object. Once an object has been created, we assume that it exists until the garbage collector can prove that no part of our program can reference it anymore, in which case it may be reclaimed. Such an object is said to have *indefinite extent*, and ideally all objects should behave this way. However, there are some situations in Common Lisp in which this is not always true.

To summarize, *scope* determines where a reference may occur and to what it refers, while *extent* determines the *lifetime* of an object and consequently the time frame during which references to that object are valid.

10.3 CATCH AND THROW PROVIDE DYNAMIC CONTROL TRANSFER

The functionality provided by binding a variable to an escape procedure, and then calling the procedure to transfer control, is already provided by Lisp with the special forms `CATCH` and `THROW`. These two special forms allow us to perform a nonlocal exit from a function, just as `BLOCK` and `RETURN-FROM` allow us to perform a local exit. The relationship of `CATCH` and `THROW` to `BLOCK` and `RETURN-FROM` is analogous to the relationship between dynamic and lexical scoping.

`CATCH` is a special form of one or more arguments. The first argument is evaluated and is called the *catch tag*. After the tag is evaluated, all remaining arguments are evaluated from left to right as if wrapped in an implicit `PROGN`. Normally the value of the last argument will be returned.

`THROW` is a special form of two arguments which allows us to transfer control to a matching `CATCH`. `THROW`'s first argument is evaluated and is called the *throw tag*. After the throw tag is evaluated, the second argument to `THROW` is evaluated, and the result is temporarily saved. Lisp then looks for a catch tag which matches the throw tag. If a matching catch tag is found, then the matching `CATCH` form *immediately* returns the saved result of evaluating `THROW`'s second argument, aborting any pending computations between it and the `THROW`. The search for a matching catch tag is dynamically scoped, and thus a call to `THROW` need not be lexically within the `CATCH` to which it wants to transfer control. Here is a simple example of `CATCH` and `THROW`:

```
Lisp> (defun outer-func ()
        (catch 'all-done (inner-func)))
OUTER-FUNC

Lisp> (defun inner-func ()
        (+ 1
           ;; return from the matching CATCH
           (throw 'all-done 7)
           (print 11)))  ; this form never gets evaluated
INNER-FUNC

Lisp> (outer-func)
7
```

`OUTER-FUNC` establishes the catch tag `ALL-DONE` and then calls `INNER-FUNC`. `INNER-FUNC` then throws the value 7 back to the matching `CATCH` in the midst of computing the arguments to `+`. We know that the evaluation of the arguments to `+` was aborted because the number 11 was never printed. This exit could not have been done by returning from a block named `ALL-DONE`, since such a block defined within `OUTER-FUNC` would not have been lexically visible from within `INNER-FUNC`.

We can also rewrite our previous example involving `*ESCAPE-PROCEDURE*` to use `CATCH` and `THROW`:

```
(defun find-fixed-point (pairs)
  (catch 'escape
    (dolist (next-entry pairs)
      (escape-if-fixed-point next-entry))))
```

```
(defun escape-if-fixed-point (next-entry)
  (when (= (car next-entry) (cdr next-entry))
    (throw 'escape next-entry)))
```

Now calling `ESCAPE-IF-FIXED-POINT` with a fixed point entry will transfer control back to the `CATCH` labeled `ESCAPE`, thus terminating the search. `CATCH` and `THROW` accept a tag argument because at any given time, many `CATCH`es may be pending, but we will want to `THROW` to a specific one. Thus, `THROW` may transfer control to a specific `CATCH` based on its tag. Don't let the simplicity of the above example fool you. Many function calls could have occurred between the `CATCH` and the `THROW`. All of those calls would have been aborted when the `THROW` occurred, and any existing dynamic variable bindings would have been undone, returning us to the dynamic and lexical environment which existed at the point of the `CATCH`.

The dynamic, nonlocal nature of `CATCH` and `THROW` is typically called for when an error or exit condition is detected deep in the middle of a complex program and it is desirable to exit an entire computation, as we will see later when we write a small Lisp interpreter. Just as we can choose between lexically or dynamically scoped variables, we can also choose between lexically or dynamically scoped block names.

10.4 MULTIPLE VALUES

Suppose that we want to convert the rectangular coordinates of a point on a plane into polar coordinates:

```
(defun rectangular->polar (x y)
  (let ((r (sqrt (+ (expt x 2) (expt y 2))))
        (theta (atan (/ x y))))
    (list r theta)))
```

`RECTANGULAR->POLAR` expects the x and y coordinates of a point and returns the corresponding radius and angle that define that point. Because all of our Lisp functions have returned only a single value so far, we must collect the values we want to return into a list and return the list. The caller of `RECTANGULAR->POLAR` must then extract the values from the list before using them.

While this method works, it has two problems. The first is that returning a list is not the clearest way of saying "this function returns more than one value." Second, we have allocated storage for a list which almost immediately becomes garbage once the values have been extracted. Thus, we are needlessly wasting time allocating and then garbage collecting a temporary list.

To solve this problem, Common Lisp provides the function `VALUES` so that we can explicitly and efficiently return multiple values from a function without consing a list:

```
Lisp> (values 'left 'right)
LEFT                                            ; value 1
RIGHT                                           ; value 2

Lisp> (values)
                                                ; no values!
Lisp> (values 'right)
RIGHT                                           ; value 1

Lisp> (values 'left 'right 'up 'down)
LEFT                                            ; value 1
RIGHT                                           ; value 2
UP                                              ; value 3
DOWN                                            ; value 4
```

The read-eval-print loops prints each value returned by a call to **VALUES** on a separate line. Notice that we return zero values if we want.

Now we can use **VALUES** to rewrite **RECTANGULAR->POLAR**:

```
Lisp> (defun rectangular->polar (x y)
        (let ((r (sqrt (+ (expt x 2) (expt y 2))))
              (theta (atan (/ x y))))
          (values r theta)))
RECTANGULAR->POLAR

Lisp> (RECTANGULAR->POLAR 4 4)
5.656854
0.7853982                                       ; pi / 4 radians = 45 degrees

Lisp> (multiple-value-bind (r theta)
          (rectangular->polar 4 4)
        (format t "Radius: ~A, Angle: ~A" r theta))
Radius: 5.656854, Angle: 0.7853982
NIL
```

We can use the special form **MULTIPLE-VALUE-BIND** to name and use the values returned by a call to **VALUES**. The first argument to **MULTIPLE-VALUE-BIND** is a list of variable names, which is not evaluated, while the second argument is a call to a potentially multiple-value producing form. The second argument is evaluated, and each variable in the list of variable names is bound to the corresponding values returned by the second argument. If there are more variables than values, than any extra variables are bound to **NIL**. Any extra values are simply discarded. Any remaining arguments to **MULTIPLE-VALUE-BIND** are then evaluated within an implicit **PROGN**, which is within the scope of the variable bindings. Thus, **MULTIPLE-VALUE-BIND** is like a variant of **LET**.

Common Lisp provides other functions that deal with multiple values. Refer to the manual for more details.

Problem. Write a function called `DECODE-TIME` which accepts a time of the form HHMMSS and returns the hours, minutes, and seconds components of the time as three separate values.

Problem. Write a function called `ADD-TIMES` which adds two times of the form HHMMSS. Your definition of `ADD-TIMES` should call `DECODE-TIME`.

CHAPTER 11

MACROS

In the previous chapter we saw how useful syntactic transformations can be for making common idioms easier to express. However, so far we have had to perform these transformations or "rewrites" by hand. Fortunately, Lisp provides *macros* which let us automatically rewrite our Lisp code using other Lisp code, once again taking advantage of the equivalence of programs and data.

11.1 PROGRAM REWRITING WITH MACROS

In Chapter 5 we examined one possible way to rewrite our programs using if-then rules. However, the system we examined was rather simplistic; Lisp provides a much more general facility. As a simple example of a macro, consider the form WHEN. WHEN is really a macro, not a special form. In fact, many of the procedures we have referred to as special forms are actually macros predefined by Common Lisp. Here is one possible definition of a macro called OUR-WHEN:

```
Lisp> (defmacro our-when (test consequent)
        `(if ,test
             ,consequent
             nil))
OUR-WHEN
```

DEFMACRO is syntactically similar to DEFUN since it accepts the name of a macro, an argument list, and a body of forms. However, a macro is handled differently than a function. When Lisp evaluates a list, it examines the first element. If that element is a symbol, then it must either name a macro or a function. If the symbol names a function, then we already know what happens. But if the symbol names a macro such as `OUR-WHEN`, then the entire list is *macroexpanded* to produce a new expression. Macroexpansion is really the same as rewriting, except that we macroexpand an expression by calling a macroexpansion function on the *unevaluated* arguments to the macro. Notice that a symbol may name either a macro or a function, but not both at the same time.

In order to expand an expression such as `(OUR-WHEN T 'A)`, Lisp calls the macroexpansion function on the unevaluated arguments in the macro call. Thus, `TEST` is bound to `T` and `CONSEQUENT` is bound to `'A`, not `A`. The body of the macroexpansion function is then evaluated just as a regular function body is evaluated. However, the macroexpansion function is expected to return a *new* expression, and this new expression is then evaluated as though it appeared in the original program where the macro call appeared. Thus, when Lisp encounters a macro call in our program, it does two things:

1. Expand the macro by calling the macroexpansion function with the unevaluated arguments.
2. Evaluate the expanded macro in place of the original macro call.

We can explicitly expand macros in our program using the function `MACROEXPAND`. `MACROEXPAND` expects a Lisp expression as an argument and it returns the macroexpansion of that expression:

```
Lisp> (trace our-when)
(OUR-WHEN)

Lisp> (macroexpand '(our-when t 'a))
1 Enter OUR-WHEN (OUR-WHEN T 'A)
1 Exit OUR-WHEN (IF T 'A NIL)
(IF T 'A NIL)
T

Lisp> (macroexpand '(our-when (atom x) (setf *flag* t)))
1 Enter OUR-WHEN (OUR-WHEN (ATOM X) (SETF *FLAG* T))
1 Exit OUR-WHEN (IF (ATOM X) (SETF *FLAG* T) NIL)
(IF (ATOM X) (SETF *FLAG* T) NIL)
T

;;; CAR is a function, not a macro
Lisp> (macroexpand '(car nil))
(CAR NIL)
NIL
```

`MACROEXPAND` also returns a second value, which is `T` if the macroexpansion was successful, or `NIL` if no expansion was possible. Hence, if we pass an expression which is not a macro to `MACROEXPAND`, then no expansion occurs and the second value returned is `NIL`. Notice that the appearance of `'A` in the expansion of `(OUR-WHEN T 'A)` makes it clear that the arguments to a macroexpansion function are passed unevaluated, unlike a regular function call.

Once a macro has been expanded, Lisp evaluates the expansion instead of evaluating the original expression:

```
Lisp> (our-when t 'a)
A

Lisp> (our-when nil 'a)
NIL
```

Recall that we use `WHEN` only to evaluate a consequent which has side effects, since it is poor style to rely on the fact that `WHEN` returns a value—instead use `IF` to make returned values explicit.

So far we have learned about many different special forms. However, most of the special forms we have seen are really macros. For example, `IF` is a special form, but `COND` is really a macro which expands into a series of nested `IF`s. In fact, even `DEFMACRO` is a macro![1] Thus, macros round out our ability to extend Lisp by allowing us to add the equivalent of new special forms just as we can add new functions using `DEFUN`.

Problem. Lisp contains a macro called `UNLESS` which is similar to `WHEN` except that the consequent is evaluated only if the test is `NIL`:

```
Lisp> (unless nil 'a)
A

Lisp> (unless t 'a)
NIL
```

Write your own version of `UNLESS`.

11.2 MACRO EXAMPLES

The only way to get a get a good grasp on macros is to examine some real macro definitions. When writing a new macro you *must* have a clear idea of what the macro call and the expansion of that call will look like, just as you must have a clear idea of what a function will accept and return before you can write it. Once you have a written a macro, it is usually best to test it using `MACROEXPAND` rather than by just calling the macro directly. When debugging a macro, remember that you are really debugging a function which rewrites some Lisp code.

---

[1] Recursive, eh? So how is `DEFMACRO` written? Read the Common Lisp manual for details.

11.2.1 LET Can Be Written as a Macro

LET can easily be written as a macro:

```
;;; This macro has 2 bugs!
(defmacro our-let (bindings &rest body)
  `((lambda ,(mapcar #'first bindings)
      ,body)
    ,(mapcar #'second bindings)))
```

This macro makes it clear that OUR-LET simply provides an alternate syntax for an anonymous function call. Our definition of LET uses backquote to provide a template of the expression we want to return, filling in slots in that template using a comma. We can use MAPCAR to separate the variables in an OUR-LET from their values. However, our definition has a bug which we could try to find by calling OUR-LET directly:

```
Lisp> (our-let ((a 3)
                (b 4))
          (list a b))
>>Error: Unknown operator 3 in (FUNCTION 3)

EVAL:
   Required arg 0 (EXPRESSION): (OUR-LET ((A 3) (B 4))
   (LIST A B))

:A    Abort to Lisp Top Level
->
```

When the bug appears, it is not at all clear what went wrong because the expansion of OUR-LET is hidden from us. However, if we use MACROEXPAND to explicitly examine the expansion, then the problem becomes clearer:

```
Lisp> (macroexpand '(our-let ((a 3)
                              (b 4))
                      (list a b)))
((LAMBDA (A B) ((LIST A B))) (3 4))
T
```
                          ↑   ↑   ↑
                          └──────┴────┴── Extra parentheses

We have left an extra level of parentheses around the arguments 3 and 4, thus causing Lisp to treat 3 as a function. Similarly, we have an extra set of parentheses around the body of the LAMBDA expression, although we never got far enough to see that bug. What we really want to do is *splice* the argument list and the body into their enclosing lists:

```
(defmacro our-let (bindings &rest body)
  (append (list (append (list 'lambda
                               (mapcar #'first
                                       bindings))
                         body))
          (mapcar #'second bindings)))
```

The call to **APPEND** removes the extra set of parentheses we were getting:

```
Lisp> (macroexpand '(our-let ((a 3)
                              (b 4))
                     (list a b)))
((LAMBDA (A B) (LIST A B)) 3 4)
T
```

Unfortunately, we must write the macro with calls to **LIST**, and this obscures the real structure of the expression we are building. However, we can achieve the splicing affect of **APPEND** by using `,@` rather than `,` within backquote:

```
(defmacro our-let (bindings &rest body)
  `((lambda ,(mapcar #'first bindings)
      ,@body)
    ,@(mapcar #'second bindings)))
```

This version of **OUR-LET** produces a macroexpansion identical to our previous definition, but it is much clearer since we have used `,@` to **APPEND** lists together.

Notice that we are needlessly creating garbage by using **APPEND** and `,@`. **LIST**, **MAPCAR**, and **&REST** all cons up fresh lists, and **APPEND** allocates even more new cons cells. We can instead perform a splice with **NCONC** rather than **APPEND** and not waste any cons cells. Similarly, we can replace `,@` with `,.` (comma-dot) within a backquote to **NCONC** lists together. Be careful when using comma-dot and **NCONC** that you are not destructively modifying a list which is shared with other parts of a program.

Problem. **LET** also accepts symbols without an initialization form and binds them to a default value of **NIL**:

```
Lisp> (let ((x nil)
            y)
        (list x y))
(NIL NIL)
```

Change **OUR-LET** to behave similarly.

11.2.2 The ITERATE Macro

In the last chapter we saw that we can use LABELS to perform iteration using tail-recursion. While DO is one alternate syntax for performing iteration, we have already seen that it is a bit limited. For example, recall that it was a bit awkward to rewrite the following function with a DO loop:

```
(defun find-fixed-point (pairs)
  (labels ((find (rest)
             (cond ((null rest) nil)
                   ((= (caar rest) (cdar rest)) (car rest))
                   (t (find (cdr rest))))))
    (find pairs)))
```

Using LABELS to define a single iteration function is so useful to we would like to capture the idiom with a macro called ITERATE:

```
(defun find-fixed-point (pairs)
  (iterate find ((rest pairs))
    (cond ((null rest) nil)
          ((= (caar rest) (cdar rest)) (car rest))
          (t (find (cdr rest))))))
```

ITERATE is sometimes called a "named let" because it looks like a LET form with a name. The argument list and the initial values of each argument are tied together as they are in a LET, but we are able to rebind the variables by calling the named function. Thus, calls to FIND in our example will bind REST to a new value and start executing the body of the ITERATE again. Here is one possible macro expansion function for ITERATE:

```
(defmacro iterate (name bindings &body body)
  `(labels ((,name ,(mapcar #'first bindings)
              ,@body))
     (,name ,@(mapcar #'second bindings))))
```

ITERATE is a simple macro, but much more complex iteration macros have become quite popular. For example, there is a macro called LOOP which offers an English-like syntax for performing complex iterations.

Some people do not like the extremely simple syntax of Lisp, and have developed alternate syntaxes which are more like Pascal. RLisp in PSL, CLisp in Interlisp, and CGOL in Maclisp are all examples of such systems. However, these systems tend to obscure the equivalence of programs and data in Lisp, and sometimes make programs more difficult to understand and manipulate.

Problem. Write a macro named OUR-DO which expands into a LABELS.

Problem. Common Lisp provides a macro named `DOTIMES` for iterating over a sequence of integers:

```
;;; Step I from 0 to 2, executing the body (PRINT I) for
;;; each value of I. Return the symbol ALL-DONE when the
;;; iteration is complete. The return value is optional,
;;; and should default to NIL if not supplied.
> (dotimes (i 3 'all-done)
    (print i))

0
1
2
ALL-DONE                              ; return value
```

Write a version of `DOTIMES` called `OUR-DOTIMES`.

11.2.3 `PROG`: Lisp History

When Lisp was first invented, goto statements were quite popular, and to this day Lisp includes a special form named `GO`. Unfortunately, the use of `GO` often leads to code that resembles spaghetti. Hopefully it is becoming clear that we can always implement whatever control constructs you need using only function calls, but as a matter of Lisp history it is worth knowing how to use `GO` in Lisp. More importantly, iteration macros such as `DO` should really expand into uses of `GO` rather than `LABELS` so that iteration can occur without consuming excessive amounts of photocopier paper in a Lisp which cannot remove tail-recursion.

The special form `GO` can only be used within the special form `TAGBODY`. `TAGBODY` is just like `PROGN` except that any symbol or number which appears as an argument to a `TAGBODY` is considered to be a *tag*, and `GO` allows us to transfer control to that tag. The macro `PROG` is a mixture of `TAGBODY`, `LET`, and `BLOCK` and thus it also allows the use of tags and `GO` within its body. Here is a simple example of a `PROG`:

```
Lisp> (defun prog-reverse (l)
        (prog ((old l) (result nil))  ; bind vars
          loop-label                  ; introduce a tag
          (when (null old)
            (return result))          ; return from the PROG
          (setf result (cons (car old) result))
          (setf old (cdr old))
          (go loop-label)))           ; transfer control to a tag
PROG-REVERSE

Lisp> (prog-reverse '(veni vidi victi))
(VICTI VIDI VENI)

Lisp> (prog-reverse '(revolution number 9))
(PAUL IS DEAD)                        ; :-)
```

This definition of `PROG-REVERSE` is equivalent to the definition of `TAIL-REVERSE` we saw in Chapter 10 with tail-recursion removed. Once upon a time, `PROG` was heavily used, but it is now virtually obsolete since we have more perspicuous ways to control the flow of execution and data in our programs.

11.2.4 SELECT: CASE with Evaluation

All of the branching constructs we have seen so far are really just macros which expand into the special form `IF`. For example, `COND` is a macro which might expand into an `IF`:

```
Lisp> (macroexpand '(cond ((eql '+ operator)
                           (deriv-add var arg1 arg2))
                          ((eql '* operator)
                           (deriv-mult var arg1 arg2))))
(IF (EQL '+ OPERATOR)
    (DERIV-ADD VAR ARG1 ARG2)
    (IF (EQL '* OPERATOR)
        (DERIV-MULT VAR ARG1 ARG2)
        NIL))
T
```

The exact expansions of macros predefined by Common Lisp are not specified, and thus the macroexpansions presented here may not look exactly like the expansions produced by your Lisp. Earlier we replaced the above usage of `COND` with the macro `CASE`. `CASE` might expand into a `COND` which in turn expands into an `IF`:

```
;;; Perform only one macroexpansion.
Lisp> (macroexpand-1 '(case operator
                        (+ (deriv-add var arg1 arg2))
                        (* (deriv-mult var arg1 arg2))))
(COND ((EQL '+ OPERATOR) (DERIV-ADD VAR ARG1 ARG2))
      ((EQL '* OPERATOR) (DERIV-MULT VAR ARG1 ARG2)))
T

Lisp> (macroexpand '(case operator
                      (+ (deriv-add var arg1 arg2))
                      (* (deriv-mult var arg1 arg2))))
(IF (EQL '+ OPERATOR)
    (DERIV-ADD VAR ARG1 ARG2)
    (IF (EQL '* OPERATOR)
        (DERIV-MULT VAR ARG1 ARG2)
        NIL))
T
```

`MACROEXPAND` will repeatedly expand its argument until it finds an expansion which is *not* a macro call. Thus, `MACROEXPAND` stops expanding `CASE` when it has been transformed into a call to the special form **IF**. However, sometimes we only want one level of expansion to occur, even if evaluating the expansion would produce another macro call. We can use **MACROEXPAND-1** to perform only one expansion, thus letting us see that **CASE** actually expands into a **COND**. **MACROEXPAND-1** is often useful when debugging macros because it shows the output of a macroexpansion function without any further transformations.

One commonly needed macro is a version of **CASE** which *does* evaluate its keys. Such a macro is not predefined in Lisp, but we can easily write our own version called **SELECT**. We want **SELECT** to behave as follows:

```
Lisp> (select (* 3 pi)
        ((* 2 pi) 'apple)
        ((* 3 pi) 'boston-cream)
        ((* 4 pi) 'blueberry))
BOSTON-CREAM
```

This **SELECT** example needs to expand into:

```
(let ((selector (* 3 pi)))
  (cond ((equal (* 2 pi) selector) 'apple)
        ((equal (* 3 pi) selector) 'boston-cream)
        ((equal (* 4 pi) selector) 'blueberry)))
```

Now that we have a clear idea of the rewrite **SELECT** must perform, we are ready to write the macro:

```
(defmacro select (selector-form &rest clauses)
  ;; only eval the SELECTOR-FORM once!
  `(let ((selector ,selector-form))
     (cond ,@(mapcar #'(lambda (clause)
                         `((equal ,(car clause) selector)
                           ,@(cdr clause)))
                     clauses))))
```

Unfortunately, there is a subtle problem with this definition of **SELECT**. Consider what happens if some code calling **SELECT** happens to already use a variable called **SELECTOR**:

```
Lisp> (let ((selector (* 2 pi)))
        (select (* 4 pi)
          ((* 2 selector) 'apple)      ; should return APPLE
          ((* 3 pi) 'lemon-meringue)))
NIL                                    ; but no keys match
```

Our example should return **APPLE**, but instead it returns **NIL**. The bug in our program becomes clear if we replace the call to **SELECT** inside the **LET** by its macroexpansion:

```
;;; The outer binding is shadowed by the binding introduced
;;; by the macroexpansion
(let ((selector (* 2 pi)))
  (let ((selector (* 4 pi)))
    (cond ((equal (* 2 selector) selector) 'apple)
          ((equal (* 3 pi) selector) 'lemon-meringue))))
```

Our macro has introduced a variable named **SELECTOR** into the macroexpanded code; however, when we replace the original call to **SELECT** with its expansion, we find that the binding of **SELECTOR** in our original program has been *shadowed* by the the binding of **SELECTOR** which is introduced by the macroexpansion. This inner binding causes all of the tests in the **COND** to fail, and therefore we get **NIL** instead of **APPLE**.

When writing **SELECT** we assumed that we were free to introduce the variable **SELECTOR**, but we never considered the possibility that the piece of code we were rewriting might already contain a reference to a *different* variable of the same name in an outer scope. Thus, we inadvertently intercepted a variable reference and introduced a tricky violation of lexical scoping.

It seems that there is no way that we can ever fix this problem, since no matter what name we choose instead of **SELECTOR**, there is always a possibility that some piece of code we expand may also be using that name. Fortunately, the function **GENSYM** allows us to generate a unique symbol which cannot possibly be referenced from another expression with Lisp:

```
Lisp> (gensym)
#:G172

Lisp> (gensym "SELECTOR-")
#:SELECTOR-173

Lisp> (eq '#:selector-173 '#:selector-173)
NIL
```

A **GENSYM**ed symbol is preceded by a sharp sign and a colon to indicate its uniqueness, although binding the variable ***PRINT-GENSYM*** to **T** will suppress the printing of the #:. **GENSYM** accepts a string as an optional argument, and it will use that string as the beginning of the name of the symbol it returns. It is good practice to always supply a string to **GENSYM** since it helps add meaning to the symbol being generated.

Notice that two **GENSYM**ed symbols of the same name are distinct objects, and thus they are not **EQ**. Now we can replace **SELECTOR** in our definition of **SELECT** with a symbol produced by **GENSYM**:

```
(defmacro select (selector-form &rest clauses)
  (let ((selector (gensym "SELECTOR-")))
    ;; only eval the SELECTOR-FORM once!
    `(let ((,selector ,selector-form))
       (cond ,@(mapcar #'(lambda (clause)
                           `((equal ,(car clause) ,selector)
                             ,@(cdr clause)))
                       clauses)))))
```

Our revised definition works correctly:

```
Lisp> (macroexpand-1 '(select (* 2 pi)
                       ((* 2 selector) 'apple)
                       ((* 2 pi) 'lemon-meringue)))
(let ((#:selector-176 (* 2 pi)))
  (cond ((equal (* 2 selector) #:selector-176) 'apple)
        ((equal (* 2 pi) #:selector-176) 'lemon-meringue)))

;;; Now our example works correctly
Lisp> (let ((selector (* 2 pi)))
        (select (* 4 pi)
          ((* 2 selector) 'apple)
          ((* 3 pi) 'lemon-meringue)))
APPLE
```

Problem. As written, the last key in a call to SELECT is not treated differently than any other key. Change SELECT so that if the last key is T, then it will be treated as a catch-all case.

Problem. Common Lisp provides a macro called ECASE which provides greater error checking than CASE:

```
Lisp> (defun color->number (color flower)
        (ecase color
          (red (eat-red flower))
          (green (eat-green flower))
          (blue (eat-blue flower))))
COLOR->NUMBER

Lisp> (color->number 'indigo)
>>Error: The value of COLOR, INDIGO is not one of:
         BLUE, GREEN or RED

COLOR->NUMBER:
   Required arg 0 (COLOR): INDIGO
```

```
:A      Abort to Lisp Top Level
->
```

Write your own version of **ECASE**.

Problem. Write your own versions of **AND** and **OR**.

11.3 MACRO-PRODUCING MACROS

We frequently will want to write macros which produce other macros. For example, suppose that we define a structure named **CYLINDER**:

```
(defstruct cylinder radius height color mass)
```

DEFSTRUCT automatically defines a function named **COPY-CYLINDER** which will create a new cylinder whose slots contain the same values as an existing cylinder. However, suppose that we have a cylinder named **C** which we wish to copy, while changing the value of the **COLOR** and **RADIUS** slots. We could use the following code to accomplish this:

```
(let ((copy (copy-cylinder c)))
  (setf (copy-color copy) "blue")
  (setf (copy-radius copy) 10)
  copy)
```

This is rather verbose and tedious for such a simple task. It would be nice if we could instead write something like:

```
(alter-copy-cylinder c :color "blue" :radius 10)
```

We would like **ALTER-COPY-CYLINDER** to make a copy of a cylinder while allowing us to specify alternate values with which to initialize specific slots. We can write a macro called **DEF-ALTER-COPIER** which accepts the name of a structure and produces an alter-copier for that structure. Thus, we can define **ALTER-COPY-CYLINDER** with the call

```
(def-alter-copier cylinder) ; define ALTER-COPY-CYLINDER
```

Our call to the macro **ALTER-COPY-CYLINDER** should expand into the several lines of explicit code we would have written by hand to create our altered copy.

Before we write **DEF-ALTER-COPIER** we need to define a function to help us construct the names of slot-accessing functions:

```
;;; Return a symbol whose print-name is the concatenation of
;;; all the NAMES.
Lisp> (defun names->symbol (&rest names)
        (intern (apply #'concatenate
                       'string
                       (mapcar #'princ-to-string names))))
NAMES->SYMBOL

Lisp> (names->symbol "COPY-" 'cylinder)
COPY-CYLINDER
NIL                     ; ignore the second value returned

Lisp> (names->symbol 'cylinder "-" "COLOR")
CYLINDER-COLOR
NIL                     ; ignore the second value returned
```

NAMES->SYMBOL uses a few new features. It returns a symbol whose print-name is the result of concatenating several names together. The function PRINC-TO-STRING prints its argument into a string, and CONCATENATE will combine strings, just as APPEND can combine lists:

```
Lisp> (princ-to-string 'alter-copy-)
"ALTER-COPY-"

Lisp> (princ-to-string "CYLINDER")
"CYLINDER"

Lisp> (princ-to-string 3)
"3"

;;; The first argument to CONCATENATE says that
;;; we want the result to be a string.
Lisp> (concatenate 'string "ALTER-COPY-" "CYLINDER")
"ALTER-COPY-CYLINDER"
```

Given a string, we can use the function INTERN to produce a symbol whose name is that string:

```
Lisp> (intern "ALTER-COPY-CYLINDER")
ALTER-COPY-CYLINDER
:INTERNAL                       ; ignore the second value

Lisp> (eq 'alter-copy-cylinder
          (intern "ALTER-COPY-CYLINDER"))
T
```

Since every symbol is unique, if we `INTERN` the string `"ALTER-COPY-CYLINDER"`, then we get back the symbol `ALTER-COPY-CYLINDER` which already exists inside of Lisp. Notice that case matters:

```
Lisp> (intern "alter-copy-cylinder")
|alter-copy-cylinder|
NIL

Lisp> (eq 'alter-copy-cylinder
          (intern "alter-copy-cylinder"))
NIL

;;; We can obtain a symbol's print-name (a string)
;;; using SYMBOL-NAME.
Lisp> (symbol-name 'alter-copy-cylinder)
"ALTER-COPY-CYLINDER"
```

Lisp uses a bar as an *escape character* to print symbols whose print-names contain lower-case characters, but normally there is never any need to use symbols with lower-case characters in their print-names. `INTERN` also accepts an optional second argument called a *package*. For now we will ignore packages, noting only that we need to use the keyword package in our macro.[2]

Now that we have written `NAMES->SYMBOL` we can write `DEF-ALTER-COPIER`:

```
;;; Given the name of a structure, define a macro named
;;; ALTER-COPY-structure-name.
;;; The macro returned will accept slot keyword/init-value
;;; pairs just as a constructor function would. The
;;; alter-copy macro will expand into code which makes a
;;; fresh copy of the structure passed to it and then
;;; alters the specified slots in that copy.
(defmacro def-alter-copier (structure-name)
  (let ((macro-name (names->symbol "ALTER-COPY-"
                                    structure-name))
        (access-function-prefix (names->symbol
                                    structure-name
                                    "-"))
        (copy-function-name (names->symbol "COPY-"
                                    structure-name)))
    `(defmacro ,macro-name (object &body
                                    slot-name-value-args)
```

---

[2]`GENSYM` produces *uninterned* symbols which do not belong to any package.

```
            (let ((keyword-package (find-package "KEYWORD"))
                  (new-obj (gensym "COPY-")))
              (labels
                ((create-slot-modifiers (remaining-pairs
                                         modifier-forms)
                   (if (null remaining-pairs)
                       (nreverse modifier-forms)
                       (let ((slot (first remaining-pairs))
                             (value (second remaining-pairs)))
                         (if (eq (symbol-package slot)
                                 keyword-package)
                             (if (and (not (null remaining-pairs))
                                      (null (cdr remaining-pairs)))
                                 (error "Value missing for slot ~A"
                                        slot)
                                 (let ((access-function
                                        (names->symbol
                                         ',access-function-prefix
                                         slot)))
                                   (create-slot-modifiers
                                    (cddr remaining-pairs)
                                    (cons `(setf (,access-function
                                                  ,new-obj)
                                                 ,value)
                                          modifier-forms))))
                             (error "slot name ~A must ~
                                     be a keyword"
                                    slot))))))
                ;; Notice that we must use ,', here!
                `(let ((,new-obj (,',copy-function-name ,object)))
                   ,@(create-slot-modifiers slot-name-value-args
                                            nil)
                   ,new-obj))))))
```

We can use **MACROEXPAND-1** to verify that the expansion of a call to **ALTER-COPY-CYLINDER** is correct:

```
Lisp> (macroexpand-1 '(alter-copy-cylinder c :color "blue"
                                              :radius 10))

(LET ((#:COPY-85 (COPY-CYLINDER C)))
  (SETF (CYLINDER-COLOR #:COPY-85) "blue")
  (SETF (CYLINDER-RADIUS #:COPY-85) 10)
  #:COPY-85)
T
```

Problem. Write a macro called `ALTER-DEFSTRUCT` which behaves exactly like `DEFSTRUCT` but also automatically defines an `ALTER-COPY` macro.

Problem. Write a macro called `ONCE-ONLY` which ensures that a macro argument is evaluated only once in the expansion of that macro. For example, we might write a macro called `SQUARE` as:

```
(defmacro square (x)
  (let ((val (gensym "VAL-")))
    `(let ((,val ,x))
       (* ,val ,val))))
```

But we can capture this idiom with `ONCE-ONLY` and rewrite `SQUARE` as:

```
(defmacro square (x)
  (once-only (x) ; ensure that X is only evaluated once.
    `(* ,x ,x))) ; even though it appears twice here
```

11.3.1 Nested Backquotes

`DEF-ALTER-COPIER` uses *nested backquotes*. Since we generally use backquote when writing macro bodies, macro-producing macros often require using backquotes within backquotes. While this sounds as though it should be no trouble at all, the rules for using nested backquotes can be quite confusing and unintuitive. For example, consider the nested backquote example in Figure 11.1.

Each backquote and comma is labeled for discussion. Consider backquote to be like an open parenthesis and comma to be like a closing parenthesis. We can match backquotes and commas like parenthesis, except that any open parentheses can be matched by zero or more closing parentheses. Thus, the backquote labeled 2 is matched by two different commas. Here is the rule for evaluating forms involving nested backquotes:

> When the form starting with backquote *n* is evaluated, then any inner forms preceded by comma *n* are also evaluated, and the resulting form is substituted for the `,FORM` which used to be there.

Unfortunately, this rule is too general to accomplish some common and simple tasks. For instance, in Figure 11.1 `FORM-A` will be successively evaluated three times and `FORM-B` will be successively evaluated twice. However, we often want a specific form to be evaluated exactly *once* within several nested

```
`(foo `(bar `(baz  , , ,form-a  , ,form-b  ,form-c ))))
 1     2     3     3 2 1        3 2        3
```

FIGURE 11.1
Nested backquote.

backquotes. For example, when defining `DEF-ALTER-COPIER` we had to substitute the value of `COPY-FUNCTION-NAME` into a piece of code nested within two backquotes. While it might seem to intuitive to use two commas to accomplish this, we actually had to use the sequence comma, quote, comma. Consider the following simpler version of the same problem:

```
Lisp> (defmacro cons-x (x)
        `(defmacro ,(names->symbol "CONS-" x) (y)
           `(cons ',',x ,y)))

Lisp> (cons-x move)
CONS-MOVE

Lisp> (cons-move '(left))
(MOVE LEFT)
```

`CONS-X` produces a new macro which conses the value of `X` onto its argument. Figure 11.2 depicts the expansion of `(CONS-X MOVE)` according the rules for nested backquote. We start by evaluating the backquote labeled 1, which in turn means that `,X` will be replaced by the value of `X`. Since no other commas are labeled 1, no other evaluations occur.

The result is that we now have `',' MOVE` where we used to have `',',X`. But the comma and the inner quote in `',' MOVE` negate each other and may be removed, thus leaving us with simply `'MOVE` and achieving the desired effect.

Nested backquotes can be extremely confusing, so do not worry if all these rules are not clear or intuitive. Just be aware that when dealing with them you should stop and think carefully.

11.4 ADVANCED MACRO ISSUES

11.4.1 Argument Destructuring

Consider trying to write our own version of `DO`. The macro definition might look something like this:

```
(defmacro cons-x (x)
  `(defmacro ,(names->symbol "CONS-" x) (y)
   1           1
     `(cons ',',x ,y)))
      2      2 1 2

(cons-x move) ==> (defmacro cons-move (y)  ==> (defmacro cons-move (y)
                    `(cons ',' move ,y))         `(cons 'move ,y))
                     2      2    2                2      2    2
```

FIGURE 11.2
Macroexpansion of `(CONS-X MOVE)`.

```
(defmacro do (var-init-step-forms termination-list
                                  &rest do-body)
  (let ((termination-test (car termination-list))
        (result-forms (cdr termination-list)))
    ;; We will omit the actual
    ;; body because it is not
    ;; relevant to this discussion.
    body))
```

The lambda-list appearing in a call to `DEFMACRO` looks similar to the lambda-lists allowed for functions. In order to write the macro, we must at some point explicitly decompose `TERMINATION-LIST` into its component parts. However, it would be much clearer if we could represent the structure of `TERMINATION-LIST` directly in the lambda-list:

```
(defmacro do (var-init-step-forms
              (termination-test . result-forms)
              &rest do-body)
  body)
```

Fortunately, we can write macro lambda-lists this way because a macro can *destructure* its arguments, just as the pattern matcher we wrote in Chapter 5 can match a pattern (the lambda-list) against some data (the arguments). Here is another simple example of argument destructuring:

```
Lisp> (defmacro poof! ((head neck) body . bottom)
        `(quote (,head ,neck ,body ,bottom)))
POOF!

Lisp> (poof! (:head :neck) (:chest :abdomen)
             :legs :feet :toes)
(:HEAD :NECK (:CHEST :ABDOMEN) (:LEGS :FEET :TOES))
```

Notice that putting a dot before the last argument in the lambda-list is equivalent to an `&REST`. Argument destructuring is a useful tool since it is easier to visualize a pattern than it is to encode that pattern into the maze of function calls which can destructure it.

Problem. We have already seen how to write `OUR-LET` and how macro argument lists can destructure their arguments. Write a macro called `DESTRUCTURING-LET` which combines these features.

11.4.2 MACROLET

Now we are ready to examine a problem with the `ITERATE` macro we wrote earlier. Sometimes we want to iterate with a large number of state variables, but on each of several recursive calls to the iteration function we may only want to change one or two variables, passing the remaining variables unchanged. The usual form of **ITERATE** requires that we explicitly pass each variable as an argument in each recursive call. However, this can be cumbersome when most of the iteration variables remain unchanged.

To avoid this problem, we can create a variant of **ITERATE** called **KEY-ITERATE** which allows us to use keyword arguments to pass only the values we wish to change in each recursive call. For example:

```
(defparameter *size-table*
  '((0 5 tiny)
    (6 10 small)
    (11 20 medium)
    (21 50 large)
    (51 100 huge))
  "List of symbolic range classifications of the form
   (LOW HIGH NAME)")

(defun size (n)
  (dolist (entry *size-table*
                 (error "No size found for ~A" n))
    (when (and (>= n (first entry)) (<= n (second entry)))
      (return (third entry)))))

(defun separate (sizes)
  (key-iterate sift ((tiny nil)
                     (small nil)
                     (medium nil)
                     (large nil)
                     (huge nil)
                     (rest sizes))
    (if (null rest)
        (list tiny small medium large huge)
        (let ((next (car rest)))
          (ecase (size next)
            (tiny (sift :tiny (cons next tiny)
                        :rest (cdr rest)))
            (small (sift :small (cons next small)
                         :rest (cdr rest)))
            (medium (sift :medium (cons next medium)
                          :rest (cdr rest)))
            (large (sift :large (cons next large)
                         :rest (cdr rest)))
            (huge (sift :huge (cons next huge)
                        :rest (cdr rest))))))))
```

DEFPARAMETER is just like **DEFVAR** except that it unconditionally sets the variable to the value of the initialization form, and thus it is useful for declaring variables whose initial values are likely to change. **SIZE** uses the ***SIZE-TABLE*** to classify numbers, and **SEPARATE** uses **SIZE** to separate a single list of numbers into sublists of each size:

```
Lisp> (separate
        '(20 7 41 9 8 34 90 12 2 65 87 12 45 92 28 76 62))
((2) (8 9 7) (12 12 20) (28 45 34 41) (62 76 92 87 65 90))
```

KEY-ITERATE should expand into code which defines a macro named **SIFT** and a **LABEL**ed function into which calls to **SIFT** will expand. **KEY-ITERATE** must not define a global macro, because then different calls to **KEY-ITERATE** with the same **NAME** argument would conflict with each other. However, just as we can define local functions using **FLET**, we can define local macros using the special form **MACROLET**. For example, consider the following definition of **KEY-ITERATE**:

```
(defmacro key-iterate (name var-init-pairs &body body)
  (let ((iteration-label (gensym (concatenate
                                   'string
                                   (symbol-name name) "-")))
        (vars (mapcar #'first var-init-pairs))
        (vals (mapcar #'second var-init-pairs)))
    `(macrolet ((,name (&key ,@(mapcar #'(lambda (var)
                                           `(,var ',var))
                                       vars))
                  (list ',iteration-label ,@vars)))
       (labels ((,iteration-label ,vars
                  ,@body))
         (,iteration-label ,@vals)))))
```

The macros defined by different calls to **KEY-ITERATE** cannot conflict with each other because they are defined by **MACROLET**. **SEPARATE** will expand into code which defines a local macro named **SIFT** which in turn expands into a call to **ITERATION-LABEL**. **MACROLET** is also useful when several macros must communicate with each other through jointly closed-over lexical variables.

Problem. The explicit manipulation of the **REST** variable in our definition of **SEPARATE** is annoying. Write a new macro called **KEY-LIST-ITERATE** which implicitly maintains the **REST** variable and performs the termination test in a manner similar to **DOLIST**.

Problem. Rewrite the **ITERATE** macro so that it expands into a **MACROLET** and a **PROG** rather than a **LABELS**, thus assuring that **ITERATE** will behave tail-recursively even in Common Lisps which cannot remove tail-recursion. Can you think of a program which will uncover a difference between these two possible implementations of `ITERATE`?

11.4.3 Macro Restrictions and Problems

Unlike a function, we cannot pass a macro to `APPLY` or `FUNCALL`, just as we cannot pass a special form to either of these functions. The reason is that *all* of the arguments passed to `APPLY` or `FUNCALL` are already evaluated, and thus the macroexpansion function has no way to get hold of the unevaluated argument forms.

Macros can also make debugging a bit difficult because what appears as a single function call within the text of a program may actually turn into many nested function calls after macroexpansion occurs. Macros must also be defined *before* they are used, because when we compile a function, all of the macro calls in it are expanded at *compile time*, and thus any macro definitions which are needed must be present.

Given some of the problems that accompany macros, some people consider them to be "semantically bankrupt" [GP88]. They should not be overused, especially when a function will do the job just as well. However, when used wisely macros offer a powerful way to extend Lisp and improve the clarity of our programs.

CHAPTER 12

ARRAYS, CHARACTERS, STRINGS, AND SEQUENCES

12.1 SIMPLE ARRAYS

12.1.1 Problems with Linked Lists

Lisp's ability to manipulate linked lists is one of its most powerful features. However, linked lists have some fundamental problems as a data structure for certain problems. For example, if we have a list of 1000 employee records and would like to access the 678th record, we must `CDR` past the first 677 records to get to the record we want. This is a direct consequence of the flexibility of a linked list. We can't find the Nth element until we can find the $(N - 1)$th element. Hence, the time required to find a given element of the list is proportional to the total number of elements in the list.

If we have a list of 100,000 elements, then it will clearly take a long time to access the 99,999th element. For many applications, this inefficiency is intolerable. It is also important to realize that a linked list of 100,000 elements will actually require 200,000 pointers, since each cons cell in the list consists of a pointer to a particular list element (the car), and a pointer to the rest of the list (the cdr).[1]

---

[1] Lists can be stored more compactly using a technique called *cdr-coding*.

Rather than storing our list this way, we could use an array. An array is an ordered sequence which is similar to a list, but is represented as a *contiguous* sequence of elements in memory. Thus, given a pointer to the start of the array, we know that we can always find a given element at a certain offset from the start of the array. Therefore, finding the 678th element in an array simply involves adding 678 "address units" to the address of the start of the array. The benefit of this approach is that we can access any element in the array in *constant* time. The length of the array does not matter. An additional benefit is that we only need half as much memory to represent a sequence of elements as an array rather than a list. The reason for this is that we don't need a cdr pointer for each element in the array, since we know that each element in the array immediately follows its predecessor in memory.

12.1.2 Using Arrays

Arrays are a widely available data type in almost all programming languages, and Common Lisp provides a dazzling (and potentially confusing) number of array features. However, most uses of arrays are quite simple. For example, to create an array of 100 elements, we can use the function **MAKE-ARRAY**:

```
Lisp> (setf a (make-array 100 :initial-element nil))
#<Simple-Vector T 100 136AB63>
```

The array we created is called a *simple vector*. One-dimensional arrays are so useful, they have been given the special name *vectors*. Common Lisp has special vector functions which we'll discuss later.

Now that we have an array, we can try to access an element in it. The **:INITIAL-ELEMENT** keyword argument to **MAKE-ARRAY** indicates that every element of the array should be initialized to **NIL**. Strictly speaking, if we did not specify the **:INITIAL-ELEMENT** keyword, then we cannot be sure what we will initially find in any array cell. However, many implementations of Common Lisp initialize all array elements to **NIL** if no explicit initial value is given.

AREF allows us to access individual cells in an array. For example, to access the 21st element in an array, we can use the following:

```
Lisp> (aref a 20)
NIL
```

In order to access the 21st cell in the array **A**, we used the number **20**. The **20** in our call to **AREF** is called the *index* into the array, and in Common Lisp array indices are zero-based. *Zero-based* simply means that the first element in the array is called element 0. Thus, array element N may be found at index $N - 1$. This may seem a bit odd at first, but it turns out to be quite consistent with other Common Lisp constructs. For example, **DOTIMES** starts its iteration variable at 0 rather than 1, thus making iteration over the contents of an array more natural.

In order to change the value of an array element, we can use `SETF`. Once again, `SETF` is used as a general updating function:

```
Lisp> (setf (aref a 20) 'element-21)
ELEMENT-21

Lisp> (aref a 20)
ELEMENT-21
```

Given the accessing form `(AREF A 20)`, `SETF` changes to `ELEMENT-21` the information the accessing form retrieves. This is convenient, since we don't need to remember another function to update the contents of an array.

If we would like to create a one-dimensional array with predetermined contents, we could use the function `VECTOR` :

```
Lisp> (setf *colors* (vector 'red 'green 'blue))
#<Simple-Vector T 3 139A8DB>

Lisp> (aref *colors* 1)
GREEN

Lisp> (svref *colors* 1)
GREEN
```

`VECTOR` is analogous to the function `LIST`, but rather than producing a list of elements, it produces a one-dimensional array of elements. We can use the function `SVREF`, which stands for Simple Vector REFerence, to access an element of a simple vector. `SVREF` is a less general version of `AREF` which can only index into simple vectors rather than any kind of array. However, `SVREF` is almost always faster than `AREF` in Lisps running on standard hardware.

12.2 EXAMPLE: GENERATING PRIME NUMBERS

Now that we can create, access, and update a simple array, we can try using one to generate all of the prime numbers from 1 to *n* using an algorithm called *the sieve of Eratosthenes*. The central data structure in the sieve is an array which contains one element for each integer we are considering. Thus, if we want to find all the primes between 1 and 1000, we need an array of 1000 elements. Each array element will hold the symbol `MARKED` or `UNMARKED` to indicate whether or not the integer index which accesses that element is prime. All non-prime numbers may be factored into prime numbers, and a `MARKED` number is one which has already been found to be a multiple of a prime number. An `UNMARKED` number is a number for which no prime factors have been found.

We start the algorithm by scanning from the second element (corresponding to the integer 2) to the last element (the last integer in which we are interested).

Initially, all array elements are set to UNMARKED. If an element is UNMARKED when we examine it, then the integer which corresponds to that number must be prime, since no factors (other than 1 and the integer itself) have been found for that number. Once we find a prime, we then proceed to mark all *multiples* of that prime number. Thus, when we find that 2 is unmarked, we add 2 to our list of prime numbers, and then mark every integer which is a multiple of 2. Next we examine 3. We find that 3 is also unmarked, so we add it to our list of primes, and mark all integers which are multiples of 3. Once we reach 4, though, we find that it has already been marked (by 2). Thus, we ignore 4 and continue, examining 5 next. The procedure continues until we have examined every element in the sieve array. When we reach the end of the array, we will have sifted all the nonprimes away, leaving us with a list of prime numbers. The Lisp code to implement SIEVE follows:

```
(defun sieve (max)
  (let ((sieve (make-array (1+ max)
                           :initial-element 'unmarked)))
    (do ((i 2 (1+ i))
         (primes nil (if (eq (aref sieve i) 'unmarked)
                         (do ((multiple i (+ multiple i)))
                             ((> multiple max)
                              (cons i primes))
                           (setf (aref sieve multiple)
                                 'marked))
                         primes)))
        ((> i max) (nreverse primes)))))
```

```
Lisp> (sieve 17)
(2 3 5 7 11 13 17)
```

The length of the SIEVE array is actually one greater than the maximum number we are considering. We do this because array indices are zero-based, and we would like to avoid subtracting 1 from all our array indices. All elements of the array start out UNMARKED. The outer DO loop iterates over the entire array, while the inner DO loop then iterates over multiples of every prime number we find, setting to MARKED the corresponding entries in the SIEVE array. When done, we have a list of primes in reverse order. We then use NREVERSE to present the list in ascending order. Note that we can safely use NREVERSE rather than REVERSE, since we explicitly consed the list of primes ourselves, and can be positive that nobody else has any pointers to the list yet. Calling REVERSE would have needlessly consed up a new list.

If we notice that all multiples of 2 are not prime, then we can use an array of half the size we were using before by considering the array to be indexed only by odd numbers, and adjusting our index calculations accordingly. It is easy to see that a linked list would not be a suitable data structure for the sieve algorithm, since the inner DO loop requires that we be able to quickly skip over many elements, touching only multiples of primes. A linked list would not allow us to access each multiple in constant time.

12.3 ADVANCED ARRAY FEATURES

In this section we will examine some of the advanced array features provided by Common Lisp.

12.3.1 Bit Arrays

Sometimes we know exactly what kind of elements will occupy the cells of an array. In such cases, it is possible to tell `MAKE-ARRAY` about what type of elements will be stored in the array, and thus potentially conserve storage. In our implementation of `SIEVE`, we really only needed a boolean (binary) value to be stored in each element of the array. This situation is so common that Common Lisp includes support for *bit arrays*. Rather than putting the symbols `MARKED` and `UNMARKED` in the array, we could have stored just 1s and 0s in a bit array, thus allowing our program to run in only a fraction of the space it used to occupy. We also could have accessed elements of the bit array more quickly using a specialized form of `AREF` called `SBIT`.

> **Problem.** Read about bit vectors in the Common Lisp manual and then rewrite the `SIEVE` function to use a bit vector rather than a general vector.

12.3.2 Multidimensional Arrays

Many problems are not one-dimensional. For example, a two-dimensional data structure provides the most natural way to represent a *matrix* of numbers. We can represent a three-by-three matrix with a three-row-by-three-column array:

```
Lisp> (setf m (make-array '(3 3)))
#<Simple-Array T (3 3) 1341D53>
```

`MAKE-ARRAY` normally expects a list of numbers as its first argument. Specifying a single number `N`, as we did earlier, is merely a shorthand notation for `'(N)`. This exception is made because one-dimensional arrays are so common. The number of elements in the list specifies the number of dimensions in the array, and is often referred to as the *rank* of the array. Each value refers to the size of a given dimension. Thus, the list `(7 10 4)` would specify a three-dimensional (rank 3) array with first dimension 7, second dimension 10, and third dimension 4. Rank is actually zero-based, just as array indices are, so it is possible to create a zero-dimensional array; that is, an array with no elements. However, this is not often useful.

Now that we have multidimensional arrays, we need to access and update them. `AREF` is actually more general than we were first led to believe, since it will accept an arbitrary number of arguments:

```
Lisp> (aref m 1 2)
NIL
```

The first argument to **AREF** must always be an array, while the remaining arguments must be integers specifying zero-based indices into the array. Thus, the above form accesses the element in the second row and third column of our matrix. Figure 12.1 illustrates the organization of our matrix.

Similarly, **SETF** will allow us to update the contents of a multidimensional array:

```
Lisp> (setf (aref m 1 2) 5)
5

Lisp> (aref m 1 2)
5
```

Sometimes we would like to view the actual contents of an array, just as we can view the contents of a list by printing it. The way in which an array is printed can be controlled by the value of *PRINT-ARRAY*. The default value of this variable is not specified by Common Lisp; however, in the above examples it was set to **NIL**. Thus, arrays were printed in the form #<*useful-information*>. However, if we set *PRINT-ARRAY* to **T**, then the actual contents of the array will be printed:

```
Lisp> (setf *print-array* t)
T

Lisp> m
#2A((NIL NIL NIL) (NIL NIL 5) (NIL NIL NIL))
```

	Column 1	Column 2	Column 3
Row 1	(aref m 0 0)	(aref m 0 1)	(aref m 0 2)
Row 2	(aref m 1 0)	(aref m 1 1)	(aref m 1 2)
Row 3	(aref m 2 0)	(aref m 2 1)	(aref m 2 2)

FIGURE 12.1
Layout of a three-by-three array.

We can now see all nine elements in our array. The notation #2A(indicates that what follows is a two-dimensional array. The contents of the array are then printed, row by row. In the case of a one-dimensional array, the #nA(...) may be replaced by just #(...). Notice that we can simulate a two-dimensional array with only one-dimensional arrays (vectors):

```
Lisp> (setf flat-matrix (make-array 3))
#(NIL NIL NIL)

Lisp> (dotimes (i 3)
        (setf (aref flat-matrix i) (make-array 3)))
NIL

Lisp> flat-matrix
#(#(NIL NIL NIL) #(NIL NIL NIL) #(NIL NIL NIL))

Lisp> (setf (aref (aref flat-matrix 1) 2) 5)
5

Lisp> flat-matrix
#(#(NIL NIL NIL) #(NIL NIL 5) #(NIL NIL NIL))
```

The array **FLAT-MATRIX** is simply an array of arrays. Initially, the contents of the one-dimensional array **FLAT-MATRIX** are all **NIL**. However, we can make each element of the vector we have created hold another vector. The printed representation of this simulated two-dimensional array is very similar to the printed representation of an actual two-dimensional array. The primary difference between the two is that we can explicitly manipulate entire rows of **FLAT-MATRIX** as vectors, while the elements of **M** are only accessible individually.

Common Lisp arrays are stored in *row-major* order, although not all languages store arrays this way (for example, Fortran stores arrays in *column-major* order). *Row-major order* means that rows are actually stored one after another in the linear memory of our computer. For example, the two-dimensional **M** array is actually stored in the memory of our computer starting at row 1, column 1. The next element is row 1, column 2, then row 1, column 3. When we reach the end of one row, we start on the next row. Therefore, the element in row 2, column 1 immediately follows the element in row 1, column 3. Hence, while Figure 12.1 reflects *our* representation of the array as an abstract matrix, Figure 12.2 depicts the array as it is actually stored in the memory of our computer.

One direct consequence of storing arrays in row-major order is that the last index in an array reference is said to vary the fastest. What this really means is that the elements of an array are stored in memory with the elements in the last dimension stored contiguously. This is an important consideration if we wish to access every element in a large array on a computer which supports virtual memory. In order to minimize the amount of paging required to access every

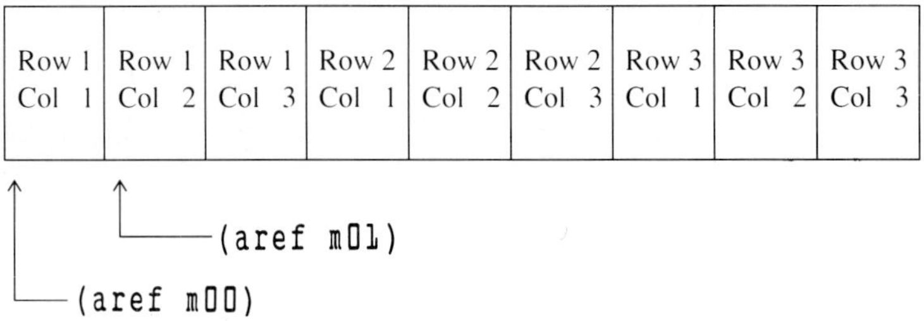

```
| Row 1 | Row 1 | Row 1 | Row 2 | Row 2 | Row 2 | Row 3 | Row 3 | Row 3 |
| Col 1 | Col 2 | Col 3 | Col 1 | Col 2 | Col 3 | Col 1 | Col 2 | Col 3 |
```
            ↑   ↑
            | └──(aref m 0 1)
            └──(aref m 0 0)

FIGURE 12.2
Linear organization of an array in the computer's memory.

element in a large array, we should scan the array by varying the last index the fastest, and the first index the slowest. Thus, to scan our matrix, we can use the following:

```
Lisp> (dotimes (row 3)
         (dotimes (col 3)
           (format t "~A " (aref m row col))))
NIL NIL NIL NIL NIL 5 NIL NIL NIL  ; values printed by FORMAT
NIL                                 ; value returned by DOTIMES
```

Of course, our matrix is so small that the order in which we scan really isn't important; however, when scanning an array which contains 100 by 100 by 100 elements, the iteration order could have a large effect on the amount of time required to access the entire array. Refer to Chapter 21 for more information about efficiently using arrays in Lisp.

12.3.3 Example: Matrix Multiplication

We can use the following algorithm to multiply the two matrices shown in Figure 12.3:

$$M3_{i,j} = \sum_{k=0}^{common-1} M1_{i,k} M3_{k,j}$$

$$\text{rows} \left\{ \begin{matrix} M1 \\ \begin{bmatrix} 0.0 & 1.0 \\ 0.0 & 0.0 \\ 1.0 & 0.0 \end{bmatrix} \end{matrix} \right. \times \begin{matrix} M2 \\ \begin{bmatrix} 1.0 & 2.0 & 3.0 \\ 4.0 & 5.0 & 6.0 \end{bmatrix} \\ \underbrace{}_{\text{cols}} \end{matrix} = \begin{matrix} M3 \\ \begin{bmatrix} 4.0 & 5.0 & 6.0 \\ 0.0 & 0.0 & 0.0 \\ 1.0 & 2.0 & 3.0 \end{bmatrix} \end{matrix}$$

FIGURE 12.3
Matrix multiplication.

Here is one way to implement the matrix multiplication algorithm:

```
(defun matrix-multiply (m1 m2 m3)
  (let ((rows-1 (array-dimension m1 0))
        (cols-2 (array-dimension m2 1))
        ;; The number of columns in M1 should equal
        ;; the number of rows in M2
        (common (array-dimension m1 1)))
    (dotimes (i rows-1)
      (dotimes (j cols-2)
        (setf (aref m3 i j)
              (do ((k 0 (1+ k))
                   (sum 0 (+ sum (* (aref m1 i k)
                                    (aref m2 k j)))))
                  ((= k common) sum)))))
    m3))
```

MATRIX-MULTIPLY expects three matrices as arguments. It multiplies the first two matrices and leaves the product in the third. **MATRIX-MULTIPLY** could accept only two matrices and allocate a new matrix for the result, but this might result in a lot of garbage being generated by temporary matrices, so we will place the burden of supplying a product matrix on the caller.

The function **ARRAY-DIMENSION** returns the length of one of the dimensions of an array:

```
Lisp> (array-dimension (make-array '(3 5)) 0)
3

Lisp> (array-dimension (make-array '(3 5)) 1)
5
```

The remainder of **MATRIX-MULTIPLY** is a straightforward implementation of the matrix multiplication algorithm. We can test our function with the following example:

```
Lisp> (matrix-multiply #2a((0 1) (0 0) (1 0))
                       #2a((1 2 3) (4 5 6))
                       (make-array '(3 3)))
#2A((4 5 6) (0 0 0) (1 2 3))
```

> **Problem.** Write a function named **TRANSPOSE** which destructively transposes a square matrix.
>
> **Problem.** Write a function named **MATRIX-ADD** which accepts three matrices as arguments, and returns the sum of the first two matrices in the third.

12.3.4 Array Displacement

Sometimes it is useful to view a problem from two different perspectives. For example, when searching a matrix for sequences of numbers, it may be more natural to consider a flattened version of the matrix. However, when adding or multiplying matrices, a two-dimensional view of a matrix may be more appropriate. Common Lisp allows us to view an array in both ways simultaneously by using *displaced arrays*. A displaced array is an array which shares storage with an already existing array. Thus, we can view the block of memory occupied by an existing array in a different way:

```
Lisp> (setf m #2a((NIL NIL NIL)
                  (NIL NIL 5)
                  (NIL NIL NIL)))
#2A((NIL NIL NIL) (NIL NIL 5) (NIL NIL NIL))

Lisp> (setf flat-matrix (make-array 9 :displaced-to m))
#(NIL NIL NIL NIL NIL 5 NIL NIL NIL)

Lisp> m
#2A((NIL NIL NIL) (NIL NIL 5) (NIL NIL NIL))

Lisp> (setf (aref flat-matrix 1) 1)
1

Lisp> flat-matrix
#(NIL 1 NIL NIL NIL 5 NIL NIL NIL)

Lisp> m
#2A((NIL 1 NIL) (NIL NIL 5) (NIL NIL NIL))

Lisp> (aref m 0 1)
1
```

The above call to **MAKE-ARRAY** asks that a vector of nine elements be created; however, rather than allocating new storage for the vector, the existing storage for **M** should be used. The array **FLAT-MATRIX** is then mapped onto **M** in row-major order. Now we can view **M** in a way which is closer to how it is actually stored in memory. Hence, when we set the second element in **FLAT-MATRIX** to 1, we are actually changing the element accessed by (**AREF M 0 1**).

12.3.5 Fill Pointers and Adjustable Arrays

Suppose we want to maintain a stack using an array. We've already seen how **PUSH** and **POP** allow us to use a list to represent a stack; however, a vector can be used to represent a stack more efficiently than a list. Pushing data onto a vector amounts to putting data into the next free location, and then incrementing a next-free-location index. Hence, at any given time, only a portion of the vector will contain data on the stack; the rest of the vector will be empty. Another way to view this is that only a portion of the vector is ever active with data; the rest is inactive, waiting to be used.

To conveniently distinguish the active from the inactive portion of the array, we can use a *fill pointer*. An array may be created with a fill pointer by specifying the keyword argument `:FILL-POINTER` to `MAKE-ARRAY`:

```
Lisp> (setf *stack* (make-array 100 :fill-pointer 0))
#()

Lisp> (fill-pointer *stack*)
0
```

The fill pointer is really the next-free-location index mentioned above. In our example, the fill pointer is initialized to index 0. We can access the fill pointer via the function `FILL-POINTER`, and we can explicitly change the fill pointer using `SETF`. However, rather than explicitly changing the fill pointer, we often use other functions to implicitly change it:

```
Lisp> (vector-push 'first *stack*)
0

Lisp> *stack*
#(FIRST)

Lisp> (fill-pointer *stack*)
1

Lisp> (vector-push 'second *stack*)
1

Lisp> *stack*
#(FIRST SECOND)

Lisp> (vector-pop *stack*)
SECOND

Lisp> *stack*
#(FIRST)
```

Initially, the vector is empty. We can treat it as a stack using `VECTOR-PUSH`, just as we could use a list as a stack using `PUSH`. `VECTOR-PUSH` sets the first element of *STACK* to FIRST, and then returns the index of the array cell it pushed the data into. VECTOR-PUSH always puts its first argument into the cell pointed to by the fill pointer of the vector it is given. It then increments the fill pointer, as shown above.

Printing the stack then shows that it does indeed contain FIRST. Notice that the other 99 elements are *not* printed out, since they are inactive; in other words, they are not contained within the portion of the array bounded by the fill pointer. We can push another element onto the stack and then remove it using VECTOR-POP. VECTOR-POP returns the last element in the active portion of the array, and decrements the fill pointer by 1. Thus, VECTOR-POP is analogous to POP. Note that it is an error to call VECTOR-PUSH or VECTOR-POP on an array which does not contain a fill pointer.

What would happen if we tried to push over 100 elements onto *STACK*? Naturally we could not do that, since there is no room for more than 100 elements. However, it is possible to create *adjustable* arrays, whose size can be dynamically varied. That is, an adjustable array can be made larger or smaller after it has been created. For example, if we try to push too much data onto an adjustable vector, then the vector should be dynamically extended as needed. We can create an adjustable array by specifying the keyword argument :ADJUSTABLE to MAKE-ARRAY:

```
Lisp> (setf *stack*
            (make-array 1 :fill-pointer 0 :adjustable t))
#()

Lisp> (vector-push 'first *stack*)
0

Lisp> *stack*
#(FIRST)
```

The arguments :ADJUSTABLE T indicate that it must be possible to dynamically extend the length of the array. The alternative :ADJUSTABLE NIL (the default) creates an array which cannot be dynamically extended. An adjustable array can be used by all the normal array manipulation functions, so we can use VECTOR-PUSH on our adjustable stack just as we used it on our nonadjustable stack. However, after pushing one element, the stack is full. Thus, another call to VECTOR-PUSH will fail:

```
Lisp> (vector-push 'second *stack*)
NIL

Lisp> *stack*
#(FIRST)
```

Rather than signaling an error, VECTOR-PUSH returns NIL to indicate that it could not push any more data onto *STACK*. We must use the function

VECTOR-PUSH-EXTEND to dynamically grow the stack and push a new element:

```
Lisp> (length *stack*)
1

Lisp> (vector-push-extend 'second *stack*)
1

Lisp> *stack*
#(FIRST SECOND)

Lisp> (length *stack*)
2
```

Notice that we can use the function **LENGTH** to determine the size of a vector after we have created it. If **VECTOR-PUSH-EXTEND** is given an adjustable vector, then it extends the length of the vector when needed. We can also explicitly grow or shrink an adjustable array by using the function **ADJUST-ARRAY**. Refer to the Common Lisp manual for more information about adjustable arrays.

Problem. Write a function called **VECTOR-REVERSE** which accepts a vector as an argument and returns a new vector containing the same elements as the original vector in reverse order.

Problem. Write a function named **ARRAY-APPEND** which accepts an arbitrary number of vectors and concatenates them just as **APPEND** concatenates lists.

Problem. One of the exercises in Chapter 3 asks you to write a function named **COUNT-OCCURRENCES**, which counts the number of times an atom appears in a list. Rewrite **COUNT-OCCURRENCES** so that it will also accept a vector, and will return the number of times an atom appears in the vector.

Problem. Write a function named **MERGE-VECTORS** which merges two ordered vectors just as the function **MERGE-LISTS** (written as an exercise in Chapter 3) merges two ordered lists.

Problem. Write a function named **VECTOR-ROTATE** which rotates the elements of a vector in the same way that the **LIST-ROTATE** function described in an exercise in Chapter 7 destructively rotates lists.

Problem. Rewrite the **INFIX->PREFIX** function described in one of the problems in Chapter 5 so that it uses vectors rather than lists to represent stacks.

12.4 CHARACTERS AND STRINGS

Lists, vectors, and strings each appear to be different data types with unique operations. However, they all represent ordered *sequences* of data. Lisp takes advantage of this commonality with a family of *sequence functions* which operate uniformly on any sequence without regard to its representation. Strings are the only kind of sequence we have not examined in detail, so we will say a bit more about characters and strings before examining the sequence functions.

12.4.1 Characters Are Objects

In some programming languages, characters are just small integers. For example, the number 65 is often the same as the character *A*. However, in Common Lisp characters are treated as a distinct data type:

```
Lisp> (characterp #\L)
T

Lisp> #\L
#\L

Lisp> #\newline
#\Newline

Lisp> #\space
#\Space

Lisp> (char> #\a #\A)
T
```

The printed representation of a character consists of #\ followed by the character. Nonprinting characters such as *space* or *newline* are explicitly written out by name. We can find out what number is used to represent a particular character with the function CHAR-CODE:

```
Lisp> (char-code #\A)
65

Lisp> (code-char 65)
#\A
```

In ASCII, the character *A* is represented by the number 65. The function CODE-CHAR converts a number back into a character. In addition to a code, characters also contain *bit* information, such as *control, alt,* or *meta,* and *font* information. Any character whose bit and font values are both zero is called a *string character*.

12.4.2 Strings Are Vectors of Characters

A string is nothing more than a vector of characters, although they are usually vectors of *string characters*, and a simple vector of string characters is called a *simple-string*.² Because strings are really vectors, we can apply the same functions we use on vectors to strings:

```
Lisp> (aref "PLUTO" 0)
#\P

Lisp> (length "PLUTO")
5

Lisp> (schar "PLUTO" 0)
#\P
```

The function `SCHAR` is a specialized version of `AREF` which accepts only simple strings rather than any kind of array. `SCHAR` will usually be faster than `AREF`, so it is often used to manipulate strings.

Problem. Common Lisp contains a function named `PARSE-INTEGER` which will convert a string of digits in a given radix into an integer:

```
Lisp> (parse-integer "123")
123
3     ; index after the last digit

Lisp> (parse-integer "FFFF" :radix 16)
65535
4     ; index after the last digit
```

Write your own version of `PARSE-INTEGER` called `STRING->INTEGER` which accepts a string and an optional radix argument and converts the string to an integer.

12.5 SEQUENCE FUNCTIONS OPERATE ON LISTS, VECTORS, AND STRINGS

Many of the functions which we have only been using on lists are actually *sequence functions* which will work on lists or vectors, including strings:

```
Lisp> (setf s1 "Less-than-")
"Less-than-"
```

---

²String characters are provided by Common Lisp because on many machines, a string is conveniently represented as a sequence of eight-bit bytes, where each byte contains the code for a single character. However, ASCII requires 7-bits for the character codes, leaving only one-bit for both the bit and font information. Thus, full-fledged characters cannot fit within a single byte. Therefore, the subtype `STRING-CHAR` was introduced to define a set of characters which fit easily within a byte and match the way other languages treat characters and strings.

```
Lisp> (length sl)
10

Lisp> (reverse sl)
"-naht-sseL"

Lisp> sl
"Less-than-"

Lisp> (nreverse sl)
"-naht-sseL"

Lisp> sl
"-naht-sseL"
```

Both REVERSE and NREVERSE behave as we would expect on a string. REVERSE conses a new string which is the reverse of the one it was given, while NREVERSE destructively reverses its argument. The operation of most sequence operations is obvious, so this section will only provide a sample of what some of them can do without much explanation:

```
Lisp> (concatenate 'list "SOON" "-" "COME")
(#\S #\O #\O #\N #\- #\C #\O #\M #\E)

Lisp> (concatenate 'string "SOON" "-" "COME")
"SOON-COME"

Lisp> (setf *print-array* t)
T

Lisp> (concatenate 'vector "SOON" "-" "COME")
#(#\S #\O #\O #\N #\- #\C #\O #\M #\E)

Lisp> (elt "ABC" 1)     ; extract an element of a sequence
#\B

Lisp> (elt '(a b c) 1)
B

Lisp> (elt #(a b c) 1)
B
```

CONCATENATE will append together different kinds of sequences, producing a result sequence whose type is specified by the first argument to CONCATENATE. ELT is a generalized sequence-accessing function. Here are some other sequence functions:

```
Lisp> (count #\o "Soon-Come")
3                ; 3 #\o characters appear in "Soon-Come"

Lisp> (position #\o "Soon-Come")
1                            ; the first #\o appears at index 1

Lisp> (elt "Soon-Come" 1) ; retrieve the first #\o
#\o

Lisp>(sort "Less-than-one-calorie" #'char>)
"tssroonnliheeecaaL---"

Lisp> (sort "Less-than-one-calorie" #'char<)
"---Laaceeehilnnoorsst"

Lisp> (search "one" "Less-than-one-calorie")
10          ; the string "one" begins at index 10

Lisp> (setf s "Less-than-one-calorie")
"Less-than-one-calorie"

;;; destructively replace part of the string S
Lisp> (replace s "two" :start 10)
"Less-than-two-calorie"

Lisp> s
"Less-than-two-calorie"
```

These examples merely hint at the variety of sequence functions available. Refer to the Common Lisp manual for more details.

CHAPTER 13

INPUT/OUTPUT AND TABLES

In this chapter we will examine functions which manipulate input and output streams of data. We will also examine several different methods for creating tables of information indexed by a key.

13.1 INPUT AND OUTPUT STREAMS

So far most of our interaction with Lisp has been through a keyboard and display, occasionally loading files of functions. However, Lisp unifies all kinds of input and output with the concept of a *stream*. Streams are characterized by whether they produce or consume data, and by the type of data they handle. For example, the read-eval-print loop normally reads data from an input stream named `*STANDARD-INPUT*` and writes data to an output stream named `*STANDARD-OUTPUT*`. Each of these streams is unidirectional, and thus we cannot write data to `*STANDARD-INPUT*` or read data from `*STANDARD-OUTPUT*`. However, Lisp also has bidirectional streams, such as `*TERMINAL-IO*`, which perform both input and output. The stream `*TERMINAL-IO*` normally connects to our console.

13.1.1 `OPEN` and Pathnames

A *file* is a sequence of data which is usually stored on some form of permanent storage such as a disk. We will specify the name of a file using a *pathname*, and we can create a stream which connects to a file with the function `OPEN`. For example, the index of this book is automatically generated by a program and written to a file. A section of the index file might look like this:

```
CONCEPT-ENTRY "Sequence Functions" 253
LISP-ENTRY "REVERSE" 253
LISP-ENTRY "NREVERSE" 253
CONCEPT-ENTRY "Stream" 255
```

Each line specifies a type of index entry, the name of an entry, and the page number where the entry appears. If this file is in the directory /u/wade/book/text/tiny.index, then we can open an input stream to it and begin reading data:

```
Lisp> (setf stream (open "/u/wade/book/text/tiny.index"))
#<Stream BUFFERED-STREAM 4BC92B>

Lisp> (read stream)
CONCEPT-ENTRY
```

The input function **READ** optionally accepts a stream as an argument. If the optional argument is not supplied, then it reads from the stream ***STANDARD-INPUT***. However, because we supplied a stream connected to our data file, it reads and returns the first form in the file. We can continue to read data with subsequent calls to **READ**:

```
Lisp> (read stream)
"Sequence Functions"

Lisp> (read stream)
253
```

READ parses its input stream according to the syntax of Lisp and returns values such as strings, integers, and lists. However, we can use the functions **READ-LINE** and **READ-CHAR** to read raw strings or individual characters without any parsing:

```
;;; double quotes within a string are
;;; preceded by the escape character '\'
Lisp> (read-line stream)
"LISP-ENTRY \"REVERSE\" 253"
NIL

Lisp> (read-char stream)
#\L
```

```
Lisp> (read-char stream)
#\I

Lisp> (read-char stream)
#\S

Lisp> (close stream)
NIL
```

READ-LINE returns the next line of characters in the stream as a string, while **READ-CHAR** will read one character at a time. When we are all done reading from a stream, we should close it with the function **CLOSE**. This releases any resources consumed by the stream and signals that we are done reading or writing to it.

13.2 EXAMPLE: READING AN INDEX FILE

Suppose that we want to represent the information in an index file as an a-list so that it can be easily manipulated and searched. We can write a function called **READ-INDEX-ENTRIES** which does this:

```
Lisp> (read-index-entries "tiny.index")
(("Stream" CONCEPT-ENTRY 255)
 ("NREVERSE" LISP-ENTRY 253)
 ("REVERSE" LISP-ENTRY 253)
 ("Sequence Functions" CONCEPT-ENTRY 253))
```

Here is the definition of **READ-INDEX-ENTRIES**:

```
;;; This macro was introduced in Chapter 11.
(defmacro iterate (name bindings &body body)
  `(labels ((,name ,(mapcar #'first bindings)
              ,@body))
     (,name ,@(mapcar #'second bindings))))

(defun read-index-entries (index-pathname)
  (let ((input (open index-pathname)))
    (iterate munch ((type (read input nil input))
                    (entries nil))
      (if (eq type input)
          (progn (close input)
                 entries)
          (let ((name (read input t input))
                (page-number (read input t input)))
            (munch (read input nil input)
                   (cons (list name type page-number)
                         entries)))))))
```

READ-INDEX-ENTRIES begins by opening an input stream which is connected to the index file. It then iterates over each line in the file, accumulating an a-list which it returns when it reaches the end of the file. In order to detect when the end of the input file is reached, each call to **READ** passes three optional arguments. **READ** has the general form:

```
(read &optional input-stream eof-error-p eof-value
              recursive-p)
```

We have already seen how the *input-stream* argument is used. If *eof-error-p* is not **NIL**, then **READ** signals an error when it detects the end of an input stream. However, if *eof-error-p* is **NIL**, then **READ** will return the value of *eof-value*. The *recursive-p* argument is rarely needed, and we will ignore it.

In **READ-INDEX-ENTRIES** there are four calls to **READ**. Two of the calls are intended to read the **TYPE** field which begins each index entry line, or to detect the end of the file when we run out of lines. Thus, these calls pass an *eof-error-p* argument of **NIL** and the input stream itself as an *eof-value*. When the end of the file is detected, the input stream is returned as the value of the call to **READ**. We return the input stream rather than something like the symbol **EOF**, because the input stream is a unique object which cannot possible be confused with an entry in the index file.

The remaining two calls to **READ** in **READ-INDEX-ENTRIES** are used to read the name and page number fields of an index entry. These calls to **READ** will signal an error if they encounter the end of the file, since end-of-file indicates that a field is missing from the index entry. For example, suppose that the index file /u/wade/book/text/bad.index contains two index entries, but the last entry is missing a page number:

```
CONCEPT-ENTRY "Sequence Functions" 253
LISP-ENTRY "REVERSE"                 ; forgot the page number!
```

If we call **READ-INDEX-DATA** on this file, **READ** will signal an error:

```
Lisp> (read-index-entry "/u/wade/book/text/bad.index")
>>Error: Unexpected end-of-file encountered during read.

READ:
   Optional arg 0 (STREAM): #<Stream BUFFERED-STREAM 4E108B>
   Optional arg 1 (EOF-ERROR-P): T
   Optional arg 2 (EOF-VALUE):
                 #<Stream BUFFERED-STREAM 4E108B>
   Optional arg 3 (RECURSIVE-P): NIL

:A    Abort to Lisp Top Level
-> :b
READ <- READ-INDEX-ENTRY <- EVAL
```

```
-> :a
Back to Lisp Top Level
Lisp>
```

Problem. The error message `Error: Unexpected end-of-file encountered during read` is not a good description of the error in the index file we just read. A better message would be `ERROR: No PAGE-NUMBER field was found on line 2 of the index file bad.index`. Modify `READ-INDEX-ENTRY` so that it will print this error message, and similar messages if any of the other fields are missing.

13.2.1 UNWIND-PROTECT

When `READ-INDEX-ENTRIES` executes without error, it explicitly closes the stream it opened before returning. However, when we entered the debugger in our last example, we abnormally exited `READ-INDEX-ENTRIES` by aborting to the top-level read-eval-print loop. Hence, the input stream was never closed, and we have no way to access it anymore.

Unfortunately, streams consume limited operating system resources such as file descriptors in UNIX. If we leave too many open streams around we will eventually be unable to open any more files. Hence, it is essential that we *always* close a stream when we are done with it. In order to *guarantee* that the input file will be closed no matter how we exit `READ-INDEX-ENTRIES`, we need to use the special form `UNWIND-PROTECT`. Here is a simple example of how it works:

```
Lisp> (block abort
        (unwind-protect (progn (print "before")
                               (print "after"))
          (print "cleanup form")))

"before"
"after"
"cleanup form"
"after"

Lisp> (block abort
        (unwind-protect (progn (print "before")
                               (return-from abort "early")
                               (print "after"))
          (print "cleanup form")))

"before"
"cleanup form"
"early"
```

The first argument to `UNWIND-PROTECT`, called the *protected form*, is evaluated, and any values returned are temporarily saved. Then any remaining arguments, called *cleanup forms*, are evaluated. After all the cleanup forms have been evaluated, the values originally returned by the protected form are returned as the result of the call to `UNWIND-PROTECT`.

`UNWIND-PROTECT` behaves exactly like `MULTIPLE-VALUE-PROG1` if the protected form does not try to abnormally transfer control ("unwind") to outside the scope of the `UNWIND-PROTECT`. However, control can abnormally transfer to outside the scope of the `UNWIND-PROTECT` in a number of ways, such as a call to `RETURN-FROM` or `THROW`, or an abort to top-level from within the debugger.[1] No matter how control is transferred, all of the cleanup forms will be executed before control is actually transferred.

We can use `UNWIND-PROTECT` to rewrite `READ-INDEX-ENTRIES` so that it always closes its input stream:

```
(defun read-index-entries (index-pathname)
  (let ((input nil))
    (unwind-protect
      (progn (setf input (open index-pathname))
             (iterate munch ((type
                                (read input nil input))
                             (entries nil))
               (if (eq type input)
                   (progn (close input)
                          entries)
                   (let ((name (read input t input))
                         (page-number
                           (read input t input)))
                     (munch (read input nil input)
                            (cons (list name type
                                        page-number)
                                  entries))))))
      (unless (null input) (close input)))))
```

Now the stream is opened within a form protected by the `UNWIND-PROTECT`. The cleanup form will always be executed no matter how the protected form exits. Notice that we check to see that the input stream is not `NIL` before closing it, since it is possible that the protected form could exit before even completing the call to `OPEN`. This could easily happen if we try to open a file which does not exist, causing us to enter the debugger. If we then choose to abort to top-level rather than continuing with a new file name, `INPUT` will still be bound to `NIL`.

---

[1] Actually, an abort to top level is usually just a `THROW` to a system-defined catch tag.

Using `UNWIND-PROTECT` to guarantee that a stream is closed when we are done with it is so common, that Lisp captures this idiom with the macro `WITH-OPEN-FILE`. Here is how we can use `WITH-OPEN-FILE` to rewrite `READ-INDEX-ENTRIES` more clearly:

```
(defun read-index-entries (index-pathname)
  (with-open-file (input index-pathname)
    (iterate munch ((type (read input nil input))
                    (entries nil))
      (if (eq type input)
          (progn (close input)
                 entries)
          (let ((name (read input t input))
                (page-number (read input t input)))
            (munch (read input nil input)
                   (cons (list name type page-number)
                         entries)))))))
```

The first argument to `WITH-OPEN-FILE` is a list containing the name of a stream and a pathname. Any remaining elements of the list are treated as options to `OPEN`. The remaining arguments to `WITH-OPEN-FILE` are sequentially executed, just as they would be by a `PROGN`. However, no matter how we exit the call to `WITH-OPEN-FILE`, the stream we opened will always be closed. There is rarely any reason to call `OPEN` directly, since we usually want the closing protection offered by `WITH-OPEN-FILE`.

Problem. The entries in the index file for this book actually have the following format:

`\indexentry{CONCEPT-ENTRY "Sequence Functions"}{253}`

The Common Lisp `READ` function is actually a user-extensible, recursive-decent parser. Read about how to define *character macros* in the Common Lisp manual, and then make open-brace and close-brace behave like open-parenthesis and close-parenthesis respectively. Also alter the behavior of backslash so that it is no longer an escape character, but just a normal constituent character. Then rewrite the function `READ-INDEX-ENTRIES` to use your modified readtable when reading an index file, restoring the default readtable when it is done.

13.3 EXAMPLE: A BINARY FILE ENCODER

Suppose that we have a binary file which we wish to send to someone via electronic mail. Unfortunately, we cannot usually send it directly because many mail programs can only manipulate text. However, we can convert a binary file into its textual representation as hexadecimal digits. For example, suppose the file `fake.bin` contains the following line:

```
Pretend that this is binary data.
Real binary data isn't pretty.
```

We would like to call a function `HEXIFY` to convert this to a text file which contains the hexadecimal representation of each byte in the binary file:

```
Lisp> (hexify "fake.bin")
#P"/u/wade/book/text/fake.hex"
```

Here are the contents of `fake.hex`:

```
50726574656E6420746861742074686973206973206269GE6172792064617461
2E0A5265616C206269GE61727920646174612069736E277420707265
7474792E
```

The definition of `HEXIFY` follows:

```
(defun hexify (input-name)
  (let ((output-name (make-pathname :defaults input-name
                                    :type "hex")))
    (with-open-file (input input-name
                           :element-type '(unsigned-byte 8))
      (with-open-file (output output-name
                              :direction :output)
        (do ((byte (read-byte input nil input)
                   (read-byte input nil input))
             (i 1 (1+ i)))
            ((eq byte input) (truename output-name))
          (write-byte-in-hex byte output)
          (when (= (mod i 30) 0)
            ;; write a #\Newline character
            ;; to the OUTPUT stream
            (terpri output)))))))
```

`HEXIFY` creates the name of the output file with the function `MAKE-PATHNAME`. The `:DEFAULTS` keyword says to make a new pathname which is just like `INPUT-NAME`, but the `:TYPE` keyword says to override the default type and use the type `hex` instead. Hence, the output file has the same name as the input file, except that the output file has the extension `hex`.

`WITH-OPEN-FILE` is used to open both the input and output streams. The `:ELEMENT-TYPE` keyword to `OPEN` specifies what kinds of elements a stream reads or writes. The element type defaults to `STRING-CHAR`, but we open the input file with an explicit element type of (`UNSIGNED-BYTE 8`) so that eight-bit, unsigned bytes (this is another way of saying numbers from 0 to 255) are read from the binary input file.

The `:DIRECTION` option to `OPEN` defaults to `:INPUT`, but we also need to open an output stream, so the second call to `WITH-OPEN-FILE` specifies a `:DIRECTION` of `:OUTPUT` so that a new text file is opened for output. `OPEN` accepts a rather elaborate set of keyword arguments whose exact behavior is sometimes implementation dependent. Refer to the Common Lisp manual for more details.

The rest of `HEXIFY` reads each byte from the binary output file, and writes it in hexadecimal to the output file. `READ-BYTE` and `WRITE-BYTE` are the only functions Common Lisp provides for dealing with binary data streams. `READ-BYTE` will read a single byte of data from an input stream, while `WRITE-BYTE` will write a single byte of data to an output stream.

After 30 bytes have been read from the input stream, and thus 60 characters have been written to the output stream, `HEXIFY` writes a newline character so that none of the output lines are too long. `READ-BYTE` accepts the same optional arguments as `READ`, so `HEXIFY` asks that `READ-BYTE` return the input stream when the end of the input file is reached. The full pathname specification for the output file is returned as the value of `HEXIFY`.

We still have to write the function `WRITE-BYTE-IN-HEX`. We can use one of the many format directives to output two digit hexadecimal numbers:

```
Lisp> (format t "~2,'0X" 47)
2F
NIL

Lisp> (format t "~2,'0X" 7)
07
NIL
```

This format directive says to write a two-character-wide hexadecimal number, padded with a leading 0 when necessary. Hence, we can define `WRITE-BYTE-IN-HEX` using `FORMAT`:

```
(defun write-byte-in-hex (byte output)
  (format output "~2,'0X" byte))
```

Although this works, it is likely to be extremely slow in most Common Lisp implementations because `FORMAT` is such a general function, and `FORMAT` control strings are usually interpreted at runtime. We can produce a faster implementation of `WRITE-BYTE-IN-HEX` if we are willing do to a little more work.

13.3.1 Byte Specifiers

Rather than letting **FORMAT** decide which digits to output, we can examine each *nibble* in a byte and output the corresponding hexadecimal digit ourselves with the function **WRITE-CHAR**. A nibble is a four-bit-wide field, and there are two nibbles in an eight-bit byte:

```
   7    6    5    4    3    2    1    0
 +-------------------+-------------------+
 |   Upper nibble    |   Lower nibble    |
 +-------------------+-------------------+
```

Given a byte, we can extract the upper and lower nibbles with the following functions:

```
Lisp> (logand #x0F #x57)
7                          ; lower nibble of #x57

Lisp> (logand #xF0 #x57)
80                         ; Clear lower nibble

Lisp> (ash 80 -4)          ; Shift 80 right by 4 bits
5                          ; to yield the upper nibble of #x57
```

The function **LOGAND** returns the logical *and* of its two arguments. The function **ASH** arithmetically shifts its first argument by the number of bits specified by the second argument. If the second argument is positive, then **ASH** shifts left, while a negative argument causes it to shift right. Hence, we can mask bit fields with **LOGAND**, and rotate them with **ASH**.

However, Common Lisp provides a more convenient way to manipulate bit fields. The term *byte* usually refers to a group of eight bits, but in Common Lisp the term byte is used to refer to an arbitrary width bit field. We can use the function **LDB**, which stands for "LoaD Byte", to extract an arbitrary width bit field from a number:

```
Lisp> (ldb (byte 4 4) #x57)
5                                      ; upper nibble of #x57

Lisp> (ldb (byte 4 0) #x57)
7                                      ; lower nibble of #x57
```

The first argument to **LDB** is a *byte specifier*, while the second is an integer. A byte specifier has the form:

(byte *width position*)

The *width* argument specifies how wide the bit field is, while the *position* argument specifies where the rightmost bit of the field begins. In our example, the first call to `LDB` extracts from the hex number 57 a four-bit-wide field beginning at bit 4, while the second call extracts a four-bit-wide field beginning at bit 0. These two calls are a clearer way of extracting the upper and lower nibbles from an eight-bit byte, and we can use them to write a faster version of `WRITE-BYTE-IN-HEX`:

```
(defun write-byte-in-hex (byte output)
  (flet ((write-nibble-in-hex (nibble)
           (write-char (schar "0123456789ABCDEF" nibble)
                       output)))
    (write-nibble-in-hex (ldb (byte 4 4) byte))
    (write-nibble-in-hex (ldb (byte 4 0) byte))))
```

`WRITE-BYTE-IN-HEX` writes each nibble individually using `WRITE-NIBBLE-IN-HEX`, which in turn uses the nibble to index into a string of hexadecimal digits, writing the appropriate digit to the output stream.

> **Problem.** `HEXIFY` could be made even faster by writing out whole lines at a time with `WRITE-STRING` rather than using `WRITE-CHAR` to write each character individually. Rewrite `HEXIFY` and `WRITE-BYTE-IN-HEX` to buffer each output line in a 60-character string, and then write the string to the hex file each time the line is complete. How much faster does your program run?

> **Problem.** Computer instructions are stored as binary data which contain various fields. For example, an extremely simple machine language may have a fixed-length instruction format with the following interpretation:

31	24 23	12 11	0
opcode	operand-1	operand-2

> Write a function called `EXTRACT-FIELDS` which expects a 32-bit instruction as an argument and returns three values: `opcode`, `operand-1`, and `operand-2`.

> **Problem.** Write a function called `DEHEXIFY` which will convert a file produced by `HEXIFY` back into a binary file. Be careful to deal with the newlines which `HEXIFY` writes after every 60 characters.

> **Problem.** Write a Huffman encoder. Refer to [Sed83] or some other algorithm book for details.

13.4 TABLES

The index file reader we wrote earlier returns an a-list containing the entries in an index file. However, an a-list is just one specific implementation of the more general concept of a *table*.[2] A table associates a key, in this case the string naming an index entry, with some information, such as an index name and a page number in our example.

However, the way a table is implemented has a significant effect on the time it takes to perform common operations such as looking up, adding, or deleting values from the table. Three techniques are commonly used to represent tables in Lisp:

- A-lists
- Hash tables
- Property lists

A-lists are simple, but they are inefficient for representing large tables which are frequently searched. They are popular because they are simple to build, manipulate, and read, and thus are ideal for small tables. They are also useful for rapid prototyping, when speed and efficiency are not major concerns.

13.4.1 Hash Tables

Suppose we have an index with 5000 entries stored as an a-list. If we want to perform many lookup and update operations on this index, then we would be better off representing the index as a *hash table*, in which lookups and updates can be performed in roughly constant time, rather than in a time proportional to the number of entries in the table. Here is a simple example of how to use a hash table to hold our index:

```
Lisp> (setf index (make-hash-table :size 5000
                                   :test #'equal))
#<Hash-Table 4FE32B>

Lisp> (gethash "Stream" index)
NIL
;; flag indicating that a value for "Stream" was not found
NIL

Lisp> (setf (gethash "Stream" index) '(CONCEPT-ENTRY 255))
(CONCEPT-ENTRY 255)

Lisp> (gethash "Stream" index)
(CONCEPT-ENTRY 255)
T   ; flag indicating that a value for "Stream" was found
```

---

[2] Tables are called sometimes called *dictionaries*.

MAKE-HASH-TABLE creates a new hash table with no entries. The two keyword options we have given are optional. The `:SIZE` argument may be passed if we have an idea about how many entries we plan to put in the table. A hash table will automatically grow to accommodate as many entries as we want to put in it, but it is usually more efficient if we can specify ahead of time how many entries we plan to have. The `:TEST` argument specifies the function used to compare keys, just like the `:TEST` argument to `ASSOC`. However, hash tables will only compare keys with the functions `EQ`, `EQL`, and `EQUAL`, with the default test being `EQL`.

The function `GETHASH` expects a key and a hash table as arguments, and returns two values: the value associated with the key, and a boolean flag indicating whether or not the key was actually found in the table. Because a freshly created table contains no entries, our first attempt to look up the value of `"Stream"` fails. `SETF` will add new entries to a hash table, and after we add an entry for `"Stream"` we can successfully retrieve it with `GETHASH`.

IMPLEMENTING OPEN HASHING. In order to understand how a hash table quickly performs lookups and updates, we will write a simple hash table implementation of our own. First we need to create a *hashing function* $h(k)$, such that given a key k, it returns a number from 0 to $p - 1$. The hash table is actually an array of size p, and we will use the value of $h(k)$ as the index into the array where the value of the key is stored. Thus, if we have an array of size $p = 23$,[3] then $h(\text{"Stream"})$ might return the number 15, indicating that the value associated with the key `"Stream"` is stored at index 15 in the array.

If we later try to store a value for a different key which also hashes to the number 15, then we will have a *collision*, because more than one key value must fit into a single array cell. There are two ways to resolve a collision. One method, called *closed hashing*, tries to *rehash* the key to find a different cell in the array to hold the value. However, a simpler method called *open hashing* simply stores an a-list of keys and values in each array cell. Once we have determined the cell to which a key hashes, we can use `ASSOC` to search the a-list in that cell for the value of the key.

In order for hashing to work well, the hashing function must evenly distribute all objects over the entire array, and finding a good hashing function is not always easy. Fortunately, Lisp already provides a hashing function called `SXHASH`:

```
Lisp> (sxhash "Stream")
239950563

Lisp> (sxhash 3)
3
```

---

[3] The size p is usually chosen to be prime for best performance.

```
Lisp> (sxhash 'stream)
16614
```

SXHASH will accept any kind of object and return a number. This number can then be reduced to a specific range of numbers with the **MOD** function. An important property of **SXHASH** is that if two objects are **EQUAL**, then they will hash to the same number.

We can use what we have just learned about hash tables to develop a simple implementation of open hashing:

```
(defstruct (table (:constructor fresh-table)
                  (:print-function
                    (lambda (table stream print-level)
                      (declare (ignore print-level))
                      (format stream
                              "#<TABLE with ~D elements>"
                              (table-value-count table)))))
  (value-count 0)
  test
  buckets)

(defun make-table (&key (test #'eql) (size 23))
  (fresh-table :test test
               :buckets (make-array size)))

(defun hash (key table)
  (mod (sxhash key) (length (table-buckets table))))

(defun add-table-value (key table value)
  (let ((bucket-number (hash key table))
        (buckets (table-buckets table))
        (test (table-test table)))
    (let ((entry (assoc key
                        (svref buckets bucket-number)
                        :test test)))
      (if (null entry)
          (progn (incf (table-value-count table))
                 (push (cons key value)
                       (svref buckets bucket-number)))
          (setf (cdr entry) value))
      value)))

(defun get-table-value (key table)
  (let ((candidates (svref (table-buckets table)
                           (hash key table))))
```

```
          (let ((entry (assoc key
                              candidates
                              :test (table-test table))))
            (if (null entry)
                (values nil nil)
                (values (cdr entry) t)))))
```

A **TABLE** structure records the number of values currently stored in the table, the comparison function used to compare keys, and a vector named **BUCKETS**. Notice that the slot specification for **VALUE-COUNT** is actually a list. The second element of that list is a *default value* which is used to initialize the **VALUE-COUNT** slot in a new table if a value for that slot is not explicitly supplied at creation time. We have also used the **:CONSTRUCTOR** option to **DEFSTRUCT** to specify that the function which creates new tables should be named **FRESH-TABLE**, rather than using the default name **MAKE-TABLE**.

We want to define **MAKE-TABLE** ourselves so that it can do some computations before actually creating a new table with **FRESH-TABLE**. Right now we do not take advantage of this possibility, but we might like to use it later. For example, although the user may specify any value for **SIZE**, we would like to be sure it is a reasonable value, and then round it up to the nearest prime number to better distribute elements over the **BUCKETS** vector.

New values are added to the table with the function **ADD-TABLE-VALUE**. The first thing this function does is to compute the hash value of the **KEY** with the function **SXHASH**. **HASH** then uses **MOD** to reduce the number returned by **SXHASH** into a number suitable for indexing into the **BUCKETS** vector.[4] The a-list in the appropriate bucket is then searched using the specified test function for a pair beginning with the key of interest. If no entry is found, then a new one is added onto the front of the a-list for that bucket. However, if an entry for that key already exists, then the value portion of the existing entry is destructively updated with the new **VALUE**.

GET-TABLE-VALUE is similar to **ADD-TABLE-VALUE**, but it only looks for an existing entry for **KEY**. If one is found, then the value of the entry and the flag **T** are returned, indicating that a value does exist. If no value exists, then the value **NIL** and the flag **NIL** are returned.

We can try our implementation on the same example we used to demonstrate the use of the hash tables built into Common Lisp:

---

[4]One potential disadvantage of using hash tables arises if the hashing function is dependent on an object's address in memory, as it sometimes is in many Lisp systems. As we will see in Chapter 19, a relocating garbage collector changes the address of an object in memory. Unfortunately, this means that any hash tables which were built using an object's address to compute its hash value are now invalid and must be rehashed! This can lead to thrashing if we have many hash tables and we cons many short-lived objects, causing the system to gc a lot and spend too much time rehashing.

```
Lisp> (setf index (make-table :size 5000 :test #'equal))
#<TABLE with 0 elements>

Lisp> (get-table-value "Stream" index)
NIL
NIL

Lisp> (add-table-value "Stream" index '(CONCEPT-ENTRY 255))
(CONCEPT-ENTRY 255)

Lisp> (get-table-value "Stream" index)
(CONCEPT-ENTRY 255)
T
```

Our implementation can be used almost exactly like the hash tables built into Lisp. However, we must explicitly use the updating function **ADD-TABLE-VALUE** rather than simply calling **SETF** to update a table entry. We can fix this problem with the macro **DEFSETF**:

```
(defsetf get-table-value add-table-value)
```

This call to **DEFSETF** says that whenever **SETF** is called with an accessing form calling the function **GET-TABLE-VALUE**, then the function **ADD-TABLE-VALUE** should be called to actually update the table:

```
Lisp> (setf (get-table-value "Stream" index)
            '(CONCEPT-ENTRY 279))
(CONCEPT-ENTRY 279)

Lisp> (get-table-value "Stream" index)
(CONCEPT-ENTRY 279)
T
```

There are several other functions provided by Common Lisp for extending the functionality of **SETF**. Refer to the Common Lisp manual for more details.

Our discussion of hashing has been rather brief and superficial. An enormous amount of effort has gone into understanding and analyzing the performance of various hashing algorithms. Refer to [Knu75] for more details.

Problem. Write a function called **DELETE-TABLE-VALUE** which can remove the value of a key from a table.

Problem. Add a slot named **REHASH-PERCENTAGE** to our **TABLE** structure. It must contain a positive number, and should default to **2.0** if the user does not specify a value when creating a new table. Change **ADD-TABLE-VALUE** so that whenever the number of elements in a table exceeds **REHASH-PERCENTAGE** times the length of the table vector, the vector is automatically doubled in size, and all the elements in the old vector are rehashed and inserted into the new vector. This way our tables will automatically grow as more elements are inserted, and thus each a-list should be short.

13.4.2 Lisp History: Property Lists

Before hash tables became popular in Lisp, *property lists* were commonly used to avoid the linear search time characteristics of a-lists. For example, recall that in Chapter 8 we used an a-list to associate math functions with corresponding derivative functions:

```
(defvar *deriv-functions*
  '((+ . deriv-add)
    (* . deriv-mult)
    (/ . deriv-div)
    (expt . deriv-expt))
  "An a-list mapping operators to deriv func names")
```

If we add many math functions to this table, then the **DERIV** function we wrote will start to slow down because it performs many table lookups. However, we can use property lists to perform this lookup more quickly. Every symbol in Lisp names a property list, just as it names a function and a value. We can retrieve the property list with the function **SYMBOL-PLIST**:

```
Lisp> (symbol-plist 'expt)
NIL
```

A property list is just a regular list with an even number of elements, and initially the property list of a symbol is the empty list. Here is a property list containing two properties:

```
(NUMBER-OF-ARGUMENTS 2 DERIV-FUNC DERIV-EXPT)
```

Recall that **NUMBER-OF-ARGUMENTS** is the zeroth element of the list. Each even numbered element of the list is an called an *indicator* (or key), while each odd numbered element is a called a *property* (or value). For example, the property list above associates the indicator **NUMBER-OF-ARGUMENTS** with the value **2**, and the indicator **DERIV-FUNC** with the value **DERIV-EXPT**. We can retrieve the value of an indicator with the function **GET**, and we can assign a value to an indicator with **SETF**:

```
Lisp> (get 'expt 'deriv-func)
NIL
```

```
Lisp> (setf (get 'expt 'deriv-func) 'deriv-expt)
DERIV-EXPT

Lisp> (get 'expt 'deriv-func)
DERIV-EXPT

Lisp> (setf (get 'expt 'number-of-arguments) 2)
2

Lisp> (get 'expt 'number-of-arguments)
2

Lisp> (symbol-plist 'expt)
(NUMBER-OF-ARGUMENTS 2 DERIV-FUNC DERIV-EXPT)
```

    `GET` expects a symbol and an indicator as arguments, and it returns the property associated with that indicator, or `NIL` if no property is found. `SETF` works as we would expect, allowing us to change the value that a call to `GET` would return. Thus, we can use property lists to replace the association list `*DERIV-FUNCTIONS*`, and the function `LOOKUP-DERIV-FUNC`:

```
(setf (get '+ 'deriv-func) 'deriv-add)
(setf (get '* 'deriv-func) 'deriv-mult)
(setf (get '/ 'deriv-func) 'deriv-div)
(setf (get 'expt 'deriv-func) 'deriv-expt)

(defun lookup-deriv-func (equation)
  (let* ((operator (first equation))
         (property (get operator 'deriv-func)))
    (if (null property)
        nil
        (symbol-function property))))
```

    Now when we look up a derivative specialist, we can find it almost immediately without linearly searching for it among all the derivative specialists in our system. Property lists are really just a convenient way to implement the special case of a table which associates symbolic keys with values. Unfortunately, property lists have many bad features.

    Because property lists are associated only with symbols, they are not nearly as general an implementation of tables as hash tables or a-lists. For example, we cannot implement our index example using property lists unless we want to create a lot of spurious symbols with mixed-case names to denote strings, solely so that we can use the symbol's property list. This is not only an obscure way to implement a table, but it wastes a lot of memory because none of the other symbol slots are needed.

Property lists are also globally visible to all the functions in our Lisp system, and thus they have the same problems associated with global variables. For example, if we choose to use an indicator called `DERIV-FUNC` and another function wants to use that same property, then there will be a conflict.[5]

Poor paging behavior is another potential problem with property lists because the cons cells of any list can be scattered across many different pages in memory. Thus, traversing a list can cause a large number of page faults, although later we will see how a good garbage collector can help to lessen this problem. Hash tables are usually stored on contiguous pages in memory, and thus they exhibit better locality.

Property lists are also linear structures, and thus the time it takes to look up a specific indicator will depend upon how many other functions have decided to store properties on the property list we are using. About the only good thing property lists have going for them is that they are sometimes a convenient way to associate a symbol with more than one value. However, they should almost always be avoided in favor of using a-lists or hash tables.

Rather than forcing us to decide what kind of table is best suited for a particular application, some versions of Common Lisp provide a generalized table facility which is independent of a particular representation. This allows us to write our programs solely in terms of tables without regard for their implementation. The table functions will choose the most efficient representation for a specific table, even dynamically switching representations as characteristics of the table change. For example, small tables may be best represented as a-lists, while larger tables might be best represented as hash tables.

Problem. Create a table facility which internally uses height-balanced binary trees (also known as AVL trees). Refer to an algorithms text for more details.

---

[5]This problem can be avoided by using different packages for the indicators.

CHAPTER
14

GAMES AND SEARCH

14.1 TIC-TAC-TOE AND MINIMAX

Game-playing programs have fascinated people since computers were invented. In fact, much of the early work in AI dealt with creating intelligent game-playing programs. Although many problems are still unsolved, several general game-playing techniques have been developed. In this chapter, we will look at how we can use some of these techniques to write a program which will play tic-tac-toe using the *minimax* search technique.

14.1.1 Trees

When playing games, it is often useful to construct a *game tree*. *Trees* are ubiquitous data structures in computer science, with many possible implementations and uses. A tree is a data structure which expresses the relationship between various objects. For example, the tree in Figure 14.1 represents the relationship between some parts of a motorcycle.

The motorcycle tree says that a motorcycle is composed of wheels, an engine, and a seat. The engine in turn consists of cylinders, an air filter, and spark plugs. Each part in the tree is called a *node*, while the lines which connect the nodes are called *edges*. For example, an edge connects `ENGINE` and `AIR-FILTER`. In this case, `ENGINE` is called the *parent* node, and `AIR-FILTER` is called the *child* node. More generally, `WHEELS`, `ENGINE`, and `SEAT` are called the *children* of `MOTORCYCLE`.

```
                        MOTORCYCLE
                        .  .  .
                     .           .
                  .                 .
                .                     .
              .                         .
            .                             .
          .                                 .
   WHEELS              ENGINE                SEAT
                       .  .  .
                     .        .
                   .            .
                 .                .
               .                    .
        CYLINDERS    AIR-FILTER    SPARK-PLUGS
```

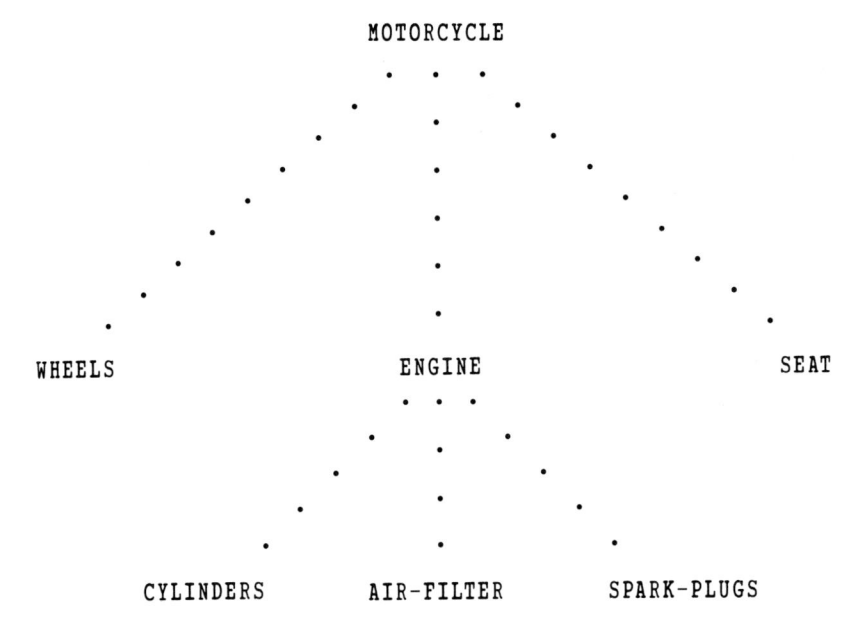

FIGURE 14.1
Motorcycle parts tree.

A sequence of edges and nodes that must be traversed when going from one node to another is called a *path* through the tree. Thus, `MOTORCYCLE`→ `ENGINE`→ `SPARK-PLUGS` is one possible path through the tree. Any node which has edges emanating from it is called an *interior* node of the tree, while a node with no edges leading away from it is called a *terminal node* or a *leaf*. Thus, `ENGINE` is an interior node, while `SEAT` is a leaf.

The motorcycle node is also called the *root* of the tree, since there is a path from `MOTORCYCLE` to all other nodes in the tree. It is important to notice that each interior node is really the root node of another tree. These other trees are *subtrees* of the larger tree we are examining; thus a tree is a recursive data structure. Every tree is either a single node (a leaf), or single node connected to several other subtrees via edges. This is analogous to the construction of lists: Every list is built out of atoms (the leaves) and other lists (the subtrees).

Problem. Try writing the following forms in tree notation:

1. `(* (- 27 (SIN X)) (+ 4 (/ 3.14 16)))`
2. `(defun fact (if (= x 0) 1 (* x (fact (1- x)))))`

14.1.2 Game Trees and Board Ranking

There is much more that we could say about trees; however, our purpose here is to use a tree to represent the state of a tic-tac-toe game. If we let each node in a game tree represent a possible board configuration, and each edge represents a single move which can take us from one board configuration to another, then we can represent an arbitrarily long sequence of moves, or even an entire game, as a path through a game tree.

Figure 14.2 depicts a portion of a possible game tree. The root node represents the state of play at some point during a tic-tac-toe game, with player X about to move. All the children of the root node represent *adjacent* boards, meaning that they can all be reached from their parent in exactly one move, with the edge connecting the boards representing that move.

At this point, we know all possible boards which can be reached from the current board in the game. If we can write a function to rank boards according to how close a particular player is to winning the game, then we could simply rank each possible move, and choose the best one.

Unfortunately, it is usually impossible to create a perfect board ranker, and the above strategy has to be based on *heuristics*. A heuristic is a general rule which is often true. In this case, we can only get a rough idea about the value of a particular board; a board which looks strong may eventually lead to much worse boards. If the computer moves to the board with the highest score, it is not guaranteed that it has made the best move, since that board may give our opponent the upper hand after several more moves.

In order to move more intelligently, we will try to look farther into the future of the game by extending the tree, drawing all the possible boards which could be reached from each of the children, and then all possible boards reachable from those boards, etc. Of course, if this were carried out indefinitely, the tree would become enormous, with all the leaves representing boards which resulted in a tie or a particular player winning. It turns out that searching such a tree

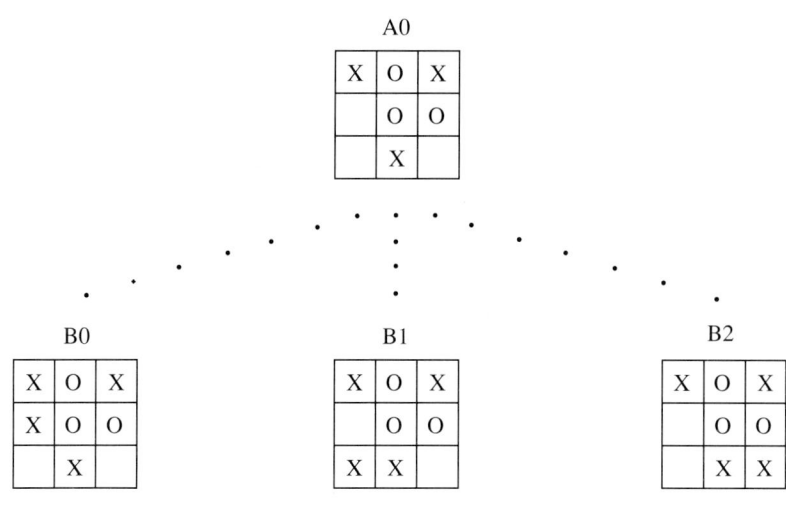

FIGURE 14.2
Partial game tree.

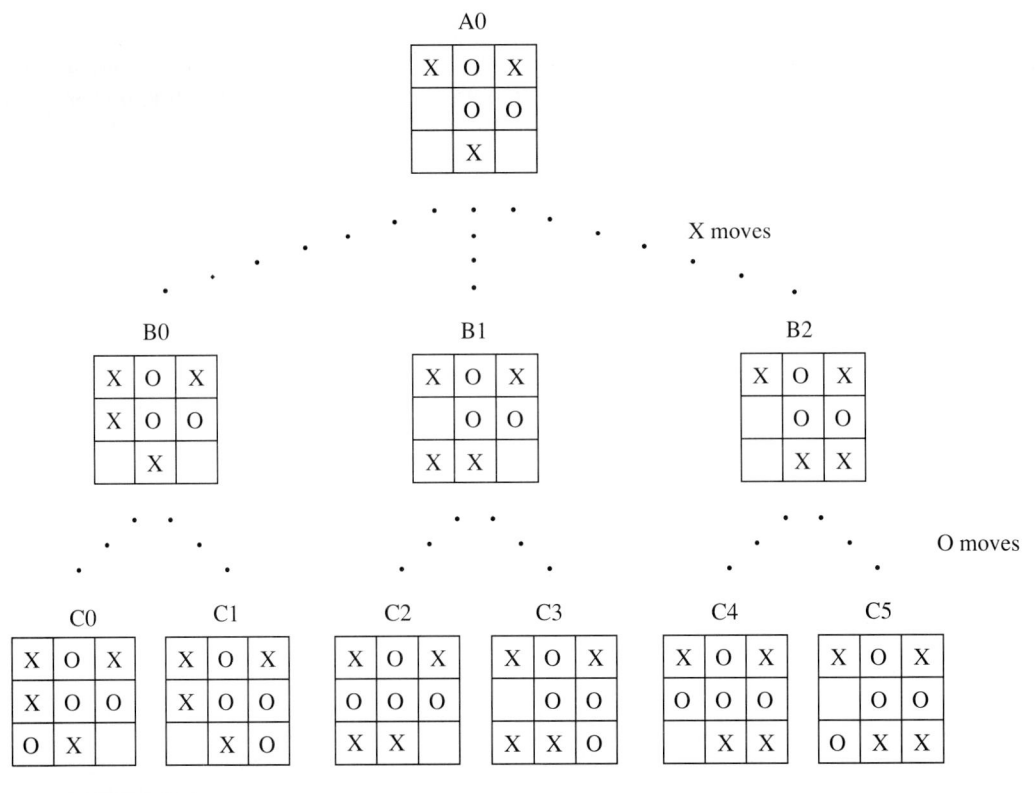

FIGURE 14.3
Game tree.

is a hopelessly overwhelming computational task. Thus, we can only extend the tree to a few levels. In game-playing parlance, each new level is called a *ply* of the game tree.

Each time we extend the game tree, we are looking ahead into many possible futures of the game. For example, Figure 14.3 represents a game tree with a two-ply look ahead. Player X is faced with moving from board A0 to one of B0, B1, or B2. Player O is then faced with moving from whichever board player X chose. If the computer is player X, though, how does it choose which board to move to, given that it has an imperfect board evaluator? To solve this problem, we will use a search algorithm known as *minimax*.

14.1.3 Minimax

In minimax, one player is called the *maximizing* player, while the other is called the *minimizing* player. The guiding idea behind minimax is that each player always wants to choose a board which is best for him and worst for his opponent. In our tic-tac-toe game, we will arbitrarily pick O as the minimizing player and X as the maximizing player. In order to use minimax with a board ranker, we want boards ranked with respect to the maximizing player to have positive scores, and boards ranked with respect to the minimizing player to have negative scores. Player O wants to choose the most negatively ranked boards, while player X wants the most positively ranked boards.

Once we have constructed the game tree, we apply the board ranker to all the leaves of the tree, since the leaves are the boards which are farthest in the future. When we rank the boards, we rank them *with respect to the player who must choose them*. In Figure 14.3, this means evaluating all the C boards with respect to player O, since player O must choose one of the C boards. Thus, we can annotate the tree as shown in Figure 14.4. We will discuss the details of the ranking function later.

Each C board has now been assigned a rank with respect to player O. Because O is the minimizing player, all the ranks must be less than or equal to zero, with the most negative boards being most valuable to player O.

Now how do we rank the B boards? Given a B board, player O must choose one of the reachable C boards. Naturally, player O wants to choose the most favorable board, thus he will choose the *minimum* scoring board because O is the

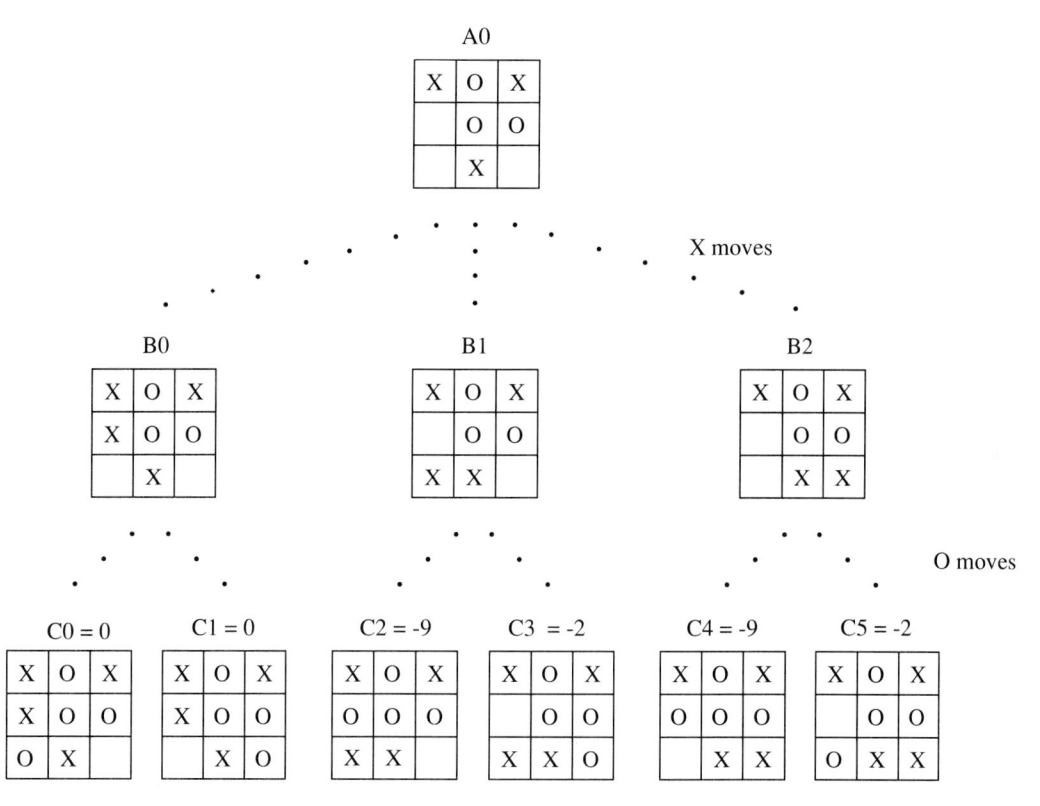

FIGURE 14.4
Ranking the leaves of a game tree.

                              A0
                          | X | O | X |
                          | | O | O |
                          | | X | |

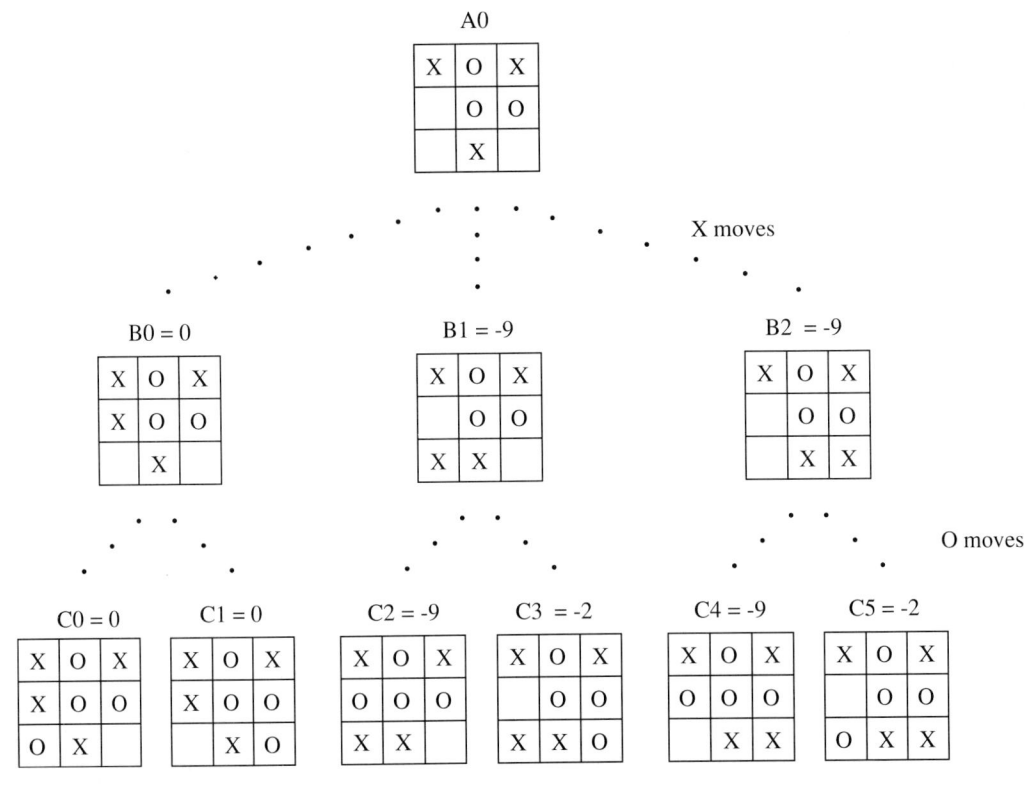

                                                        X moves

     B0 = 0   B1 = -9   B2 = -9
X	O	X		X	O	X		X	O	X
X	O	O			O	O			O	O
	X			X	X				X	X

                                                        O moves

   C0 = 0   C1 = 0   C2 = -9   C3 = -2   C4 = -9   C5 = -2
X	O	X		X	O	X		X	O	X		X	O	X		X	O	X		X	O	X
X	O	O		X	O	O		O	O	O			O	O		O	O	O			O	O
O	X				X	O		X	X			X	X	O			X	X		O	X	X

FIGURE 14.5
Bubbling minimum values up from the leaves to interior nodes.

minimizing player. We assign the rank of this minimum scoring C board to the parent B board. Figure 14.5 illustrates this step.

By "bubbling up" the ranks of the C boards to the B boards, we have ranked the B boards without actually calling our board evaluator on any of the B boards. We have indicated the desirability of each B board to player O, though, which is the purpose of assigning rank. Clearly player O would prefer that player X move from A0 to either B1 or B2, since from either of these positions player O could choose a C level board with a rank of -9.

However, player X wants to give player O the worst possible selection of boards. Thus, rather than choosing the board with the minimum score, player X wants to choose the board with the *maximum* score; that is, the board which is best for X and worst for O. To rank board A0, we repeat the bubbling up of ranks from B to A, realizing that player X gets to choose a B board. Figure 14.6 depicts the resulting tree, in which we have assigned a score of 0 to A0.

The bubbling-up process takes into account the fact that any competitive game is really a tug-of-war, with each player alternately trying to push the game in a direction which is best for him. For a more detailed description of minimax, refer to [Ric83].

GAMES AND SEARCH **227**

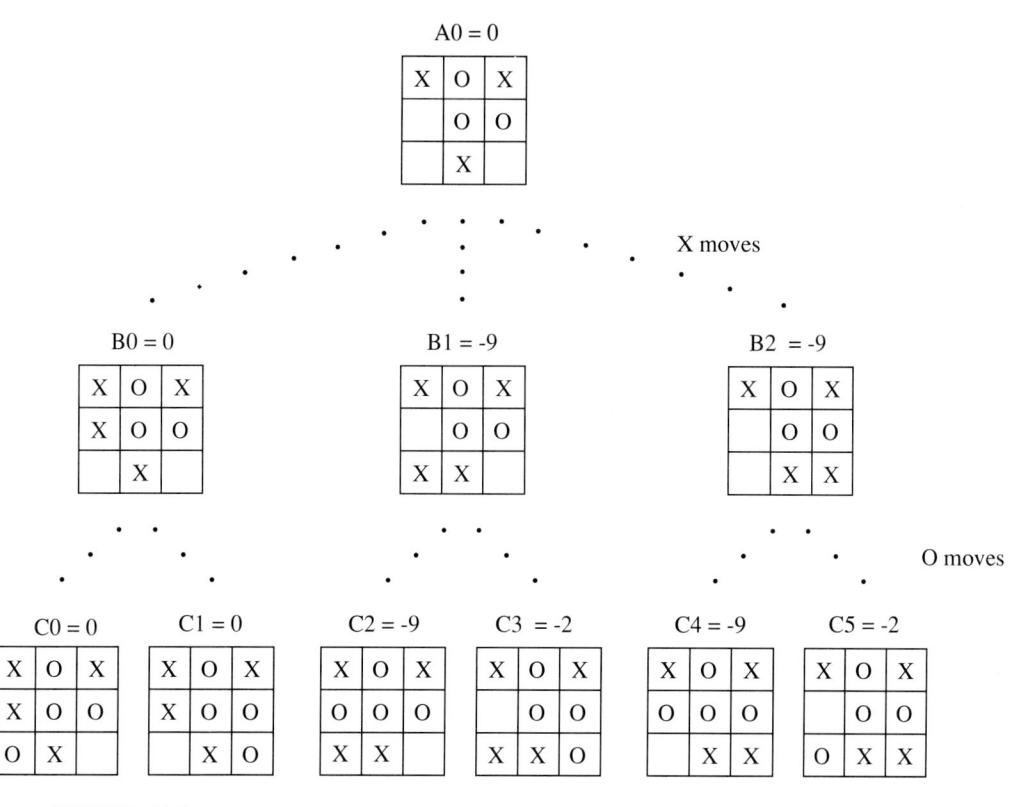

$A0 = 0$

X	O	X
	O	O
	X	

X moves

$B0 = 0$

X	O	X
X	O	O
	X	

$B1 = -9$

X	O	X
	O	O
X	X	

$B2 = -9$

X	O	X
	O	O
	X	X

O moves

$C0 = 0$

X	O	X
X	O	O
O	X	

$C1 = 0$

X	O	X
X	O	O
	X	O

$C2 = -9$

X	O	X
O	O	O
	X	

$C3 = -2$

X	O	X
	O	O
X	X	O

$C4 = -9$

X	O	X
O	O	O
	X	

$C5 = -2$

X	O	X
	O	O
O	X	X

FIGURE 14.6
Result of applying minimax to the entire tree.

14.2 IMPLEMENTING A TIC-TAC-TOE GAME USING MINIMAX

Now we are ready to actually implement the tic-tac-toe game we have been discussing.

14.2.1 Declarations

We will represent a game board as a structure with two slots:

```
(defstruct board
   squares                ; current board configuration
   player)                ; player who gets to move
```

The **SQUARES** slot will hold a vector which contains the current board pieces. The vector will represent the two-dimensional game board in row-major order as shown in Figure 14.7. Each cell in the vector will contain a symbol representing

0	1	2
3	4	5
6	7	8

FIGURE 14.7
Vector indices of the cells in a three-by-three tic-tac-toe board.

one of the players, or **NIL** if the corresponding square is not occupied. We are representing the board as a one-dimensional rather than a two-dimensional array because it simplifies most of the board manipulating functions we need to write.

Our program will also use the following four global variables:

```
(defvar *board-width* 3 "Width of a tic-tac-toe board")

(defvar *look-ahead* 3 "Number of plies to look ahead")

(defvar *min-player* 'o "The minimizing player")

(defvar *max-player* 'x "The maximizing player")
```

The width of the board can be varied by changing *BOARD-WIDTH*. Thus, we can play tic-tac-toe on any size board we like. The number of plies in the game tree will be controlled by the variable *LOOK-AHEAD*. More look-ahead should produce better moves, but it will also make our program run more slowly. We have also defined the variables *MIN-PLAYER* and *MAX-PLAYER* so that we do not have to hard-wire the symbols O and X into our code.

We will need the following two macros in functions we write later:

```
(defmacro iterate (name bindings &body body)
  `(labels ((,name ,(mapcar #'first bindings)
             ,@body))
     (,name ,@(mapcar #'second bindings))))

(defmacro select (selector-form &rest clauses)
  (let ((selector (gensym "SELECTOR-")))
    `(let ((,selector ,selector-form))
       ;; only eval the SELECTOR-FORM once!
       (cond ,@(mapcar #'(lambda (clause)
                           `((equal ,(car clause) ,selector)
                             ,@(cdr clause)))
                       clauses)))))
```

Each of these macros is described in detail in Chapter 11. We must list them *before* they are used so that the compiler can correctly expand calls to them when we compile all of our code.

Here is one of the functions which uses **SELECT**:

```
(defun opponent (player)
  (select player
    ((*min-player* *max-player*)
    (*max-player* *min-player*)
    (nil nil))))
```

OPPONENT expects a player or **NIL** as an argument, and returns the opponent of that player or **NIL**.

14.2.2 A Heuristic Tic-Tac-Toe Board Ranker

Now we are ready to write the actual board evaluator. [Ric83] suggests the following heuristic for ranking tic-tac-toe boards with respect to a player P:

> One point for each row in which P could win and in which P already has one piece, plus two points for each such row in which P has two pieces.

We can state this rule more concisely as:

> Assign N points for each row in which P has N pieces and can still win.

In each of the above rules, *row* really refers to a row, column, or a diagonal. Using this rule, the board shown in Figure 14.8 would have a rank of -4 when scored with respect to O (the minimizing player), and a rank of 2 when scored with respect to X (the maximizing player).

Our board ranking function is called **RANK-BOARD**:

```
;;; Rank a board with respect to the player who will choose
;;; that board.
;;; *MAX-PLAYER* wants positive scores.
;;; *MIN-PLAYER* wants negative scores.
(defun rank-board (board)
  (funcall (if (eq (board-player board) *min-player*)
               #'+                          ; adjust sign for
               #'-)                         ; the CHOOSING player
           (apply #'+ (mapcar #'(lambda (sequence)
                                  (rank-possible-win
                                    board
                                    sequence))
                              (possible-tic-tac-toe-wins
                                *board-width*)))))
```

FIGURE 14.8
Sample tic-tac-toe board.

`RANK-BOARD` generates a list of *all* possible winning sequences for a given size board using `POSSIBLE-TIC-TAC-TOE-WINS`. For example, a three-by-three board has the following winning sequences:

```
Lisp> (possible-tic-tac-toe-wins 3)
((0 1 2) (3 4 5) (6 7 8) (0 3 6) (1 4 7) (2 5 8) (0 4 8)
 (2 4 6))
```

The function `RANK-POSSIBLE-WIN` implements our heuristic ranking rule. For each such sequence, `RANK-POSSIBLE-WIN` is called to assign a rank to that sequence for a particular board. For example, the sequence (0 1 2) ranked against the board in Figure 14.8 has a value of 0 to either X or O since neither player can win with this sequence. However, the sequence (0 3 6) has a value of 1 to X, and the sequence (3 4 5) has a value of 2 to player O.

`RANK-BOARD` collects the scores of every possible winning sequence into a list using `MAPCAR`, and then applies `#'+` to the list to sum the scores. The sign of the total score is then adjusted so that the score will be negative for the minimizing player and positive for the maximizing player. Remember that we rank the board with respect to the player who will *choose* the board, not the player who will move from it.

In order to write the other functions which `RANK-BOARD` uses, we will first define the function `ENUMERATE`, which was presented as an exercise in Chapter 3. `ENUMERATE` accepts a starting number, an increment, and a count as arguments and returns the corresponding list of enumerated numbers:

```
Lisp> (enumerate 1 1 5)
(1 2 3 4 5)

Lisp> (enumerate 0 2 5)
(0 2 4 6 8)

Lisp> (enumerate 0 10 7)
(0 10 20 30 40 50 60)
```

Here is one possible definition of `ENUMERATE`:

```
(defun enumerate (start increment count)
  (do ((n start (+ n increment))
       (l nil (cons n l))
       (i count (1- i)))
      ((= i 0) (nreverse l))))
```

The `DO` loop maintains two counters and collects the desired sequence into the list L in reverse order. The list is reversed and returned when the iteration completes. `ENUMERATE` is heavily used by `POSSIBLE-TIC-TAC-TOE-WINS` to generate winning sequences of numbers:

```
(defun possible-tic-tac-toe-wins (*board-width*)
  (append
    (mapcar #'(lambda (n)                      ; across
                (enumerate n 1 *board-width*))
            (enumerate 0 *board-width* *board-width*))
    (mapcar #'(lambda (n)                      ; down
                (enumerate n *board-width* *board-width*))
            (enumerate 0 1 *board-width*))
    (list (enumerate 0 (1+ *board-width*) *board-width*)
          (enumerate (1- *board-width*)      ; diagonals
                     (1- *board-width*)
                     *board-width*))))
```

A winning sequence consists of all the squares in a row, column, or diagonal. The first call to MAPCAR in POSSIBLE-TIC-TAC-TOE-WINS generates a list of all winning rows by enumerating the squares in the first column, and then for each of these enumerating each square which follows in the row. Similarly, all the winning column and diagonal sequences are generated, and all these lists are appended together to produce a list of all possible wins.

RANK-POSSIBLE-WIN expects a board and a potentially winning sequence of squares. It uses our heuristic scoring rule to rank the possibility of winning with the given sequence:

```
(defun rank-possible-win (board squares)
  (iterate loopy ((rest squares)
                  (number-of-occupied-squares 0)
                  (no-opponents? t))
    (if (null rest)
        (if no-opponents?
            (if (= number-of-occupied-squares
                   *board-width*)             ; a win?
                (winning-score board)
                number-of-occupied-squares)
            0)
        (let ((square (svref (board-squares board)
                             (car rest))))
          (loopy (cdr rest)
                 (+ number-of-occupied-squares
                    (if (eq square (opponent (board-player
                                               board)))
                        1
                        0))
                 (and no-opponents?
                      (not (eq square (board-player
                                        board)))))))))
```

```
(defun winning-score (board)
  (length (board-squares board)))
```

RANK-POSSIBLE-WIN uses the **ITERATE** macro we wrote in Chapter 11 to iterate over each square in the list of **SQUARES**. As it examines each square, it keeps track of how many squares the choosing player occupies in the sequence, and whether or not the choosing player's opponent occupies a blocking square. Once every square has been examined, the number of occupied squares is returned as the rank, unless an opponent's piece was seen, in which case 0 is returned because a win is not possible. As a special case, the number returned by the function **WINNING-SCORE** is returned if every square in the sequence is occupied by the choosing player. The winning score is much higher than any nonwinning score so that a board in which several *possible* wins exist cannot be ranked more highly than any board in which one or more actual wins exist.

In order for the computer to know when the game has ended, we will also define a function named **TERMINAL-BOARD-P**. This function accepts a board and returns the player who wins with this board, the symbol **:TIE** if the game is a draw, or **NIL** if no one has won and the game can still continue:

```
;;; Return *MAX-PLAYER*, *MIN-PLAYER*, :TIE, or NIL if the
;;; game can continue.
(defun terminal-board-p (board)
  (or (winning-board-p board)
      (if (position nil (board-squares board))
          nil
          :tie)))

(defun winning-board-p (board)
  (dolist (possible-win (possible-tic-tac-toe-wins
                          *board-width*))
    (iterate loopy ((rest (cdr possible-win))
                    (player (svref (board-squares board)
                                   (car possible-win))))
      (if (null rest)
          (unless (null player)
            (return-from winning-board-p player))
          (loopy (cdr rest)
                 (if (eq player (svref (board-squares board)
                                       (car rest)))
                     player
                     nil))))))
```

TERMINAL-BOARD-P returns immediately with the name of a player if **WINNING-BOARD-P** finds a win. If not, then we call the sequence function **POSITION** to see if any free squares still exist on the board. If a free square is found, then `NIL` is returned to indicate that play may continue, otherwise we return the symbol `:TIE`.

`WINNING-BOARD-P` iterates over all possible winning sequences using `DOLIST`. `ITERATE` is used to examine each square within a particular sequence. If the player in the first square of a sequence also occupies each succeeding square, then that player has a win and so we abnormally transfer control out of the entire call to `WINNING-BOARD-P` using `RETURN-FROM`. If a winner is not found, then the `DOLIST` continues. If no winning sequence is found, then the `DOLIST`, and thus `WINNING-BOARD-P`, returns `NIL`.

Problem. Write a ranker for an N-by-N checkerboard. Your ranker should use at least the following heuristics to rank a board with respect to player P:

- 1 point for each square P occupies.
- −1 point for each square P's opponent occupies.
- 1 point for each king that P has.
- −1 point for each king that P's opponent has.

What other heuristics do you think might be useful when ranking checkerboards?

Problem. Write the equivalent of `TERMINAL-BOARD-P` for an N-by-N checkerboard.

14.2.3 Generating and Searching the Game Tree

Now that we can rank game boards and detect the end of a game, we are ready to generate and search a game tree. We will use lists to represent game trees. The car of a list will contain the root of a tree, while the cdr of the list will be a list of children. Of course, the list of children may contain subtrees. Thus, the tree

```
(A0 (B0 ((C0)
         (C1)))
    (B1 ((C2)
         (C3)))
    (B2 ((C4)
         (C5))))
```

represents the game tree in Figure 14.3. We will manipulate trees with the following functions:

```
(defun make-tree (root children)
  (cons root children))
```

```
(defun make-leaf (node)
  (make-tree node nil))

(defun tree-parent (tree)
  (car tree))

(defun tree-children (tree)
  (cdr tree))

(defun leafp (tree)
  (null (tree-children tree)))
```

Notice that a leaf is just a tree with a root and no children.

The function GROW-TREE will create a game tree emanating from a particular board:

```
(defun grow-tree (board depth)
  (if (= depth 0)
      (make-leaf board)
      (make-tree board
                 (mapcar #'(lambda (child)
                             (grow-tree child (1- depth)))
                         (adjacent-boards board)))))
```

The DEPTH argument to GROW-TREE specifies the number of plies to generate in the tree. When DEPTH reaches 0, we return a leaf containing the current board. If DEPTH is greater than 0, then a tree is created with the current board at the root, and all of the subtrees which are reachable in one move as children.

The function ADJACENT-BOARDS accepts a game board and returns a list of all game boards which are accessible in one move by the current player:

```
(defun adjacent-boards (board)
  (if (terminal-board-p board)
      nil
      (do ((i 0 (1+ i))
           (moves nil (if (null (svref (board-squares board)
                                       i))
                          (cons (make-move board i) moves)
                          moves)))
          ((= i (length (board-squares board))) moves))))

(defun make-move (from-board square)
  (let ((new-squares (make-array (length (board-squares
                                           from-board)))))))
```

```
       (dotimes (i (length new-squares))
         (setf (svref new-squares i) (svref (board-squares
                                             from-board) i)))
       (setf (svref new-squares square) (board-player
                                         from-board))
       (make-board :squares new-squares
                   :player (opponent (board-player
                                      from-board)))))
```

If the board is terminal, then no further moves are possible. If the board is not terminal, then a `DO` loop iterates over each square on the board, creating a new board to represent a move every time an empty square is found in the current board. Once every square on the current board has been examined, the list of new boards is returned. `MAKE-MOVE` creates a copy of the board it is given, with the current player added to the given square. The player for the new board is also changed to the opponent of the previous player.

Next we will define the minimax algorithm:

```
;;; Return two values: a rank and a board
(defun minimax (tree)
  (if (leafp tree)
      (values (rank-board (tree-parent tree))
              (tree-parent tree))
      (let* ((child-ranks (mapcar #'(lambda (subtree)
                                      (minimax subtree))
                                  (tree-children tree)))
             (best-rank (apply (if (eq (board-player
                                        (tree-parent tree))
                                       *min-player*)
                                   #'min
                                   #'max)
                               child-ranks)))
        (values best-rank
                (tree-parent (elt (tree-children tree)
                                  (position best-rank
                                            child-ranks)))))))
```

Our `MINIMAX` function accepts a game tree and returns two values: the rank of the board that should be moved to, and the board itself. The base case of `MINIMAX` checks to see if the tree it is given is a leaf. If so, it calls the board ranker on the leaf board and returns the rank and the board.

If the tree is not a leaf, then `MINIMAX` is applied to all of the children of the tree, and the ranks assigned to the boards at the root of each subtree are collected into a list using `MAPCAR`. Notice that the second value returned by the recursive call to `MINIMAX` is ignored since we are only interested in the ranks at this point.

The best rank is then chosen from the list of ranks by applying either `MAX` or `MIN` to list, depending upon which player will be choosing the child boards. The best rank and the corresponding board are then returned as the values of `MINIMAX`.

Problem. Write a move generator for an *N*-by-*N* checkerboard.

14.2.4 Putting It All Together

Now that we have created all of the major functions in our tic-tac-toe game, we need to glue them all together with a top-level function and a crude user interface:

```
(defun ttt (&optional (first-player *max-player*))
  (format t
          "~&The computer will play ~A, You will play ~A.~%"
          *min-player*
          *max-player*)
  (let ((initial-board (make-board
                         :squares (make-array
                                    (expt *board-width* 2))
                         :player first-player)))
    (iterate loopy ((board initial-board))
      (print-board board)
      (let ((board-status (terminal-board-p board)))
        (select board-status
          (*min-player* (format t "The computer wins.~%"))
          (*max-player* (format t "You win.~%"))
          (:tie (format t "The game is a draw."))
          (nil (loopy (if (eq (board-player board)
                              *min-player*)
                          (computer-move board)
                          (human-move board)))))))))
```

`TTT` starts a tic-tac-toe game in which the user may optionally specify which player should go first. The computer will be the minimizing player, while the user will be the maximizing player. After the initial game board is created, each player is given a chance to move until someone wins or the game is a tie. The computer moves with the following function:

```
(defun computer-move (board)
  (format t "Computer moves. Searching...")
  (let ((game-tree (grow-tree board *look-ahead*)))
    (multiple-value-bind (rank board)
                         (minimax game-tree)
      ;; Avoid compiler warnings about unused var
      (declare (ignore rank))
```

```
     (format t "done.~%")
     board)))
```

Given the current game board, a game tree is grown with the appropriate number of plies, and then **MINIMAX** is run on the tree to determine which board the computer should choose.

The function **HUMAN-MOVE** asks the user for the number of the square to which he wants to move:

```
(defun human-move (board)
  (format
   t
   "Your move. Please enter the number of a square: ")
  (let ((square (read)))
    (if (null (svref (board-squares board) square))
        (progn (setf (svref (board-squares board)
                            square)
                     *max-player*)
               (setf (board-player board)
                     (opponent (board-player board)))
               board)
        (progn
          (format t "Square ~A is occupied. Try again.~%"
                    square)
          (human-move board)))))
```

The square number is read using **READ**, and then checked to see if the square is actually free. If so, then the board is destructively modified to represent the effect of the move, and then returned. However, if the user tries to enter the number of a square which is already occupied, then an error message is printed and **HUMAN-MOVE** is tail-recursively called to ask for a new move.

The only remaining function is the board printer:

```
(defun print-board (board)
  (labels ((divider ()
             (dotimes (i *board-width* (format t "|~%"))
               (format t "|-----"))))
    (terpri)
    (divider)
    (dotimes (i (length (board-squares board)))
      (let ((square (svref (board-squares board) i)))
        (format t "| ~A " (if (null square) " " square)))
      (when (= (mod (1+ i) *board-width*) 0)
        (format t "|~%")
        (divider)))))
```

PRINT-BOARD prints out each row of the board separated by a dividing line.

Here is a sample run of the complete program:

```
Lisp> (ttt)
The computer will play O, You will play X.

   |-----|-----|-----|
   |     |     |     |
   |-----|-----|-----|
   |     |     |     |
   |-----|-----|-----|
   |     |     |     |
   |-----|-----|-----|
Your move. Please enter the number of a square: 0

   |-----|-----|-----|
   |  X  |     |     |
   |-----|-----|-----|
   |     |     |     |
   |-----|-----|-----|
   |     |     |     |
   |-----|-----|-----|
Computer moves. Searching...done.

   |-----|-----|-----|
   |  X  |     |     |
   |-----|-----|-----|
   |     |  O  |     |
   |-----|-----|-----|
   |     |     |     |
   |-----|-----|-----|
Your move. Please enter the number of a square: 8

   |-----|-----|-----|
   |  X  |     |     |
   |-----|-----|-----|
   |     |  O  |     |
   |-----|-----|-----|
   |     |     |  X  |
   |-----|-----|-----|
Computer moves. Searching...done.

   |-----|-----|-----|
   |  X  |     |     |
   |-----|-----|-----|
   |     |  O  |     |
   |-----|-----|-----|
   |     |  O  |  X  |
   |-----|-----|-----|
```

```
Your move. Please enter the number of a square: 1
|-----|-----|-----|
|  X  |  X  |     |
|-----|-----|-----|
|     |  O  |     |
|-----|-----|-----|
|     |  O  |  X  |
|-----|-----|-----|
Computer moves. Searching...done.
|-----|-----|-----|
|  X  |  X  |  O  |
|-----|-----|-----|
|     |  O  |     |
|-----|-----|-----|
|     |  O  |  X  |
|-----|-----|-----|
Your move. Please enter the number of a square: 6
|-----|-----|-----|
|  X  |  X  |  O  |
|-----|-----|-----|
|     |  O  |     |
|-----|-----|-----|
|  X  |  O  |  X  |
|-----|-----|-----|
Computer moves. Searching...done.
|-----|-----|-----|
|  X  |  X  |  O  |
|-----|-----|-----|
|  O  |  O  |     |
|-----|-----|-----|
|  X  |  O  |  X  |
|-----|-----|-----|
Your move. Please enter the number of a square: 5
|-----|-----|-----|
|  X  |  X  |  O  |
|-----|-----|-----|
|  O  |  O  |  X  |
|-----|-----|-----|
|  X  |  O  |  X  |
|-----|-----|-----|
The game is a draw.
NIL
```

We now have a general framework for playing many more games than just tic-tac-toe. For example, the techniques we have used in this program could also be used to develop a checker or chess playing program.

Problem. Write a checker-playing program using the board evaluator, end game detector, and move generator you wrote earlier. Reuse as many parts of the tic-tac-toe program as you can.

Problem. Play the example game with a look-ahead of two plies rather than three. Does the program still play as well? Explain.

Problem. Try putting an X in square zero of a four-by-four tic-tac-toe board and then let the computer play with two-ply look-ahead. Repeat with three-ply look-ahead. Does the computer make the same move each time? Which game is better? Explain.

Problem. Read in an AI text such as [Ric83] about how to add *alpha-beta* cutoffs to the minimax algorithm. Modify our `MINIMAX` function to incorporate alpha-beta cutoffs.

Problem. As our program is currently written, it regenerates parts of the game tree which have already been created. Replace `GROW-TREE` with a function named `EXTEND-TREE` which extends an existing tree to to a specified depth. Change the tic-tac-toe program to use `EXTEND-TREE` rather than `GROW-TREE`.

Problem. If your Lisp implementation supports graphics, replace our crude user interface with a more pleasant visual one.

CHAPTER 15

MISSIONARIES AND CANNIBALS, BACKTRACKING SEARCH

In this chapter we will learn about streams and backtracking search while solving the missionaries and cannibals problem.

15.1 THE PROBLEM: MISSIONARIES AND CANNIBALS

Three missionaries and three cannibals are on the left side of a river and want to get to the other side. There is one boat available and it is capable of holding either one or two people. However, the number of cannibals on one side of the river or in the boat may never exceed the number of missionaries, lest the cannibals devour the missionaries. Find a sequence of river crossings which will safely move all six people and the boat to the other side of the river while satisfying all of the above constraints.

15.2 A SOLUTION TO THE PROBLEM

15.2.1 A Backtracking Search Algorithm

The *search space* for this problem may be viewed as a tree, with the initial state, all six people, and the boat on the left side of the river at the root. Every node in the tree represents a particular *state* of the problem (the exact location of all six people and the boat), while every branch from a node represents a possible legal move from that node. There are many illegal moves which are not represented by the tree. For example, from the initial state we could try to move two missionaries to the other bank, but that would leave three cannibals and one missionary alone, thus violating one of the problem constraints. Our objective is to find a sequence of legal moves from the initial state to a leaf in the tree which represents the *goal state*, in which all of the people and the boat have been moved to the other bank. Figure 15.1 depicts a portion of the search space.

We can solve this problem with a *backtracking search* which starts from the initial node, trying a potential move to a legal state. If this new state is the

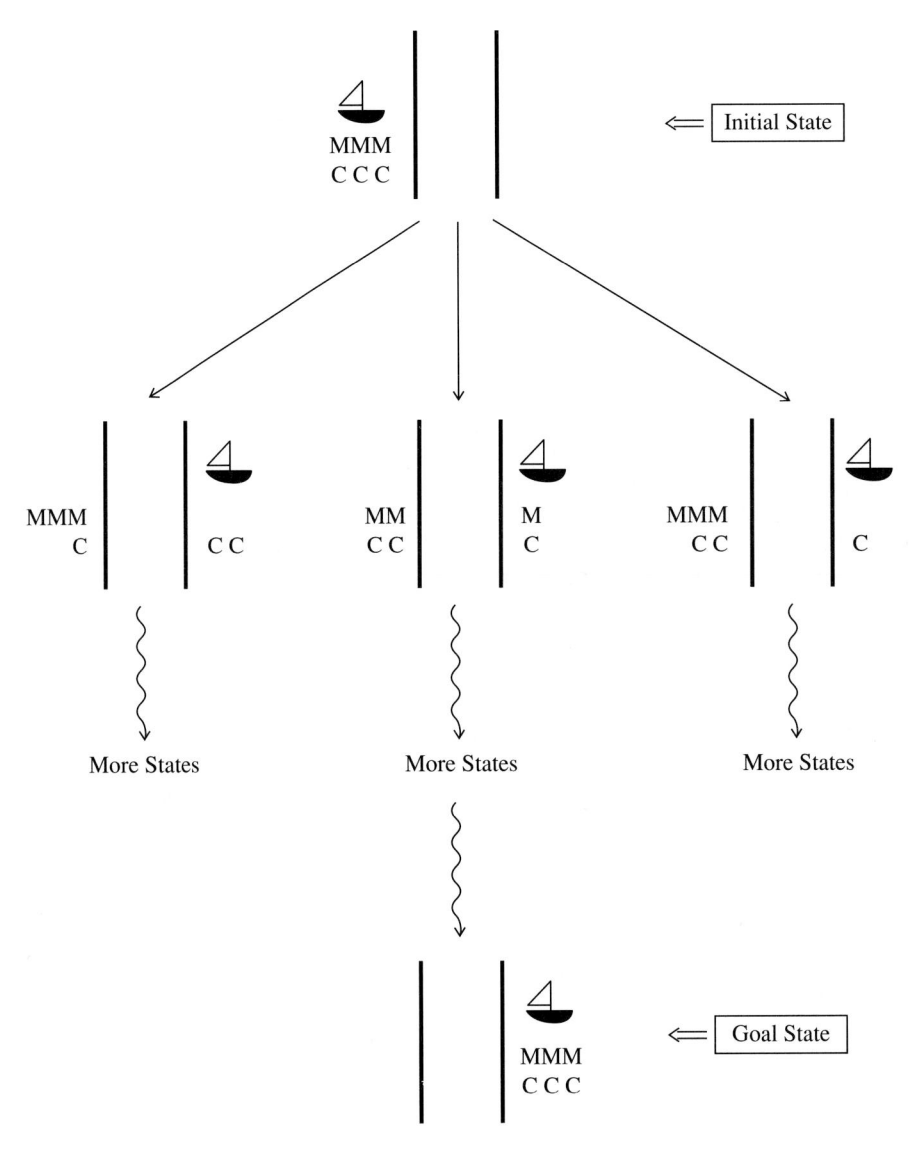

FIGURE 15.1
The search space of the missionaries and cannibals problem.

goal state, then we are done and need only return the path we took to arrive there; however, if the state we arrive at is not the goal state, then we need to recursively repeat the above procedure, starting from the current state. If there are no moves possible from the current state, we have reached a dead end and must have made an incorrect move earlier. Thus, we should *backtrack* to the state which brought us to the current state, and try the next available legal move from that state. If no more legal moves are available, then we backtrack once again, etc. In the worst case we will repeatedly backtrack all the way up to the initial node, only to find that there are no more legal moves from there which do not at some point terminate at a dead end. If we ever reach this point, then the problem is unsolvable. We must also be sure to never visit a state which we have already visited, or we will enter an infinite loop, traversing a *cycle* in what has become a graph rather than a tree.

We will generalize the statement of our problem by making the initial number of people, the boat capacity, and the starting bank parameters in our solution. The main function in our program is called **SOLVE** and it should accept these three parameters as optional arguments which default to the values in our original problem statement. **SOLVE** will then search for a solution, printing out a readable "map" of the sequence of crossings which represents the solution, or a failure message if no solution was found. Thus, **SOLVE** might print the following:

```
Solution found in 11 crossings

            \____/ |         |
    MIS MIS MIS    |         |
    CAN CAN CAN    |         |


                   |         | \____/
        MIS MIS    |         | MIS
        CAN CAN    |         | CAN


            \____/ |         |
    MIS MIS MIS    |         |
        CAN CAN    |         | CAN


                   |         |
    MIS MIS MIS    |         | \____/
                   |         | CAN CAN CAN


            \____/ |         |
    MIS MIS MIS    |         |
            CAN    |         | CAN CAN


                   |         | \____/
            MIS    |         | MIS MIS
            CAN    |         | CAN CAN
```

```
          \____/  |              |
        MIS MIS   |              |  MIS
        CAN CAN   |              |  CAN


                  |              |  \____/
                  |              |  MIS MIS MIS
        CAN CAN   |              |  CAN


           \____/ |              |
                  |              |  MIS MIS MIS
      CAN CAN CAN |              |


                  |              |  \____/
                  |              |  MIS MIS MIS
              CAN |              |  CAN CAN


           \____/ |              |
              MIS |              |  MIS MIS
              CAN |              |  CAN CAN


                  |              |  \____/
                  |              |  MIS MIS MIS
                  |              |  CAN CAN CAN
```

15.2.2 Data Structures and Declarations

The first step in implementing our search algorithm is to decide upon a representation for states. Many representations are possible, but we will represent a state as a structure consisting of three slots:

```
(defstruct state
  bank      ; bank where the boat is (either :LEFT or :RIGHT)
  mis       ; number of missionaries on the current bank
  can)      ; number of cannibals on the current bank
```

A state in our problem is uniquely determined by the number of missionaries and cannibals on a given bank of the river, since the number of people on the other bank can be deduced from the total number of people in the problem. At this point we might want to start defining functions which can manipulate states; however, we will first list a few global variables in our program:

```
(defvar *num-of-each* 3
  "The number of missionaries or cannibals in the problem")
```

```
(defvar *boat-capacity* 2
  "How many people the boat can hold")

(defvar *start-bank* :left
  ":LEFT or :RIGHT to indicate bank everyone starts from")
```

The initial values of these three variables may be passed as optional arguments to the main function **SOLVE**. However, these variables are used by so many parts of our program that it would become cumbersome to continue passing them around as arguments between functions. Thus, we use **DEFVAR** to declare that all bindings of these variables and all references to them will be *special*. Thus, we can *dynamically* bind the variables upon entering **SOLVE**, and refer to those dynamic bindings with special references in our program. Since we bind the variables upon entering **SOLVE** we could recursively call **SOLVE** from within itself. Notice that this would not be possible if we used **SETF** to assign values to the variables upon entering **SOLVE**.

We must also define any macros before they are used in our program. The iteration macro **ITERATE** which we wrote in Chapter 11 will be used later in the program:

```
(defmacro iterate (name bindings &body body)
  `(labels ((,name ,(mapcar #'first bindings)
              ,@body))
     (,name ,@(mapcar #'second bindings))))
```

Now that we have all the declarations required by our program out of the way, we can proceed to define state-manipulating functions.

15.2.3 State Manipulation Functions

In this section we will write some of the state manipulation functions which we will need to perform a state space search. We at least need to know what state to start from and when we have reached the goal state. Thus, we define the following functions:

```
;;; Give the number of missionaries or cannibals
;;; on one bank, return the number of those
;;; people on the opposite-bank.
(defun opposite-bank-count (current-bank-count)
  (- *num-of-each* current-bank-count))

(defun opposite-bank (bank)
  (ecase bank
    (:left :right)
```

```
             (:right :left)))

(defun make-initial-state ()
  (make-state :bank *start-bank*
              :mis *num-of-each*
              :can *num-of-each*))

(defun goal-state-p (state)
  (and (eq (state-bank state) (opposite-bank *start-bank*))
       (= (state-mis state) *num-of-each*)
       (= (state-can state) *num-of-each*)))
```

We can create the root node in the search tree by calling **MAKE-INITIAL-STATE** and we can determine if we have reached the goal using **GOAL-STATE-P**.

In order to go from the current state to an adjacent state, we must introduce the idea of a *move*. We can represent a move from a state as a pair of numbers describing the number of missionaries and the number of cannibals to move from the current bank to the opposite bank using the boat. Thus, there are 16 possible moves from the initial state which range from moving no one—(0, 0)—to moving everyone—(3, 3). However, most of these moves are illegal, since they will violate one or more constraints in the problem specification. Thus, given a state and the number of people to move from that state, we want to know if we can legally perform a move:

```
(defun legal-move-p (from move-mis move-can)
  ;; Add new people to the other bank
  (let* ((new-mis (+ move-mis (opposite-bank-count
                                (state-mis from))))
         (new-can (+ move-can (opposite-bank-count
                                (state-can from))))
         (remaining-mis (opposite-bank-count new-mis))
         (remaining-can (opposite-bank-count new-can)))
    ;; avoid identity moves
    (and (not (and (= move-mis 0) (= move-can 0)))
         ;; don't overload boat
         (<= (+ move-mis move-can) *boat-capacity*)
         ;; safe new bank?
         (or (= new-mis 0) (>= new-mis new-can))
         ;; safe old bank?
         (or (= remaining-mis 0)
             (>= remaining-mis remaining-can)))))
```

The predicate **LEGAL-MOVE-P** checks to be sure that we are not overloading the boat and that the cannibals will not be able to eat the missionaries. If all of the conditions are satisfied, then the predicate returns **T**.

Once we have found a legal move to an adjacent state, we often want to create the new state which results from the move:

```
(defun make-move (from num-mis num-can)
  (make-state :bank (opposite-bank (state-bank from))
              :mis (+ num-mis (opposite-bank-count
                                (state-mis from)))
              :can (+ num-can (opposite-bank-count
                                (state-can from)))))
```

Finally, we want to have a graphic representation for printed states so that we can print our final solution out nicely:

```
(defun print-state (state)
  (flet ((print-row (num-people-on-left person-string)
           (format t
                   "~3T~V@{~A ~:*~}~* ~V@{~A ~:*~}~
                   |     | ~3:*~V@{~2*~A ~3:*~}~%"
                   (opposite-bank-count num-people-on-left)
                   "  "
                   num-people-on-left
                   person-string))
         (get-people-count (state accessor bank)
           (funcall (if (eq (state-bank state) bank)
                        #'identity
                        #'opposite-bank-count)
                    (funcall accessor state))))
    (if (eq (state-bank state) :left)
        ;; Note that we have to escapify
        ;; backslashes in strings because
        ;; backslash *is* the escape character.
        (format t "~%~VT \\____/ |        |~%"
                (* 4 (1- *num-of-each*)))
        (format t "~%~VT  |        | \\____/~%"
                (* 4 *num-of-each*)))
    (print-row (get-people-count state #'state-mis :left)
               "MIS")
    (print-row (get-people-count state #'state-can :left)
               "CAN")))
```

Here is how our printer prints the initial state:

```
Lisp> (print-state (make-initial-state))

         \____/ |        |
   MIS MIS MIS  |        |
   CAN CAN CAN  |        |
NIL
```

PRINT-STATE is a bit complicated, especially because it makes extensive use of some rather obscure **FORMAT** features. If you are interested in finding out what the format strings in **PRINT-STATE** mean, consult the Common Lisp manual. They are used here to hint at the power and complexity of **FORMAT** as well as its potential for confusion.

15.2.4 A Backtracking Search

Now that we can manipulate states, we need to somehow drive our search procedure. Given a state, we would like to know all of the adjacent states, since any solution must go through one of them (or more than one if there are multiple solution paths). Thus, given a state, we would like to be able to generate a list of all states which can be reached from that state in exactly one move:

```
(defun make-adjacent-state-stream (from)
  (iterate count-mis ((num-mis (min *boat-capacity*
                                    (state-mis from))))
    (if (< num-mis 0)
        nil
        (iterate count-can ((num-can (min *boat-capacity*
                                          (state-can from))))
          (if (< num-can 0)
              (count-mis (1- num-mis))
              (if (legal-move-p from num-mis num-can)
                  (cons (make-move from num-mis num-can)
                        (count-can (1- num-can)))
                  (count-can (1- num-can)))))))))
```

MAKE-ADJACENT-STATE-STREAM iterates over all possible moves, collecting only the legal ones and returning a list of them:

```
Lisp> (make-adjacent-state-stream (make-initial-state))
(#S(STATE BANK :RIGHT MIS 1 CAN 1)
 #S(STATE BANK :RIGHT MIS 0 CAN 2)
 #S(STATE BANK :RIGHT MIS 0 CAN 1))
```

Now that we can look one level ahead to all possible moves from our current state, we are ready to write **SEARCH-FOR-SOLUTION**, which will actually implement a backtracking search. **SEARCH-FOR-SOLUTION** expects a list of states which represents a partial path from the initial state to some point in the middle of the search space, with the current state at the front of the list and the initial state at the end of the list. **SEARCH-FOR-SOLUTION** will return a new path which extends the argument path all the way to the goal state, or **:FAIL** if no such extension is possible:

```
(defun search-for-solution (path-so-far)
```

```
      (dolist (next-state (make-adjacent-state-stream
                            (car path-so-far)) :fail)
        (let ((extended-path (cons next-state path-so-far)))
          (unless (seen-state-p next-state path-so-far)
            (if (goal-state-p next-state)
                (return extended-path)
                (let ((solution-path
                        (search-for-solution extended-path)))
                  (unless (eq solution-path :fail)
                    (return solution-path)))))))))

(defun seen-state-p (state seen-states)
  ;; We must use EQUALP to compare structures.
  (member state seen-states :test #'equalp))
```

We start by attempting to extend the **PATH-SO-FAR** to the first adjacent state, unless that state has already been visited, in which case we must discard it and try another adjacent state. If we have never seen the next state, then we test to see if it is the goal state. If so, then we are done and can return immediately. If not, then we recursively call **SEARCH-FOR-SOLUTION** to continue the search with our newly extended path. If the recursive search succeeds, then we are done and can return immediately. However, if the recursive search fails then we must continue trying other adjacent states until we either find a solution or run out of adjacent states. When we run out of adjacent states, then we must also return **:FAIL**.

We *backtrack* whenever a recursive call to **SEARCH-FOR-SOLUTION** fails, causing us to discard the current **NEXT-STATE** in order to consider another adjacent state. The net result is that we will either find a solution or return **:FAIL** because all potential solutions brought us to a dead end.

Finally we can write a front end to **SEARCH-FOR-SOLUTION** called **SOLVE**:

```
(defun solve (&optional (*num-of-each* 3)
                        (*boat-capacity* 2)
                        (*start-bank* :left))
  (let ((solution (search-for-solution (list
                    (make-initial-state)))))
    (if (eq solution :fail)
        (format t "No solution was found~%")
        (progn (format
                 t
                 "Solution found in ~A crossings~%"
                 (1- (length solution)))
               (mapc #'print-state (reverse solution))))))
```

SOLVE dynamically binds the three global variables defining our problem and then attempts to find a solution. If a solution is found, then it is printed using `PRINT-STATE`. The final result is a printout like the one shown at the beginning of this section in which a solution was given in 11 crossings.

15.3 STREAMS

There is one major inefficiency in our search program as it is currently written. Each time we call `MAKE-ADJACENT-STATE-STREAM`, we generate a complete list of *all* adjacent states. However, we may never use many of these states unless we need to backtrack a lot. For example, there are three possible moves from the initial state. Our search procedure will try to find a solution by trying the first move and recursively calling itself. If the first move eventually leads to the goal state, then we will never examine the other two moves, and thus computing them only wastes time and memory. Since this process occurs each time `SEARCH-FOR-SOLUTION` is called, we may needlessly compute many adjacent states. We will call this *eager* evaluation.

Instead of eagerly computing all the adjacent states, we would rather compute each state as we need it. Thus, when searching for a move from the first state we should only generate the first legal move we can find. If that move does not eventually lead to the goal state, then we will backtrack. Only then should we generate the next possible move—but how can we do this? We have to somehow remember exactly where we were in the computation of adjacent states so that we may resume that computation at a later time if we decide that we need more information. Delaying a computation until we are sure that we will need its result is called *lazy* evaluation.

In order to solve our problem, it helps to view `MAKE-ADJACENT-STATE-STREAM` as a producer of *streams*. So far streams and lists appear to be identical. However, we can formalize the notion of a stream as any sequence of objects. We can lazily compute adjacent states if we can invent a representation for streams which only computes elements as we need them. Before we do this, we will first separate the concept of a stream from its implementation by defining some stream primitives.

15.3.1 We Can Think of Lists as Eager Streams

Here are some simple stream primitives which are defined in terms of lists:

```
(defun make-empty-stream ()
  nil)

(defun empty-stream-p (stream)
  (null stream))

(defun make-stream (next rest)
  (cons next rest))
```

```
(defun stream-next (stream)
  (car stream))

(defun stream-rest (stream)
  (cdr stream))
```

These primitives allow us to write our programs in terms of streams without having to know that they are implemented in terms of lists. For example, here is a simple stream generator:

```
Lisp> (defun n-stream (n)
        "Return a stream of numbers from N to 0"
        (if (< n 0)
            (make-empty-stream)
            (make-stream n (n-stream (1- n)))))
N-STREAM

Lisp> (n-stream 10)
(10 9 8 7 6 5 4 3 2 1 0)
```

Even if we change our implementation of streams to use something other than lists, functions such as **N-STREAM** should still work correctly since they rely on the defined external behavior of a stream.

15.3.2 Changing Our Implementation to Use Streams

Now that we have defined some stream primitives, we can change parts of our original solution so that they are independent of the representation of streams. First we have to change **MAKE-ADJACENT-STATE-STREAM**:

```
(defun make-adjacent-state-stream (from)
  (iterate count-mis ((num-mis (min *boat-capacity*
                                    (state-mis from))))
    (if (< num-mis 0)
        (make-empty-stream)                              ; changed
        (iterate count-can ((num-can (min *boat-capacity*
                                          (state-can from))))
          (if (< num-can 0)
              (count-mis (1- num-mis))
              (if (legal-move-p from num-mis num-can)
                  (make-stream                           ; changed
                    (make-move from num-mis num-can)
                    (count-can (1- num-can)))
                  (count-can (1- num-can))))))))
```

The changes are quite minor, replacing the list primitives `NIL` and `CONS` with their corresponding stream primitives.

Problem. Write a function which generates pairs of numbers by combining streams produced by `N-STREAM` rather than by using nested calls to `ITERATE`.

Problem. Restructure `MAKE-ADJACENT-STATE-STREAM` into two distinct pieces: a move stream generator and a move stream filter. Rather than checking for legal moves as we are generating pairs, simply generate a stream of all potential move pairs and then filter out any illegal moves, producing a new stream consisting only of valid moves. What are the advantages and disadvantages of this approach?

The only other function we have to change is `SEARCH-FOR-SOLUTION`:

```
(defun search-for-solution (path-so-far)
  (do ((stream (make-adjacent-state-stream      ; changed
                 (car path-so-far))              ; changed
               (stream-rest stream)))            ; changed
      ((empty-stream-p stream) :fail)            ; changed
    (let* ((next-state (stream-next stream))    ; changed
           (extended-path (cons next-state path-so-far)))
      (unless (seen-state-p next-state path-so-far)
        (if (goal-state-p next-state)
            (return extended-path)
            (let ((solution-path (search-for-solution
                                   extended-path)))
              (unless (eq solution-path :fail)
                (return solution-path))))))))
```

We cannot use `DOLIST` anymore because our iteration must be expressed entirely in terms of stream primitives. Other than that, the translation to streams is quite mechanical, for example replacing `NULL` by `EMPTY-STREAM-P`.

Problem. Write a macro called `DOSTREAM` to capture the idiom of stream iteration, just as `DOLIST` captures the idiom of list iteration.

Now that we have rewritten our solution, we are free to use lists to represent streams, in which case our program will behave exactly as it did before, eagerly computing all states which are adjacent to the current state. However, now we can work on implementing *lazy streams*.

15.3.3 Lazy Streams

The key to implementing a lazy stream is to only perform a computation when we are forced to do so. The term *stream* normally refers to what we are now explicitly calling a lazy stream. Recall that in Chapter 9 we saw how we could

use lexical closures to delay the evaluation of the *then* and *else* arguments to our
BRANCH primitive, later forcing the evaluation of either one or the other, but not
both. We can formalize this notion as follows:

```
(defmacro delay-evaluation (form)
  `(function (lambda () ,form)))

(defun force-evaluation (thunk)
  (funcall thunk))
```

DELAY-EVALUATION must be a macro, because the arguments to a function are always evaluated, thereby defeating our original purpose! A call to DELAY-EVALUATION will expand into an argumentless lexical closure which we will call a *thunk*.[1] We can force the evaluation of a thunk by simply calling it as a function, thereby evaluating the body of the thunk in the correct lexical environment. Here is an example of delayed evaluation:

```
Lisp> (setf thunk (let ((x 'outer-contour))
                    (delay-evaluation (print x))))
#<Interpreted-Function (LAMBDA ()
                         (PRINT X))
                       [closed over X = OUTER-CONTOUR]
                       10D063F>

Lisp> (force-evaluation thunk)

OUTER-CONTOUR                          ; printed value
OUTER-CONTOUR                          ; return value
```

Notice that we must use a lexical closure to be sure that the value of X is available when we force the evaluation of (PRINT X).

Now we can embed our delay mechanism in a new implementation of streams built upon structures:

```
(defstruct (lazy-pair (:print-function print-lazy-pair))
  next
  rest)

(defun print-lazy-pair (pair output-stream current-level)
  (when (or (not (numberp current-level))
```

---

[1] The name *thunk* was introduced by the computer language Algol, which passed arguments as thunks to implement call-by-name semantics.

```
              (not (numberp *print-level*))
              (<= current-level *print-level*))
    (format output-stream
            "#<LAZY-STREAM ~A and [promise-to-compute-more]>"
            (lazy-pair-next pair))))

(defun make-empty-stream ()
  nil)

(defun empty-stream-p (stream)
  (null stream))

(defun stream-next (stream)
  (lazy-pair-next stream))

(defmacro make-stream (next rest)
  `(make-lazy-pair :next ,next
                   :rest (delay-evaluation ,rest)))

(defun stream-rest (stream)
  (force-evaluation (lazy-pair-rest stream)))
```

A stream is now a structure with two slots. **DEFSTRUCT** allows us to specify our own function for printing **LAZY-PAIR** structures so that we can print lazy streams nicely. **PRINT-LAZY-PAIR** expects as arguments the object to be printed, an output stream (do not confuse this with the streams we are building!), and the current print level. Rather than printing out a potentially messy-looking closure as the rest of a **LAZY-STREAM**, it simply prints the message [promise-to-compute-more]. Refer to the Common Lisp manual for more details about specifying a structure-specific **PRINT** function.

Our lazy streams are quite similar to our list implementation of streams, except that **MAKE-STREAM** is a macro which delays the evaluation of its **REST** argument until it is asked for with a call to **STREAM-REST**. Notice that **MAKE-STREAM** must be a macro since the **REST** argument would already have been evaluated if it were a function.

We can test our new stream implementation with the function **N-STREAM**, but we will get very different results than before:

```
Lisp> (defun n-stream (n)
        "Return a stream of numbers from N to 0."
        (if (< n 0)
            (make-empty-stream)
            (make-stream n (n-stream (1- n)))))
N-STREAM

Lisp> (setf s (n-stream 10))
#<LAZY-STREAM 10 and [promise-to-compute-more]>
```

```
Lisp> (stream-next s)
10

Lisp> (setf s (stream-rest s))
#<LAZY-STREAM 9 and [promise-to-compute-more]>

Lisp> (stream-next s)
9
```

    Rather than computing a list of 11 numbers, `(N-STREAM 10)` computes a stream of one number with a promise to compute the remaining numbers if they are needed. The state of the iteration variable `N` is captured by the thunk stored in the `REST` slot of a `LAZY-STREAM` so that all the information needed to continue the computation is available.

    Now we can return to our original motivation for implementing lazy streams. We have already rewritten our original solution to the missionaries and cannibals problem in terms of streams, so we can simply substitute our lazy stream implementation for our eager stream implementation. The result is that our search will lazily compute adjacent nodes only as they are needed. This change may not significantly speed up the execution of `SOLVE`, but consider applying the same technique to a problem in which the branching factor at each level of the tree is much higher than it is in our current problem. In these cases, the advantages of lazy evaluation are much greater.

    Problem. Write a program to solve the Eight Queens problem described in [Ric83].

    Problem. Write a program to solve the Water Pot problem described in [Ric83].

    Problem. Generalize `SEARCH-FOR-SOLUTION` and `MAKE-ADJACENT-STATE-STREAM` so that these procedures can be used to solve other problems involving backtracking search without rewriting our generate and search procedures each time.

    Problem. Rewrite the `SIEVE` function introduced in Chapter 12 to produce a lazy stream of prime numbers. Notice that this is effectively equivalent to computing an infinite stream of primes.

    Problem. If we repeatedly force the evaluation of a thunk, then we will repeatedly perform the same computation. However, if the computation has a side effect or is time-consuming, this may not be desirable. Change the behavior of `DELAY-EVALUATION` by adding a *memoizer* so that evaluation only occurs the first time `FORCE-EVALUATION` is called on a thunk. The result of this evaluation should be saved, and future calls to `FORCE-EVALUATION` on the same thunk should immediately return the result of the first evaluation.

CHAPTER 16

DATA TYPES AND OBJECT-ORIENTED PROGRAMMING

Lisp is significantly different from languages such as C or Pascal because *data* rather than *variables* are typed. For example, in Lisp the variable `*MR-TOAD*` may have a value of any type. There is no need to restrict it to holding a specific type of data because we can determine the data type of any object at runtime. In this chapter we will examine functions which manipulate data types and how we can improve the way our functions deal with types.

16.1 THE COMMON LISP TYPE HIERARCHY

Figure 16.1 graphically depicts the Common Lisp type hierarchy. The type `T` is a *supertype* of all other types, while the type `NIL` is a *subtype* of all other types. Notice that we can extend the type hierarchy by defining our own structures. The relationship between types is important because functions often will behave correctly only when passed values which are of specific types. For example, most numeric functions will produce reasonable results when passed any kind of number:

```
Lisp> (sqrt -1)
;; a complex number with real part = 0, imaginary = 1
#C(0.0 1.0)
```

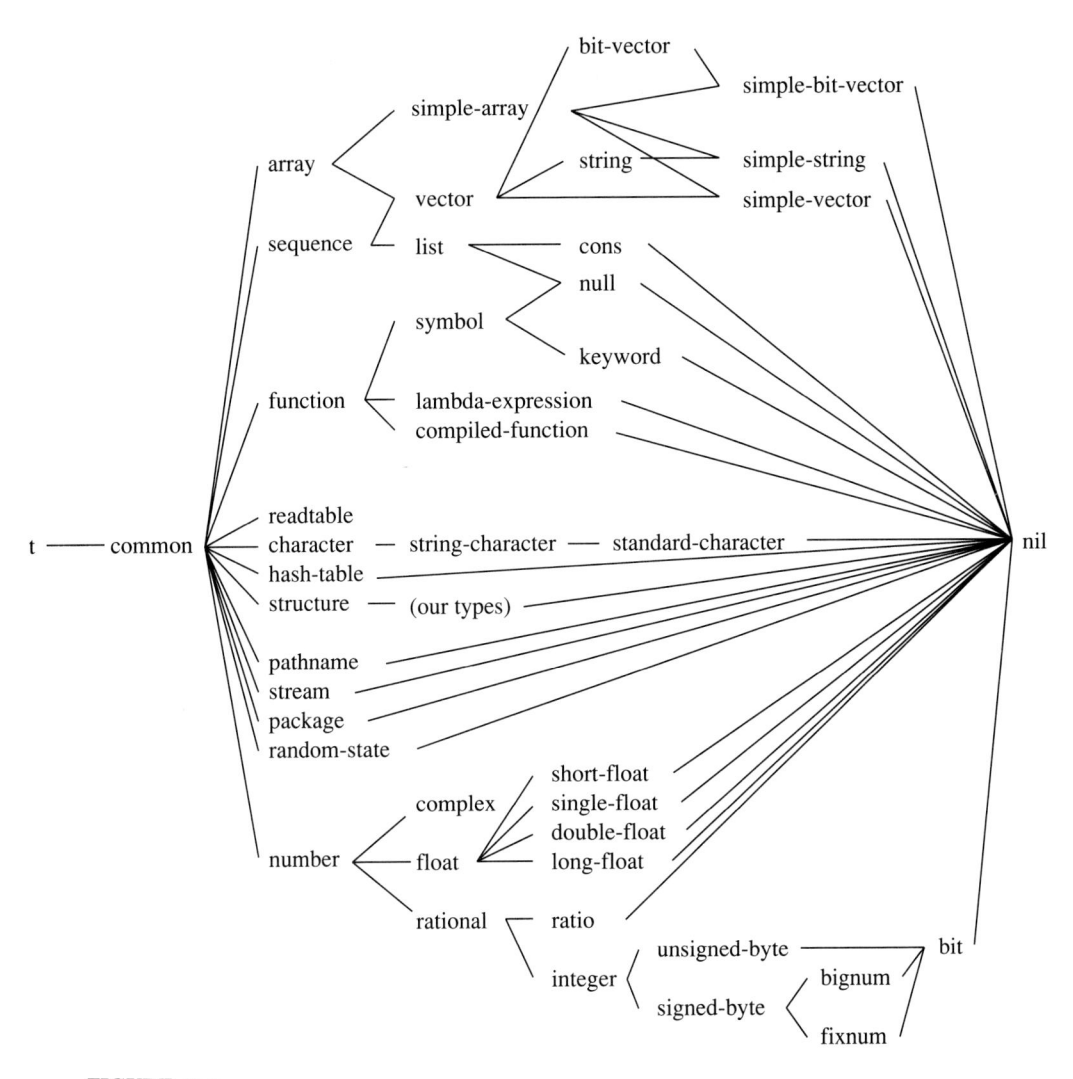

FIGURE 16.1
The Common Lisp type hierarchy. The type **ATOM** is a subtype of **COMMON** and a supertype of all types but **CONS**.

```
Lisp> (expt 2 150)
;; Large integer, usually called a BIGNUM
1427247692705959881058285969449495136382746624

Lisp> (/ 1 3)
1/3              ; a ratio with numerator = 1, denominator = 3

Lisp> (+ 1/3 2/3)
1
```

```
Lisp> (/ 1.0 pi)
0.31830987         ; a floating point number

Lisp> (+ #\B 3)    ; characters are not numbers!
>>Error: #\B should be of type NUMBER

+:
   Rest arg (RESTARG): (#\B 3)

:A    Abort to Lisp Top Level
:C    Supply a new value
->
```

The function + checks the type of each argument it is passed, and signals an error if any argument is not a number. The predicate TYPEP is a general way to test the type of any object, whether it is predefined by Lisp or by us. TYPEP expects two arguments—an object and a type specifier. It returns T if the object is of the specified type, otherwise it returns NIL:

```
Lisp> (typep 34 'integer)
T

Lisp> (typep 'johnny-be-good 'symbol)
T

Lisp> (typep '(6 feet high and inflatable) 'list)
T

Lisp> (typep #2a((1 0) (0 1)) 'array)
T
```

TYPEP is just a more general way of invoking specific type predicates such as INTEGERP or LISTP. For example, + could determine the types of its arguments by calling TYPEP:

```
Lisp> (typep 3 'number)
T

Lisp> (typep 3 'integer)
T

Lisp> (typep 3 'signed-byte)
T

Lisp> (typep 3 'fixnum)
T
```

```
Lisp> (typep #\b 'number)
NIL
```

For each data type, there is a path through the type hierarchy which starts at T and ends at that data type. Each type which lies on this path is a supertype of the data type at the end of the path. For example, 3 is of types T, COMMON, NUMBER, RATIONAL, INTEGER, SIGNED-BYTE, and FIXNUM. FIXNUM is the most specific type specifier for 3, but TYPEP will tell us that 3 is also an instance of each other data type we passed through on our way to FIXNUM. We can use the function SUBTYPEP to ask questions about the relationship between two types in the hierarchy:

```
Lisp> (subtypep 'fixnum 'integer)
T
T

Lisp> (subtypep 'integer 'number)
T
T

;; The SUBTYPE relationship is transitive
Lisp> (subtypep 'fixnum 'number)
T
T

;; all INTEGERS are NUMBERS
Lisp> (subtypep 'integer 'number)
T
T

;; but not all NUMBERS are INTEGERS
Lisp> (subtypep 'number 'integer)
NIL
T
```

SUBTYPEP returns two values: the first value is T if the first type is a subtype of the second type, while the second value is T if the relationship between the two types could be determined, or NIL if the relationship is unknown.

16.1.1 Contagion and Coercion

Notice what happens when + is given three different types of numbers:

```
Lisp> (+ 1/3 (sqrt 2) 5)
6.747547
```

Numeric functions use a set of *contagion* rules to decide what kind of number to return when given several different types of numbers as arguments. In this example, + decides to return a floating point number. In order to do this, each argument is *coerced* into a floating point number, and all the floating point results are then added together.

```
Lisp> (float 1/3)
0.33333334

Lisp> (sqrt 2)
1.4142135623730951

Lisp> (float 5.0)
5.0
```

We can coerce a number into a floating point number with the function **FLOAT**, or we can use the more general coercion function **COERCE**. Just as **TYPEP** is a general way to perform type tests, **COERCE** is a general way to coerce data from one type to another:

```
Lisp> (coerce 5 'float)
5.0

Lisp> (coerce 1/3 'float)
0.3333333333333333

;; coerce from one sequence type to another
Lisp> (coerce "ALOHA" 'list)
(#\A #\L #\O #\H #\A)

;; this coercion does not make sense to Lisp
Lisp> (coerce "ALOHA" 'integer)
>>Error: Cannot coerce to type INTEGER

COERCE:
   Required arg 0 (OBJECT): "ALOHA"
   Required arg 1 (RESULT-TYPE): INTEGER

:A    Abort to Lisp Top Level
->
```

COERCE tries to convert its first argument to the type specified by the second argument, and it signals an error if we try to perform a type coercion which does not make sense.

16.1.2 Extending the Type System

`DEFSTRUCT` not only allows us to define new structures, but it integrates these structures into the type system. For example, recall our definition of a `CYLINDER` in Chapter 6:

```
Lisp> (defstruct cylinder radius height color)
CYLINDER
```

This call to `DEFSTRUCT` defines many functions, including a predicate named `CYLINDER-P`. Additionally, the type `CYLINDER` has been added to the type hierarchy as a subtype of `STRUCTURE`, and we can treat it like any of the predefined types we have seen already.

```
Lisp> (setf c (make-cylinder :radius 2
                             :height 25
                             :color "yellow"))
#S(CYLINDER RADIUS 2 HEIGHT 25 COLOR "yellow")

Lisp> (typep c 'cylinder)
T

Lisp> (subtypep 'cylinder 'structure)
T
T
```

So far all the type specifiers we have seen are symbols. However, more complex type specifiers may be written as lists. For example, we can combine type specifiers with `AND`, `OR`, and `NOT`:

```
Lisp> (typep c '(and cylinder (not list)))
T

Lisp> (typep 3 '(or cylinder (and number unsigned-byte)))
T

Lisp> (typep -3 '(or cylinder (and number unsigned-byte)))
NIL
```

Boolean combinations of type specifiers work as you would expect. For example, The first call to `TYPEP` asks if the cylinder we created earlier is of type `CYLINDER` and not of type `LIST`.

Other list type specifiers accept arguments which specialize certain types. For example, we can create a type specifier which denotes a specific *range* of integers:

```
Lisp> (typep 3 '(integer 0 255))
T
```

```
Lisp> (typep 1000 '(integer 0 255))
NIL

Lisp> (typep 1000 '(integer 256 *))
T

Lisp> (typep 1000 '(integer))
T

Lisp> (typep 1000 'integer)
T
```

The general form of the `INTEGER` type specifier is (`INTEGER` *low high*). We can use the symbol * as a wildcard to represent any possible value for a type specifier argument. Thus, the specification (`INTEGER 256 *`) denotes all integers from 256 to infinity. If an argument is not supplied, then it defaults to *, and if a type specifier list consists of a single symbol with no arguments, then the list may be replaced by just the symbol. Thus, the type specifiers `INTEGER`, (`INTEGER`) and (`INTEGER * *`) are all equivalent.

Similarly, we can specify the element type and dimensions in an array specifier. The type specifier for an array has the general form (`ARRAY` *element-type dimension-list*). The arguments *element-type* and *dimension-list* are optional, and if omitted default to *:

```
Lisp> (typep #2a((1 0) (0 1)) '(array t (2 2)))
T

Lisp> (typep #2a((1 0) (0 1)) '(array * (* *)))
T

Lisp> (typep #2a((1 0) (0 1)) '(array t))
T

Lisp> (typep #2a((1 0) (0 1)) '(array))
T

Lisp> (typep #2a((1 0) (0 1)) 'array)
T

Lisp> (subtypep '(array t (2 2)) '(array * (* *)))
T
T
```

`ARRAY` is a shorthand notation for (`ARRAY`), which is shorthand for (`ARRAY * *`). The specifier (`ARRAY * (* *)`) denotes all two-dimensional arrays of any size and element type.

We can define new type specifiers with the macro `DEFTYPE`. `DEFTYPE` is similar to `DEFMACRO`:

```
Lisp> (deftype matrix (&optional element-type row col)
        `(array ,element-type (,col ,row)))
MATRIX

Lisp> (typep #2a((1 2 3) (4 5 6)) 'matrix)
T

Lisp> (typep #2a((1 0) (0 1)) '(matrix))
T

Lisp> (typep #2a((1 0) (0 1)) '(matrix t 2 2))
T
```

A type specifier list which begins with `MATRIX` is expanded into a new type specifier, just as a call to a macro is expanded into new code by a macroexpansion function. Unlike `DEFMACRO`, optional arguments which are not supplied automatically default to * rather than `NIL`. Thus, the type specifiers `MATRIX` and `(MATRIX)` are equivalent to `(ARRAY * (* *))`. In other words, any two-dimensional array is a matrix. As you have probably guessed, the Common Lisp type system is rather complicated. Refer to the Common Lisp manual for more details.

Problem. Define the type `SQUARE-MATRIX`.

Problem. Read in the Common Lisp manual about how to use `SATISFIES` in type specifications, and then write a type specification for `ORTHONORMAL-MATRIX`. An orthonormal matrix is a matrix whose columns are mutually perpendicular unit vectors.

16.2 GENERIC FUNCTIONS

Now that we understand how types are defined and how they are related, we are ready to examine in more detail how functions deal with different data types. We have already seen that numeric functions such as + or * operate on all types of numbers. Because they operate on such a wide range of data types, we call them *generic functions*.[1] Rather than explicitly calling specialized functions such as `FIXNUM-*` and `RATIO-*`, we can simply call * and let it decide which more specific operation should be invoked to actually multiply its arguments. The sequence functions we examined in the last chapter are other examples of generic functions, because they operate on sequences which can be either lists or vectors.

---

[1] The use of generic functions in Lisp is similar to *function overloading* in languages such as Ada or C++.

We might write a simple, two-argument version of `*` that handles only `FIXNUM`s and `FLOAT`s as follows:

```
(defun */2 (x y)
  (cond ((fixnump x)
         (cond ((fixnump y)
                (fixnum-fixnum-*/2 x y))
               ((floatp y)
                (float-float-*/2 (float x) y))
               (t (error "~A must be a FIXNUM or a FLOAT"
                         y))))
        ((floatp x) (float-float-*/2 x (float y)))
        (t (error "~A must be a FIXNUM or a FLOAT" x))))
```

This function simply examines the type of each argument and decides which type-specific version of `*/2` to call. We will use the convention that the fixed-number-of-arguments version of an *n*-ary function is written as `FUNC/N`, where `FUNC` is the name of the *n*-ary function, and `N` is the fixed number of arguments accepted by `FUNC/N`. Thus, `*/2` is a version of `*` which accepts exactly two arguments.

Dispatching to a subfunction based on the type of one or more arguments is so common that Lisp supplies the macro `TYPECASE` to make such code simpler. `TYPECASE` it similar to `CASE`, but it branches based on the *type* of its key. Also, rather than allowing a list of keys at the start of a clause, `TYPECASE` only allows a single type to appear:

```
Lisp> (defun typecase-test (n)
        (typecase n
          (fixnum 'integer)
          (float 'real)
          (t 'you-lose)))
TYPECASE-TEST

Lisp> (typecase-test 3)
INTEGER

Lisp> (typecase-test 3.14)
REAL

Lisp> (typecase-test 'foo)
YOU-LOSE
```

The macro `ETYPECASE` is a version of `TYPECASE` which automatically supplies a default error-handling case, just as `ECASE` is the error-handling version of `CASE`:

```
Lisp> (defun etypecase-test (n)
        (etypecase n
          (fixnum 'integer)
          (float 'real)))
ETYPECASE-TEST

Lisp> (etypecase-test 'foo)

>> The value of N, FOO, should be a FLOAT or a FIXNUM

ETYPECASE-TEST:
   Required arg 0 (N): FOO
:A  0: Abort to Lisp Top Level

->
```

We can use **ETYPECASE** to simplify `*/2`:

```
(defun */2 (x y)
  (etypecase x
    (fixnum (etypecase y
              (fixnum (fixnum-fixnum-*/2 x y))
              (float  (float-float-*/2 (float x) y))))
    (float (float-float-*/2 x (float y)))))
```

This definition of `*/2` is far from complete because it ignores many of the numeric data types which `*` must handle. However, the basic structure of a complete version of `*/2` which handles all numeric data types should be clear.

16.2.1 N-ary Functions

Common Lisp normally provides *n*-ary versions of functions such as `*` or **APPEND**, even though the basic functionality is provided by a two-argument function. For example, calls to `*` which pass more than two arguments can be converted by a compiler into a nested set of calls to `*/2`:

`(* 1.0 3.14 1/3) => (*/2 (*/2 1.0 3.14) 1/3)`

This process is sometimes called *dyadicizing*. Similarly, we can define the function `*` as follows:

```
(defun * (&rest numbers)
  (if (null numbers)
      1
      (collect #'*/2 numbers)))
```

```
(defun collect (func args)
  (do ((rest (cdr args) (cdr rest))
       (result (car args) (funcall func result (car rest))))
      ((null rest) result)))
```

The function `*` and many other *n*-ary functions are really just front ends to two-argument functions such as `*/2` which do the real work.

16.3 OBJECT-ORIENTED PROGRAMMING

So far we have taken the view that each time we write a new *function*, it is that function's responsibility to handle all reasonable data types. Unfortunately, there is a significant problem associated with this style of programming. Suppose that we want to extend `*/2` so that it knows how to multiply matrices. In order to add this functionality, we first have to locate the source code for `*/2`, assuming we even have access to it, and then we must understand how it works. Once we understand how it works, we can add some new cases to the `ETYPECASE` so that `*/2` will call a matrix multiplication function when passed two matrices. This is an unfortunate violation of modularity, because we are required to understand and alter a piece of code in which we are not even interested, and we might break the existing functionality if we are not careful.

However, *object-oriented programming* takes the view that each *data type* is responsible for describing how all possible operations on that data type should be handled. The following quote from [SS76b] provides a comparison of these two views:

> Instead of considering the single problem of how to compute the GCD(111, 259), we [could] have generalized the problem and have regarded this as a specific instance of the wider class of problems of how to compute GCD(*X*, *Y*). It is worthwhile to point out that we could have generalized the problem of computing GCD(111, 259) in a different way: we could have regarded the task as a specific instance of a wider class of tasks, such as the computation of GCD(111, 259), SCM(111, 259), 111*259, 111 + 259, 111/259, 111 − 259, 111 ↑ 259, the day of the week of the 111th day of the 259th year B.C., etc. This would have given rise to a "111-and-259" processor and in order to let that produce the originally desired answer, we should have had to give the request "GCD, please" as its input!

We can generalize operations by extending the types of data they can handle, or we can generalize data types by extending the kinds of operations that can operate on them. Of course, this is really two different ways of doing the same thing, but the method we choose affects how we develop programs.

Modularity is one of the primary benefits of object-oriented programming. Since each data type "definition" is responsible for describing how to perform operations on itself, we can easily extend the functionality of existing functions without actually altering or even understanding how the current functionality is implemented.

16.3.1 Using DEFMETHOD to Define Generic Functions

As a concrete example of object-oriented programming, we will examine how we might rewrite */2. As part of the "definition" of the data types FIXNUM and FLOAT, we must describe how */2 will work with these types. We will use the macro DEFMETHOD to describe a function which accepts only arguments of a specific type:

```
(defmethod */2 ((x fixnum) (y fixnum))
  (fixnum-fixnum-*/2 x y))

(defmethod */2 ((x fixnum) (y float))
  (float-float-*/2 (float x) y))

(defmethod */2 ((x float) (y fixnum))
  (float-float-*/2 x (float y)))

(defmethod */2 ((x float) (y float))
  (float-float-*/2 x y))
```

DEFMETHOD looks like DEFUN, but each required argument in the lambda-list may actually be a *list* rather than a symbol. If an argument is a list, then the first element of the list is the name of an argument, while the second element of the list is the type that argument must have in order for this method to apply. Thus, when Lisp sees the the call (*/2 2.71 3.14), it examines the four methods we have provided for dealing with the operation */2 to see if one of them can handle the call.

The first method only handles calls to */2 in which the first and second arguments are FIXNUMs. However, the first and second arguments in our call are floating point numbers, so this method does not apply. Similarly the next two methods do not apply either because one of the arguments is of the wrong type. Only the last method definition can handle the call (*/2 2.71 3.14), because it handles calls in which both arguments are floating point numbers. The real work is then handled by the function FLOAT-FLOAT-*/2, just as it was when we defined */2 using TYPECASE.

The important point about this example is that we have replaced one monolithic ETYPECASE with a sort of distributed etypecase which is more easily extended. For example, earlier we saw how to use DEFTYPE to define a new matrix type of the form (MATRIX &OPTIONAL ELEMENT-TYPE ROW COL). Now we can use DEFMETHOD to extend */2 to handle matrices, and we will not have to alter or even understand how any of the other methods for */2 are written.

In Chapter 12 we wrote the function MATRIX-MULTIPLY which multiplies two matrices, leaving their product in a third matrix. Rather than calling

`MATRIX-MULTIPLY` explicitly, we can extend `*/2` to handle matrices:

```
(defmethod */2 ((x matrix) (y matrix))
  (matrix-multiply x
                   y
                   (make-array (list (array-dimension x 0)
                                     (array-dimension y 1))
                               :element-type
                               (array-element-type x))))
```

Lisp will invoke this method whenever it sees a call to `*/2` with two matrices as arguments:

```
Lisp> (*/2 #2a((0 1) (0 0) (1 0))
           #2a((1 2 3) (4 5 6)))
#2A((4 5 6) (0 0 0) (1 2 3))
```

Notice that we did not have to alter or understand how `*/2` deals with any other data types.

Problem. Define a new method for `*` which can multiply a matrix by a constant.

Problem. Extend `+` and `*` so that they can deal with the `GIANT-INTS` we introduced in Chapter 4.

Problem. Add support for infinite precision floating point numbers.

16.3.2 Generic Function Examples

Arithmetic functions are only one of many kinds of generic functions in Lisp. For example, `PRINT` is really a generic function which knows how to display every type of object. In Chapter 5 we saw that `DEFSTRUCT` provides a mechanism for defining our own `PRINT` function. However, this is not a general method for changing how `PRINT` works. For instance, suppose that we want to change `PRINT` so that hash tables are printed differently. Right now we have no way to do that without understanding and actually changing the code for `PRINT`, and the code for `PRINT` is usually not even available. However, we can use `DEFMETHOD` to alter how `PRINT` handles hash tables:

```
Lisp> (defmethod print ((x hash-table) &optional (stream t))
        (format stream
                "~%#<A hash table with ~D elements>"
                (hash-table-count x))
        x)
PRINT
```

```
Lisp> (print (make-hash-table))  #<A hash table with 0 elements>
#<Hash-Table 98B83B> ; the repl doesn't call PRINT
```
Even though `PRINT` accepts a stream as an optional argument, we will only allow type discrimination on required arguments. Thus, the `DEFMETHOD` above says that the required argument `X` must be of type `HASH-TABLE` to invoke this method, and the optional argument `STREAM` will default to `T` when unsupplied.

Unfortunately, many read-eval-print loops do not actually call the function `PRINT` to perform output, so our method definition does not affect the behavior of our top-level read-eval-print loop. However, an explicit call to `PRINT` with a hash table as an argument invokes our method. Changing the behavior of the read-eval-print loop would require knowledge about the internals of our Lisp system.

Notice that the default `PRINT` function is still invoked if none of our method definitions can handle a particular call to `PRINT`:
```
Lisp> (print 3)
3 3
```
In this case, we have not defined a `PRINT` method for integers, so `PRINT` behaves as usual, although we could change this behavior too if we wanted.

As another example of object-oriented programming, consider the `CYLINDER-VOLUME` function we wrote in Chapter 6. This function accepts a cylinder as an argument and returns its volume as a result. However, we would rather define a single generic function named `VOLUME` which can compute the volume of any geometric object such as a pyramid or a cone. `DEFMETHOD` makes it easy to define a new method for the generic function `VOLUME` each time we add a new kind of geometric object to our system.

By now the flexibility and advantages of object-oriented programming should be clear, although we have conveniently ignored many problems which might arise in an object-oriented system. For example, what if the type constraints of two or more methods can be satisfied—which method should handle the call? We will not address such issues here, although any robust object-oriented system must.

> **Problem.** Define a new method for `+` which can add *video times*. Video time is of the form HH:MM:SS:FF where HH is hours, MM is minutes, SS is seconds, and FF is frames. There are 30 frames per second, 60 seconds per minute, and 60 minutes per hour. You may signal an error if an addition would require a result greater than or equal to 24 hours of video time.

16.3.3 Message Passing

The term *object* is used to denote the collection of both a data type and the operations which deal with that type. Some object-oriented systems, notably

Smalltalk-80 [GR83] [Gol84] [Kra83] and old Flavors [DM84], like to view the act of calling a generic function as sending a *message* to an *object*. For example, we just saw how to invoke a specific `PRINT` method for hash tables in our generic functions system:

```
;;; Define method
(defmethod print ((x hash-table) &optional (stream t))
  (format stream
          "~%#<A hash table with ~D elements>"
          (hash-table-count x))
  x)

;;; Invoke method
(print (make-hash-table) *terminal-io*)
```

However, a *message passing* system would view this function call as sending a message named `:PRINT` to an object of type hash table:

```
;;; Define  method
(defmethod (:print hash-table) (&optional (stream t))
  (format stream
          "~%#<A hash table with ~D elements>"
          (hash-table-count self))
  self)

;;; Invoke method
(send (make-hash-table) :print *terminal-io*)
```

A `:PRINT` "message" is "sent" to an object with the function `SEND`. Any other arguments appear after the message. Within the method definition, the object to which the message is being sent is implicitly named `SELF`, while any other arguments are explicitly named by the lambda-list of the `DEFMETHOD`.

Sending a message to an object is really an awkward and asymmetric way of calling a generic function which discriminates only on the type of its first argument. Message passing does not fit cleanly into Lisp because the function is passed as the second argument to `SEND`, and only the first argument is subject to type discrimination. We only mention message passing here because of its historical importance.

16.4 IMPLEMENTING OUR OBJECT-ORIENTED SYSTEM

Now we are ready to implement the generic function system we have been examining. Although an object-oriented programming system is not part of Common Lisp at the time this is being written, the Common Lisp Object System (CLOS) is being standardized, and should be widely available in a few years. The system presented here implements a simple subset of the functionality offered by CLOS.

16.4.1 Representing and Applying Methods

Each method for a generic function will be represented by a `METHOD` structure:

```
(defstruct method
  ;; A list of type constraints for each argument
  type-constraints
  ;; function to call to invoke the method
  handler)
```

The `TYPE-CONSTRAINTS` slot is a list of type specifiers for each of the required arguments in the method. For example, consider the following `DEFMETHOD`:

```
(defmethod */2 ((x fixnum) (y float))
  (float-float-*/2 (float x) y))
```

This method would be represented by a structure whose `TYPE-CONSTRAINTS` slot contains the list `(FIXNUM FLOAT)` and whose `HANDLER` slot contains the function `#'(LAMBDA (X Y) (FLOAT-FLOAT-*/2 (FLOAT X) Y))`.

We will represent each distinct method we define for `*/2` by a method structure, and the symbol `*/2` will be associated with a list of all its methods in a table named `*GENERIC-FUNCTION-METHODS*`:

```
(defvar *generic-function-methods*
  (make-hash-table)
  "Hash table mapping a generic func to a list of methods")

(defmacro lookup-methods (generic-name)
  `(gethash ,generic-name *generic-function-methods*))
```

The macro `LOOKUP-METHODS` retrieves the list of all the methods associated with a generic function. Thus, if we define four methods for `*/2`, then the call `(LOOKUP-METHODS '*/2)` will return a list of four method structures.

Normally we would write an accessor such as `LOOKUP-METHODS` as a function. However, we have written it as a macro so that we can easily update a method list with macros such as `SETF` and `PUSH` which accept generalized variables as arguments. For example, we can say `(LOOKUP-METHODS 'PRINT)` to retrieve a list of print methods, and we can use the form `(PUSH NEW-METHOD`

`(LOOKUP-METHODS 'PRINT))` to add a new method to the front of the list of `PRINT` methods.[2]

The function `APPLY-METHOD` is used to select which method should be used to handle a generic function call. `APPLY-METHOD` expects as arguments the name of a generic function and the argument list to which the function should be applied, and it is responsible for invoking the correct method for those arguments. For instance, Lisp should handle the call (`*/2 3.14 2`) by calling the function `APPLY-METHOD` with the symbol `*/2` and the list (`3.14 2`) as arguments:

```
(defun apply-method (generic-name arg-list)
  (dolist (method
            (lookup-methods generic-name)
            (error "No method found for ~A with args ~A"
                   generic-name
                   arg-list))
    ;; Do the args satisfy method type constraints?
    (do ((args arg-list (cdr args))
         (type-constraints (method-type-constraints method)
                           (cdr type-constraints)))
        ((null type-constraints)
         (return-from apply-method
           (apply (method-handler method) arg-list)))
      (unless (typep (car args) (car type-constraints))
        (return)))))
```

`APPLY-METHOD` iterates over all the methods in the method list for `GENERIC-NAME`. For each method, `APPLY-METHOD` compares the type of each argument to the type constraint for that argument. If all the type constraints for a particular method are satisfied, then the handler function for that method is applied to the arguments. If a suitable method cannot be found, then `APPLY-METHOD` signals an error.

16.4.2 Representing Generic Functions

In order for a generic function such as `*/2` to call `APPLY-METHOD`, the function cell of `*/2` should contain a function which will accept any number of arguments and will in turn call `APPLY-METHOD` with the symbol `*/2` and those arguments. We will use the function `ENSURE-GENERIC` to install such an intermediary function in the function cell of a symbol if one is not already present:

---

[2] As an alternative to this approach, we could write `LOOKUP-METHODS` as an inlineable function, and then define our own `SETF` "method" for `LOOKUP-METHOD` using the macro `DEFSETF`. This is how the accessing functions defined by `DEFSTRUCT` work.

```
;;; Bletch! This loses because's it's slow, takes a lot of
;;; space and it prevents the gc from reclaiming dead
;;; generic functions.  However, we need the functionality.
;;; We'd really like to set a bit in the procedure header to
;;; distinguish between generic and non-generic procedures.
(defvar *all-generic-functions*
  (make-hash-table)
  "Hash table of all known generic functions")

(defun generic-function-p (function)
  (gethash function *all-generic-functions*))

;;; Install a generic function in the function cell of of
;;; GLOBAL-FUNCTION-NAME. If a nongeneric function is
;;; already there, then use it as the default method handler
;;; for the generic function with which we are replacing it.
;;; This lets us make functions like PRINT generic.
(defun ensure-generic (generic-name)
  (unless (and (fboundp generic-name)
               (generic-function-p
                 (symbol-function generic-name)))
    (let ((default-method (if (fboundp generic-name)
                              (list (make-method
                                      :type-constraints '()
                                      :handler
                                        (symbol-function
                                          generic-name)))
                              nil)))
      (setf (lookup-methods generic-name) default-method)
      (let ((generic-function #'(lambda (&rest args)
                                  ;; Notice that we close
                                  ;; over GENERIC-NAME
                                  (apply-method generic-name
                                    args))))
        (setf (gethash generic-function
                       *all-generic-functions*)
              t)
        (setf (symbol-function generic-name)
              generic-function)))))
```

The predicate **FBOUNDP** returns **T** if the function cell of a symbol contains a function, otherwise it returns **NIL**. **ENSURE-GENERIC** first checks to see if the symbol it is passed already contains a generic function in its function cell. If so, there is no need to install a new one.

Unfortunately, there is no efficient and portable way to distinguish between a generic function created by `ENSURE-GENERIC` and any other function in the system. Therefore, we use a brute force approach which records every generic function ever created in a table. The predicate `GENERIC-FUNCTION-P` returns `T` if its argument appears in the table of all generic functions, otherwise it returns `NIL`. One problem with this approach is that generic functions will never be garbage collected because the hash table will always contain a pointer to each one.

In order to be be able to add new methods to functions such as `PRINT` without disturbing any existing functionality, we must create a default method with no type constraints and a handler which is the default `PRINT` function. This `DEFAULT-METHOD` should appear as the last method in the method list. Because the method list is searched from first to last, the default method will only be invoked when a more type specific method cannot be found.

Installing a new generic function in a symbol's function cell requires that we initialize the method list for that symbol to either a list containing the default method, or `NIL` if no default behavior exists. The generic function is then created and recorded in the hash table named `*ALL-GENERIC-FUNCTIONS*` so that we can recognize it later.

16.4.3 Defining Methods

Now we have seen all the functions which do the real work in our generic function system. However, we still need to write `DEFMETHOD`, the front end we use to add new methods:

```
(defmacro defmethod (generic-name arg-list &body body)
  (multiple-value-bind (lambda-list type-constraints)
      (collect-lambda-list-and-types arg-list)
    `(progn (ensure-generic ',generic-name)
            (add-method ',generic-name
                        ',type-constraints
                        #'(lambda ,lambda-list ,@body))
            ',generic-name)))
```

`DEFMETHOD` first decomposes the `ARG-LIST` into a lambda-list suitable for `LAMBDA` and a corresponding list of type constraints. Then it ensures that the function cell of the symbol naming this function contains a generic function, and it adds a new method to the list of existing methods.

`ADD-METHOD` expects as arguments the name of a generic function, the type constraints for a method, and a handler for that method:

```
(defun add-method (generic-name type-constraints handler)
  (let ((existing-methods (lookup-methods generic-name)))
```

```
         (dolist (method existing-methods
                  ;; like SETF, PUSH accepts a
                  ;; generalized variable
                  (push (make-method :type-constraints
                                              type-constraints
                                     :handler handler)
                        (lookup-methods generic-name)))
           (when (equal (method-type-constraints method)
                        type-constraints)
             (return (setf (method-handler method) handler))))))
```

In the simplest case we can just create a new method and push it onto the list of existing methods. However, if we are redefining the handler for an existing method, then we locate that method and destructively update the handler function, rather than pushing a new method onto the front of the method list.

Finally, we have **COLLECT-LAMBDA-LIST-AND-TYPES**. It takes the argument list passed to **DEFMETHOD** and returns the lambda-list and type specifiers as two values:

```
(defun collect-lambda-list-and-types (arg-list)
  ;; ITERATE is defined in Chapter 11
  (iterate loopy ((rest arg-list)
                  (lambda-list nil)
                  (types nil))
    (let ((arg (car rest)))
      (if (or (null rest)
              (member arg '(&optional &rest &key &aux)))
          (values (append (nreverse lambda-list) rest)
                  (nreverse types))
          (loopy (cdr rest)
                 (cons (if (atom arg)
                           arg
                           (first arg))
                       lambda-list)
                 (cons (if (listp arg)
                           (second arg)
                           t)    ; Everything is of type T
                       types))))))
```

For each element of the **ARG-LIST**, we separate the variable name from the type specifier and add them to the lists **LAMBDA-LIST** and **TYPES** respectively. If a type specifier is not supplied for a required argument, then we pretend that the type **T** was specified, indicating that any type of object is acceptable. We are done as soon as we reach the end of the argument list or we see a lambda-list keyword, signaling that we have examined all of the required arguments.

16.5 INHERITANCE

Earlier we saw that the type structure is a lattice in which types such as `INTEGER` are a subset of `NUMBER`, and any structure we define with `DEFSTRUCT` is a subtype of `STRUCTURE`. Similarly, we would like to be able to create our own tree of structures, all of which are a subtype of the type `STRUCTURE`. For example, suppose that we want to write a window system which supports text and graphics windows as well as pop-up and pull-down menus. We might define a text window as a structure:

```
(defstruct text-window x-pos y-pos superior width height
                       font)
```

The slots in the text-window hold information which will be needed to display, move, resize, and draw characters in the window. Similarly, we will also want to define a structure to represent a graphics window and a menu:

```
(defstruct graphics-window x-pos y-pos superior width height
                           bitmap)

(defstruct menu x-pos y-pos superior width height
                items current-selection)
```

Notice that because these three kinds of windows are so similar, we have to repeat the same basic information three times. Rather than duplicating information, we would like all three structures to share the slot and method information which is common to all windows.

16.5.1 Single Inheritance

`DEFSTRUCT` allows us to *inherit* structures with the `:INCLUDE` option:

```
(defstruct window x-pos y-pos superior)

(defstruct (rectangular-window (:include window))
  width height)

(defstruct (text-window (:include rectangular-window)) font)
```

The `:INCLUDE` used in the definition of a `RECTANGULAR-WINDOW` says that rectangular windows are a subtype of `WINDOW` and should contain all the slots that a `WINDOW` contains:

```
Lisp> (subtypep 'rectangular-window 'window)
T
T

Lisp> (subtypep 'text-window 'rectangular-window)
T
T

Lisp> (setf tw (make-text-window :x-pos 0
                                 :y-pos 0
                                 :font "Helvetica 10"))
#S(TEXT-WINDOW X-POS 0 Y-POS 0 SUPERIOR NIL WIDTH NIL
               HEIGHT NIL FONT "Helvetica 10")

Lisp> (text-window-x-pos tw)
0

Lisp> (rectangular-window-x-pos tw)
0

Lisp> (window-x-pos tw)
0
```

Notice that we can access the **X-POS** slot of a **TEXT-WINDOW** with the accessing functions **TEXT-WINDOW-X-POS**, **RECTANGULAR-WINDOW-X-POS**, or **WINDOW-X-POS**. We can use any of these functions because a **TEXT-WINDOW** is also a **RECTANGULAR-WINDOW** and a **WINDOW**. Including all the attributes of one structure in another is called *single-inheritance*.

In CLOS, structures are largely superseded by *classes*. Classes are similar to structures, but they are a more versatile and complicated way of grouping related pieces of information. We can simulate some of the functionality of CLOS classes with Common Lisp structures:

```
(defmacro defclass (name parent slots)
  (case (length parent)
    (0 `(defstruct ,name ,@slots))
    (1 `(defstruct (,name (:include ,(car parent)))
                   ,@slots))
    (t (error "Multiple inheritance is not supported"))))
```

Our version of **DEFCLASS** is just a limited form of **DEFSTRUCT** that provides a simpler syntax for expressing single inheritance. For example, we can use **DEFCLASS** to define our entire window system hierarchy:

```
(defclass window () (x-pos y-pos superior))

(defclass rectangular-window (window) (width height))

(defclass text-window (rectangular-window) (font))

(defclass menu (rectangular-window) (items))

(defclass pop-up-menu (menu) ())

(defclass pull-down-menu (menu) ())

(defclass graphics-window (rectangular-window)
                         (resolution image))
```

The type hierarchy represented by these forms is more clearly depicted by the graph in Figure 16.2. Notice that because text windows, menus, and graphics windows are all subtypes of rectangular-window, we can define a single method called **MOVE** which knows how to drag rectangular-windows around on the screen, and this method will work on all the specialized windows we have developed. Thus, we can share not only slots but methods using inheritance.[3] Inheritance is clearly a useful method for eliminating the duplication of information in our programs.

16.5.2 Multiple Inheritance

Unfortunately, single inheritance is not quite as flexible as we might like. For example, we have forgotten that both text and graphics windows usually have a

---

[3]Notice that we could also define a special **MOVE** method just for menus. In this case, the system must either decide which method to select, or decide how the methods should be combined.

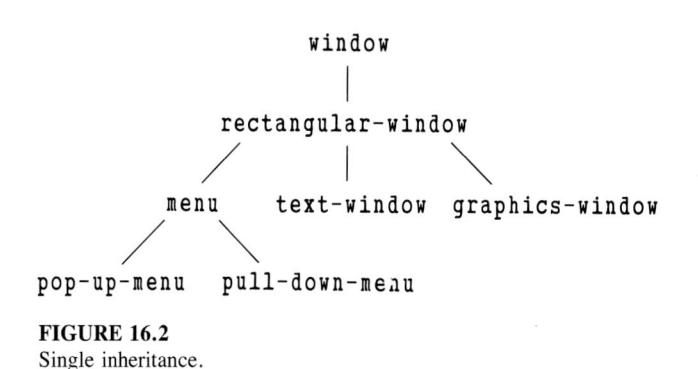

```
                         window
                            |
                   rectangular-window
                   /        |        \
            menu     text-window   graphics-window
           /    \
    pop-up-menu  pull-down-menu
```

FIGURE 16.2
Single inheritance.

cursor to indicate where the next character will be drawn or where the current point is located. However, we do not want all windows, such as menus, to contain a cursor.

We could add new slots to hold cursor information to both the definition of a text window and the definition of a graphics window. We would also have to define new methods to manipulate the cursor in each kind of window. However, because cursors are common to *both* kinds of windows, we would rather factor this information out and create a new class called CURSOR. Now both TEXT-WINDOW and GRAPHICS-WINDOW should inherit slots and methods from *both* RECTANGULAR-WINDOW and CURSOR:

```
(defclass cursor () (x-offset y-offset blinking?))

(defclass text-window (rectangular-window cursor) (font))

(defclass graphics-window (rectangular-window cursor)
                          (resolution image))
```

These changes are graphically depicted in Figure 16.3. Inheriting the attributes of two or more classes as we have done in this example is called *multiple inheritance*. We always want the data structures in our program to accurately represent objects in our problem domain, and multiple inheritance is obviously a more flexible method of combining information than single inheritance. Unfortunately, Common Lisp does not provide support for multiple inheritance of structures. However, CLOS does provide multiple inheritance of classes.

We have not discussed the efficiency implications of the object-oriented programming techniques we have seen in this chapter. However, object-oriented programming features such as multiple inheritance can have severe performance penalties unless they are cleverly implemented in either hardware or software. We have also not discussed some of the complicated details of CLOS because

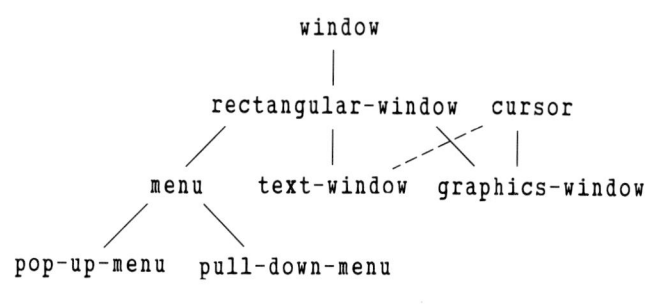

```
                        window
                          |
              rectangular-window   cursor
              /       |      ⟋⎯⎯X  |
         menu      text-window   graphics-window
         /   \
pop-up-menu  pull-down-menu
```

FIGURE 16.3
Multiple inheritance.

its definition has not yet been finalized. However, it should be clear that object-oriented programming is an important method for organizing and extending both data structures and functions in our programs.

Problem. A graphics window and a laser printer can both be treated as raster devices consisting of discrete pixels. Show how you might define a new class called `RASTER-IMAGE` which is inherited by the class `GRAPHICS-WINDOW` and the new class `RASTER-PRINTER`.

CHAPTER 17

LOGIC PROGRAMMING

So far all of our programs have been collections of functions, which describe *how* to compute something. For example, the function OUR-APPEND in Chapter 3 tells Lisp how to concatenate two lists:

```
(defun our-append (head tail)
  (if (null head)
      tail
      (cons (car head)
            (our-append (cdr head) tail))))
```

Because OUR-APPEND provides a sequence of commands describing *how* to concatenate two lists, it is called an *imperative* or a *procedural* program.

17.1 IMPERATIVE VERSUS DECLARATIVE PROGRAMMING

Unfortunately, if we want to perform the inverse of OUR-APPEND, we need to write a new function called UNAPPEND. It should accept a single list as an argument and should return all pairs of lists which concatenate to the original list. Because there may be many such pairs, UNAPPEND will return a stream of answers:

```
;;; This function uses the ITERATE macro of Chapter 11 and
;;; the stream functions defined in Chapter 15.
(defun unappend (l)
  (iterate loopy ((head nil)
                  (tail l)
                  (i (length l)))
    (if (< i 0)
        (make-empty-stream)
        (make-stream (list head tail)
                     (loopy (snoc (car tail) head)
                            (cdr tail)
                            (1- i))))))

;;; Add X to the end of L. The reverse of CONS.
(defun snoc (x l)
  (append l (list x)))
```

Here is a simple example of how **UNAPPEND** works:

```
Lisp> (unappend '(a b c))
#<LAZY-STREAM (NIL (A B C)) and [promise-to-compute-more]>

;;; The variable * is bound to the last object printed by
;;; the READ-EVAL-PRINT Loop.
Lisp> (stream-rest *)
#<LAZY-STREAM ((A) (B C)) and [promise-to-compute-more]>

Lisp> (stream-rest *)
#<LAZY-STREAM ((A B) (C)) and [promise-to-compute-more]>

Lisp> (stream-rest *)
#<LAZY-STREAM ((A B C) NIL) and [promise-to-compute-more]>

Lisp> (stream-rest *)
NIL
```

The variable * is always bound to the last object the read-eval-print loop printed, making it convenient for us to apply **STREAM-REST** in succession. **UNAPPEND** is not complicated, but it demonstrates a fundamental problem with a programming language which requires us to describe exactly *how* to perform a given operation. Suppose we want to go one step further and write another variant of **APPEND** which accepts two lists and returns a list which when appended to the first list produces the second:

```
Lisp> (head-unappend '(c d) '(a b c d))
(A B)
```

We would have to write yet another function to perform this special task. The problem is that we are not telling the computer anything fundamental about `APPEND`. We understand what `APPEND` means, so we can write sequences of commands which compute a specific variant of list concatenation. However, we would like to express our understanding of `APPEND` directly to the computer by *declaring* a set of axioms which describe the basic meaning of list concatenation. From this logical description of `APPEND`, the computer should be able to infer how to perform variants of `APPEND` that we might have written as functions. This style of programming is usually called *declarative programming* or *logic programming* because we are stating facts about the world rather than giving the computer imperative commands describing how to perform an operation.

17.2 PROLOG IN LISP

In the remainder of this chapter we will examine some simple logic programs written in a subset of the programming language Prolog [bFP87].

17.2.1 Facts

In order to better understand logic programming, we will leave `APPEND` alone for a while and examine a simpler problem. Suppose that we want to maintain a database of facts about people:

```
(init-db '((warlock maurice)
           (witch endora)
           (witch samantha)
           (human darin)
           (male darin)
           (witch tabatha)
           (warlock brian)
           (mother endora samantha)
           (mother samantha tabatha)
           (mother samantha brian)))
```

The function `INIT-DB` will initialize a database with a set of facts. A fact such as `(WITCH SAMANTHA)` has no intrinsic interpretation. It is simply a piece of data which we can interpret in any way we want. In this case, we will interpret `(WITCH SAMANTHA)` to represent the statement "Samantha is a witch." We will use the function `PROLOG` to interactively ask questions about the contents of the database:

```
Lisp> (prolog)
Prolog> (witch tabatha)    ; Is the pattern (WITCH TABATHA)
Yes.                       ; in the database? Prolog says yes.
```

```
;; Does it appear more than once?
Search for next solution?  (Y or N) y
No.                                              ; Prolog says no.
Prolog> (witch endora)
Yes.

Search for next solution?  (Y or N) y
No.
```

Each question we ask is called a *goal*, and Prolog searches through the database to see if any facts match our goal. Each time a match is found, Prolog prints out `Yes` and asks if we would like to search for more matches. Prolog uses a pattern matcher similar to the one we built in Chapter 5, and our goal may contain logical variables which start with a dollar sign:

```
Lisp> (prolog)
;;; Are there any WITCHes in the database?
Prolog> (witch $person)

Yes.
$PERSON = ENDORA
Search for next solution? (Y or N) y

Yes.
$PERSON = SAMANTHA
Search for next solution? (Y or N) y

Yes.
$PERSON = TABATHA
Search for next solution? (Y or N) y

No.
Prolog>
```

When Prolog finds a match, it prints the value each variable in the goal needs to assume in order for the goal to match a particular assertion in the database. Prolog tries to match the goal against each element of the database, starting with the first element and working forward.

17.2.2 Rules

If we want to state that each witch in the database is also a female, we could add the following three assertions:

```
;;; ADD-ASSERTIONS adds new data to the database.
(add-assertions '((female endora)
```

```
          (female samantha)
          (female tabatha)))
```

This is rather painful because each time we add a new witch to the database, we must also add a new fact stating that the witch is a female. We really want to state the more general *rule* that *every* witch is a female. For example, rather than adding the three assertions above, we could add the single rule:

```
(add-assertions '((<= (female $person) (witch $person))))
```

This rule says that *if* a person is a witch, *then* that person is a female. Rules have the general form

```
(if (and antecedent-1 antecedent-2 . . . antecedent-n)
    then consequent)
```

However, we will transpose the antecedents and the consequent and write rules in the form:

```
;;; The conjunction of the antecedents
;;; implies the consequent
(<= consequent antecedent-1 antecedent-2 . . . antecedent-n)
```

If all of the antecedents are true, then Prolog may infer that the consequent is true. Rules written in this form are called *horn clauses*. Facts may be viewed as rules that are always true and may be written as horn clauses with no antecedents. For example, the fact `(WITCH TABATHA)` may be written as `(<= (WITCH TABATHA))`. Therefore, every fact or rule in our database can be written as a horn clause.

Now we can try the rule (<= (FEMALE $PERSON) (WITCH $PERSON)):

```
Lisp> (prolog)
Prolog> (female samantha)

Yes.
Search for next solution? (Y or N) y

No.
Prolog>
```

Even though we never entered the fact `(FEMALE SAMANTHA)` into the database, Prolog was able to infer this fact from the fact `(WITCH SAMANTHA)` and the rule `(<= (FEMALE $PERSON) (WITCH $PERSON))`.

We can also write a slightly more complicated set of rules to express what it means to be a parent and a grandmother:

```
(add-assertions '((<= (parent $person $child)
                      (mother $person $child))
                  (<= (grandmother $grandmother $child)
                      (mother $grandmother $parent)
                      (parent $parent $child))))
```

The first rule says that the mother of a child is also a parent of that child:

```
Prolog> (parent samantha $child)

Yes.
$CHILD = TABATHA
Search for next solution? (Y or N) y

Yes.
$CHILD = BRIAN
Search for next solution? (Y or N) y

No.
```

The second rule says that someone who is the mother of a parent of a child is the grandmother of the child:

```
Prolog> (mother endora $child)

Yes.
$CHILD = SAMANTHA
Search for next solution? (Y or N) y
No.

Prolog> (grandmother endora $grandchild)

Yes.
$GRANDCHILD = TABATHA
Search for next solution? (Y or N) y

Yes.
$GRANDCHILD = BRIAN
Search for next solution? (Y or N) y

No.
```

Although there is no fact which directly says that ENDORA is the grandmother of TABATHA, the Prolog system can *infer* this fact from the other facts and the rules we have given it. We will see how it does this later.

17.2.3 A Declarative Definition of APPEND

Now that we have a basic understanding of how facts and rules work, we can define APPEND with the following two rules:

```
(add-assertions '((append nil $l $l)
                  (<= (append ($x . $l1) $l2 ($x . $l3))
                      (append $l1 $l2 $l3))))
```

The first rule says that we can append NIL onto the front of any list $L and get $L as a result. This corresponds to the base case in the imperative version of APPEND.

The second rule is more complicated. It says that if appending $L1 to $L2 produces $L3, then we can cons a new element called $X onto the front of $L1 and the front of $L3 and still maintain the APPEND relationship. This may seem confusing at first, but it is just a way of stating a fundamental property of APPEND. Compare this rule to the recursive case of the imperative version of APPEND.

Now we can use our declarative version of APPEND to solve the same problems solved by the imperative version:

```
Prolog> (append nil (a b c) $l)

Yes.
$L = (A B C)
Search for next solution? (Y or N) y

No.
Prolog> (append (a) (b c) $l)

Yes.
$L = (A B C)
Search for next solution? (Y or N) y

No.
```

We can also use our declarative APPEND to solve problems which the imperative APPEND could not do:

```
Prolog> (append $l1 $l2 (a b c))

Yes.
$L1 = NIL
$L2 = (A B C)
Search for next solution? (Y or N) y
```

```
Yes.
$L1 = (A)
$L2 = (B C)
Search for next solution? (Y or N) y

Yes.
$L1 = (A B)
$L2 = (C)
Search for next solution? (Y or N) y

Yes.
$L1 = (A B C)
$L2 = NIL
Search for next solution? (Y or N) y

No.
```

We no longer need to write a new function to find out all the different ways in which a list can be UNAPPENDed because Prolog can infer how to UNAPPEND from the facts and rules we have told it about APPEND. As Figure 17.1 shows, *imperative programs* designate specific inputs called arguments, perform a computation with those arguments, and return one or more results; however, a *declarative program* does not predesignate inputs and outputs.

Problem. Write the function REVERSE in Prolog.

Problem. Write the function MEMBER in Prolog.

17.3 IMPLEMENTING PROLOG IN LISP

In this section we will examine one way to implement in Lisp the Prolog system we used in the last section. Some of the material in this section is more detailed

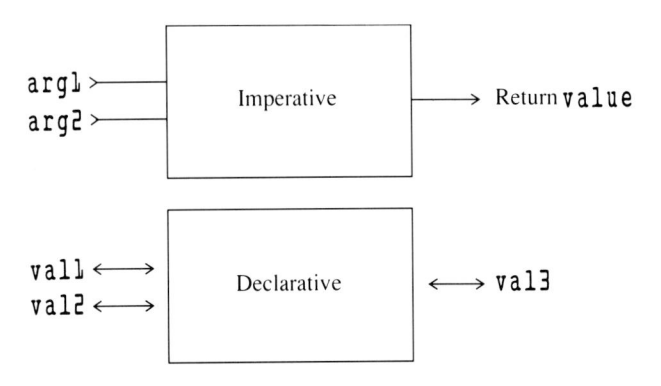

FIGURE 17.1
Imperative versus declarative programming.

and complicated than anything else we have encountered so far in this book. Do not worry if some of it seems confusing at first.

17.3.1 Unification Is Similar to Pattern Matching

The heart of our Prolog system is called a *unifier*. As shown in Figure 17.2, a unifier is a generalization of the pattern matcher we wrote in Chapter 5, which in turn is a generalization of the `EQUAL` function we wrote. We will use the word *term* to refer to either a pattern or a piece of data.

`UNIFY` expects three arguments: two terms and an a-list of bindings. Variables in a term are still denoted by symbols which start with a dollar sign. `UNIFY` will try to extend the set of bindings passed with bindings under which the two terms passed to `UNIFY` are equal. A binding is now represented as an a-list of dotted pairs:

```
Lisp> (unify '(mother endora $x)
             '(mother endora samantha)
             nil)
(($X . SAMANTHA))                       ; example 1

Lisp> (unify '(mother endora $x)
             '(mother $parent samantha)
             nil)
(($X . SAMANTHA) ($PARENT . ENDORA))    ; example 2

Lisp> (unify '(mother endora $x)
             '(mother $parent $child)
             nil)
(($X . $CHILD) ($PARENT . ENDORA))      ; example 3

Lisp> (unify '(mother endora $x)         ; example 4
             '(mother $parent $child)
             '(($x . samantha)))
(($CHILD . SAMANTHA) ($PARENT . ENDORA) ($X . SAMANTHA))

;;; UNIFY returns the symbol FAIL
;;; if it cannot unify the two terms.
Lisp> (unify '(mother endora $x)         ; example 5
             '(mother samantha $y)
             nil)
FAIL
```

```
EQUAL:    Compare DATA to DATA
MATCH:    Compare TERM to DATA
UNIFY:    Compare TERM to TERM
```

FIGURE 17.2
Comparison functions.

In the first example, the two terms are unified by binding $X to SAMANTHA. The pattern matcher could also handle this example because the second term does not contain any variables. However, in the next example both terms contain variables, and the unifier correctly determines that the terms can be unified by binding $X to SAMANTHA and $PARENT to ENDORA. The third example is similar, but this time $X is bound to the variable $CHILD. Binding a variable to a variable makes sense in this case because it represents the most general unification of the two terms, and we always want the unifier to return the minimum set of constraints under which the two terms are equal. In the fourth example we have explicitly told UNIFY that $X must be bound to SAMANTHA, so the unifier correctly determines that $CHILD must also be bound to SAMANTHA. If two terms cannot be unified, then UNIFY returns the symbol FAIL.

Here is a more complicated unification involving APPEND:

```
Lisp> (unify '(append $u $v (a b c))
             '(append ($x . $l1) $l2 ($x . $l3))
             nil)
(($L3 B C) ($X . A) ($V . $L2) ($U $X . $L1))
```

Just like the pattern matcher, the unifier is capable of destructuring lists like (A B C) into subparts. In this case, $X unifies with the car of (A B C), while $L3 unifies with the cdr of (A B C).[1] The complete set of bindings represents the minimum set of constraints needed to unify the two terms. Unification is similar to solving a set of simultaneous equations. Just as there are often many solutions for an underconstrained set of equations, there may also be many possible unifications for a set of terms.

Here is all the code for UNIFY:

```
(defun unify (term-1 term-2 bindings)
  (cond ((eq bindings 'fail) bindings)
        ((variablep term-1)
         (maybe-extend-bindings term-1 term-2 bindings))
        ((variablep term-2)
         (maybe-extend-bindings term-2 term-1 bindings))
        ((or (atom term-1)
             (atom term-2))
         (if (equal term-1 term-2)
             bindings
             'fail))
        (t (unify (cdr term-1)
                  (cdr term-2)
```

---

[1] Do not forget that ($L3 B C) is another way of saying ($L3 . (B C)).

```
              (unify (car term-1)
                     (car term-2)
                     bindings)))))

;;; Add a new binding for VARIABLE to BINDINGS unless
;;; VARIABLE is already bound.
(defun maybe-extend-bindings (variable value bindings)
  (multiple-value-bind (present-value found?)
      (variable-value variable bindings)
    (if found?
        ;; We recursively call unify because VALUE may
        ;; contain variables.
        (unify present-value
               value
               bindings)
        ;; no occurs check!
        (acons variable value bindings))))

(defun variable-value (variable bindings)
  (let ((binding (assoc variable bindings)))
    (values (binding-value binding)
            ;; style point: use (NOT (NULL BINDING))
            ;; rather than BINDING
            (not (null binding)))))

(defun binding-value (binding)
  (cdr binding))

(defun variablep (v)
  (and (symbolp v)
       (char= (schar (symbol-name v) 0) #\$)))
```

We will not examine this code in detail because it is similar to the pattern matcher we wrote earlier, although it is a bit more complicated. The primary difference is the check in **UNIFY** to see if **TERM-2** is a variable. We never had to worry about this case in the pattern matcher because **TERM-2** was always a constant. **MAYBE-EXTEND-BINDINGS** is also different because it contains a recursive call to **UNIFY**. We need this recursive call because **VALUE** may now be a complicated term containing variables, whereas before it was always a constant.

Notice that **VARIABLE-VALUE** returns two values: the value of **VARIABLE**, and a boolean flag indicating whether or not a **VARIABLE** is bound in **BINDINGS**. When **VARIABLE** is unbound, we cannot simply return **NIL** to represent the boolean value false because **NIL** is also a valid value for **VARIABLE**. This is one instance in which the overloading of **NIL** makes our code more complicated.

Problem. Our unifier has the following problem:

```
Lisp> (unify '$x '(father $x) nil)
(($X FATHER $X))
```

The binding returned by **UNIFY** makes no sense because **$X** is bound to an expression containing **$X**. In order to fix this, **MAYBE-EXTEND-BINDINGS** needs to include an *occurs check* to prevent a variable from being bound to an expression containing itself. Add an occurs check to **MAYBE-EXTEND-BINDINGS**.[2]

17.3.2 Maintaining the Database

Now that we have a unifier, we need some way to maintain a database of facts. In order to keep our system simple, we will represent the database as a list of horn clauses:

```
(defparameter *database* nil "Database of horn clauses")

(defun clear-db (&optional (db '*database*))
  (set db nil))
```

The default database will be stored in the global variable ***DATABASE***. We can clear the database by calling the function **CLEAR-DB**. However, we would also like to be able to store databases in global variables other than ***DATABASE***, so **CLEAR-DB** optionally accepts the name of another database. We can add new information to the database with the following functions:

```
(defun add-assertions (assertions
                       &optional (db '*database*))
  (flet ((add-assertion (assertion)
           ;; A horn clause has the form
           ;; (<= (head) (body1) (body2) ...)
           (let ((horn-clause (if (eq (first assertion) '<=)
                                  assertion
                                  '(<= ,assertion))))
             ;; Rules must appear in the
             ;; order they were asserted.
             (set db (snoc (symbol-value db)
                           horn-clause)))))
    (mapc #'add-assertion assertions)
    "Done"))

;;; Add X to the end of L.
(defun snoc (l x)
  (append l (list x)))
```

---

[2] Prolog does not perform an occurs check because it is computationally expensive. However, the omission of the check can lead to nasty programming errors if we are not careful.

```
(defun init-db (assertions &optional (db '*database*))
  (progn (clear-db db)
         (add-assertions assertions db)))
```

ADD-ASSERTIONS expects a list of assertions. An assertion can either be a fact or a rule, so **ADD-ASSERTION** must explicitly convert all facts to rules before adding them to the database. That way, the database consists entirely of horn clauses. Each fact is added to the *end* of the database so that rules will appear in the order in which they were asserted.

INIT-DB first clears the database and then adds a list of assertions. This is the most commonly used function when debugging a logic program, because we want to be careful to avoid adding the same rule to the database multiple times. For example, if we are debugging a program with 100 assertions, we will probably want to change only a few of them at a time as we debug the program. After making a few changes, we will discard the old database and reinitialize it with the latest version of our program in order to avoid inadvertently adding the same rule more than once.

We will also define the following two accessing functions:

```
(defun head (rule)
  (second rule))

(defun body (rule)
  (cddr rule))
```

The conclusion of a rule is often called the *head*, while the conjunction of terms which imply the conclusion is called the *body*.

17.3.3 Rules and Backtracking

Now that we have a unifier and some database functions, we can build a simple Prolog system to ask questions about a database containing only facts (rules with no body). Prolog should try to unify the goal we supply with each fact in the database, starting with the first fact and working forward until it reaches the last fact. Each time the unifier succeeds and returns a binding list rather than the symbol **FAIL**, Prolog will print **Yes** followed by the value each goal variable has in the binding list. When it runs out of facts, Prolog will print **No** and ask us for another goal.

However, the database also contains rules with terms in their body. We can treat rules like conditional facts. The conclusion of each rule is listed first, followed by the set of conditions which must be true in order to reach the conclusion. Handling these rules requires that we modify our idea of what constitutes the goal. So far the goal has been a single term which we have tried to match against facts in the database, but now it will be a conjunction of terms which must be satisfied from left to right.

Prolog searches the database from the first rule to the last, trying to unify the first term in the goal with the conclusion of a rule in the database. When the first goal term unifies with the conclusion of a rule, Prolog replaces the goal term with all of the terms in the body of the rule, thus forming a new goal. In this way, Prolog uses rules *backwards*. It then repeats the entire process as though this new set of goals was posed by the user, so it starts searching again from the *beginning* of the database.

Because facts are rules with no body, unifying with a fact allows us to remove one of the terms from the goal. Eventually Prolog must unify each term in the goal with a fact, thereby eliminating every term in the goal and producing a set of bindings which satisfy the original goal posed by the user.

However, Prolog might reach a point at which the next term in the goal does not unify with the head of any rule in the database. In this case, it must *backtrack* and undo its attempt to satisfy the last rule it tried. It will then continue to search the database starting with the rule following the one which just failed. Eventually it will either succeed in satisfying all the terms in the goal, or it will run out of rules to try, in which case the original goal posed by the user cannot be satisfied.[3]

In order to understand this rather complicated description of how Prolog works, we will follow the example presented in Figure 17.3. The abbreviation M stands for MOTHER and GM stands for GRANDMOTHER. The database we are using is presented on the left, the current conjunction of goal terms is in the middle, and the current set of bindings is on the right. An arrow points to the current goal term and another arrow points to the rule which is being used to satisfy that term.

The initial goal is (GM ENDORA $C). In other words, we want to find out the names of all the children of whom ENDORA is the grandmother. The goal does not unify with the head of the first three rules, but it does unify with the head of the fourth, provided that $X is bound to ENDORA and $C is bound to $Z. Because the goal matches the head of this rule, we replace the goal with the body of the rule, and begin searching the database from the beginning as though the original goal never existed. Therefore, we start a new search labeled 2. However, we have *not* forgotten the state of the search labeled 1, because we will eventually have to resume it.

We begin search 2 by trying to unify the term (M ENDORA $Y) in the goal with the head of a rule in the database. This term immediately unifies with the first rule, so we can remove the term and replace it by the body of the rule. However, this time the rule is actually a fact, so there is no body. Therefore, we have eliminated the term from the goal and will start a new search labeled 3, with only one term left in the goal.

This time the first term in the goal unifies with the second rule in the database. However, this rule is also a fact, so we have eliminated another term from the goal. This leaves us with an empty goal, and an empty goal means that

---

[3]This is not really true, since the Prolog program may not terminate.

```
         Database                    goals                 current bindings
        ----------------------------------------------------------------
   1.
      (<= (m endora samantha))    > (gm endora $c)         nil
      (<= (m samantha tabatha))
      (<= (m samantha brian))
   >  (<= (gm $x $z)
              (m $x $y)
              (m $y $z))
      (<= (gm endora jethro))

   2.
   >  (<= (m endora samantha))    > (m endora $y) and      (($c . $z)
      (<= (m samantha tabatha))     (m $y $z)               ($x . endora))
      (<= (m samantha brian))
      (<= (gm $x $z)
              (m $x $y)
              (m $y $z))
      (<= (gm endora jethro))

   3.
      (<= (m endora samantha))    > (m samantha $z)        (($c . $z)
   >  (<= (m samantha tabatha))                             ($x . endora)
      (<= (m samantha brian))                               ($y . samantha))
      (<= (gm $x $z)
              (m $x $y)
              (m $y $z))
      (<= (gm endora jethro))

                                  Solution found:          (($c . $z)
                                  (gm endora tabatha)       ($z . tabatha)
                                                            ($x . endora)
                                                            ($y . samantha))
```

FIGURE 17.3
How Prolog searches a database.

we have nothing left to prove. Therefore, Prolog will announce that a solution has been found in which $C assumes the value **TABATHA**.

At this point we will be asked if we want to continue the search. If so, then Prolog continues the search labeled 3 starting with the rule *after* the one at which we just paused, as shown in Figure 17.4.

Now the first term in the goal immediately unifies with the head of the rule (<= (M SAMANTHA BRIAN)). Because this rule has no head, we are once

```
   Database                              goals                    current bindings
   ----------------------------------------------------------------------------
3. (continued)
   (<= (m endora samantha))    > (m samantha $z)                  (($c . $z)
   (<= (m samantha tabatha))                                       ($x . endora)
 > (<= (m samantha brian))                                         ($y . samantha))
   (<= (gm $x $z)
       (m $x $y)
       (m $y $z))
   (<= (gm endora jethro))

                               Solution found:                    (($c . $z)
                               (gm endora brian)                   ($z . brian))
                                                                   ($x . endora)
                                                                   ($y . samantha))

3. (continued)
   (<= (m endora samantha))    > (m samantha $z)                  (($c . $z)
   (<= (m samantha tabatha))                                       ($x . endora)
   (<= (m samantha brian))                                         ($y . samantha))
   (<= (gm $x $z)
       (m $x $y)
       (m $y $z))
   (<= (gm endora jethro))
 > No more unifications, backtrack to 2:
```

FIGURE 17.4
Prolog continues searching for more solutions.

again left with an empty conjunction of goals, so we have found a new solution in which $C is bound to BRIAN.

We can continue the search again by examining more rules in the database. However, no more rules unify with the goal (M SAMANTHA $Z). Therefore, we must *backtrack* and continue the search labeled 2, as shown in Figure 17.5.

Now we are back to a goal which contains two terms, and we will continue the search by trying to unify the term (M ENDORA $Y) with the head of a rule. However, this term does not unify with any subsequent rules in the database, so search 2 also fails. Therefore we must backtrack to the initial search.

Now we must try to unify the original goal with any remaining rules in the database. There is one more rule in the database, and it does unify with the goal term. Once again the rule has no body, so we have eliminated our goal term and found another solution, in which $C is bound to JETHRO. When we try to continue the search, there are no more rules left and no other suspended search to which we can backtrack, so all the solutions to the original goal have been found. The search strategy we have just seen is called a *depth-first, chronologically backtracking search*.

2. (continued)
```
   (<= (m endora samantha))      > (m endora $y) and        (($c . $z))
   (<= (m samantha tabatha))       (m $y $z)                 ($x . endora)
   (<= (m samantha brian))
   (<= (gm $x $z)
       (m $x $y)
       (m $y $z))
   (<= (gm endora jethro))
> No more unifications, backtrack to 1:
```

1. (continued)
```
   (<= (m endora samantha))      > (gm endora $c)            nil
   (<= (m samantha tabatha))
   (<= (m samantha brian))
   (<= (gm $x $z)
       (m $x $y)
       (m $y $z))
>  (<= (gm endora jethro))
```

```
                                 Solution found:             (($c . jethro))
                                 (gm endora jethro)
```

1. (continued)
```
   (<= (m endora samantha))      > (gm endora $c)            nil
   (<= (m samantha tabatha))
   (<= (m samantha brian))
   (<= (gm $x $z)
       (m $x $y)
       (m $y $z))
   (<= (gm granny jethro))
> No more unifications, no more backtracking. Original goal fails now.
```

FIGURE 17.5
Prolog performs a backtracking search.

Problem. Present a trace similar to the one in this section showing how the goal **(APPEND $L1 $L2 (A B))** is satisfied using the definition of **APPEND** given earlier.

17.3.4 The Inference Engine

In this section we will see how we can implement the search algorithm described above using the implementation of streams we wrote in Chapter 15. The function **SOLUTION-STREAM** expects a single goal term as an argument, and it will return a stream of bindings which satisfy the goal. However, the real work is done by the function **SOLVE**:

```
(defun solve (goals rest-db bindings continuation)
  (cond ((null goals) (make-stream
                         bindings
                         (funcall continuation)))
        ((null rest-db) (funcall continuation))
        (t (flet ((continue-search ()
                    (solve goals
                           (rest rest-db)
                           bindings
                           continuation)))
             ;; Notice rename
             (let* ((next-rule (rename-term
                                 (first rest-db)))
                    (new-bindings (unify (first goals)
                                         (head next-rule)
                                         bindings)))
               (if (eq new-bindings 'fail)
                   (continue-search)
                   ;; Replace head by body.
                   ;; This corresponds to depth 1st search.
                   (solve (append (body next-rule)
                                  (rest goals))
                          *database*
                          new-bindings
                          #'continue-search)))))))

(defun solution-stream (goal)
  (solve (list goal)
         *database*
         nil
         ;; explicit continuation
         #'(lambda () (make-empty-stream))))
```

SOLVE expects four arguments. The first argument is the current set of goals, which must be satisfied from left to right. The second argument is the remaining portion of the database which has not yet been searched. The third argument is the current set of bindings, and the fourth argument is a *continuation function*.[4] The **CONTINUATION** is a lexical closure which captures the state of a suspended search. Calling the continuation will resume the search.

SOLVE begins by examining the current set of **GOALS**. If it is empty, then a solution has been found, so **SOLVE** returns a stream consisting of the current set of bindings, followed by any solutions produced by resuming the suspended search represented by the continuation function. Remember that streams are *lazy*,

---

[4]We will discuss the general concept of continuations in greater detail in the next chapter.

so the continuation function will not actually be called until someone asks to see the rest of the stream.

If any goal terms remain to be solved, then `SOLVE` checks to see if any unexamined rules remain in `REST-DB`. If not, then `SOLVE` cannot do anything more, so it backtracks and resumes the previous search by calling the `CONTINUATION`. However, if there are more rules to examine, then we get to the heart of `SOLVE`.

`SOLVE` tries to unify the next term in `GOALS` with the head of the next rule in the database. However, `SOLVE` first calls `RENAME-TERM` on the rule in order to uniquely rename every variable which appears in it. We need to do this in case a goal happens to contain variables which are also used in a rule. The variables in the goal are in separate scope than those of the rule, so we rename the rule variables to assure that the scoping rules are obeyed.[5]

If the unification fails, then we continue searching `REST-DB` by calling a *new* continuation function named `CONTINUE-SEARCH`. `CONTINUE-SEARCH` discards from `REST-DB` the rule that failed to unify with the goal term, and recursively calls `SOLVE`, thereby driving us closer to the second base case in `SOLVE`.

If the unification succeeds, then we also recursively call `SOLVE`, but this time with a completely new set of arguments. We first replace the goal term with the body of the rule that unified with it, and then we start searching the database from the beginning. We also pass along the latest set of bindings and the new continuation function. If the recursive call to `SOLVE` eventually needs to backtrack and undo the current rule, it will do so by calling this new continuation.

`SOLUTION-STREAM` is used as a front end to `SOLVE` to start a search consisting of a single goal term. The search starts at the beginning of the current database with no bindings and a continuation function which returns the empty stream and does not attempt any further search.

`SOLVE` is rather complicated, so do not worry if you do not understand all of the details presented here. It is more important that you understand the general search strategy used by Prolog rather than this particular implementation of that strategy. In fact, there are far more efficient ways to implement a depth-first, backtracking search than the method presented here.

The function `PROLOG` is just an interactive front end for the function `SOLUTION-STREAM`:

```
(defun prolog (&optional (*database* *database*))
  (loop (format t "~&Prolog> ")
        (let ((goal (read)))
          (if (equal goal '(quit))
              (return 'quit)
              (do ((rest (solution-stream goal)
                         (stream-rest rest)))
                  ((empty-stream-p rest)
```

---

[5]Renaming rule variables is analogous to the process of *alpha conversion* described in Chapter 20.

```
              (format t "~%No.~%"))
            (let ((next-bindings (stream-next rest)))
              (print-search-result goal next-bindings)
              (unless (y-or-n-p
                        "~&Search for next solution?")
                (return)))))))))
```

DATABASE is a special variable bound to the database supplied by the user, or to the default database if a database is not explicitly passed as an argument to **PROLOG**. **PROLOG** asks for a goal and calls **SOLUTION-STREAM** on it, offering to print out each solution found. Once all the solutions have been found, or the user indicates that she does not want to search for any more solutions, the process repeats in an infinite loop until the goal (**QUIT**) is entered, at which point the call to **PROLOG** returns the symbol **QUIT**. Notice that because the stream returned by **SOLUTION-STREAM** is lazy, the search for solutions proceeds incrementally, performing only as much of the search as is needed to find the next solution.

All that remains to the Prolog system are various auxiliary functions used by the code we have already seen. Here are the functions related to renaming terms:

```
(defvar *level* 0
  "Number used to uniquely rename variables")

(defun rename-term (term)
  (labels ((rename (term)
             (cond ((variablep term)
                    (rename-variable term *level*))
                   ((atom term) term)
                   (t (cons (rename (car term))
                            (rename (cdr term)))))))
    (incf *level*)
    (rename term)))

(defun rename-variable (variable level)
  (intern (concatenate 'string
                       (symbol-name variable)
                       "-"
                       (princ-to-string level))))
```

A global variable named ***LEVEL*** is used to uniquely name each variable. **RENAME-TERM** increments ***LEVEL*** and then performs a tree walk over **TERM**, renaming each variable it finds. A variable is renamed by concatenating a dash followed by the current value of ***LEVEL*** to the variable's name.

Finally, here are the functions used by the **PROLOG** function to print out solutions in a readable form:

```
;;; Return a list of all the atoms in TREE.
```

```
(defun flatten (tree)
  (cond ((null tree) tree)
        ((atom (car tree)) (cons (car tree)
                                 (flatten (cdr tree))))
        (t (append (flatten (car tree))
                   (flatten (cdr tree))))))

;;; Print the value of each variable which appears in GOAL.
(defun print-search-result (goal bindings)
  (format t "~%Yes.")
  (let ((variables-in-goal (if (atom goal)
                               (if (variablep goal)
                                   (list goal)
                                   nil)
                               (remove-if-not
                                #'variablep
                                (flatten goal)))))
    (dolist (var variables-in-goal)
      (format t "~&~A = ~A" var
        (plug-in-values var bindings)))))

;;; Replace all variables in FORM by their values.
(defun plug-in-values (form bindings)
  (if (atom form)
      (if (variablep form)
          (multiple-value-bind (value found?)
              (variable-value form bindings)
            (if found?
                (plug-in-values value bindings)
                form))         ; It's ok to have unbound vars
          form)
      (cons (plug-in-values (car form) bindings)
            (plug-in-values (cdr form) bindings))))
```

A solution will consist of *all* the bindings needed to satisfy the goal, but we are only interested in seeing the values of variables which appear in the original goal. PRINT-SEARCH-RESULT expects a GOAL and a set of BINDINGS as arguments, and it prints out the value of each variable in the GOAL:

```
Lisp> (print-search-result '(gm endora $c)
                           '(($c . $z)
                             ($z . tabatha)
                             ($y . samantha)))

Yes.
$C = TABATHA
NIL
```

Problem.
How many solutions are there to the goal `(APPEND (A B) $Y $L)`? How does our Prolog system handle this goal? How many solutions are there to the goal `(APPEND $X (A B) $L)`? How does our Prolog system handle this goal? Do the answers to each of these problems seem consistent?

17.4 LOGIC PROGRAMMING EXAMPLES

In this section we will examine two examples of logic programming which are a bit longer than what we have seen so far.

17.4.1 A Simple Natural Language Parser

Parsing and understanding natural language has long been a goal of AI, and natural language processing was one of Prolog's earliest applications. We can write a simple grammar for English sentences as follows:

sentence → np vp
np → noun
np → det noun
vp → verb
vp → verb np
noun → gilligan
noun → coconuts
verb → eats
det → the
det → a

The grammar says that a sentence is a noun phrase (np) followed by a verb phrase (vp). A noun phrase is either a noun, or a determiner (det) followed by a noun. Similarly, a verb phrase is either a verb, or a verb followed by a noun phrase. Nouns, verbs, and determiners are terminals which cannot be further decomposed. This simple grammar clearly does not describe the structure of many sentences, but it does describe some basic grammatical rules.

Now we would like to write a program which can examine a sentence such as "Gilligan eats coconuts" and determine whether or not it is a valid sentence according to our grammar. One possible Prolog program for doing this is represented by the following database:

```
(init-db '((<= (append nil $1 $1))
           (<= (append ($x $l1) $l2 ($x . $l3))
               (append $l1 $l2 $l3))

           ;; Grammar rules
           (<= (sentence $sent)
               (append $np $vp $sent)
               (np $np)
               (vp $vp))
```

```
(<= (np $noun)
    (noun $noun))
(<= (np $np)
    (append $det $noun $np)
    (determiner $det)
    (noun $noun))

(<= (vp $verb)
    (verb $verb))
(<= (vp $vp)
    (append $verb $np $vp)
    (verb $verb)
    (np $np))

;;; Words
(noun (gilligan))
(noun (skipper))
(noun (minnow))
(noun (lagoon))
(noun (coconuts))
(verb (swims))
(verb (wrecked))
(verb (eats))
(determiner (the))
(determiner (a)))
'*grammar*)
```

Here is an example of how we can use this grammar:

```
Lisp> (prolog *grammar*)
Prolog> (sentence (Gilligan eats coconuts))

Yes.
Search for next solution? (Y or N) y

No.
Prolog> (sentence (Gilligan eats swims))

No.
Prolog> (sentence (The skipper wrecked the minnow))

Yes.
Search for next solution? (Y or N) y

No.
```

Notice that the grammar rules can be given to Prolog with almost no changes, except that most rules contain a call to `APPEND`. Our program uses the fact that `APPEND` can find all the possible ways to split a list into two pieces:

```
Lisp> (prolog *grammar*)
Prolog> (append $np $vp (gilligan eats coconuts))

Yes.
$NP = NIL
$VP = (GILLIGAN EATS COCONUTS)
Search for next solution? (Y or N) y

Yes.
$NP = (GILLIGAN)
$VP = (EATS COCONUTS)
Search for next solution? (Y or N) y

Yes.
$NP = (GILLIGAN EATS)
$VP = (COCONUTS)
Search for next solution? (Y or N) y

Yes.
$NP = (GILLIGAN EATS COCONUTS)
$VP = NIL
Search for next solution? (Y or N) y

No.
```

The sentence rule uses this property of `APPEND` to search for the correct way to parse a sentence:

```
(<= (sentence $sent)
    (append $np $vp $sent)
    (np $np)
    (vp $vp))
```

The first term in the body of the rule is a call to `APPEND` which will produce a binding for `$NP` and `$VP` when `$SENT` is bound to a sentence. Prolog tries to satisfy the next two terms using these bindings. The rules for `NP` and `VP` are analogous to the sentence rule, and will also try to divide their sentence fragments into pieces. If either the call to `NP` or the call to `VP` fails, then Prolog will backtrack to `APPEND` and produce a new set of bindings for `$NP` and `$VP` and try again. It will continue to do this until a valid noun phrase and a valid verb phrase are found, at which point our goal will succeed, or until **APPEND** runs out of ways to divide the sentence, at which point our goal will fail.

We can also use our grammar to ask for all the possible sentences we can make from a sentence template:

```
Prolog> (sentence (The skipper $verb the minnow))

Yes.
$VERB = SWIMS
Search for next solution? (Y or N) y

Yes.
$VERB = WRECKED
Search for next solution? (Y or N) y

Yes.
$VERB = EATS
Search for next solution? (Y or N) y

No.
```

Prolog thinks that we can make three different sentences from the term **(THE SKIPPER $VERB THE MINNOW)**. Of course, some of the sentences do not make any sense because our grammar says nothing about the *meaning* of sentences. Our parser is also extremely inefficient, and much better parsing algorithms exist. However, the grammar is still interesting, because we did not have to explicitly tell the computer *how* to parse a sentence. Instead, we gave it the grammar rules we would have used to write a parser, and let Prolog figure out how to use those rules to actually parse sentences.

> **Problem.** Extend the grammar to handle *prepositional phrases*. For example, it should be able to accept the sentence "The skipper wrecked the minnow in the lagoon."

> **Problem.** Repeat the problem in Chapter 5 which asks you to convert infix to prefix notation, but this time write your solution as a Prolog program.

17.4.2 Prolog Implements Resolution

Many books about artificial intelligence discuss how to use predicate calculus to represent knowledge, and how to use *resolution* to answer questions about such a knowledge base. For example, the following problem appears at the end of Chapter 5 in [Ric83]:

Consider the following sentences:

- John likes to eat all kinds of food.
- Apples are food.
- Chicken is food.
- Anything anyone eats and isn't killed by is food.
- Bill eats peanuts and is still alive.
- Sue eats everything Bill eats.

1. Translate these sentences into clause form.
2. Prove that John likes peanuts using resolution.
3. Use resolution to answer the question "What food does Sue eat?"

Prolog uses resolution to answer questions about a database represented as horn clauses, so we should be able to use Prolog to automatically perform the resolution proofs that this problem asks us to perform manually. The first step in solving this problem is to convert the given sentences into horn clauses:

```
(init-db '((<= (eats john $food) (food $food))
           (food apples)
           (food chicken)
           ;; Left recursion bug in the next rule!
           (<= (food $food) (eats $person $food)
                            (alive $person))
           (eats bill peanuts)
           (alive bill)
           (<= (eats sue $food) (eats bill $food)))
         '*food*)
```

Now we have a database upon which Prolog can perform resolution. The first question in the problem asks us to prove that John likes to eats peanuts. Unfortunately, there is a problem with one of our rules:

```
Lisp> (prolog *food*)
Prolog> (eats john peanuts)

>>Error: Stack Overflow

RENAME-VARIABLE:
   Required arg 0 (VARIABLE): $FOOD
   Required arg 1 (LEVEL): 14406
:A    Abort to Lisp Top Level
:C    Attempt to grow the stack and continue
->
```

Rather than answering Yes, the Prolog system has gone into an infinite loop, causing a stack overflow. We can see the loop by following the steps that Prolog takes to try to prove our goal.

Prolog first unifies `(EATS JOHN PEANUTS)` with the head of the first rule, binding `$FOOD` to `PEANUTS`. It must then prove the goal `(FOOD PEANUTS)`. This goal unifies with the head of the fourth rule, so Prolog now tries to prove the two terms in the body of the rule. The first term to prove is `(EATS $PERSON PEANUTS)`, which unifies with the head of the first goal in the database if we bind `$PERSON` to `JOHN`. Unfortunately, this was our original goal! At this point we are in an infinite loop, and Lisp eventually signals a stack overflow error.

The problem is due to the way our fourth rule is written, and is generally known as *left recursion*. Left recursion means that a recursive goal occurs as the first (leftmost) term in the body of a rule. Because Prolog uses depth-first search, it ends up in an infinite loop as we have just seen. We can avoid the problem by reordering the terms in the body of the broken rule:

```
Change: (<= (food $food) (eats $person $food)
                         (alive $person))
To:     (<= (food $food) (alive $person)
                         (eats $person $food))
```

The recursive goal starting with `EATS` now occurs as the *second* goal in the body. Now `$PERSON` will be bound to `BILL` *before* we attempt to satisfy the `EATS` goal, thus preventing the infinite recursion:

```
;;; Try the problem again using the new version of rule 4.
Lisp> (prolog *food*)
Prolog> (eats john peanuts)

Yes.
Search for next solution? (Y or N) y

No.
```

Now Prolog successfully uses resolution to prove that John eats peanuts. Similarly, we can ask Prolog to answer the second question in the problem: What kind of food does Sue eat?

```
Prolog> (eats sue $food)

Yes.
$FOOD = PEANUTS
Search for next solution? (Y or N) y

No.
```

There is a great deal of theory behind logic programming which we have not discussed in this chapter. For more extensive coverage of resolution and logic programming, refer to [GN87] and [SS83].

Problem. Rather than rearranging our database to avoid left recursion, we could change the search strategy used by our Prolog system. Change the Prolog interpreter to perform a breadth-first rather than a depth-first search of the database. Does this fix the left recursion problem? Why?

17.5 ADVANCED LOGIC PROGRAMMING TOPICS

In this section we will examine a few other important logic programming topics.

17.5.1 Procedural Attachment

So far we have avoided dealing with numbers in our Prolog programs. However, if we want to write **LENGTH** in Prolog, then we need to have some way of performing arithmetic. We could describe the Peano arithmetic system presented in Chapter 4 as a set of facts and rules, and let Prolog infer how to perform arithmetic from this database. While this approach has an appealing elegance, it is appallingly inefficient because it ignores the fact that most computers can implement common arithmetic operations in a single instruction.

Similarly, we also need to provide some way for Prolog to perform I/O. One answer to these problems is to interpret some terms as function calls rather than as patterns to be unified. For example, when Prolog encounters a term such as (+ $X 1 $ANSWER), rather than calling the unifier, we would like to call the Lisp function + with the value of the variable $X and 1 as arguments. Prolog should then bind $ANSWER to the value returned by the function call to +. Mixing imperative programming into our declarative programming language in this way is usually called *procedural attachment*. Procedures act like escape hatches into the imperative world.

Unfortunately, we have already seen that, unlike logic programs, procedures have specific inputs and outputs. Thus, procedures do not fit neatly into logic programming when we are presented with a goal such as (+ $X $Y 10). Any two bindings of $X and $Y which add to 10 should satisfy this goal. However, the procedural version of + cannot deal with this query. Our answer to this is that goals which represent calls to functions *must* have certain arguments instantiated and others unbound. In the case of +, we will require that the first two arguments be either literals or bound variables, while the last argument must be a variable.

Problem. Add procedural attachment to our Prolog system. Implement + and **QUIT** using procedural attachment. Write **LENGTH** in Prolog using your implementation of +.

17.5.2 Search and Efficiency

One of the most important aspects of a declarative programming language is how it searches its database. We have examined Prolog's depth-first, chronologically backtracking algorithm in detail, but other alternatives exist. *Meta-level* programming [Gen84] offers an interesting way for us to control the search strategy with rules, while *dependency directed backtracking* [Zab87] provides a more sophisticated alternative to chronological backtracking. Logic programming is also amenable to parallel search.

When our Prolog system tries to unify a goal term with the head of a rule, it examines *every* rule in the database. This is extremely inefficient because the unification usually fails. In order to speed up the rule search, we would like to reduce the number of rules which must be examined. One way to filter out rules which will obviously fail is called *clause indexing*. Clause indexing stores rules according to the symbol which appears as the first element in the head of a rule. For example, all rules whose heads start with the symbol **APPEND** would be stored together, but separately from all the other rules in the database. In this way, the database is presorted. Now when **SOLVE** tries to unify a goal term with a rule in the database, it should only examine rules whose heads contain the symbol which appears as the first element of the goal term. For instance, when **SOLVE** encounters a goal term which begins with **APPEND**, it can immediately retrieve and examine only rules whose head begins with **APPEND**.

In order to keeps things simple, we have not implemented clause indexing or many other common techniques for making Prolog an efficient language. For more details about efficient implementation, refer to [MW88]. Many of our logic programs are also needlessly inefficient. For more information about writing logic programs, refer to [SS83]. Ultimately, the goal of logic programming is to write a specification for a program and to directly execute that specification. Unfortunately, many program specifications make terrible programs, but in some cases declarative programs provide an elegant alternative to imperative ones.

> **Problem.** Add clause indexing to our Prolog system by rewriting the database functions and **SOLVE**. Store the database in a hash table rather than in a single list.

> **Problem.** Read about the *cut* operator in [SS83] and add it to our Prolog interpreter.

> **Problem.** It is difficult to debug Prolog programs with our interpreter because we cannot see what is happening. A facility analogous to the Lisp **TRACE** function would be helpful. Read about *spy* in [SS83] and add it to our interpreter.

CHAPTER 18

A LISP INTERPRETER

In this chapter we will once again take advantage of the equivalence of programs and data by building our own Lisp interpreter. We will call the interpreter `OUR-EVAL`, and it will behave much like the `EVAL` which is built into Lisp. The idea of writing a Lisp interpreter in Lisp might seem odd at first, but a Lisp interpreter accepts some arguments and returns a value just like any other function.

18.1 EXAMPLE: AN EVALUATOR WITH IMPLICIT CONTROL FLOW

The main function in our interpreter is called `OUR-EVAL`. The `EVAL` function in Lisp accepts a single form and evaluates it in the null lexical environment. However, `OUR-EVAL` accepts not only a form, but an optional argument called a *lexical environment*. If an environment is not specified, then it defaults to the null lexical environment:

```
(defun our-eval (form &optional env)
  (if (atom form)
      (if (symbolp form)
          (lookup-variable-value form env)
          form)
      (eval-application form env)))
```

Our interpreter represents an environment as an a-list of variable name and value pairs. For example, **NIL** is the null lexical environment, while **((GUMBY . GREEN))** is a lexical environment in which **GUMBY** is bound to **GREEN**. If a variable is not bound in the lexical environment, then we will assume that it is a free variable reference and look for a value in the value cell of the referenced symbol. Thus, the variable **ENV** in **OUR-EVAL** corresponds to the sheets of paper in the photocopier model of function calling. Our interpreter will not handle special variable bindings right now.

If **FORM** is a symbol, then **OUR-EVAL** will return the value of that symbol in the current lexical environment. Environment-handling functions such as **LOOKUP-VARIABLE-VALUE** will be defined after we have examined more of the interpreter. For now we will assume that environment-manipulating functions do what their names suggest.

Other atomic forms such as numbers or strings evaluate to themselves. If **FORM** is a list, then we need to apply the function or special form at the beginning of the list to the arguments in the remainder of the list:

```
(defun eval-application (form env)
  (case (first form)
    (quote (eval-quote form))
    (if (eval-if form env))
    (function (eval-function form env))
    (defun (eval-defun form env))
    (setq (eval-setq form env))
    (exit (eval-exit))
    (t (eval-function-call form env))))
```

EVAL-APPLICATION first checks to see if **FORM** is a call to a special form. Because our Lisp does not have macros, **EVAL-APPLICATION** must also explicitly check for **DEFUN** and other symbols which would normally be treated as macros. For each special form or macro, there is an interpreter function which can evaluate a call to it. Here is how some common special forms are handled:

```
(defun eval-quote (form)
  (second form))

(defun eval-if (form env)
  (if (our-eval (second form) env)
      (our-eval (third form) env)
      (our-eval (fourth form) env)))

(defun eval-setq (form env)
  (set-variable-value (second form)
                     (our-eval (third form) env)
                     env))
```

`EVAL-QUOTE` prevents further evaluation by immediately returning the quoted piece of data. `EVAL-IF` recursively calls `OUR-EVAL` on the *test* portion of a call to `IF`, and then recursively evaluates either the *then* or the *else* form in the `IF`. Notice that we must pass the current lexical environment along in each recursive call to `EVAL`.

We can change the value of a variable using the special form `SETQ`. So far we have always used `SETF` to modify the value of a variable or data structure. However, `SETF` is really a macro which expands into a more primitive destructive operation:

```
Lisp> (macroexpand '(setf grinch 'mean))
(SETQ GRINCH (QUOTE MEAN))
T
```

We will continue to use `SETF` to alter variable values in our Lisp code, but our interpreter will only implement the more primitive operation `SETQ`.[1] `EVAL-SETQ` works by evaluating the value portion of the call to `SETQ` in the current lexical environment, and then setting the given variable to that value.

Because our interpreter does not currently handle macros, we must also treat `DEFUN` specially:

```
(defun eval-defun (form env)
   (setf (symbol-function (second form))
         ;; Notice how we use FUNCTION to make
         ;; sure that the body of the DEFUN
         ;; captures its lexical environment.
         (eval-function `(function (lambda ,(third form)
                                    ,@(cdddr form)))
                        env))
   (second form))
```

As a matter of style, rather than using functions such as `SECOND` and `THIRD` to extract subparts of `FORM`, it would be simpler to use the `DESTRUCTURING-LET` macro presented as an exercise in Chapter 11:

```
(defun eval-defun (form env)
  (destructuring-let ((name lambda-list . body) (cdr form))
    (setf (symbol-function name)
          (eval-function
            `(function (lambda ,lambda-list ,@body))
            env)))
  (second form))
```

---

[1] There is a good argument for *not* allowing `SETF` to change variable values, because altering the value of a variable is fundamentally different than updating a slot in a data structure.

Regardless of how it is implemented, `EVAL-DEFUN` stores the result of the call to `EVAL-FUNCTION` in the function cell of the symbol being defined. We build a lambda expression from the lambda-list and the body of the `DEFUN`, and then we wrap that lambda expression inside a call to `FUNCTION` to be sure to create a lexical closure over the current environment. It is important that recursive calls to `OUR-EVAL` pass the current lexical environment along, or else calls to `FUNCTION` will not close over the correct environment. Rather than calling `EVAL` recursively and letting it figure out that the real work needs to be done by `EVAL-FUNCTION`, we call `EVAL-FUNCTION` directly from `EVAL-DEFUN`. Here is how `EVAL-FUNCTION` works:

```
(defun eval-function (form env)
  (let ((formal-args (second (second form)))
        (body (third (second form))))
    #'(lambda (&rest evaled-args)
        (our-eval body
                  ;; Close over definition ENV
                  (extend-env env
                              formal-args
                              evaled-args)))))
```

In our interpreter, *all* functions are represented as a lexical closure in the underlying Lisp. Recall that when we define a function, we must capture the current lexical environment. When the closure returned by `EVAL-FUNCTION` is called, it recursively evaluates the body of the lambda expression passed to `FUNCTION`. However, it also *extends* the lexical environment which was present at the time of definition by binding the formal parameters of the lambda expression to the evaluated arguments. This may be a bit difficult to grasp at first, but it corresponds exactly to the verbal description of closure and function calling presented in Chapter 9.

Now that we have examined all the special forms our interpreter knows about, we are ready to see how regular function calls are handled:

```
(defun eval-function-call (form env)
  (let ((function (if (symbolp (first form))
                      (lookup-function-value (first form)
                                             env)
                      (eval-function
                        `(function ,(first form))
                        env)))
        (evaled-args (mapcar #'(lambda (arg)
                                 (our-eval arg env))
                             (rest form))))
    (apply function evaled-args)))
```

The function portion of a function call may be either a symbol which names a function or a lambda expression. If it is a symbol, then we call

LOOKUP-FUNCTION-VALUE to retrieve the actual function object; otherwise we assume that a lambda expression is being called directly, so we recursively evaluate it. Notice that we once again wrap the lambda expression inside a call to **FUNCTION**, just as we did in **EVAL-DEFUN**, to be sure to create a lexical closure over the current environment.

Once we have a valid function object we can evaluate all the arguments from left to right, collecting the results into a list. Since all functions created by **EVAL-FUNCTION** are represented as functions in the underlying Lisp, we can use **APPLY** to call the function on the evaluated arguments.

Because we are using **APPLY** to call functions, we can call primitives, such as **CAR** or **CDR**, which are already defined in the underlying Lisp just as easily as we can call functions defined by our own interpreter. Likewise, we can call functions defined in our interpreter directly from the host Lisp! Our interpreter fits rather seamlessly into the underlying Lisp system.

In order to try **OUR-EVAL**, we will define a simple read-eval-print loop:

```
;;; The Read-Eval-Print-Loop
(defun repl ()
  (catch 'done
    (loop (format t "~&~%Our-Lisp> ")
          (let ((result (our-eval (read) nil)))
            (princ result)))))

(defun eval-exit ()
  (throw 'done 'done))
```

We establish a **CATCH** tag around the looping part of **REPL** so that a call to the function **EXIT** can throw out of the loop and escape back to the host Lisp interpreter:

```
Lisp> (repl)

Our-Lisp> (* 3 4)     ; call the function * defined in
12                    ; the host Lisp from OUR-EVAL

Our-Lisp> (defun fact (x)
            (if (= x 0)
                1
                (* x (fact (- x 1))))))
FACT

Our-Lisp> (fact 5)    ; Call the fact defined by
120                   ; OUR-EVAL from OUR-EVAL

Our-Lisp> (exit)
DONE
```

```
Lisp> (fact 5)          ; Call the fact defined by
120                     ; OUR-EVAL from the host Lisp
```

Representing functions defined by `OUR-EVAL` as regular functions in the host Lisp allows us to freely mix code defined by either the host or `OUR-EVAL`. Here is a more complex example to prove that `OUR-EVAL` can really create lexical closures. Recall that in Chapter 9 we saw how we could simulate the functionality of `CONS` with a closure:

```
Lisp>(repl)

Our-Lisp> (defun make-pair (castor pollux)
            #'(lambda (selector)
                (if (eq selector :castor)
                    castor
                    (if (eq selector :pollux)
                        pollux
                        (error "Unknown message ~A"
                               selector)))))
MAKE-PAIR

Our-Lisp> (defun castor (closure)
            (funcall closure :castor))
CASTOR

Our-Lisp> (defun pollux (closure)
            (funcall closure :pollux))
POLLUX

Our-Lisp> (setq p1 (make-pair 'left 'right))
#<Interpreted-Function
  (LAMBDA (&REST EVALED-ARGS)
    (OUR-EVAL BODY
              (EXTEND-ENV ENV FORMAL-ARGS EVALED-ARGS)))
  [closed over BODY, ENV, and FORMAL-ARGS]
  109E65F>

Our-Lisp> (functionp p1)
T

Our-Lisp> (castor p1)
LEFT

Our-Lisp> (pollux p1)
RIGHT
```

Notice that we are using closures in the underlying Lisp to represent closures in our interpreter. This may seem like cheating, but we are only using the underlying Lisp's closures as a data structure to hold the environments which we are explicitly maintaining in our interpreter.

18.1.1 Environment Manipulation

Now we will examine the environment manipulation functions. Because Common Lisp supports separate function and value namespaces, we will use separate accessing and updating functions for each namespace. Here is the code to manipulate the value namespace:

```
(defun lookup-variable-value (symbol env)
  (let ((entry (assoc symbol env)))
    (if (null entry)
        (symbol-value symbol)
        (cdr entry))))

(defun set-variable-value (symbol value env)
  (let ((entry (assoc symbol env)))
    (if (null entry)
        (setf (symbol-value symbol) value)
        ;; destructively modify the environment
        (setf (cdr entry) value))))

(defun extend-env (current-env new-vars new-vals)
  (pairlis new-vars new-vals current-env))
```

In **LOOKUP-VARIABLE-VALUE**, we use **ASSOC** to look up a binding for a variable in the current lexical environment. If a binding is found then we return it; otherwise we return the variable's global value. Similarly, we can destructively alter a global value with **SET-VARIABLE-VALUE**. Notice that the a-list entry which represents a binding is destructively changed, and thus multiple functions which have closed over the same environment will all see the change. This is the correct behavior for multiple closures over the same binding. Finally, **EXTEND-ENV** is used to augment an existing environment with a new set of variables and values.

The support for the function namespace is similar to that for the value namespace, but it is simpler because our interpreter does not support lexical function definitions:

```
(defun lookup-function-value (symbol &optional env)
  ;; Tell Lisp that we do not want to use the ENV
  ;; argument right now. It will be used when
  ;; the interpreter can define local functions.
  (declare (ignore env))
  (symbol-function symbol))
```

```
(defun set-function-value (symbol value &optional env)
  (declare (ignore env))
  (setf (symbol-function symbol) value))
```

The function namespace functions manipulate only the function cell of a symbol.

Problem. Add support for local functions in the function namespace. One way to do this is to represent an environment as a structure consisting of two a-lists: one for values and the other for functions. Then extend `OUR-EVAL` so that it can handle `LABELS` and `FLET`.

Problem. Extend `OUR-EVAL` so that we can define macros. Write `DEFUN` as a macro so that it does not appear as an explicit case in `EVAL-APPLICATION`.

Problem. Change the representation of an environment from an a-list to a linked series of *frame* structures. Each frame should contain an a-list representing the lexical environment needed by a function, the name of that function (if it has one), and a pointer to the previous frame.

Problem. Write a simple debugger for `OUR-EVAL` which can examine individual frames and display their contents.

18.1.2 Problems with Implicit Control

Although our interpreter works, it does not have some of the functionality we have discussed so far:

- Tail-recursion removal—All function calls allocate new storage for bindings whether they need to or not. This means that even tail-recursive calls allocate memory, so our interpreter does not remove tail-recursion.
- Abnormal control flow—Our interpreter does not support special forms like `RETURN-FROM` or `GO` which alter the flow of control.

Both of these problems stem from the fact that the control flow in our interpreter is *implicit*. All functions must return to their caller, and there is currently no way to change this without altering `OUR-EVAL`. In order to introduce constructs such as `RETURN-FROM` or `GO` we will make the flow of control in our programs *explicit* with the idea of *continuation passing*.

18.2 CONTINUATION PASSING MAKES CONTROL FLOW EXPLICIT

In order to make the flow of control in our programs explicit, we will eliminate the rule that functions *return* one or more values to their caller. Instead, each primitive function like `CAR` or `CONS`, as well as new functions we define, will accept an extra argument called a *continuation*. Instead of returning one or more values, a function should call the given continuation function with those values. Thus, functions *never* return—they only transfer control to another function. Of course, the continuation functions themselves do not expect a continuation argument, but all other functions do.

For example, `CAR` now expects two arguments: a pointer to a cons cell and a continuation function. In order to "return" the car pointer of the cons cell, `CAR` calls the continuation function with the car as an argument. The continuation function represents a *complete* continuation of the computation which needed to call `CAR`, and thus the call to `CAR` never returns.

Programs which are written to explicitly accept continuations are said to be written in *Continuation-Passing Style*, or CPS for short. Here are some simple examples of how we could write the CPS version of some typical primitive functions:

```
(defun cps-car (x cont)
  (funcall cont (car x)))

(defun cps-= (x y cont)
  (funcall cont (= x y)))

(defun cps-- (x y cont)
  (funcall cont (- x y)))

(defun cps-* (x y cont)
  (funcall cont (* x y)))
```

Each of these functions has the same structure. We perform some computation with all the arguments except the continuation, and we call the continuation with the result of that computation when we are done:

```
Lisp> (identity 4) ; same as ((lambda (x) x) 4)
4

Lisp> (cps-* 4 5 #'identity)
20

Lisp> (cps-= 0 0 #'identity)
T
```

In order to test our CPS primitives, we can pass them the `IDENTITY` function as a continuation. `IDENTITY` accepts a single argument and returns it unchanged. Of course, this is a bit odd since we just agreed that functions would not return, but we still need to transfer control to the underlying Lisp in order to test our CPS functions.

18.2.1 A CPS Version of Factorial

Now we can examine a more elaborate example: the CPS version of **FACT**. Unlike the version of **FACT** we usually use, the flow of control is explicit in **CPS-FACT**:

```
(defun cps-fact (n cont)
  (cps-= n
         0
         #'(lambda (test-true?)
             (if test-true?
                 (funcall cont 1)
                 (cps-- n
                        1
                        #'(lambda (temp-2)
                            (cps-fact temp-2
                                      #'(lambda (temp-3)
                                          (cps-* n
                                                 temp-3
                                                 cont)))))))))
```

Since every function we define takes a continuation, **CPS-FACT** expects a second argument named **CONT**.[2] The implicit left-to-right evaluation rules have been made explicit in **CPS-FACT**. Hence, the order of argument evaluation in a CPS program cannot affect the meaning of the program because the arguments to every function are always variables or constants such as 1. Here is a simple test of **CPS-FACT**:

```
Lisp> (cps-fact 5 #'identity)
120
```

CPS-FACT starts by calling **CPS-=** to see if we have a base case. **CPS-=** returns its boolean result by calling the continuation function we have passed as a third argument. Notice that this continuation function contains *all* the information needed to compute factorial, so we will never need to return from **CPS-=** because calling the continuation *is* the return.

The continuation function names the result of calling **CPS-=** as **TEST-TRUE?**, and calls **IF** to decide how to proceed. If the result is true,

---

[2]It is actually easier to think of the continuation as the "zeroth" argument to a function so that it always come first in the argument list. This convention makes it easier to define functions which accept an arbitrary number of arguments, but it makes the code more difficult to read. Putting the continuation last makes the CPS code easier to read, so we will adopt that convention in our examples.

then `CPS-FACT` is done and can call its continuation function with the value 1. However, if the result is false we continue computing by subtracting 1 from `N`. The result of the subtraction is used as an argument in a recursive call to `CPS-FACT` along with a new continuation argument. This new continuation will be called with the factorial of `(- N 1)` as an argument. Finally, we call `CPS-*` to multiply that answer by `N` to finish the original computation (`FACT N`).

Notice that we pass the original continuation named `CONT` as the continuation argument to `CPS-*`. Thus, `CPS-*` will not return its result to `CPS-FACT`. Instead, it will return the result *directly* to the caller of `CPS-FACT`. This corresponds exactly to tail-recursion removal.

We could have written the call to `CPS-*` differently:

```
...
   (cps-* n
          temp-3
          #'(lambda (temp-4)
              (funcall cont temp-4)))
```

This version needlessly passes a continuation function which forces control to return back to `CPS-FACT` when the multiplication is done. This is effectively what our interpreter does now. The advantage of this is that debugging is easier if an error occurs within `CPS-*` because a record of the call to `CPS-FACT` still exists. However, no useful computation is performed upon returning to `CPS-FACT` because we then proceed to call `CONT` ourselves, thus wasting time and space. The point of all this is that converting our programs to CPS can easily remove tail-recursion for us as long as function calls never return. In fact, we have to go to some extra effort to *not* remove tail-recursion!

18.2.2 Using CPS to Express Abnormal Control Transfer

Our next example does not exemplify good programming style, but it illustrates a nontrivial case of how CPS can express the kind of control transfers provided by `BLOCK` and `RETURN-FROM`:

```
(defun twisty (x)
  (let ((y (block yow
             (print (if (< x 0)
                        (return-from yow 0)
                        x)))))
    (* x y)))
```

If `X` is negative, then the call to `PRINT` is prematurely aborted and `Y` is bound to `0`. Otherwise, `X` is printed and `Y` is bound to `X`. `X` times `Y` is then returned:

```
Lisp> (twisty 5)

5
25

Lisp> (twisty -5)
0
```

We can eliminate the calls to **BLOCK** and **RETURN-FROM** by rewriting **TWISTY** using continuation passing:

```
(defun cps-twisty (x cont)
  ((lambda (yow)
     (cps-< x 0 #'(lambda (test-true?)
                    (if test-true?
                        (funcall yow 0)
                        (cps-print x yow)))))
   #'(lambda (y)
       (cps-* x y cont))))

(defun cps-< (x y cont)
  (funcall cont (< x y)))

(defun cps-print (x cont)
  (funcall cont (print x)))
```

BLOCK is really just a way to name continuations, so the first thing **CPS-TWISTY** does is bind the name **YOW** to the continuation function which wants the result returned by **BLOCK**. Once the continuation is named, we call **CPS-<** to see if **X** is less than zero. If so, then we "return" the number **0** from the block by calling the continuation function named **YOW**, and the call to **CPS-PRINT** is never executed.

If **X** is not negative, then we call **CPS-PRINT** on **X** and **YOW**. When **CPS-PRINT** is done, it will call **YOW** with the value of **X**. Either way we end up calling the continuation **YOW**. **YOW** merely binds **Y** to the value it is passed and then multiplies **X** by **Y**. Just as in **CPS-FACT**, the original continuation passed to **CPS-TWISTY** is passed to **CPS-*** so that tail-recursion is removed and **CPS-*** will directly call the continuation which wants the value of **CPS-TWISTY**. The end result is that **CPS-TWISTY** behaves identically to **TWISTY**:

```
Lisp> (cps-twisty 5 #'identity)

5
25

Lisp> (cps-twisty -5 #'identity)
0
```

Continuation passing can be a bit difficult to get used to, but it provides a simple, regular way to make explicit many of the implicit semantics of Lisp. We can use this to our advantage in our interpreter by first converting Lisp to CPS and then using `OUR-EVAL` to interpret the converted code. Later we will see that this technique is also useful when building a Lisp compiler.

Problem. Convert the following function into CPS.

```
(defun ugly-assoc (key a-list)
  (dolist (e a-list)
    (when (eq (car e) key)
      (return e))))
```

Problem. Rewrite the version of `TAIL-REVERSE` presented in Chapter 10 into CPS.

Problem. Rewrite the definition of `PROG-REVERSE` in Chapter 11 by replacing each tag by a function introduced by `LABELS`, and each `GO` by a call to that function. Convert this version of the function to CPS.

Problem. Is there any difference between the CPS versions of `TAIL-REVERSE` and `PROG-REVERSE`?

18.2.3 Upward Continuations

In light of continuation passing, `BLOCK` really provides another namespace in which to name functions. However, the functions which `BLOCK` names are continuation functions which the system creates for us. Although convenient, this is a rather obscure way of naming continuations.

A clearer way to name a continuation is to invent a new function called `CALL-WITH-CURRENT-CONTINUATION`, which we will abbreviate to `CALL-CC`. `CALL-CC` is really the same thing as `BLOCK`,[3] but the semantics of `CALL-CC` fit in better with our understanding of how continuation passing works:

```
Lisp> (defun call-cc (func)
        (funcall func #'(lambda (&rest values)
                          (return-from call-cc
                            ;; Be sure to pass multiple
                            ;; values on to the continuation
                            ;; function as arguments
                            (values-list values)))))
CALL-CC
```

---

[3]Except that first-class continuations have indefinite extent, rather than the dynamic extent of `BLOCK` names.

```
Lisp> (defun ugly-assoc (key a-list)
        (call-cc #'(lambda (escape)
                     (dolist (e a-list)
                       (when (eq (car e) key)
                         (funcall escape e))))))
UGLY-ASSOC
```

CALL-CC expects a function of one argument, and it calls that function with the *current continuation*. The current continuation is the implicit continuation function which expects to be called by CALL-CC itself. However, we can rewrite the body of the DOLIST to prematurely call the continuation when it wants to exit.

As we saw at the end of Chapter 10, it is illegal to try to return from a BLOCK after the call to BLOCK has exited because blocks have *dynamic* rather than *indefinite* extent. This restriction also affects what we can do with CALL-CC:

```
Lisp> (print (call-cc #'(lambda (continuation)
                          (setf *continuation* continuation)
                          3)))

3
3

Lisp> (funcall *continuation* 4)
>>Error: Attempt to RETURN-FROM block CALL-CC
         occurred from within a closure which
         no longer exists!

unnamed function:
   Required arg 0 (VALUE): 4

:A    Abort to Lisp Top Level

->
```

A continuation which is passed out of the CALL-CC which established it is called an *upward continuation*. Because of Common Lisp's restrictions on blocks, continuations can only be passed *downward*, not upward. If upward continuations did work, then the call to *CONTINUATION* would have printed the number 4. Upward continuations would have allowed us to return from the original call to CALL-CC as many times as we liked!

A similar situation exists with TAGBODY. The tags in a tagbody have dynamic extent, so that it is illegal to GO to a tag once the tagbody establishing it has exited. Common Lisp has these restrictions because it is difficult to implement upward continuations efficiently. Unfortunately, in declining to implement upward continuations, we lose the power and semantic consistency offered by them.[4] For more information about CPS, refer to [Ste78b], [KKR+86], [SS76a], and [SS76a]. For information about interpreters refer to [AS85] and [Ste78a].

Problem. Write your own version of `CATCH` and `THROW` in terms of `BLOCK` and `RETURN-FROM`.

Problem. Write a version of `UNWIND-PROTECT` that works with the versions of `CATCH` and `THROW` that you just wrote.

Problem. Can you think of any uses for upward continuations?

Problem. Write a function called `LISP->CPS` which accepts two arguments: a Lisp form and a continuation which wants the result of evaluating that form. `LISP->CPS` should return the CPS version of the form it is passed.

---

[4]Other dialects of Lisp, notably Scheme, do support upward continuations.

CHAPTER 19

LISP IMPLEMENTATION

Unlike most of the previous chapters in this book, the remaining chapters cover Lisp implementation, compilation, and efficiency issues. In order to understand this material, it helps to have a basic understanding of computer architecture and assembly language programming. This is not meant to scare you off, but merely to warn you that some of the material ahead is not for everyone and assumes a bit more background than previous chapters.

Why should you learn about Lisp implementation? After all, a high-level programming language provides an abstraction which insulates us from the gory details of the underlying hardware. Unfortunately, no programming language is perfect, and some level of implementation knowledge is often necessary to write efficient programs on standard hardware. Another possibility is that you are simply curious about how the semantics of Lisp are usually implemented.

The topics in these few chapters really deserve a book of their own. Therefore, the coverage of them will necessarily be more of an overview than an in-depth discussion of all the issues. If you are especially interested in a topic, you should use the references at the end of the book to find more information.

19.1 COMPILING LISP CODE

So far we have run all of our Lisp programs using an interpreter. However, it is also possible to *compile* our Lisp code into a faster form. In the most general sense, compilation translates one language into another. For example, the "source code" for this book is written in a typesetting language called L^{A}T$_E$X [Lam86]. In order to print the book, it is compiled by the L^{A}T$_E$X compiler into a more primitive representation called a *DVI* (Device Independent) file. The DVI file is then compiled into another language, such as PostScript [ASI85], which a printer can understand. Similarly, we can compile Lisp programs from their representation as lists into a lower-level representation which executes more efficiently on a particular machine.

The function `COMPILE` will compile a single Lisp function:

```
Lisp> (defun add1 (x) (1+ x))
ADD1

Lisp> (compile 'add1)
;;; Compiling function ADD1...done
ADD1

Lisp> (add1 3)
4
```

`ADD1` behaves as we expect, but now it will run more quickly than the interpreted version. Some Lisps do not even have an interpreter, instead compiling everything. An expression which is typed into the read-eval-print loop is immediately compiled and then executed. If the compiler is fast, such an implementation can provide many of the benefits of an interpreter, while at the same time reducing the complexity of the Lisp and assuring that there is no difference between compiled and interpreted code.

In Chapter 4 we saw how to compile an entire file of Lisp code with the function `COMPILE-FILE`.

```
;;; The file ADD-CONSTANTS.LISP contains the functions
;;; ADD1 and ADD2 which add 1 and 2 respectively to their
;;; single arguments.

Lisp> (compile-file "add-constants.lisp")
;;; Reading input file #P"$DISK1:[WADE]add-constants.lisp"
;;; Compiling function ADD1...done
;;; Compiling function ADD2...done
;;; Wrote output file #P"$DISK1:[WADE]add-constants.bin"
#P"$DISK1:[WADE]add-constants.bin"

Lisp> (load "add-constants.bin")
#P"$DISK1:[WADE]add-constants.bin"

Lisp> (add2 3)
5
```

The result of compiling a Lisp file is a binary file which usually contains machine instructions. Binary files are sometimes called Fast Load or *fasl* files because they can also be loaded more quickly into Lisp than the original source file.

Sometimes we want to examine the compiled code for a function to try to determine where time is being wasted or simply because we are curious. The function **DISASSEMBLE** will print the machine code for a function. For example, here is the result of disassembling **ADD1** in Lucid Common Lisp on a VAX:

```
Lisp> (disassemble 'add1)
          0:       CMPL 515(SQ), SP   ; SQ-STACK-OVERFLOW-FRONTIER
          5:       BLEQU L1
          7:       MOVL 519(SQ), R7   ; SQ-STACK-OVERFLOW-HANDLER
         12:       JSB 5(R7)
L1:      15:       CMPW COUNT-REG, #1
         18:       BEQLU L2
         20:       MOVL 227(SQ), R7         ; SQ-INCORRECT-NO-ARGS
         25:       JSB 5(R7)
L2:      28:       MOVL -12(LISP-FP), R5 ; Required argument X
         32:       MOVL #4, R6
         35:       MOVB R5, R2
         38:       BISB2 R6, R2
         41:       BITB #3, R2
         44:       BNEQU L3
         46:       ADDL2 R6, R5
         49:       BVC L4
         51:       SUBL2 R6, R5
L3:      54:       MOVL 167(SQ), R7         ; SQ-GENERIC-BINARY-+
         59:       JSB 5(R7)
L4:      62:       MOVL R5, 4(LISP-FP)      ; return-value
         66:       MOVL -4(LISP-FP), CP     ; old CP
         70:       MOVAL -8(LISP-FP), SP    ; return PC
         74:       JMP @0(SP)
NIL
Lisp>
```

Of course, this machine code is implementation specific, but it can be useful to understand what it is doing. As we will see later, we can often improve the efficiency of compiled code on standard hardware by adding *declarations* to our Lisp code. **DISASSEMBLE** is often essential to determining if the compiler is using those declarations to make the optimizations we think (hope!) it is making.

19.2 STORING TYPE INFORMATION

One of Lisp's distinctive features is its ability to determine the type of any object at runtime. In Chapter 7 we saw that any object may be represented as a contiguous sequence of bytes in memory, but we did not mention how we could determine the type of an object given only a pointer to it.

```
                                    s   n
                                    e   -
 O   O   O   7   O   5              v   -
                                    e   -

 ↓       ↓       ↓                  FIGURE 19.1
CONS  FIXNUM  SIMPLE-STRING         The cons cell (7 . "seven").
```

19.2.1 Storing the Type in the Object

The simplest way to store data types is to devote an extra slot in every object to holding type information. Figure 19.1 shows how the cons cell (7 . "seven") might look.

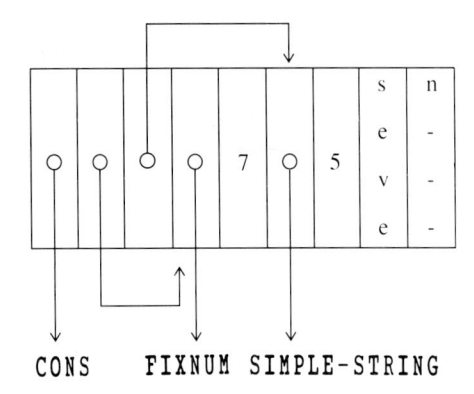

The cons cell actually has three slots: a type, a car, and a cdr. The integer 7 can fit in a single machine word and is called a *fixnum*. Thus, we need one slot to hold the type specifier FIXNUM and another slot to hold the integer itself. The simple string "seven" needs a slot for the type SIMPLE-STRING, a slot to hold the number of characters in the string, and slots to hold the character codes for the characters in the string. Most character encodings, for example ASCII, can fit in a single byte, so we can store four characters per word. Because all objects are aligned on four-byte boundaries, only the first byte in the last word of the string "seven" is actually used. The remaining bytes are filled with nulls.

Notice that the interpretation of an object slot is completely dependent on the type information, which is always stored at the beginning of the object. Once we see that an object is a cons cell, we know that the next two words are pointers, while a fixnum consists of a type slot followed by a single word which contains the binary representation of a 32-bit integer.

19.2.2 Tagged Pointers

While putting the data types directly into each object is simple and regular, it is also inefficient. For example, it took three words of memory to hold the number 7 in the car of a cons cell: one word to point to the number and two words to hold the number itself.

We could save memory by storing the number directly in the car of the cons cell. However, in order to do that we need some special way of saying that the car should *not* be interpreted as a pointer to another object, but instead as the object itself. In this case, we want to represent the number 7 as an *immediate* fixnum.

We can distinguish pointers from immediate objects by encoding the type of an object in all the *pointers* which point to that object. We will reserve a few bits in each pointer as *tag bits* which encode the type of the object. Ideally, these bits would be extra and tacked onto every single pointer. Unfortunately, only special-purpose hardware such as Lisp machines generally provide such extra tag bits.

A pointer can actually point to any *byte* in the machine, but we require that all objects be *word* aligned. Therefore, we really only need to be able to point to every fourth byte in the machine. This means that the two least significant bits of a pointer are not needed and can be used as tag bits. This scheme is usually called *low-tag*.[1] If we use the two least significant bits of every pointer as tag bits, then we can assign them the following meanings:

```
Tag bits         Type of object pointed at
--------         -------------------------
   00              Immediate fixnum
   01              Other immediate
   10              Cons cell
   11              Other pointer
```

If the tag bits are both zero, then the remaining 30 bits may be treated as the fixnum itself rather than wasting memory and pointing at a number somewhere else. Similarly, a type code of `01` means that some other immediate data type, such as a character or a byte specifier, is represented in the remaining 30 bits of the word. Of course, the rest of the word must also contain a *secondary tag* to describe *which* other immediate data type is being represented.

A tag of `10` means that the pointer points to a cons cell. Therefore, we do not have to put a type slot in every cons cell since every pointer to the cell already contains the type information. This is an important case because cons cells are so prevalent in Lisp that putting a type slot in every cons cell seems excessive.

However, we are now left with all the other data types in Lisp, with only the tag `11` unused. At this point we must revert back to the original scheme of encoding the type of an object directly in the object itself. A string will still look like it did before, as will arrays, bignums, structures, etc. However, rather than putting a pointer to a symbol at the beginning of each object which contains a type slot, we will instead put a special kind of immediate data type (tag `01`) called a *header*. The header will encode the actual type and length of the object in the remaining bits of the header word. Figure 19.2 shows what the cons cell (7 . "seven") looks like using low tag.

Immediate objects are drawn inside a box, while pointers are drawn as before. The values of the tag bits are listed below each word, even though the tag bits are contained in the word itself. The header which begins the simple string `"seven"` not only encodes the fact that the object is a simple string, but it

---

[1] Many implementations of low tag actually use three tag bits rather than two. These implementations must align all objects on eight-byte boundaries.

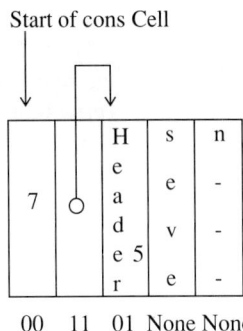

FIGURE 19.2 The cons cell `(7 . "seven")` using low tag.

also contains the length of the string. Because a simple string contains characters, the next two words are treated as 32-bit immediate data, and thus their low-order two bits are not treated as tags but instead as parts of characters.

Putting a header at the beginning of each object other than a cons or an immediate object means that we can linearly scan memory and determine the beginning, ending, and type of every object contained in it. Later we will see that this is important to the correct functioning of many garbage collectors.

Using type bits may seem to make it difficult to dereference a pointer, because the pointer no longer contains the correct address. However, we can use the indexed addressing mode provided by virtually all computers to cancel the type code and dereference a pointer in a single instruction. For example, if register `R1` contains a pointer to a cons cell, then we can move the car of the cell to `R2` with the instruction `MOVE 2(R1),R2`. This assumes that every *untagged* pointer actually points four bytes *before* the word to which we really want to point. Then, because a *tagged* cons pointer points $4 - 2 = 2$ bytes *before* the actual start of the cons cell, we can access the car of the cons cell by adding 2 to the pointer. The same sort of scheme will work for any data structure accessing and updating functions.

Putting tag bits in the low-order portion of the word and using a tag of `00` to mean fixnum also means that we can use native machine instructions to perform fixnum arithmetic in one or two machine instructions. For example, adding or subtracting two lowtag fixnums will produce another fixnum.

Although we will discuss one other way of representing type information, we will assume a low tag implementation for the duration of the book.

19.2.3 Big Bag of Pages (BIBOP)

Sometimes we do not want to give up any of our address bits to represent type information, particularly on machines which are not byte addressable. Instead we would like to derive the type of object pointed to from the object's address. We can do this if we only allocate a single kind of object in a given chunk of memory. For example, if a page of memory contains 1024 bytes and we agree to store only objects of a certain type on each page, then we can look up the type of an object by ignoring the 10 least significant bits (which index into a page) and use only the upper portion of the pointer as an index into a table which describes the type of object stored on each page.

Each time we want to allocate an object of type x, we should first check to see if we already have a page holding other objects of type x. If so, then we can allocate the new object on the same page. If not, then we should grab a new page of memory and insert a new entry into the type table describing the kind of objects which will be stored on this page. All the free pages of memory which have not yet been designated to hold a particular kind of object are called a BIg Bag Of Pages in the PDP-10 implementation of Maclisp [Ste77a], hence this scheme has been given the name BIBOP.

19.3 DIVIDING MEMORY INTO STORAGE AREAS

No matter what data-typing scheme we use, all Lisp systems allocate space for new objects from a pool of free memory called a *heap*. However, rather than having a single heap inside of Lisp, most Lisp systems have several different kinds of heaps called *areas* or *spaces*. They can be distinguished by how the data within them is used.

Most data is created in a *dynamic* area of memory which is garbage-collected when it becomes full. However, this can lead to inefficiency. For example, the compiled code for built-in functions and the literal objects they reference will never change, and every Lisp process on our computer must contain these immutable objects. Rather than making each Lisp process contain its own copy of these constant objects, we can allow them to all share a single copy by storing the objects in a *read-only* area of memory. Read-only objects may be referenced but never updated, and therefore they may be safely shared by all processes which want to use them. This scheme conserves memory and has the effect of reducing paging in a virtual memory system, allowing more of each process's address space to stay in physical memory.

Because literals referenced by compiled code are treated as constants, they are put into read-only space. However, consider how this affects the following program:

```
;;; CIRCULARIZE is introduced at the end of Chapter 7
(defun circularize! (l)
  (if (null l)
      l
      (setf (cdr (last l)) l)))

(defun infinite-zeros ()
  (circularize! '(0)))        ; '(0) is treated as a constant
```

Although it is poor programming style to ever try to alter a constant, `INFINITE-ZEROS` will usually work correctly when interpreted. However, it will usually not work when compiled because the constant `'(0)` will be in read-only space and cannot be altered. We can avoid this problem by replacing the constant `'(0)` with the expression `(LIST 0)`, which will guarantee that storage is allocated in dynamic space at runtime.

Another area of memory is considered *static*. Data placed in a static area may be both read and written, but it is never subject to garbage collection. For example, most interned symbols will never become garbage and should live in static space so that the garbage collector does not waste time trying to reclaim their memory.

Other kinds of area classifications are usually based on how the garbage collector should treat data in that area. We will briefly discuss some of these areas later when we examine garbage collection.

19.4 FUNCTION CALL CONVENTIONS

We can select any one of a number of conventions for how function calls will work. However, we must strike a balance between two opposing desires: we want our code to run as fast as possible, but we also want it to retain as much information as possible so that our programs will be easier to debug.

A function call consists of two components: argument passing and control transfer. In order to simulate the photocopier model of function calling, each time we perform a non-tail-recursive function call we need to somehow create a new frame to hold arguments and locals. Ideally we would allocate these frames in dynamic space just like any other object and allow the garbage collector to periodically reclaim the memory occupied by dead frames.

Unfortunately, function calls and returns occur with such high frequency that we would spend too much time heap-allocating and later garbage-collecting frames. However, frame allocation and deallocation generally follow a *stack*-like discipline, and thus we can use a stack to quickly create new frames and destroy old ones.[2] We will store the stack pointer in a register and use machine instructions to push and pop data onto the stack. Offset addressing can be used to access arguments and local variables in a stack frame.

In order to call a function, we can create a new stack frame by pushing the arguments, including a continuation, onto the stack. Next we must look up the starting address for the function code, often by looking in the function cell of the symbol which names the function. We can then transfer control by jumping to the start of the function code. When the function is done, it should pop the stack frame and call the continuation argument with the result of the function. Thus, a function call is really nothing more than a *goto* which passes arguments [SS76b].

---

[2]Correctly implementing upward closures and upward continuations requires extra work in a system which stack-allocates frames.

Instead of passing arguments on the stack we could also pass them in registers. This will usually be faster than using the stack, but it will also make debugging compiled code more difficult because we will have to figure out which registers are actually in use at any given time.

Recall that Lisp must allow interpreted and compiled code to freely call each other. We can accomplish this by making *all* code look compiled, which is exactly what the interpreter we wrote in Chapter 18 does once it has been compiled. Recall that the function `EVAL-FUNCTION` represented an interpreted function as a lexical closure. The interpreter itself must be compiled at some point, and all of the lexical closures which it returns will also be compiled functions. We do not have to do anything special to make interpreted code look like compiled code. Therefore, the function cell of any symbol should contain only compiled code, and compiled and interpreted functions may freely call each other.

19.5 DYNAMIC SCOPING

In this section we will examine the two most common methods for implementing special variable bindings. Both of these techniques can be implemented entirely at Lisp level, although they are usually implemented at a lower level to improve efficiency.

19.5.1 Shallow Binding

Referencing a special variable is really the same thing as calling `SYMBOL-VALUE` on that variable. For example, a reference to `*PRINT-BASE*` in the body of a program is just a shorter way of saying `(SYMBOL-VALUE '*PRINT-BASE*)`. A symbol typically has six parts (including the header).[3] One possible symbol layout is as follows:

Header	Package	Value	function	plist	name

Each of the accessing functions `SYMBOL-PACKAGE`, `SYMBOL-VALUE`, `SYMBOL-FUNCTION`, `SYMBOL-PLIST`, and `SYMBOL-NAME` can retrieve the value

---

[3]In order to open code the functions `CAR` and `CDR` in one instruction, we have to be careful about how we lay out a symbol so that `CAR` and `CDR` of `NIL` will both return `NIL`. How would you arrange a symbol or change the tagging scheme to make this possible?

of a symbol slot, while `SETF` can update the slot. In a *shallow bound* implementation of special variables, the current dynamic value of a variable is stored in the value cell. Thus, `SYMBOL-VALUE` and `SETF` can be used to access and update a special variable value.

When we want to create a new special binding, we have to save the current value stored in the value cell and install the new value. We can undo the binding by putting the saved value back in the value cell. This idea can be implemented directly in Lisp as a source code rewrite. For example, the code fragment

```
Lisp> (defun special-demo (n)
        (let ((*print-base* 16))
          (print n)
          (return-from special-demo n)))
SPECIAL-DEMO

Lisp> (special-demo 15)

F
15
```

can be implemented with the following rewrite:

```
Lisp> (defun special-demo (n)
        ;; save old value
        (let ((old-value (symbol-value '*print-base*)))
          (unwind-protect
              ;; install new value
              (progn (setf
                       (symbol-value '*print-base*)
                       16)
                     (print n)
                     (return-from special-demo n))
            ;; no matter how we exit, *always*
            ;; restore the old value.
            (setf (symbol-value '*print-base*)
                  old-value))))
SPECIAL-DEMO

Lisp> (special-demo 15)

F
15
```

Notice that we need the `UNWIND-PROTECT` to *always* restore the old binding value, even if we abnormally exit the special binding code. The advantage of shallow binding is that variable references are fast because we know exactly where to look for the variable's value. However, variable binding is rather slow because of all the overhead involved in saving and restoring values no matter how the scope of the binding is exited.

19.5.2 Deep Binding

An alternative to shallow binding is called *deep binding*. In a deep binding system, dynamic variable/value pairs are stored on a *binding stack*. This method works nicely because dynamic bindings have dynamic extent. Each time we want to create a binding, we push a new variable/value pair onto the stack, and to undo a binding we pop the pair from the stack. To look up the value of a special variable, we search the binding stack from top (most recent bindings) to bottom (least recent bindings), stopping at the first binding for the variable in which we are interested. Hence, we do not need a symbol value cell in a deep binding scheme because `SYMBOL-VALUE` is essentially like `ASSOC`, searching for a variable/value pair.

The disadvantage of deep binding is that the time it takes to look up a binding is proportional to the number of bindings. However, we can quickly create and undo bindings using push and pop. Even better, we can undo a large number of bindings all at once simply by changing the binding stack pointer. Later we will see that deep binding also works better than shallow binding in a multiprocessing system.

> **Problem.** Rewrite the special binding example given above to explicitly implement deep binding. Global variables which are globally set to a value and never bound are often useful, but under a deep binding scheme it may take a long time to look up those values. Can you think of a way to improve the performance of deep binding for such variables?

> **Problem.** Implement special variable binding and lookup in the interpreter we wrote in the last chapter. You may use any method you like.

19.6 GARBAGE COLLECTION

The term *garbage collection* is actually a bit of a misnomer, since most modern garbage collectors work by *abandoning* garbage rather than collecting it. In this section we will examine several different garbage collection techniques. Although all figures depicting heaps in this section assume a low-tag implementation, the tag bits are not displayed to avoid cluttering up the diagrams.

19.6.1 Stop and Copy

One of the most important and popular methods for garbage collection, especially in a virtual memory system, is called *stop and copy*. In its simplest form, stop and copy works by dividing dynamic space into two equal sized *semispaces*. We will call one section *new space* and the other *copy space*. At first, copy space

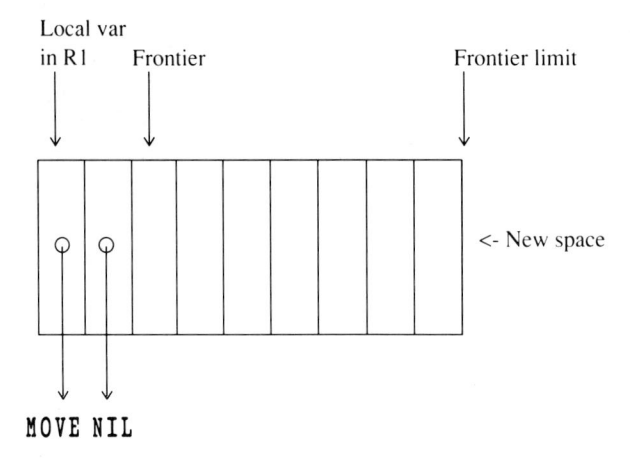

FIGURE 19.3
New space contains the list (**MOVE**).

will be unused and we will allocate new objects in new space. Figure 19.3 shows new space with the single cons cell (**MOVE**) in it. A local variable stored in **R1** contains a pointer to this cons cell.

In order to allocate new objects, we will maintain two pointers called a *frontier* and a *frontier limit*. The frontier is a pointer to the next available word in the heap. The frontier limit is a pointer to the first word *after* the end of the heap. We can use the following algorithm to allocate a new object of size *n* bytes:

```
(defun heap-allocate (n)
  (let ((new-frontier (+ n frontier)))
    (if (> new-frontier frontier-limit)
        ;; try to get more space and try allocation again
        (progn (if (gc)
                   (heap-allocate n)
                   (error "Out of memory!")))
        ;; PROG1 is like PROGN, but it
        ;; returns its first argument
        (prog1 frontier
               (setf frontier new-frontier)))))
```

We can allocate a new object by bumping the **FRONTIER** up by the specified number of bytes to create a **NEW-FRONTIER**. If the **NEW-FRONTIER** exceeds the **FRONTIER-LIMIT**, then we try to reclaim space with a garbage collection. A garbage collection may not reclaim enough space if too many objects are in use, in which case we can ask the operating system for more memory. If it still cannot find memory, then we signal an error. If the gc succeeds, then we try to allocate space again. If there is already enough space, then we update the actual

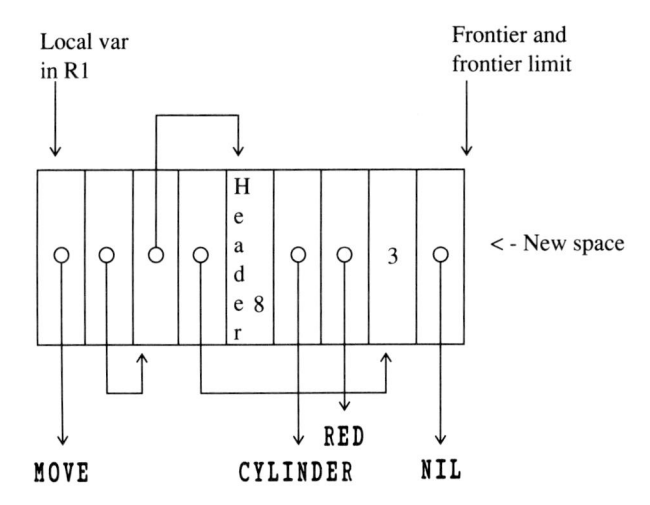

FIGURE 19.4
New space contains (`MOVE #S(CYLINDER COLOR RED) 3`).

FRONTIER and return its original value as the beginning of the allocated object. Now suppose that we run an imaginary program for a while, and we fill our tiny heap with more data until it looks like Figure 19.4. Now the heap contains the list (`MOVE #S(CYLINDER COLOR RED) 3`). At this point the heap is full and all objects are in use. However, pretend that our program keeps running and performs some list surgery, producing the heap shown in Figure 19.5.

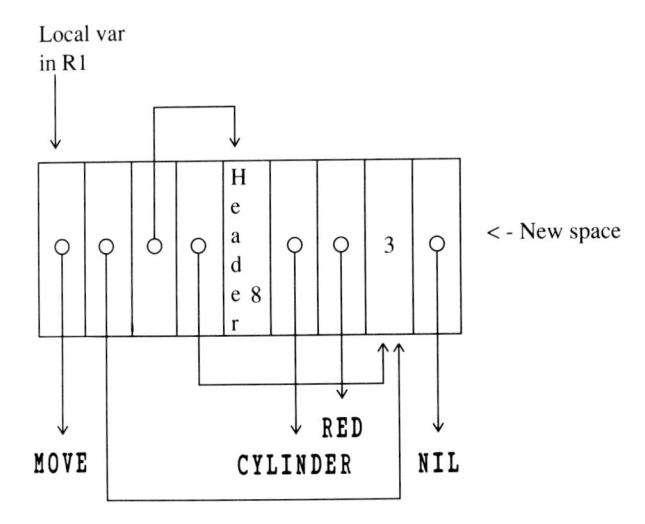

FIGURE 19.5
New space contains (`MOVE 3`) and two garbage objects.

At this point only the list (MOVE 3) is reachable by our program. There are no longer any pointers to the second cons cell, and therefore it and the structure it references are garbage. However, if we now try to call HEAP-ALLOCATE to allocate eight bytes for a new cons cell, we will exceed the FRONTIER-LIMIT. Hence, HEAP-ALLOCATE will try to garbage-collect to reclaim space.

Now we need to perform a garbage collection. We will rename new space *old space* and will copy all live objects from old to copy space. We must also update all pointers to those objects so that they point to objects in copy space rather than the objects in old space. Once all good objects have been copied, we no longer need old space and we can *flip*. Copy space will now be called new space, and we may continue to allocate new objects beginning after the copied objects. Old space will become copy space and will be used the next time we need to garbage-collect. Figure 19.6 shows what the copy space looks like when all good objects have been copied into it and we are ready to flip.

We can start to find all the live objects in old space by *scanning* a *root set* of references. The root set consists of any machine registers[4] which can hold pointers into the heap, as well as any frames on the call stack. We scan by looking for references from the root set to old space. If we find either a register or a stack location which points into old space, then we should copy the referenced object into copy space and update the reference.

As shown in Figure 19.7, we will use two pointers into copy space to remember the state of the copy from old space to copy space. The first pointer

---

[4]Registers which hold Lisp data are sometimes called *marked registers*, while registers holding raw (untagged) bits are called *unmarked* registers.

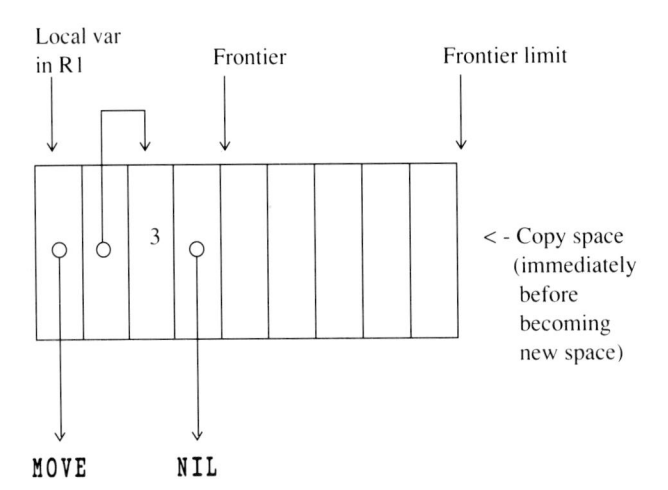

FIGURE 19.6
Stop and copy garbage collection leaves only the list (MOVE 3).

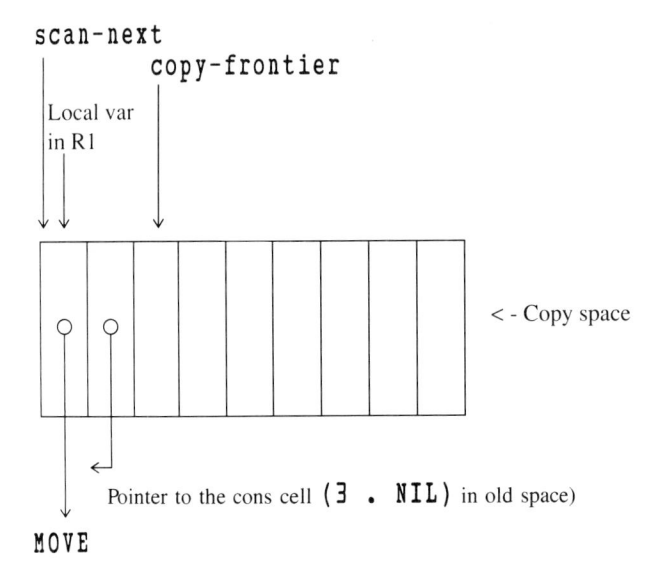

FIGURE 19.7
Copying objects from old space to copy space.

will be called `COPY-FRONTIER` and will point to the next available word in copy space. It will be used just as the frontier pointer was used in old space.

After copying an object from old space to copy space, we must also scan the object to recursively copy all of its *subparts*. The second pointer will be called `SCAN-NEXT` and will point to the next object in copy space which has *not* been scanned.

After the entire root set of objects has been copied, the `SCAN-NEXT` pointer will be initialized to point at the first object in copy space, while the `COPY-FRONTIER` pointer will already point to the next free word in copy space. We will then start to copy each subpart of the object pointed to by `SCAN-NEXT` into the free space pointed to by `COPY-FRONTIER`. Once the entire object has been scanned, we can increment `SCAN-NEXT` to point to the next object. Thus, `SCAN-NEXT` will always be trying to catch up to `COPY-FRONTIER`. When `SCAN-NEXT` is actually equal to `COPY-FRONTIER`, then all the live objects in old space have been copied, and the garbage collection is complete. At this point we can flip, renaming copy space to new space and `COPY-FRONTIER` to `FRONTIER`.

Stop and copy is a fairly simple algorithm, but there are two problems we have overlooked. The first is the possibility of copying the same object twice. The first time we encounter a pointer to an object in old space, we will copy the object into copy space. However, if we later encounter *another* pointer to the same object, we will copy it again, thereby producing multiple copies of the same object. However, if we do this, multiple references to the same object will no longer be `EQ`.

To avoid this problem, we will create a new data type called a *forwarding pointer*. Once an object has been copied from old space to new space, we will replace the object in old space with a forwarding pointer. The forwarding pointer will point to the new copy of the object in copy space. We will also modify the copying algorithm to first check if an object in old space starts with a forwarding pointer. If so, then we do not need to perform another copy. Instead, we only have to update references to the old object with the value contained in the forwarding pointer, thus ensuring that all pointers to an object in old space will be changed to point to a single copy of that object in copy space. We will represent a forwarding pointer in the first two words of an object. The first word will contain an immediate header with secondary tag bits indicating that it is a forwarding pointer. The second word will contain the actual pointer. This scheme works because all objects must be at least two words long: either a cons cell, or an object with a header followed by one or more words.

A second problem involves scanning the root set. So far we have ignored static space, the region of memory which is never garbage collected. However, it may contain pointers into old space. Even though static space itself is not subject to garbage collection, we must consider it as part of the root set because it may contain pointers to a space which *is* subject to garbage collection. We need to linearly scan static space from beginning to end, examining every object in it. Any object in old space referenced by an object in static space must be copied and the pointer updated, just as we did when scanning the stack.

In order to linearly scan static space, we rely on the fact that all objects, besides immediates and cons cells, start with an immediate header. Starting at the beginning of static space we can identify each object and its type, and therefore we know which words contain pointers to be examined and which words contain immediate data to be ignored. We do *not* have to sweep read-only space, because read-only space can never be changed and thus it cannot point to anything in old space.

There are two major advantages to stop and copy:

- Virtual memory performance—It is extremely important that we examine only the root set and memory containing live objects. If we have a 20-megabyte old space, we do *not* want to have to examine every byte. If we have only 8 megabytes of real memory, then we cannot hold the entire virtual address space in memory and must page most of it in from the disk. This will take a long time and would quickly become intolerable. However, if only 10 percent of the objects in the heap are in use, then we need only examine the root set and 2 megabytes worth of old space. Of course, we will also have to hold 2 megabytes of copy space in memory so that we can copy the objects, but this amounts to only 4 megabytes of memory rather than 22.
- Compaction—All of the live objects in old space are copied into consecutive locations in copy space. This means that we are *compacting* the working set of objects into the smallest chunk of contiguous memory possible. This reduces fragmentation and paging because objects which point to each other are more likely to lie on the same page in memory. In fact, it is usually advantageous to use a depth-first copying algorithm to put related objects on the same page of memory. Even if we did not collect any garbage at all, reordering objects in

memory can have a dramatic effect on the performance of a virtual memory system.

There are also two disadvantages to stop and copy:

- Memory waste—We essentially waste half of our total heap memory at any given time, although this is not too bad in a virtual memory system because we are primarily wasting disk space rather than real memory.
- Delay—Unfortunately, stop and copy as we have just seen it requires that we stop all Lisp computation in order to perform a garbage collection which may potentially take several minutes. This is not only annoying, but it is often unacceptable in systems which have response time requirements. You do not want to call an airline to make a reservation only to be told that they cannot help you at the moment because their computer is garbage collecting. Fortunately, as we will see in the next section, there are ways to avoid this problem.

Problem. Does stop and copy perform a depth-first or a breadth-first copy? What are the advantages and disadvantages of the kind of copy it performs?

19.6.2 Incremental Stop and Copy

In order to avoid long garbage collection delays we need an *incremental* garbage collector which interleaves garbage collection with Lisp computations. A nice description of incremental collection is given in [BH79].

The trick to making incremental collection work is *pretending* that we have copied all of new space into copy space, when in reality we have only copied the root set. We will then call the partially collected new space *old* space and introduce a third space called *new* space. Hence, we now have old, copy, and new space. Only the set of objects reachable directly from the root set have been transported from old to copy space.[5] We will also *invalidate* old space so that any references to it are now illegal.

At this point we may resume computation. Since the root set has been scanned, the stack, registers, and static space all point into copy space, so it appears that a full gc has occurred. However, many objects *in* copy space still point back to old space because we have not scanned any of them. Therefore, every time we *fetch* a pointer from memory, we must check to see if it points to the invalidated old space. If so, then the garbage collector must be invoked to transport that object from old space to new space. Additional objects may also be copied at this time in order to distribute the overhead of invoking the transporter. Now our program can never see references to old space, because any such references are immediately changed to copy space references as the program is running.

---

[5]Transporting an object is the same as copying an object.

We must also be sure that the garbage collection will complete before our program (which is often called a *mutator*) has allocated all of new space and requires another garbage collection. To ensure that the gc will finish before new space is full, every time we allocate an n-word object in new space, we will transport $k \times n$ words worth of objects from old to copy space. If we make k a constant such as 4, then there is no way that the rate of allocation in new space can "outrun" the transport rate from old to copy space.

Because only a small number of objects are copied at a time, the longest garbage collection delay is proportional to the time it takes to copy the largest object in the system, because now only object copying, not the entire gc, is an atomic operation. Hence this scheme is incremental and does not need to stop for long intervals.

Unfortunately, the overhead involved in performing an incremental copy is higher than performing the copy all at once as we did before. Even worse, checking *every* single pointer fetch is not cheap! Some special-purpose Lisp machines contain special hardware which performs this check automatically, taking a trap similar to a page fault trap when an invalid reference occurs. However, checking every pointer reference on standard hardware is not so cheap. What was previously a simple instruction now becomes several instructions to check the pointer and call the transporter if the pointer is invalid. In fact, no production Lisp system on standard hardware has ever used an incremental garbage collector because of this performance penalty.

19.6.3 Generation Scavenging

The last section makes the prospects for limiting garbage collection delays sound grim. However, there is another modification to the stop and copy algorithm called *generation scavenging*[6] which can help to reduce garbage collection pauses as well as the total amount of time spent garbage collecting. When running a Lisp program, objects exhibit different *lifetime* characteristics. Many objects are created and used for only a short time before becoming garbage, while other objects stay around for a long time.

The garbage collectors we have examined so far pay no attention to how long an object lives. They simply copy all live objects back and forth from one space to another. This means that the garbage collector will waste a lot of time copying long-lived objects back and forth. This can consume a significant amount of time if there are many such objects.

To avoid this waste, we can modify the garbage collector to pay attention to how long an object has been alive. Once an object is created, it will generally either die quickly or live a long time. Thus, it makes sense for the gc to spend most of its time trying to find objects that have died young and less time trying to collect old objects.

---

[6]The term *scavenging* is sometimes used to describe the process of collecting garbage, and generation scavenging is often called *ephemeral garbage collection*.

Instead of having a single new space, we will have several different *ephemeral* spaces. Most objects will initially be allocated in a rather small *first* ephemeral space on the assumption that most of those objects will die quickly. When the first ephemeral space fills, the garbage collector will scan only the registers and the stack looking for references to objects in ephemeral space, copying any live objects into the *second* ephemeral space. If our assumption is correct, then only a few objects will actually graduate to the second space, and the gc should not take too long. Once the few live objects have been transported, we can reuse all of the first ephemeral space.

We can have as many different levels of ephemeral space as we want, although the optimal number is difficult to determine and varies from program to program. When the second level is full, then any live objects in it will be copied into the third level. Eventually some long-lived objects graduate from the last ephemeral space into a *dynamic* space which is garbage collected by regular stop and copy only as a last resort, and perhaps never.

The generation scavenging algorithm is more intelligent than the previous algorithms because it takes advantage of the observed characteristics of object lifetimes. The greatest effort is focused on the objects which are most likely to be garbage. Eventually long-lived objects migrate into dynamic space so that they are rarely, if ever, examined again. Not only is the garbage collector more efficient, but the pauses caused by a generation scavenger are usually small because only a small root set is scanned, and only a few objects will actually be copied. Delays on the order of a few tenths of a second rather than tens of seconds can usually be expected. Of course the garbage collections occur more frequently, but they are much less annoying.

However, like all good schemes, generation scavenging has a problem. Notice that we only use the registers and the stack as a root set. How can we ignore static space? Similarly, what happens if someone destructively modifies a pointer in a later ephemeral level or dynamic space to point *back* into an *earlier* ephemeral level? As our algorithm stands now, these references will not be seen and a live object will inadvertently be declared dead. However, scanning all spaces during every garbage collection would destroy the advantages offered by generation scavenging.

We can avoid this problem by explicitly checking every pointer *setting* operation. If an object in static space is modified to reference an object in an ephemeral space, then that object must be explicitly remembered and scanned as part of the root set when a garbage collection occurs. Similarly, we must record any destructive pointer operations which cause a pointer from one ephemeral space to point back into an earlier space. This scheme works because there are generally not too many of these kinds of pointer updates and it is possible to efficiently record them. However, actually checking every pointer set is expensive, just as checking every pointer reference is expensive. Once again, most Lisp machines contain special hardware to perform the pointer-setting checks, while standard hardware has to use many explicit instructions. But generation scavenging has been successfully implemented on standard hardware because pointer updates are far less frequent than pointer references, so we can afford to increase the cost of an update.

Generation scavenging is the state of the art right now on standard hardware. Lisp machines go one step further and combine incremental collection and generation scavenging. Garbage collection is interleaved with Lisp computation *and* the gc concentrates its time where it will do the most good. There are two other garbage collection methods worth examining, but they are used less frequently than the techniques we have just seen because of various performance problems.

19.6.4 Mark and Sweep

One of the simplest methods of garbage collection is called *mark and sweep*. The big advantage that mark and sweep has over other methods is that it does not reserve large portions of memory for copying objects, and so it is possible to make better use of available physical memory. For this reason, mark and sweep is popular on machines such as personal computers with small physical memories and no virtual memory.

We will consider mark and sweep in its simplest form. Imagine that we want to allocate only cons cells. The system will maintain a *free list* of available cells, which are linked together by their cdrs. The head of the list is pointed to by a variable named *FREE-LIST*. CONS will work as follows:

```
(defun cons (x y)
  (when (null *free-list*)          ; free list empty
    (when (null (gc))               ; try to get more memory
      (error "No more memory!")))
  (let ((cons-cell *free-list*))
    (setf *free-list* (cdr cons-cell))   ; unhook next cell
    (setf (car cons-cell) x)             ; initialize
    (setf (cdr cons-cell) y)
    cons-cell))
```

To allocate a cons cell, we first check the free list. If a cell is available, then we unhook it from the list, initialize its car and cdr, and return it. When the free list is empty, the mark and sweep garbage collector is invoked to try to put dead cons cells back on the free list. The algorithm used by the garbage collector is roughly outlined by the following code:

```
(defun gc ()
  (mark-root-set)
  (sweep))

(defun mark-root-set ()
  ;; Call MARK-CELL on every cons cell directly
  ;; reachable from the root set
  ...)
```

```lisp
(defun mark-cell (cons-cell)
  ;; Don't check already marked cells
  (unless (markedp cons-cell)
    (setf (markedp cons-cell) t)
    (when (consp (car cons-cell))      ; recursively mark car
      (mark-cell (car cons-cell)))
    (when (consp (cdr cons-cell))      ; recursively mark cdr
      (mark-cell (cdr cons-cell)))))

;;; Linearly Sweep memory from low to high,
;;; calling CHECK-CELL on each cons cell.
(defun sweep ()
  (do ((i first-cons-cell-in-heap (next-cons-cell i)))
      ((> i end-heap) 'done)
    (check-cell i)))

(defun check-cell (cons-cell)
  (unless (markedp cons-cell)
    ;; add an unreachable cell to the free list
    (setf (cdr cons-cell) *free-list*)
    (setf *free-list* cons-cell)))
```

The first step is to *mark* all accessible cons cells. Marking is conceptually like putting a check mark next to every cons cell which is still live. We mark cons cells referenced by the root set, and recursively mark the subparts of these cells. Thus, when the mark phase is over, all accessible cons cells have check marks next to them. In order to avoid an infinite loop, we do not try to mark a cell which has already been marked.

The next step is to examine *every* cons cell in memory by linearly sweeping from the beginning to the end of the heap. Every cons cell which is *not* marked can be put back on the free list.

The basic idea behind mark and sweep is quite simple. However, we have glossed over several problems:

- Stack space—We will need a lot of memory devoted to a call stack in order to execute the recursive Lisp code presented above. However, we call the gc only when we are *out* of memory! Fortunately, there is a clever algorithm which uses the pointers in the objects being marked to replace the stack.
- Linear sweep—Examining the *entire* heap is acceptable if the heap is small and contained in physical memory. However, trying to examine a large heap in virtual memory could cause immense amounts of paging.
- Memory fragmentation—We no longer have a single heap from which we can allocate various-sized objects. Instead, we will have to maintain many free lists for different-sized objects. Allocating variable-sized objects like arrays is inefficient, and it may be difficult to find large blocks of contiguous space.

- Reference locality—Objects will quickly become scattered throughout memory as they are taken from and returned to the free list. This means that mark and sweep will require a larger working set than a compacting collector would.
- Mark table—This is not too much of a problem, but we will have to find some way to record which cells are marked and which are not. Because there may not be a free bit available in each pointer, we might have to build a table of size *heapsize/wordsize* words. Each bit in the table will serve as the mark bit of a corresponding word in the heap.

There is a *compacting* version of mark and sweep used by PSL [GB82] which does not require that we devote half of our memory to copy space, but offers the compaction advantages of stop and copy. However, because of the problems with mark and sweep, some variation of stop and copy is currently the most popular way to perform garbage collection on systems employing virtual memory.

19.6.5 Reference Counting

Another way to perform garbage collection is to remember how many pointers point to each object in the system. This technique is called *reference counting* and has been successfully used by Interlisp [Tei78]. Whenever a pointer is made to point at an object, the object's reference count is increased by one. Similarly, when a pointer is changed so that it no longer references an object, that object's reference count is decreased by one. When an object's reference count drops to zero, then the object must be garbage and is reclaimed by decreasing the reference counts of the objects to which it points and returning the object's memory to a free list. Reference counting has the advantage of being incremental by nature, so it does not require a linear sweep of the heap.

Reference counting has several drawbacks. One of the most significant problems with reference counting is illustrated by the following quote:

> One day a student came to Moon and said, "I understand how to make a better garbage collector. We must keep a reference count of the pointers to each cons." Moon patiently told the student the following story—"One day a student came to Moon and said, 'I understand how to make a better garbage collector . . ." (Danny Hillis, quoted in [LH80])

Reference counting cannot reclaim circular structures. Consider a circular list of 10,000 elements. Because the cdr of the last cons cell points back to the first one, every cons cell in the list will have a reference count of at least 1. Even if there are no other pointers in the system to these cons cells, they will never be garbage-collected because they think they need each other.

Because a free list is used to hold free chunks of memory, we will encounter the same problems we had with a free list using mark and sweep. Another problem is *where* to store the reference counts. If a fixed number of bits are set aside for each reference count, what should we do if we need to store a reference count larger than the bits can hold? There is also a significant amount of overhead involved in doing the bookkeeping needed to maintain the reference counts. Because of these disadvantages, reference counting is not widely used.

Problem. Change the Lisp interpreter we built in Chapter 18 by implementing your own object allocation, accessing, and updating functions. Represent memory as a vector of *word* structures. Each word structure should contain a pointer slot and a tag slot. Depending on the value of the tag slot, the pointer slot will be interpreted as the index of another word in the vector or as an immediate piece of data.

Problem. Implement a garbage collector for your memory vector using one of the garbage collection schemes described above. You should change the interpreter to explicitly maintain its own stack so that it can be included in the root set. Try building a visual garbage collector which shows an animated picture of a small heap undergoing garbage collection.

CHAPTER 20

LISP COMPILATION

Now that we understand most of the basic machine-level conventions needed to run compiled Lisp code, we are ready to outline one possible implementation of a good Lisp compiler. Our compiler must accept a Lisp program and convert it into another language, usually the machine language for a particular processor. Fortunately, we do not even have to consider the issue of how to *parse* the textual representation of a Lisp program into an internal representation, because the READ function does this for us already.

20.1 REDUCING COMMON LISP TO THE ESSENTIALS

Our goal is to express all of Common Lisp in terms of an extremely simple *basis set* of Lisp constructs, just as we can express any vector in three-space as a combination of three basis vectors (usually the x, y, and z axes). If we can do a good job compiling this small basis set of constructs, then we can do a good job compiling the whole language. Almost all Lisp compilers employ this idea to varying degrees. The greatest benefit of this approach is that we will avoid duplicating knowledge in different parts of the compiler which deal with related constructs.

The minimum subset of Lisp which we need to write all other Lisp programs is amazingly small. In fact, we can funnel *all* Lisp programs into equivalent programs consisting of only the following three kinds of basic *nodes*:[1]

---

[1] Most Lisp compilers do not go to this extreme, although some do.

1. `LAMBDA` nodes represent functions.
2. `REFERENCE` nodes refer to constants and variable bindings.
3. `CALL` nodes apply a function to some arguments.

Each node can be represented as a structure which contains subparts of that node as well as other information needed to compile the node. For example, a `CALL` node would consist of at least a function and a list of arguments. Although these three nodes are sufficient to represent all Lisp programs, we will add the following three node types:

4. `IF` nodes
5. `LABELS` nodes
6. `SETQ` nodes

We could express the last three node types in terms of the first three, but it will make the structure of our compiler cleaner if we include these three additional node types. Once we have succeeded in converting all Lisp programs into equivalent programs which are combinations of these six node types, then we can concentrate on writing a compiler which knows a great deal about how to generate efficient code for these simpler programs.

Problem. Describe how to convert a program using `IF`, `LABELS`, or `SETQ` into a program which uses only the first three node types. (`SETQ` is a bit tricky. Try to make it look like a data structure update.)

20.2 SOURCE CODE REWRITING AND ALPHATIZING

As the first step in compiling code, we must expand any macros we find. This step already starts to funnel Lisp into a subset of itself, especially because many of the special forms listed in the Common Lisp manual can be implemented as macros. For example, `LET` is considered a special form, but we have already seen how to write it as a macro which expands into an anonymous function call.

Earlier in the book we have either discussed or presented as problems various program transformations. For example, suppose we have to compile this ugly-looking version of `REVERSE` which uses a `PROG`:

```
(defun prog-reverse (l)
  (prog ((old l)                      ; bind vars
         (result nil))
    loop-label                        ; introduce a tag
    (when (null old)
      (return result))                ; return from the PROG
    (setf result (cons (car old) result))
    (setf old (cdr old))
    (go loop-label)))                 ; transfer control to a tag
```

PROG is really a macro which expands into a mixture of **LET**, **BLOCK**, and **TAGBODY**. The **LET** will be macroexpanded into an anonymous function call, the **BLOCK** can be converted into a function call to the primitive **CALL-CC**, while the **TAGBODY** can be converted into equivalent form using **LABELS**:

```
(defun prog-reverse (l)
  (call-cc #'(lambda (escape)
              ((lambda (old result)
                 (labels ((loop-label ()
                            ((lambda (ignore)
                               ((lambda (ignore)
                                  ((lambda (ignore)
                                     (loop-label))
                                   (setq old (cdr old))))
                                (setq result
                                      (cons
                                        (car old)
                                        result))))
                             (if (null old)
                                 (funcall escape
                                          result)))))
                   (loop-label)))
               l
               nil))))
```

We have successfully transformed a **PROG** into a combination of the six basic nodes listed earlier, thereby eliminating the need to consider **PROG** specially.

There is a problem with this approach. Consider what would happen if the tag in our example was named **CAR** rather than **LOOP-LABEL**. In the process of rewriting the **PROG**, we would have inadvertently merged the tag and function namespaces, and conflicts might arise.

20.2.1 Single versus Multiple Namespaces

At this point it is useful to summarize the various namespaces we have seen:[2]

```
Lexical namespaces       Dynamic namespaces
_____      _____

  1. Variables             5. Variables
  2. Functions             6. (Global) functions
  3. Blocks                7. Catch tags
  4. Tags                  <No counterpart>
```

---

[2]Later we will see that *packages* offer a way to control the mapping from names to symbols at *read time*.

Here is a rather ridiculous example of the name FOO being used in seven different namespaces simultaneously:

```
(defun foo (foo)          ; global function, lexical variable
  (catch 'foo             ; dynamic catch tag
    (block foo            ; lexical block
      (tagbody foo        ; lexical tag
        (flet ((foo (x y) ; lexical function, lexical vars
                 (return-from
                   foo        ; lexical block ref
                   (go foo))))  ; lexical tag ref
          (foo (funcall      ; lexical function ref
                ;; global function ref
                (symbol-function 'foo)
                (symbol-value 'foo)) ; dynamic variable ref
               foo)))))) ;   lexical variable ref
```

While code like this is legal, it can be confusing. About the only advantage multiple namespaces offer is the ability to use a name like LIST as both a variable and the name of a function at the same time. It is generally poor style to take advantage of the multiple namespaces that Common Lisp offers.

We would like to avoid dealing with so many different namespaces inside our compiler, so we will merge them all into a *single* variable namespace. In order to avoid conflicts, we must generate a unique name for each variable we encounter. For example, when converting a TAGBODY into a LABELS, we must replace each tag with a unique name and replace every reference to that tag by the same name. We can use GENSYM to generate unique names, just as we did when writing macros. For instance, the tag, and hence the function, named LOOP-LABEL in our earlier example should be renamed by GENSYM to something like LOOP-LABEL-987. Any GO to that tag should also be changed to use the new name.

20.2.2 Alpha and Beta Conversion

Once we have converted Common Lisp into a single-namespace Lisp, it would seem that the rules of lexical scoping are all we will need to resolve further naming conflicts. For example, consider the following program:

```
Lisp> (let* ((y (print 'outer))
             (x y))
        (let ((y 'inner))
          (cons (print y) x)))

OUTER
INNER
(INNER . OUTER)
```

Even though there are two variables with the name Y, the rules of lexical scoping allow us to determine the binding to which a reference refers. Macroexpansion will transform this code into a simpler subset of Lisp:

```
Lisp> ((lambda (y)
        ((lambda (x)
           ((lambda (y)
              (cons (print y) x))
            'inner))
         y))
       (print 'outer))

OUTER
INNER
(INNER . OUTER)
```

There is one obvious simplification which we can apply to this code. Rather than binding X to the value of the outer Y, we can perform a *beta substitution*[3] by replacing the reference to X by the value of X, thereby eliminating the need to bind X:

```
Lisp> ((lambda (y)
        ((lambda (y)
           ;; replace ref to X by its value
           (cons (print y) y))
         'inner))
       (print 'outer))

OUTER
INNER
(INNER . INNER)
```

Unfortunately, our substitution has changed the meaning of the program! The problem is that we cannot reorder the code without affecting the rules of lexical scoping. However, the meaning of our programs is independent of the names we choose for variables. Therefore, we can uniformly generate unique names for each variable in our program:

```
Lisp> ((lambda (y-1498)
        ((lambda (x-1499)
           ((lambda (y-1500)
```

---

[3]Sometimes called *beta conversion*.

```
            (cons (print y-1500) x-1499))
          'inner))
      y-1498))
  (print 'outer))
```

```
OUTER
INNER
(INNER . OUTER)
```

Uniformly renaming a variable and all references to that variable is called *alpha conversion*. Alpha conversion assures that we no longer have to worry about disobeying the rules of lexical scoping because there are no possible ambiguities in our program—each variable reference can only refer to one possible binding. Now if we apply beta substitution to our alphatized program, we will no longer change its meaning:

```
Lisp> ((lambda (y-1498)
         ((lambda (y-1500)
            (cons (print y-1500) y-1498))
          'inner))
        (print 'outer))
```

```
OUTER
INNER
(INNER . OUTER)
```

Notice that we cannot replace references to the outer Y by its value because Y is bound to the value of (PRINT 'OUTER), and calls to PRINT produce a side effect. If we were to replace the reference to Y-1498 by (PRINT 'OUTER), then INNER would be printed before OUTER, which is incorrect. Beta substitution changes the order of evaluation in our programs, and so we have to be careful to apply it only in situations in which evaluation order does not affect the meaning of our program.[4]

20.3 USING CONTINUATION-PASSING STYLE AS AN INTERMEDIATE LANGUAGE

Once we have converted a source program into an alphatized, single-namespace program in our small subset of Lisp, we will convert it to continuation-passing

---

[4]The ideas of alpha and beta conversion come from the lambda calculus upon which Lisp is based. Alpha conversion replaces the scoping block mechanisms used by traditional compilers to obey the rules of lexical scoping.

style (CPS). In the last chapter we saw how CPS makes the implicit order of evaluation in Lisp explicit. This meant that a simple interpreter could interpret any Common Lisp program once it had been converted to CPS. Similarly, CPS is a useful language for our compiler to use internally. CPS also has features which were not useful to our interpreter, but are useful to our compiler. Recall the definition of `CPS-FACT`:

```
(defun fact (n cont)
  (= n
     0
     #'(lambda (test-true?)
         (if test-true?
             (funcall cont 1)
             (- n
                1
                #'(lambda (temp-2)
                    (fact temp-2
                          #'(lambda (temp-3)
                              (* n
                                 temp-3
                                 cont))))))))))
```

We have dropped the `CPS-` prefix from the functions because all functions now take explicit continuations. The CPS version of `FACT` is more suitable for compilation than the usual definition of `FACT` for several reasons described below.

20.3.1 CPS Makes All Temporary Quantities Explicit

CPS code makes all intermediate values in our program explicit. For example, the form `(* N (FACT (- N 1)))` contains two implicit temporary quantities: one called `TEMP-2` to hold the value of `(- N 1)` and another called `TEMP-3` to hold the value of `(FACT - N 1)`.

Making every temporary quantity explicit is useful because the machine for which we generate code can only deal with operations applied directly to variables stored in registers or memory locations, and each temporary variable corresponds exactly to a storage location in our computer.

20.3.2 Reordering Argument Evaluation

We do not really need CPS to make all temporary quantities explicit. Regular Lisp code will suffice:

```
(defun fact (n)
  (let ((test-true? (= n 0)))
```

```
(if test-true?
    1
    (let* ((temp-2 (- n 1))
           (temp-3 (fact temp2)))
      (* n temp-3)))))
```

However, this approach still leaves the order of evaluation implicit, while CPS also makes a particular sequence of execution explicit. Although Common Lisp specifies that argument evaluation occurs from left to right, we might sometimes decide to reorder the evaluation to improve the usage of registers or memory in our target machine. CPS provides a convenient way to represent in Lisp the precise evaluation order we decide upon.

20.3.3 Function Calls and Tail-Recursion Removal

A function call is nothing more than a *goto* that passes some arguments. Once all the arguments (including the continuation) are in the right places, then the control transfer portion of a function call can be implemented by a single JUMP instruction.[5]

The continuation is a more general name for what is usually called a *return address*. Because the continuation is a complete lexical closure, we do not have to make a special case out of saving and restoring registers across function calls. A closure must capture all the variables that it needs from its creation environment, so preserving variables across calls is a special case of lexical closure.

Passing the continuation as an argument and treating function calls as *gotos* also means that tail-recursion is easily removed, so we can implement iteration using only function calls. If we want more debugging information, then we have already seen how we can inhibit tail-recursion removal by passing unnecessary intermediate continuations.

20.3.4 CPS Makes Multiple Values Simple

Continuation passing also makes the symmetry between multiple argument function calls and multiple value returns clear. Returning multiple values is nothing more than calling a continuation function with more than one argument. There is no difference between call and return in CPS.[6]

---

[5] Often passing the continuation and transferring control are merged into a single JUMP-TO-SUBROUTINE instruction.

[6] We are ignoring Common Lisp's loose rules for returning too few or too many values in this discussion, but those rules do not change the underlying symmetry; it just makes the continuation function more complicated.

The net result is that CPS code satisfies most of our needs for a good intermediate language *and* it still lets us manipulate only Lisp code! This is unusual, because most compilers generate an intermediate language which is much closer to the language understood by the underlying machine.

20.4 META-EVALUATION AND ANALYSIS

Once we have CPS code, the front end of our compiler is done. Now we will turn our attention to the back end, which must understand the CPS program and decide how it can be efficiently implemented on our target machine.

20.4.1 Meta-evaluation

Meta-evaluation will try to perform at compile time computations which would normally be done at runtime. Here are some typical opportunities for meta-evaluation:

- *Constant folding*—Many function calls involving only constant arguments can be evaluated at compile time. For example, we can replace the expression (+ 3 4) by 7. This is an example of meta-evaluation because we can evaluate the call to + and replace it by the result at compile time without changing the meaning of the program. Of course, we could not do the same thing with a call to PRINT.
- *Dead code elimination*—We can partially evaluate any IF expression whose *test* is a constant. If the constant is NIL, then we can replace the IF by the *else* expression, otherwise by the *then* expression.
- *Beta substitution*—We already examined beta substitution when discussing alpha conversion. Beta substitution is an example of meta-evaluation because we are essentially performing an evaluation—binding X to Y in the example given earlier—at compile time rather than waiting until runtime.
- *Common Subexpression Elimination (CSE)*—If a variable is bound to the result of a complex expression, it does not make sense to replace every reference to that variable by the expression. In fact, it makes sense for us to try to find identical expressions which appear more than once in a program and evaluate the expression only once by binding a variable to the result. For example:

   (* (* x x) (* x x)) ===> (let ((temp (* x x)))
                              (* temp temp))

   Rather than computing (* X X) twice, we can compute it once and bind TEMP to the result. Hence, CSE is the inverse of beta conversion.
- *Dyadicizing*—The function call (+ X Y Z) is expensive to execute not only because + is a generic function, but because + must be able to handle *any* number of arguments. In Chapter 16 we saw that it is easy to convert such calls

into an equivalent set of nested calls to a binary version of an *n*-ary function. For example, we can rewrite `(+ X Y Z)` as `(+/2 (+/2 X Y) Z)`. Now we have eliminated the overhead associated with handling an arbitrary number of arguments because `+/2` expects exactly two arguments.
- *Eliminating generic function calls.* Whenever possible we would also like to perform type-dispatching computations at compile time rather than runtime. For example, if we know that the variable `X` and the result of the expression `(+/2 X 1)` are both of type `FIXNUM`, then we can rewrite the call as `(FIXNUM-+/2 X 1)`.

This is certainly not an exhaustive list, but it describes some of the optimizations you can expect from a good compiler.

20.4.2 Analysis

In order to perform many of the optimizations described in the previous section, a compiler must analyze the CPS code to understand how data and control flow through a program. There is a vast amount of literature on these subjects and we will not discuss it in detail here. However, here is an outline of the basic ideas:

- Data flow analysis—We need to analyze the source program to determine when variables are bound and referenced in our programs. We also need to understand all the possible paths of execution which can occur in a function. This information will also be used later in deciding where and when to store variables in registers or in memory.
- Representation analysis—We would like to avoid consing and needlessly converting data from Lisp to machine format whenever possible. For example:

```
(defun simple-string-copy (source destination)
  (dotimes (i (length s1))
    (setf (schar destination i) (schar source i))))
```

This function expects as arguments two `SIMPLE-STRING`s which contain "raw" character codes. We expect `SCHAR` to extract a specific character code from the `SOURCE` string. However, that character code is an untagged byte, so `SCHAR` must convert the byte to an immediate tagged Lisp object. Unfortunately, we must immediately convert the tagged Lisp object *back* into a raw character code so that it can be inserted into the `DESTINATION` string. Converting data from raw to Lisp format is sometimes called *boxing*, while converting from Lisp to raw format is called *unboxing*.

In order to avoid this problem, the compiler can perform *representation analysis* to determine when boxing and unboxing steps would negate each other and are unnecessary. In the next chapter, we will see how representation analysis can also be used to generate efficient floating-point code.

20.5 REGISTER ALLOCATION AND CODE GENERATION

When we are done optimizing a program at Lisp level, we must decide how to actually implement it on the target machine. This involves understanding how variables are used, where they will be stored in the machine, and the exact machine instructions which will implement the program.

20.5.1 Primitive Operations

All Lisp programs are expressed as combinations of a few *primitive* operations. In order to compile a program, we must know the exact machine instructions which implement each primitive. For example, the primitive `CAR` might be described as follows:

```
(define-primitive car (l result)
  :type-constraints (l cons)
  :must-constraints (registerp l)
  :wish-constraints (registerp result)
  :code `((move (offset ,car-offset ,l) ,result)))
```

`DEFINE-PRIMITIVE` is like an elaborate form of `DEFUN`. It contains a body which can generate machine code to implement `CAR`, but it also describes restrictions on the type, location, and representation of the arguments passed to `CAR`. The `:CODE` option provides the body of the primitive and will return a Lisp Assembly Program or *lap* code when the primitive is actually called upon to generate code. Lap code is essentially assembly language written using list notation. For example, `(MOVE (OFFSET 2 R0) R1)` represents a single lap instruction.

The `:TYPE-CONSTRAINTS` option says that the argument L must always be a cons cell. This can be used by the compiler to perform type checking at compile time or to emit type-checking code. The `:MUST-CONSTRAINTS` option lists any restrictions on where variables can reside in the machine, or what representation they must have. For example, many machines can only perform a two-operand operation such as a `MOVE` or an `ADD` when one of the arguments is a register, while the other may be either a register or a memory location.

Because the `CAR` primitive is implemented by a `MOVE` instruction which uses the offset addressing mode of our machine to reference the car slot of a cons cell, the pointer to the cons cell must reside in a register. Similarly, the `:WISH-CONSTRAINTS` option indicates it would be preferable, although not necessary, if the destination was also a register so that the `MOVE` instruction could execute as quickly as possible.

Because most of the strange details that make a machine unique are described in the primitive definitions, retargeting our compiler for a new machine primarily amounts to writing new primitive definitions for that machine.

20.5.2 Register Allocation

Before generating code, we must decide where variables will actually reside in the machine at all times. For example, we want to keep frequently used variables in registers because registers can be accessed more quickly than any other storage in the machine. In order to perform register allocation, we need to use the information gained from the previous analysis phases. This information tells us when we must save a register across a function call, or whether a piece of data is tagged and should be placed in a location which is part of the root set scanned by the garbage collector.

20.5.3 Code Generation

So far we have presumed that we will convert Lisp to machine code. However, we actually have several choices when it comes to deciding what kind of code our compiler should generate. For instance, it could generate code for C, and then let a C compiler turn our output into machine code. Kyoto Common Lisp [YH85] uses this approach to achieve portability with minimal effort. However, it is difficult to generate top-notch code with this method because we are at the mercy of the intermediate C compiler.

We can also generate code for a simple *virtual machine*. For example, Lisp is most naturally run on a stack-based machine which contains instructions to perform generic arithmetic, accessing functions like `CAR` and `CDR` with type checking, etc. Usually only Lisp machines provide these conveniences, though, so we must simulate such a machine if we want to run virtual machine code on standard hardware. We can easily write a portable interpreter for a virtual machine in a high-level language, and thus we can run the code generated by our compiler simply by porting the abstract machine interpreter.

Most Smalltalk systems and the GNUemacs editor contain a compiler which generates code for a virtual machine. These compilers actually generate *byte codes* which correspond to virtual machine instructions. By generating code for a virtual machine which is well suited to Lisp, we can achieve good code density and use a simple compiler because Lisp code can easily be mapped onto the target machine. However, there is an enormous degradation in performance when running a byte code interpreter on standard hardware. For each byte of code, the interpreter must execute many machine-level instructions to figure out what the byte code should do and then do it. The net result is that byte code interpreters typically run several times slower than native machine code.

Ultimately, any high-quality, optimizing compiler must deal directly with *native* machine code if maximum efficiency is desired. Generating assembly language rather than some other intermediate language will usually make the compiler more difficult to write and to port to new machines, but it allows us to generate more efficient code.

As we saw earlier, each primitive knows how to generate a *code stream* of lap instructions. We can generate machine code from the CPS code by generating lap code for each primitive call and concatenating the resulting streams. The code generator must also know how to set up the arguments for a function call and transfer control, but the bulk of the machine-specific knowledge is embedded in the primitive definitions.

Because primitives emit code independently of each other, a compiler will sometimes emit silly looking code sequences:

```
                 ((JUMP  LABEL-1483)
LABEL-1483        (MOVE R0 R0)
                  (RETURN))
```

In order to improve this code we can submit it to a *peephole* optimizer. The purpose of the peephole optimizer is to analyze small windows of code and to remove obvious inefficiencies. The instruction stream above can be rewritten by the peephole optimizer:

```
((RETURN))
```

We could try to write the compiler so that it never emitted bad code in the first place, but it is often easier to just use a peephole optimizer to clean up the output.

20.6 SAMPLE COMPILATION OF FACT

As an example of the techniques described in the previous sections, we will briefly examine some of the steps involved in compiling **FACT**:

```
(defun fact (n)
  (if (= n 0)
      1
      (* n (fact (1- n)))))
```

First we must expand macros, convert to a single namespace, and perform alpha conversion:

```
(set-symbol-function 'fact
  (labels ((fact6 (n5)
             (if (= n5 0)
                 '1             ; all literals should be quoted
                 (* n5 (fact6 (1- n5))))))
    fact6)) ; single namespace Lisp
```

Because **FACT** is so simple, there really isn't any need to perform alpha conversion, but it does no harm. We have also converted to a single-namespace Lisp, so **LABELS** now acts like a version of **LET** which allows recursive definitions.

We use **LABELS** to name the function **FACT6** because it provides a uniform way of naming locations in our code. When the compiler generates code for the recursive call to **FACT6**, it can emit a jump directly back to the point in the code labeled **FACT6** rather than taking extra time to look in the function cell of the symbol **FACT**.

Now we are ready to convert our simplified Lisp to CPS:

```
(labels ((fact6 (n5 cont)
          (= n
             '0
             (lambda (test-true?)
               (if test-true?
                   (cont 1)
                   (1- n
                       (lambda (temp-2)
                         (fact6 temp-2
                                (lambda (temp-3)
                                  (* n
                                     temp-3
                                     cont)))))))))))
  (set-symbol-function 'fact fact6 outer-cont))
```

This CPS code has already been beta converted to avoid trivial renamings. We no longer need to prefix functions with #' because **LAMBDA** nodes represent functions in our compiler. Notice how reading the CPS code from top to bottom indicates the order in which the program is evaluated.

Our next step is to perform source code rewrites and meta-evaluation:

```
(labels ((fact6 (n5 cont)
          (=/2
            n
            '0
            (lambda (test-true?)
              (if test-true?
                  (cont 1)
                  (-/2
                    n
                    '1
                    (lambda (temp-2)
                      (fact6 temp-2
                             (lambda (temp-3)
                               (*/2
```

```
                                        n
                                        temp-3
                                        cont))))))))))
(set-symbol-function 'fact fact6 outer-cont))
```

The call to `1-` has been rewritten into a call to `-`, while calls to generic primitives such as `=`, `-`, and `*` have been converted into calls to generic primitives which accept only a fixed number of arguments. Unfortunately, we are still performing generic operations. However, if we knew that N5 and the result returned by all numeric functions applied to N5 would always be a FIXNUM, then we could call type-specific versions of the functions `*`, `=`, and `-`. In the next chapter we will see how we can specify the types of variables at compile time by adding *declarations* to our code, but for now we will assume that the appropriate declarations have already been added to the code. Therefore, we can rewrite our program to call type-specific functions:

```
(labels ((fact6 (n5 cont)
           (fixnum-=/2
             n
             '0
             (lambda (test-true?)
               (if test-true?
                   (cont 1)
                   (fixnum--/2
                     n
                     '1
                     (lambda (temp-2)
                       (fact6 temp-2
                              ;; labeled as CONT-1 later
                              (lambda (temp-3)
                                (fixnum-*/2
                                  n
                                  temp-3
                                  cont))))))))))
  (set-symbol-function 'fact fact6 outer-cont))
```

Because we have replaced generic functions which accept an arbitrary number of arguments by type-specific functions which accept a fixed number of arguments, we can emit more efficient code. Decisions which normally would have been made at runtime have been performed at compile time.

At this point the compiler must perform the analysis and register allocation phases we discussed earlier. These phases are beyond the scope of this chapter, so we will skip ahead to the generated code. Remember that we are assuming a two-bit low-tag implementation, so the fixnum 1 is represented by the raw machine number 4:

```
label      machine-instruction   operands         comments
-----      -------------------   --------         --------
(FACT6     (COMPARE              R1 0)            ;does N5 =
                                                  ;fixnum 0?

           (BRANCH-IF-NOT-=      ELSE)            ;if not, then
                                                  ;not done

           (MOVE                  4 R1)           ;put fixnum 1
                                                  ;into arg1 reg

           (RETURN)                                ;call CONT with
                                                  ;result = 1
ELSE       (PUSH R1)                               ;save n
                                                  ;(lifetime
                                                  ;analysis)

           (SUBTRACT              4 R1)           ;compute fixnum
                                                  ;(- N5 1)

           (JUMP-TO-SUBROUTINE   FACT6)           ;push CONT-1,
                                                  ;jmp FACT6
CONT-1     (MULTIPLY             (POP SP) R1)     ;(* N5 (FACT6
                                                  ;(- N5 1)))

           (RETURN))                               ;call CONT with
                                                  ;result in r1
```

This code should be heap-allocated in read-only space and be preceded by an immediate header. We have omitted the code fragment which sets the function cell of the symbol FACT so that we can concentrate on the code which actually implements the function FACT. Our compiler generates code which passes the first few arguments in the registers R1, R2, etc., and returns the first few values in those registers, since a return is really a continuation call. However, the continuation argument will always be passed on the stack because virtually all machines support a single instruction to push a continuation and transfer control. Our calling method uses the *caller saves* convention, which says that any function is free to use any registers it wishes. Therefore, the caller of a function must preserve any register it needs to use when the function call returns. Caller saves is really another way of saying that the continuation must close over its lexical environment.

Now we can examine the code itself. What appeared as a call to = in our original function has been compiled into a single COMPARE instruction. The branching operation of the IF is implemented by the BRANCH-IF-NOT-= instruction. Notice how the representation analysis phase of the compiler has determined that the condition codes set by the COMPARE instruction can be used immediately by the BRANCH-IF-NOT-= instruction.

If the *then* branch of the IF is taken, then the continuation to FACT6 is popped from the stack and called with the fixnum 1 as an argument. If the *else* branch is taken, the current value of N5 must be saved because it is needed after the recursive call to FACT6. The call to 1- in the original code is implemented by the machine instruction `SUBTRACT` which leaves (1- N5) in R1. Now we push a *new* continuation and jump to the beginning of `FACT6` (now you can see why we labeled it).

When `CONT-1` is called, we complete the original call to `FACT6` by multiplying the number in R1 by the value of N5 that we saved earlier, simultaneously popping the saved N5 from the stack (this can be done using the post-increment addressing mode provided by many machines). Now we can pop the original continuation from the stack and call it with the result contained in R1. Notice that continuations are not really full-fledged functions in our system. They cannot be freely returned and passed around like full closures, but they are an efficient implementation of downward closures.

Because our code does not perform type checking, does not check for overflow, and does not check the number of arguments it is passed, we can easily produce incorrect results if we are not careful to call `FACT` with a fixnum argument which produces a fixnum result.

Unfortunately, there is no free lunch. There are special-purpose machines which are better suited to running Lisp than standard machines because they can perform various checks in parallel with other operations. However, these machines are still fairly expensive and not available to most people. Ultimately, matching the efficiency of a language such as C on standard hardware will require that we insert declarations into our Lisp code and sacrifice much of the type and safety checking which we normally expect from Lisp.

For more information about Lisp compilation, refer to [Ste78b], [BP82], [KPO86], [BGJ82], and [KKR[+]86].

CHAPTER 21

EFFICIENCY AND LARGE SYSTEMS

So far we have only examined small Lisp programs which operate in isolation, and we have not been too concerned with making our programs run efficiently once we have chosen an algorithm. In this chapter we will examine a few of the most important issues involved in building large systems which can run efficiently on standard hardware.

21.1 DECLARE AND EFFICIENCY

While generic operations such as + and SORT simplify our programs, they also bring with them an inherent slowdown on standard hardware. In this section we will see how to use declarations to perform at compile time operations which are normally performed at runtime.

21.1.1 Example: Matrix Multiplication

Recall the MATRIX-MULTIPLY example from Chapter 12:

```
;;; Multiply M1 by M2, placing the result in M3.
;;; We require that M3 be passed as an
;;; argument to avoid consing.
```

```
(defun matrix-multiply (m1 m2 m3)
  (let ((rows-1 (array-dimension m1 0))
        (cols-2 (array-dimension m2 1))
        ;; The number of columns in M1 should
        ;; equal the number of rows in M2
        (common (array-dimension m1 1)))
    (dotimes (i rows-1)
      (dotimes (j cols-2)
        (setf (aref m3 i j)
              (do ((k 0 (1+ k))
                   (sum 0 (+ sum (* (aref m1 i k)
                                    (aref m2 k j)))))
                  ((= k common) sum)))))
    m3))
```

Although this code works, it will not run on standard hardware nearly as quickly as the same function written in Fortran or C. The difference is that Lisp defers decisions about how to perform generic operations such as +, *, and AREF until runtime, whereas many other languages make these decisions at compile time. Unless we have special hardware to facilitate runtime type dispatching, we will have to provide Lisp with the same kind of declarations that we would give to a comparable Fortran or C program in order to attain similar performance.

21.1.2 Declaring Variable Types

In Chapter 9 we saw how to use the special form DECLARE to locally declare that a variable was special. Although it is not required, we can also declare that a variable will only be bound to values of a certain type:

```
(defun double-1 (x)
  (declare (type fixnum x))
  ;; Lisp also needs to know that the sum is a FIXNUM
  ;; in order to open code this addition as a single
  ;; ADD instruction.
  (+ x x))

(defun double-2 (x)
  (declare (fixnum x))              ; shorthand type declaration
  ;; Now the types of both the arguments and the result are
  ;; declared to be FIXNUMs.
  (the fixnum (+ x x)))
```

In the example above we have declared that the variable X will *always* have a value which is of type FIXNUM. Notice that there are two equivalent ways to declare that X is a FIXNUM. The method used in DOUBLE-1 is the most general, while the method used in `DOUBLE-2` is shorter. We can also use the special form `THE` to declare the type of unnamed values such as the result returned by the call to `+`.

In order for a Lisp compiler to avoid calling the generic `+` function, it must know not only the type of arguments passed to `+`, but also the type of the result. For example, if we try to add the constant `MOST-POSITIVE-FIXNUM` to itself, the result would be of type `BIGNUM`. Hence, the result of the addition must be checked at runtime in order to see if it is really a fixnum. By telling the compiler that we *know* ahead of time that the result will always be a fixnum, it can perform the addition with a single `ADD` instruction.

Similarly, in order to speed up array accesses, we should declare the dimensions of the array and the type of elements it can hold at runtime. We should also use only simple arrays for maximum efficiency on standard hardware, because arrays which may be displaced or dynamically adjusted or may contain a fill pointer involve more overhead than simple arrays. The following example shows how to quickly double the value of every element of a vector containing floating-point numbers:

```
Lisp> (defun double-vector (v)
        (declare (type (simple-array single-float '(*)) v))
        (dotimes (i (length v) v)
          (declare (fixnum i))
          (setf (aref v i) (* 2.0 (aref v i)))))
DOUBLE-VECTOR

Lisp> (double-vector (make-array '(3)
                                 :element-type 'single-float
                                 :initial-contents
                                 '(1.0 2.0 3.0)))
#(2.0 4.0 6.0)
```

The first type declaration in `DOUBLE-VECTOR` says that the variable `V` will always be bound to a simple array of single-precision floating point numbers. The list `'(*)` is actually a list of dimensions, where `*` means that the actual size of a dimension is unknown. For example, `(SIMPLE-ARRAY SINGLE-FLOAT '(3 3))` specifies a three-by-three matrix of single floats, while `(SIMPLE-ARRAY SINGLE-FLOAT '(*))` specifies a one-dimensional array of single floats, where the length of the dimension is unknown at compile time. The `(DECLARE (FIXNUM I))` in the body of the `DOTIMES` should not really be necessary, because the length of any vector must be a fixnum in virtually all implementations of Lisp. Unfortunately, most compilers are not smart enough to realize this fact.

Many implementations of Lisp on standard hardware must heap-allocate floating-point numbers. This is clearly inefficient, especially when we consider the overhead of garbage collection. However, a good compiler can avoid heap allocation of intermediate floating-point numbers by using *pdlnums*.[1] Pdlnums are floating-point numbers which are stored as raw (as opposed to tagged Lisp) numbers which may be used directly as arguments to a machine instruction. For example, `DOUBLE-VECTOR` can fetch a single float directly from the heap-allocated vector `V`, multiply the raw floating-point number by 2.0, and immediately place the result back in the vector. No dynamic memory needs to be allocated and no generic functions need to be called. Any intermediate results may be kept in raw format on a stack or in registers which are intended to hold untagged data.

21.1.3 Speed versus Safety and Time over Space

Although we may put type declarations into our program, that alone is not enough to guarantee that we will get the fastest possible code. Common Lisp allows us to choose between various code optimization tradeoffs with the following optimization parameters:

- `SPEED`—How important is the speed of our code?
- `SAFETY`—How important is type checking, debugging information, number-of-arguments checking on function entry, etc.?
- `SPACE`—Do we care how much memory the code occupies?
- `COMPILATION-SPEED`—Does it matter to us how long the compilation takes?

Each parameter has a value from 0 to 3, where 0 means least important and 3 means most important. The default optimization settings are implementation dependent. However, we can alter them with the `OPTIMIZE` declaration. For example, when aiming for the fastest possible code, we should either `PROCLAIM` the following declaration or include it at the beginning of a function:

```
(declare (optimize (safety 0) (speed 3) (space 0)
                   (compilation-speed 0)))
```

The primary decision we must make is between fast code which does no type checking, or slower code which is safer and performs full type checking. The danger involved in removing type checking is that our programs may fail in mysterious ways which are difficult to track down.

A less important decision involves trading time for space. For example, it is often faster to replace each call to a function by the body of the function in order to eliminate the overhead of the function call itself. However, this means that we are replicating the same piece of code many times rather than sharing

---

[1] The term *pdlnums* comes from Maclisp, where they were first used. PDL stands for Push Down List and is just another name for a stack.

it. This technique is useful for short functions such as `CAR` and `CDR`, but it is usually not useful for larger functions where the overhead of the function call is relatively insignificant compared to the actual computation.

21.1.4 Adding Declarations to `MATRIX-MULTIPLY`

Now we are ready to add declarations to `MATRIX-MULTIPLY`:

```
(defun matrix-multiply (m1 m2 m3)
  (declare (optimize (safety 0) (speed 3) (space 0)
                     (compilation-speed 0)))
  (declare (type (simple-array single-float (* *))
                 m1 m2 m3))
  (let ((rows-1 (array-dimension m1 0))
        (cols-2 (array-dimension m2 1))
        ;; The number of columns in M1 should
        ;; equal the number of rows in M2
        (common (array-dimension m1 1)))
    (declare (fixnum rows-1 cols-2 common))
    (dotimes (i rows-1)
      (dotimes (j cols-2)
        (setf (aref m3 i j)
              (do ((k 0 (1+ k))
                   ;; Notice the floating point 0.0!
                   (sum 0.0 (+ sum (* (aref m1 i k)
                                      (aref m2 k j)))))
                  ((= k common) sum)
                (declare (fixnum k) (single-float sum))))))
    m3))
```

The primary difficulty is deciding where *not* to put declarations. Aside from the `OPTIMIZE` declaration, we should only *have* to include the array declaration. Any remaining declarations should be deducible from this declaration and the rules of Common Lisp. Unfortunately, most compilers are not capable of making all the type inferences we might expect, and therefore we will usually have to add other declarations as well. Finding the minimum number of declarations which obtain the maximum amount of optimization possible is difficult. Often the only way to really be sure about what is being optimized is to `DISASSEMBLE` the compiled code.

Problem. Explain how the other type declarations we have included in `MATRIX-MULTIPLY` could be inferred by a sufficiently smart compiler.

Here is a simple test of our new version of `MATRIX-MULTIPLY`:

```
Lisp> (setf m1 (make-array '(3 2)
```

```
                              :element-type 'single-float
                              :initial-contents
                              '((0.0 1.0)
                                (0.0 0.0)
                                (1.0 0.0))))
#2A((0.0 1.0) (0.0 0.0) (1.0 0.0))

Lisp> (setf m2 (make-array '(2 3)
                              :element-type 'single-float
                              :initial-contents
                              '((1.0 2.0 3.0)
                                (4.0 5.0 6.0))))
#2A((1.0 2.0 3.0) (4.0 5.0 6.0))

Lisp> (setf m3 (make-array '(3 3)
                              :element-type 'single-float))
#2A((0.0 0.0 0.0) (0.0 0.0 0.0) (0.0 0.0 0.0))

Lisp> (matrix-multiply m1 m2 m3)
#2A((4.0 5.0 6.0) (0.0 0.0 0.0) (1.0 2.0 3.0))
```

When this example is compiled by a sufficiently smart Lisp compiler, it should execute as efficiently as the code generated by a good C or Fortran compiler.

21.1.5 Additional Declarations

Here is a quick summary of some other useful declarations:

- **:TYPE** option to **DEFSTRUCT**—**DEFSTRUCT** allows you to specify type constraints for each slot in a structure. Putting declarations on structure slots means that a more efficient representation may be used for the structure, and the compiler can efficiently code accesses and updates.
- **FTYPE** and **FUNCTION**—These allow us to specify the type of arguments a function accepts and the type of values it will return.
- **INLINE** and **NOTINLINE**—These declarations can be used to control whether or not a function call is replaced by the body of the function being called. A compiler is not obligated to obey **INLINE** declarations, although it must obey **NOTINLINE** declarations. A disadvantage of inlining, aside from the increase in code space, is that you cannot trace an inline function. You should never use a macro to achieve function inlining because macros are more difficult to read and write and they cannot be funcalled or applied.

You should refer to the Common Lisp manual for complete details about these and other declarations.

All Lisp declarations (other than **SPECIAL**) are optional, and therefore we can quickly get a program running without them. Only later should we tune time critical functions for performance. In order to find out *where* in the program we should take the time to insert declarations, it helps to use the *performance monitoring* tools provided by some Lisps. These tools analyze a running program and can tell us which functions are consuming the most time. It is often the case that 90 percent of the running time of a program is spent executing only 10 percent of the code, so we usually only need to concentrate on speeding up a small portion of the entire program.

Getting the best performance out of a particular Common Lisp can be difficult, and you should consult the manual for your particular Lisp implementation to determine which optimizations you can expect of it. Refer to [Gab85] and [Ste77b] for information about making Lisp programs run fast.

Problem. Try timing a loop which performs 10,000 calls to **MATRIX-MULTIPLY** under the following conditions:

1. Interpreted
2. Compiled with no declarations and maximum safety
3. Compiled with minimum safety
4. Compiled with full declarations and minimum safety

Try to find all the declarations needed to make **MATRIX-MULTIPLY** run as quickly as possible in your implementation of Lisp.

Problem. Add declarations to the factorial function presented in the previous chapter. Try to get the fastest code possible. Disassemble **FACT** and try to understand the machine code generated by the Lisp you are using and how it could be improved.

Problem. Write a function which sorts arrays of integers. Repeat the timing problem on this new function.

21.2 GARBAGE AVOIDANCE

Because garbage collection takes time, we must sometimes avoid generating lots of objects which die quickly. This section discusses two common techniques for "manually" garbage-collecting objects in order to improve system performance.

21.2.1 Taking Advantage of Dynamic Extent— Stack Allocation

Sometimes we know when writing a program that an object need only have dynamic rather than indefinite extent. **&REST** argument lists are a typical example. We need **&REST** arguments to write functions like +, but once + has added all the numbers up and returned a result, the **&REST** list is no longer needed. Unfortunately, it takes time to allocate an **&REST** list, and after we are done with it the garbage collector must eventually spend some time trying to reclaim it. This sort of waste can have a detrimental effect on system performance.

We can avoid the problem by *stack-allocating* objects which are known to have dynamic extent, just as we stack-allocate function call frames. For example, the &REST list to + could be allocated on a stack for the duration of the call to + and deallocated along with the stack frame when the call to + is over. That way no garbage is left in the heap. Many implementations understand special dynamic extent declarations or provide macros which allow us to stack-allocate data. Of course, we have to be careful to obey the restrictions imposed by stack allocation. Returning a pointer to a stack-allocated &REST list after it has been destroyed is a good way to introduce invalid objects and nasty bugs into our Lisp system.

21.2.2 Explicit Resource Allocation and Deallocation

Sometimes we want to frequently allocate and free objects which must have indefinite extent. For example, buffers in a file system, network, or window system fall into this category. Although these objects do not typically have dynamic extent, we often know at what point in our program they have become garbage and may be safely reclaimed. Thus, we would like to manually free these objects so that the garbage collector does not waste time trying to reclaim them.

In order to assist with manual storage management, some Lisp systems provide a *resource* facility. Most resource systems maintain a pool of free objects. When a new object is needed, the pool is checked. If it contains an object of the right type and size, the object is removed from the pool, initialized, and returned. If the pool is empty, then a new object must be allocated from the heap. When a program knows that a resource is no longer needed, it can be freed by returning it to the pool of available objects.

> **Problem.** Rewrite the tic-tac-toe game in Chapter 14 so that it explicitly allocates and deallocates storage for boards rather than letting the garbage collector reclaim them.

21.3 PACKAGES

So far we have not considered the problem of building a large software package in Common Lisp. For example, suppose five people are working on different modules in a large computer-aided design (CAD) program. A specification for the functionality provided by each module should be agreed upon so that each person can test and debug her particular module individually. However, if two different people both decide to define a function named FLATTEN, then when all five people try to combine their modules, one of the modules might break because two different definitions of FLATTEN cannot exist at once.

Until now, we have treated top-level functions as though they are all defined in the same namespace, but Common Lisp provides a *package system* to allow the same symbol to simultaneously exist in different namespaces. Unlike the other namespaces we have seen, the package a symbol belongs to is determined at *read time* rather than *runtime*.

So far we have been using a shorthand notation for referring to symbols. The full specification of a symbol describes the symbol's name *and* its package. For example, the symbol `LISP:APPEND` refers to the symbol named `APPEND` in the `LISP` package. The character `:` is used to separate the package name from the symbol name. All symbols which do not contain an explicit *package qualifier* are interned at read time in the package given by the current value of `*PACKAGE*`. By default, `*PACKAGE*` is bound to the package named `USER`. Thus, all the examples in this book have been implicitly defined in the `USER` package.

As a concrete example of how the package system is used, suppose that one of the modules in our CAD system is a math package which contains 700 symbolic algebra and matrix functions. However, of these functions perhaps only 100 are defined by the specification of the module. The remaining functions are all internal to the module and exist only to support the 100 functions that are meant to be used by everyone. Each source file in the `MATH` package should begin with the line

```
(in-package "MATH")
```

The call to `IN-PACKAGE` will bind the symbol `*PACKAGE*` to the package named `MATH` while the file is being loaded. Hence, beginning a file with `(IN-PACKAGE "MATH")` means that all symbols in the file without explicit package qualifiers will be interned in the `MATH` package. A symbol which is interned in a package is called an *internal symbol* in that package. However, any symbols which should be made available to other packages must be explicitly *exported*:

```
;; This example exports 2 of the 100 symbols which should be
;; made external in the MATH package
(export '(matrix-multiply cholesky) "MATH")
```

The function `EXPORT` expects a list of symbols and a package or the name of a package. Each symbol named in the list will be made an *external symbol* in the given package. External symbols are intended to be used by functions in other packages.

Someone writing a `DESIGN-ANALYZER` package will probably want to use the external functions provided by the `MATH` package. For example, the name `MATH:MATRIX-MULTIPLY` refers to the external symbol `MATRIX-MULTIPLY` in the `MATH` package. Unfortunately, explicitly package-qualifying every symbol which appears in another package can be cumbersome, so the function `USE-PACKAGE` can be used to make the external symbols of a particular package *accessible* to another package by inheritance:

```
(use-package "DESIGN-ANALYZER" "MATH")
```

This call to USE-PACKAGE makes all the external symbols in MATH accessible without explicit package qualification when DESIGN-ANALYZER is the current *PACKAGE*. Thus, the symbol MATRIX-MULTIPLY can now be referenced without explicit package qualification from a file in the DESIGN-ANALYZER package.

Common Lisp predefines the following packages:

- "LISP"—This package exports *only* the standard symbols defined in the Common Lisp manual.
- "SYSTEM"—Implementation-dependent functions and extensions often reside here.
- "USER"—The default package when Lisp starts. It uses the "LISP" package, and usually the "SYSTEM" package, so that Common Lisp and any extensions can be used without explicit package qualification.
- "KEYWORD"—This package is unusual because it neither uses nor is used by another package. All symbols in the "KEYWORD" package are bound to themselves, and they may be referenced by prefixing the symbol name with a colon.

In addition to the packages defined above, most implementations of Lisp provide other packages which provide enhancements to Common Lisp.

Notice that we have been using upper-case strings as package names. It is sometimes acceptable to use symbols as package names, but it is poor style and can lead to confusing problems, so we will avoid the practice. The package system contains many complexities, imperfections, and nuances which we have not even begun to cover. Furthermore, the behavior of the package system is one of the least portable aspects of Common Lisp, because it is often unclear how it should behave in complicated situations. However, it is an essential tool which can help improve the structure of our programs when understood and used carefully.[2]

21.4 EXTENSIONS TO COMMON LISP

By this time you have probably noticed that the implementation of Common Lisp you are using supports many features which are not described in the Common Lisp reference manual or this book. Many useful extensions to Lisp have not

---

[2]A better alternative to packages might seem to involve LABELS. Each module could be written inside a giant LABELS, and then only particular functions would be exported. All functions internal to the module will be invisible by the rules of lexical scoping. Experimental systems like this have been built, but none have proven entirely satisfactory. Currently, packages are the only way Common Lisp provides to express clean interfaces between different modules in a program.

yet been standardized, usually because they are not understood well enough or because people cannot agree on a single standard, especially when it comes to dealing with programming environment and operating system issues. This section briefly describes some of the more popular ways to extend Lisp's capabilities.

21.4.1 Foreign Function Calls

Sometimes we need to call, from Lisp, functions written in another language. For example, we might like to implement part of the **MATH** package mentioned earlier by calling a function in a library of Fortran routines which already exist on our computer. A function defined in a language other than Lisp is usually called a *foreign function*. For instance, in order to call a function written in Fortran, Lisp must be able to pass Lisp data to Fortran and receive Fortran data returned to Lisp. Some Lisps also provide a means for foreign functions to call Lisp functions.

Because Lisp stores data with tag bits or other unusual conventions, it must usually be converted to and from the form required by a foreign language. Lisp must also know the function-calling conventions used by a foreign language routine. Almost all Lisps on standard hardware provide some sort of foreign-function-calling facility to take care of these problems.

Data passed to foreign languages should be allocated in static space, because otherwise a garbage collection might occur and transport an object referenced by foreign code. Because the garbage collector has no way of updating foreign pointers, the foreign code could be left with pointers to invalid data if data is allocated in a dynamic space.

21.4.2 Error Handling

So far we have signaled errors with **ERROR**, which always put us in the debugger. However, sometimes we would like our program to detect that an error has occurred and handle it without forcing us into the debugger. Many Lisps provide complex *error handling* mechanisms for defining classes of errors using an object-oriented programming system. There are usually several ways for programs to explicitly signal and handle different classes of errors. An error-handling standard has been proposed for Common Lisp, but it has not yet been universally adopted.

21.4.3 LOOP

In Chapter 11 we learned how we could extend the syntax of Lisp with macros like **DO**. Although we can perform complex iterations using **DO**, it is often cumbersome. Because iteration is so common, a popular macro called **LOOP** [DM84] is frequently provided to make it simpler. The extended **LOOP** macro is upwardly compatible with the **LOOP** macro in Common Lisp, which does nothing more than execute its body in an infinite loop. Here are some simple examples of how to use the extended **LOOP**:

```
;;; Create a list of the numbers from 1 to 5.
Lisp> (loop for x from 1 to 5 collect x)
(1 2 3 4 5)

;;; Add the numbers from 0 to 9
Lisp> (loop for x from 0 below 10 summing x)
45

;;; Count the number of nonnegative numbers in a list
Lisp> (loop for x in '(1 -2 3 -4 5) when (> x 0) count x)
3
```

LOOP code is intended to be easy to read. As a more realistic example of LOOP, here is the MATRIX-MULTIPLY function we wrote earlier using DOTIMES and DO:

```
(defun loopy-matrix-multiply (m1 m2 m3)
  (let ((rows-1 (array-dimension m1 0))
        (cols-2 (array-dimension m2 1))
        ;; The number of columns in M1 should
        ;; equal the number of rows in M2
        (common (array-dimension m1 1)))
    (loop for i from 0 below rows-1 do
       (loop for j from 0 below cols-2 do
          (setf (aref m3 i j)
                (loop for k from 0 below common
                      summing (* (aref m1 i k)
                                 (aref m2 k j))))))
    m3))
```

Notice how the single word SUMMING replaces the uninteresting details of the DO loop we used in the original function. Just as FORMAT provides a language within Lisp for describing how output should look, LOOP provides a language for describing iteration. One of Lisp's greatest advantages is its extensibility and the ease with which we can devise new languages for specific problems. However, rather than having 50 different kinds of iteration languages, it is better to standardize upon one which everyone can use. It appears that LOOP is likely to become part of Common Lisp, so it is fairly safe to use in portable programs.

21.4.4 Interrupt Handling

Earlier we saw that it is usually possible to interrupt Lisp at any time by typing control-c or some other key. This kind of interrupt is *asynchronous*, because it may occur at any time with respect to a program's execution. Most Lisp systems allow us to define our own interrupt handlers to deal with other kind of interrupts. For example, we might want to execute some Lisp code every time a timer interrupt occurs or each time we move a mouse. *Synchronous* events, such as an attempt to divide by 0 or an attempt to reference an illegal part of memory, may also generate an interrupt. These interrupts are synchronous because they always occur at a specific point in our program.

Sometimes we do not want a critical section of code to be interrupted, so most interrupt systems provide a way of queuing and *deferring* asynchronous interrupts until after the critical section is complete. For example, we cannot usually interrupt a garbage collection, so all asynchronous interrupts which occur during a gc must be deferred and handled when it is complete. Synchronous interrupts such as an illegal memory reference usually indicate that there is something wrong with our program, so they must be handled immediately and cannot be deferred.

21.4.5 Multiprocessing

Multiprocessing[3] allows us to concurrently execute several programs which use a single shared set of objects. Unlike traditional multiprocessing systems, which provide each process with separate address spaces, multiple Lisp processes may execute in a single address space, and can therefore reference the same set of objects.

The advantage of having a single address space for all processes is that all the processes can communicate with each other very easily in complex ways. For example, a Lisp editor might run in one process, while an interpreter might run in another. The editor can easily redefine functions which can then be run by the interpreter.

One disadvantage of this approach is that an errant process can destroy the entire Lisp system or leave it in an inconsistent state. Fortunately, we can often have the best of both worlds. Operating systems usually provide multiple "jobs" with distinct address spaces, while Lisp provides multiple "processes" within each operating system process.

At this point it is interesting to recall our earlier discussion of deep and shallow binding. Deep binding is better suited to multiprocessing systems because all the special variable bindings for a particular process are stored on a single stack unique to that process. In order to switch processes, we need only switch stack pointers. However, in a shallow bound system, there is a *single* global value cell which holds the current dynamic value of a symbol. When switching from one process to another, we must undo all the special bindings currently in effect and restore the bindings for the process to which we are about to switch. This problem arises because all the processes share a single global value cell. Therefore, the time it takes to perform a context switch in a shallow-bound system is proportional to the number of special bindings on the stack. In practice, both systems have been successfully used.

---

[3]Also known as *stack groups* or *threads*.

21.4.6 Parallel Processing

So far we have only considered running Lisp on a single processor. However, it is interesting to think about how Lisp can run on multiple processors simultaneously (we will call this *parallel processing*). The functional style of Lisp seems especially well suited to parallel processing because of how function calls work. Rather than evaluating each argument from left to right, we can sometimes evaluate *all* the arguments to a function in parallel. Because each argument to a function is often another function call, there is potentially a good deal of parallelism.

Unfortunately, there are many complications involved with this idea. For example, if the arguments to a function have side effects which interact, then they cannot be evaluated in parallel without unpredictable results. For example, if two arguments to a function print a number as a side effect, then the order of evaluation affects the meaning of the program.

The subject of parallel processing is an active area of research, and it is more difficult than it might first appear to devise parallel algorithms. However, Lisp looks like one interesting way to take advantage of the continually falling price and size of processors. Some interesting parallel Lisps are described in [Hil85], [Hal87], and [GoLI88].

21.4.7 Object-Oriented Programming

We have already examined the subject of object-oriented programming in Chapter 16. Although many different experimental object systems have been written in Lisp, the Common Lisp Object System (CLOS) will become a standard.

21.4.8 Environment Issues

There are a myriad of environment issues which are hotly debated by the proponents of particular Lisp implementations. In this section we will briefly mention some of them.

TEXT VERSUS STRUCTURE EDITORS. In this book we have decided to store functions in text files which can be read by Lisp, compiled, and edited as text. However, rather than editing the textual representation of a function, it is possible to edit the *structural* representation of a program as it exists in memory. Structure editing involves destructively modifying the cons cells or other objects which describe a Lisp function, rather than the textual representation of those objects. Thus, there is no way to accidentally delete a needed parenthesis when editing because the parenthesis is only part of the text which represents a function. Of course, at some point the system must be able to save all of our functions in a file, but we need not be concerned with the format of those files.

DATA INSPECTORS. The Common Lisp function **INSPECT** is the standard way to invoke an implementation-dependent object inspector. The inspector can interactively examine and alter objects inside of Lisp, and is extremely useful for trying to figure out the state of a large and complicated data structure. A data inspector is really another kind of structure editor.

SYSTEM BUILDING. An issue related to how we edit and redefine functions is how we maintain all the source code for a large programming system. For example, there are usually complex dependencies describing the order in which files must be compiled and loaded. The Unix operating system provides a utility called **MAKE** which is designed to solve this problem. Similarly, many Lisps provide some sort of *system building* facility which describes how to build, patch, and distribute all the files in a complex system.

WINDOW SYSTEMS AND GRAPHICS. Many Lisp systems provide window and graphics facilities based on an object-oriented programming paradigm. Unfortunately, there is no clear standard in this area yet.

21.5 DELIVERING APPLICATIONS

Once we have written a useful Lisp program, what is the best way to deliver it to its users? So far we have considered how to develop programs in a complicated environment which contains dozens of tools to interactively edit, compile, debug, and maintain our programs. Unfortunately, these tools usually consume a great deal of memory, and the end user of our application does not need them. For example, if our imaginary CAD application tries to take the car of the string **"YOU LOSE!"** while a mechanical engineer is using it, the engineer is unlikely to suddenly start trying to edit and debug the source code for the program.

In order to deliver the smallest, most efficient program possible, some Lisp systems provide ways to statically link Lisp object files together into a single executable image just as more traditional programming systems do. The **LOAD** function provided by Lisp is really an incremental linker which is useful for program development.

As we saw when discussing stop-and-copy garbage collection, the ordering of objects in virtual memory can have a significant effect on performance. Therefore, some Lisps also provide delivery tools which reorganize the layout of objects in memory in order to improve reference locality, and consequently paging behavior.

21.6 CONCLUSION

We could have written any of the programs presented in this book in almost any language. However, the features provided by Lisp allow us to spend more time concentrating on the problem we are trying to solve and less time worrying about mundane details. Nevertheless, Lisp is not particularly good at solving any particular problem. Instead, it is good at devising problem-specific languages.

The key to solving difficult new problems is to devise a language which can easily express the solution to those problems. For instance, a spreadsheet is really a language which makes it easy to describe the relationship between columns of numbers, while logic is a language which helps us to prove facts from a set of axioms and rules. Solving new problems really amounts to a search for a language that makes the expression of our problem elegant, clear, and concise. At the same time, we should be able to embed all of our problem-oriented languages in the same basic framework so that they can easily build upon each other. Lisp provides a convenient environment in which to experiment with a variety of different problem-specific languages, while at the same time offering the potential to deliver efficient applications.

BIBLIOGRAPHY

[AS85] Harold Abelson and Gerald Sussman. *The Structure and Interpretation of Computer Programs.* McGraw-Hill Book Company, New York, 1985.

[BCE84] Glenn S. Burke, George J. Carrette, and Christoper Eliot. *NIL Reference Manual.* LCS Technical Report 311, MIT, 1984.

[bFP87] Fernando Pereira, editor. *C-Prolog User's Manual.* SRI International, 1987.

[BGJ82] Rodney Brooks, Richard Gabriel, and Guy L. Steele, Jr. An optimizing compiler for a lexically scoped Lisp. In *Conference on Compiler Construction.* ACM, June 1982.

[BH79] Henry Baker and Carl Hewitt. *The Incremental Garbage Collection of Processes.* AI Memo 454, MIT, 1979.

[BP82] Rodney Brooks and David Posner. Design of an optimizing, dynamically retargetable compiler for Common Lisp. In *Conference on Lisp and Functional Programming,* 1982.

[Chu41] Alonzo Church. *The Calculi of Lambda-Conversion.* Princeton University Press, Princeton, New Jersey, 1941.

[DM84] Daniel Weinreb, David Moon, Richard M. Stallman. *Lisp Machine Manual.* MIT AI Lab, Cambridge, Massachusetts, 1984.

[Gab85] Richard P. Gabriel. *The Performance and Evaluation of Lisp Systems.* The MIT Press, Cambridge, Massachusetts, 1985.

[GB82] Martin Griss and Eric Benson. PSL: A portable Lisp system. In *ACM Lisp and Functional Programming Conference,* 1982.

[Gen84] Michael Genesereth. *The MRS Dictionary.* Heuristic Programming Project Report HPP-80-24, Stanford, 1984.

[GN87] Michael Genesereth and Nils Nillson. *Logical Foundations of Artificial Intelligence.* Morgan Kaufmann, Los Altos, California, 1987.

[Gol84] Adelle Goldberg. *Smalltalk-80: The Interactive Programming Environment.* Addison-Wesley Publishing Company, Reading, Massachusetts, 1984.

[GoLI88] Ron Goldman and Richard Gabriel (of Lucid Inc.). Preliminary results with the initial implementation of Qlisp. In *ACM Lisp and Functional Programming Conference, 1988.*

[GP88] Richard P. Gabriel and Kent Pitman. Issues of separation of function cells and value cells. *The Journal of Lisp and Symbolic Computation* 1, 1988.

[GR83] Adelle Goldberg and David Robson. *Smalltalk-80: The Language and Its Implementation.* Addison-Wesley Publishing Company, Reading, Massachusetts, 1983.

[Gro83] The Mathlab Group. *MACSYMA Reference Manual*. MIT Laboratory for Computer Science, 1983.

[Hal87] R. Halstead. *A Multithreaded Processor Architecture for Parallel Symbolic Computation*. LCS Technical Report 338, MIT, 1987.

[Hil85] Daniel Hillis. *The Connection Machine*. MIT Press, Cambridge, Massachusetts, 1985.

[KKR + 86] David Kranz, Richard Kelsey, Jonathan Rees, Paul Hudak, James Philbin, and Norman Adams. Orbit: An optimizing compiler for scheme. In *Conference on Compiler Construction*. ACM, June 1986.

[Knu75] Donald Knuth. *The Art of Computer Programming: Searching and Sorting*. Addison-Wesley Publishing Company, Reading, Massachusetts, 1975.

[KPO86] R. Kessler, J. Peterson, and others. Epic—a retargetable, highly optimizing Lisp compiler. In *Conference on Compiler Construction*. ACM, June 1986.

[Kra83] Glenn Krasner. *Smalltalk-80: Bits of History, Words of Advice*. Addison-Wesley Publishing Company, Reading, Massachusetts, 1988.

[Lam86] Leslie Lamport. L^AT_EX User's Guide and Reference Manual. Addison-Wesley Publishing Company, Reading, Massachusetts, 1986.

[LH80] Henry Lieberman and Carl Hewitt. *A Real Time Garbage Collector That Can Recover Temporary Storage Quickly*. LCS Technical Report 184, MIT, 1980.

[Mos70] Joel Moses. *The Function of Function in Lisp*. AI Memo 199, MIT, 1970.

[MW88] David Maier and David S. Warren. *Computing with Logic—Logical Programming with Prolog*. Benjamin Cummings Publishing, Menlo Park, California, 1988.

[Pit83] Kent Pitman. *The Revised Maclisp Manual—Saturday Evening Edition*. LCS Technical Report 295, MIT, 1983.

[RC86] Jonathan Rees and William Clinger. *Revised, Revised, Revised Report on the Algorithmic Language Scheme*. SIGPLAN Notices 21(12), New Haven, Connecticut, 1986.

[Ric83] Elaine Rich. *Artificial Intelligence*. McGraw-Hill Book Company, New York, 1983.

[Sed88] Robert Sedgewick. *Algorithms*. Addison-Wesley Publishing Company, Reading, Massachusetts, 1988.

[ASI85] Adobe Systems Incorporated. *PostScript Language Reference Manual*. Reading, Massachusetts, 1985.

[SS76a] Guy L. Steele and Gerald Sussman. *Lambda: The Ultimate Declarative*. AI Memo 379, MIT, 1976.

[SS76b] Guy L. Steele and Gerald Sussman. *Lambda: The Ultimate Imperative*. AI Memo 353, MIT, 1976.

[SS83] Leon Sterling and Ehud Shapiro. *The Art of Prolog*. MIT Press, Cambridge, Massachusetts, 1983.

[Sta81] Richard M. Stallman. *EMACS: The Extensible, Customizable Self-documenting Display Editor*. AI Memo 519A, MIT, 1981.

[Sta87] Richard M. Stallman. *The Gnuemacs Manual*. Free Software Foundation, Cambridge, Massachusetts, 1987.

[Ste77a] Guy L. Steele, Jr. *Data Representations in PDP-10 Maclisp*. AI Memo 420, MIT, 1977.

[Ste77b] Guy L. Steele, Jr. *Fast Arithmetic in Maclisp*. AI Memo 421, MIT, 1977.

[Ste78a] Guy L. Steele, Jr. *The Art of the Interpreter or, The Modularity Complex (Parts Zero, One, and Two)*. AI Memo 453, MIT, 1978.

[Ste78b] Guy L. Steele, Jr. *Rabbit: A Compiler for Scheme*. AI Memo 474, MIT, 1978.

[Ste84] Guy L. Steele, Jr. *Common Lisp the Language*. Digital Press, Bedford, Massachusetts, 1984.

[Tei78] Warren Teitelman. *INTERLISP Reference Manual*. Xerox Corporation, 1978.

[YH85] Taiichi Yuasa and Masami Hagiya. *Kyoto Common Lisp Report*. Kyoto University, Japan, 1985.

[Zab87] Ramin Zabih. Non-deterministic Lisp with dependency-directed backtracking. In *Proceedings of AAAI*, 1987.

INDEX

#', 111, 130, 131, 136, 361
#(...), 191
#2A(, 191
#:, 173
#<, 132
#<*useful-information*>, 132, 191
#S, 81
#nA(...), 191

:, 373
*, 10–14
', 17, 111, 130, 136
`, 106, 107
`,`X, 180
`,`MOVE, 180
,, 168, 179, 180
,., 168
,@, 168

-, 12–13, 362
->, 15
-AUX, 50
-P, 25, 81

+, 4, 12
/, 73
+/2, 357
*/2, 264–275

<, 24
<-, 79
<=, 24
=, 24, 25, 362, 363
>, 24, 31, 136
>=, 24
1+, 12
1-, 12, 362, 363

:A (debugger abort), 15
a-list, 67
Accessing
   functions, 18, 70, 76
   symbols from packages, 374
ACONS (*cl function*), 89
ADD, 48, 50, 51, 110, 358, 367
ADD-ASSERTION, 293
ADD-ASSERTIONS, 293
ADD-METHOD, 274
ADD-NEGATIVE, 48
ADD-POINTS, 78
ADD-POSITIVE, 48, 51
ADD-TABLE-VALUE, 216, 217
ADD-TIMES, 163
ADD1, 326, 327
Address (of memory), 84, 92
Adjacent state, 223
ADJACENT-BOARDS, 234
:ADJUSTABLE
  argument to MAKE-ARRAY, 197
ADJUST-ARRAY (*cl function*), 198
AIR-FILTER, 221

383

384 INDEX

`ALL-DONE`, 160
`*ALL-GENERIC-FUNCTIONS*`, 274
Alpha conversion, 299, 353
Alpha-beta cutoff in a search, 240
`ALTER-COPY`, 179
`ALTER-COPY-CYLINDER`, 175, 177, 178
`ALTER-DEFSTRUCT`, 179
`AND` (cl macro), 62, 63, 64, 112, 175, 261
Anonymous function, 124
`APPEND` (cl function), 39–42
`APPLE`, 173, 174
`APPLY` (cl function), 119, 120, 184, 314
`APPLY-METHOD`, 272
Areas (of storage), 331
`AREF` (cl function), 186, 187, 189, 190, 199, 366
`ARG-LIST`, 274, 275
`ARG1`, 110, 111
`ARG2`, 110, 111
Argument list of a function, 27
Arguments to a function, 10
Array
  adjustment, 197–198
  displacement, 194
  row-major order, 192
`ARRAY` (cl type specifier), 262, 263
`ARRAY-APPEND`, 189
`ARRAY-DIMENSION` (cl function), 194
`ASH` (cl function), 211
`ASSOC` (cl function), 67, 70, 112, 158, 214, 316, 335
Association list, 67
Asynchronous interrupt, 376
`ATOM` (cl function), 61, 257
`ATOMP`, 61
Automatic storage allocation, 3
Auxiliary function, 50

`:B` (debugger backtrace), 79
Backquote, 106
Backtrace, 79
Backtracking search, 242, 248, 294, 296
`BASE`, 138
`:BASE` (cl keyword), argument to `WRITE`, 138
Base case in recursion, 35
`BEAVER`, 68
`BEGIN`, 96
Beta conversion, 352
Beta substitution, 352
`BIGNUM`, 367
`BILL`, 307

Binding
  deep, 335
  shallow, 334
  stack, 335
  a variable, 28
`BINDINGS`, 70, 291, 301
`BINDING-VALUE`, 70
`BIT` (cl type specifier), 199
bit-arrays, 189
`BLOCK` (cl special form), 154–159, 170, 320–321, 322–323, 350
`BLUE`, 16
`*BOARD-WIDTH*`, 228
Body
  of a function, 28
  of a rule, 293
Box and pointer notation, 86
Boxing data, 357
`BQ-LIST`, 107
`BRANCH`, 133, 253
`BRANCH-IF-NOT-=`, 363
`BREAK`, 143
`BRIAN`, 295, 296
broken computation, 15
`BUCKETS`, 216
`BYTE` (cl function), 211
byte
  codes, 359
  specifier, 211

`:C` (continue from debugger), 15
`CADDR` (cl function), 20
`CADR` (cl function), 89
`CALL`, 349
`CALL-ARGUMENTS-LIMIT` (cl constant), 13
`CALL-CC`, 322, 323
`CALL-WITH-CURRENT-CONTINUATION`, 322
Caller saves convention, 363
Calling a function, 10
`CAR` (cl function), 17–21
car pointer, 86
`CASE` (cl macro), 104, 105, 108, 171, 172, 174, 264
`CASTOR`, 131, 132, 133
`CATCH` (cl special form), 159, 160, 161, 314, 324
Catch tag, 160
`CDR` (cl function), 18–21
cdr pointer, 86
Cdr-coding, 185
Character macros in the Lisp reader, 208
`CHAR-CODE` (cl function), 198

Children in a tree, 221
CIRCULARIZE!, 98
Classes in object-oriented programming, 277
CLASSIFY-CYLINDER, 30, 31, 32, 33
Clause indexing of a database, 309
Cleanup forms in **UNWIND-PROTECT**, 207
CLEAR-DB, 292
CLOSE (*cl function*), 204
Closed hashing, 214
:CODE, 358
Code stream, 360
CODE-CHAR (*cl function*), 199
COERCE (*cl function*), 260
COLLECT-LAMBDA-LIST-AND-TYPES, 275
Collision while hashing, 214
COLOR, 123, 175
Column-major order of array storage, 192
Comment, 11
COMMON (*cl type specifier*), 256-257
Common subexpression elimination, 356
COMMON-TAIL, 43
Compacting garbage collector, 340
COMPARE, 363
COMPILATION-SPEED (*cl declaration*), 368
COMPILE (*cl function*), 325–326
COMPILE-FILE (*cl function*), 46, 326
Compiler, 10, 99
Compile time, 184
COMPLETELY, 79
Computed function call, 111
CONCATENATE (*cl function*), 176, 201
COND (*cl macro*), 49, 50, 63, 69, 104, 166, 171, 172, 173
CONS (*cl function*), 18, 37, 76, 86
Cons cell, 86
CONS-X, 180
CONSEQUENT, 165
CONSEQUENT-1, 105
Constant folding, 104, 356
:CONSTRUCTOR (*cl keyword*), argument to **DEFSTRUCT**, 216
Constructor function, 18, 76
CONSUME, 92
CONT, 319–320
CONT-1, 364
Contagion of data types, 260
CONTINUATION, 298, 299
Continuation
  function, 298, 299
  passing style, 318
CONTINUATION, 323
Continue (from debugger), 15
CONTINUE-SEARCH, 299

CONTRIVED-SCOPE-EXAMPLE, 125
Copy space (in garbage collection), 335
COPY-CYLINDER, 81, 175
COPY-FRONTIER, 339
COPY-FUNCTION-NAME, 180
COPY-LIST (*cl function*), 81
COPY-TREE (*cl function*), 65
COUNT-OCCURRENCES, 43, 198
CPS, 322, 356, 360
  See also continuation
CPS-*, 320, 321
CPS-<, 321
CPS-=, 319
CPS-FACT, 319, 320, 321, 354
CPS-PRINT, 321
CPS-TWISTY, 321
CUBE-VOLUME, 28
Current continuation, 323
CURSOR, 279
Cut, 309
Cycle, 243
CYLINDER, 76, 80, 175, 261
CYLINDER-COLOR, 76, 81
CYLINDER-HEIGHT, 76, 81, 83
CYLINDER-P, 81, 82, 261
CYLINDER-RADIUS, 79, 81
CYLINDER-VOLUME, 28, 32, 33, 75, 77, 78, 80, 269
CLINDERP, 76, 80

DATA, 70, 124
Data
  boxing, 357
  unboxing, 357
  type, 3
Data driven programming, 108
DATABASE, 292, 340
Datum, 67
Dead code elimination, 356
Debugging and programming environment, 4, 14–15
Declarations, 327, 362
Declarative programming, 283, 288
DECLARE (*cl special form*), 141, 365, 366
DECODE-TIME, 163
Deep binding, 335
DEF-ALTER-COPIER, 175, 177, 179, 180
Default value, 122, 216
DEFAULT-METHOD, 274
:DEFAULTS, argument to **MAKE-PATHNAME**, 209
DEFCLASS, 278
DEFCONSTANT (*cl macro*), 141

Deferring interrupts, 377
`DEFINE-PRIMITIVE`, 358
Definition of a function, 128
`DEFMACRO` (cl macro), 164, 166, 181, 263
`DEFMETHOD`, 267–271, 274–275
`DEFPARAMETER` (cl macro), 183
`DEFSETF` (cl macro), 217, 272
`DEFSTRUCT` (cl macro), 80–82, 88-89, 118
`DEFTYPE` (cl macro), 263, 267
`DEFUN` (cl macro), 27–32
`DEFVAR` (cl macro), 52, 141, 142, 183, 245
`DEHEXIFY`, 212
`DELAY-EVALUATION`, 253, 255
`DELETE-TABLE-VALUE`, 217
Dependency directed backtracking, 309
`DEPTH`, 234
Depth-first, chronologically backtracking search, 296
`DERIV`, 101–115
`DERIV-ADD`, 103
`DERIV-EXPT`, 218
`DERIV-FUNC`, 110, 111, 218, 220
`*DERIV-FUNCTIONS*`, 109, 219
`DERIV-SIN`, 108
`DESIGN-ANALYZER`, 373
`DESTINATION`, 357
Destructive operation, 90, 91
Destructively modifying a data structure, 82
Destructuring in macro definitions, 181
`DESTRUCTURING-LET`, 182, 312
Dictionaries, 213
`DIGITS`, 53
`*DIGITS*`, 52, 53, 58, 141
`:DIRECTION` (cl keyword), argument to `OPEN`, 210
`DISASSEMBLE` (cl function), 327, 369
Dispatching to a function, 48, 103
Displaced arrays, 194
`DISTANCE`, 78
`DIVIDE`, 51
`DO` (cl macro), 151–158, 169-170
Documentation string, 52
`DOLIST` (cl macro), 157, 184, 233, 252, 323
`DOSTREAM`, 252
`DOTIMES` (cl macro), 186, 367, 376
Dotted pair, 67, 86
`DOUBLE-1`, 366
`DOUBLE-2`, 367
`DOUBLE-VECTOR`, 367, 368
`DOWN`, 49
Downward
 continuation, 323
 funarg, 131
`DUMB-SQUARE`, 138
`DUMP-BINARY-IMAGE`, 140, 141

`DUMP-IMAGE`, 139, 140, 141
dvi file, 326
Dyadicizing, 265
Dynamic
 extent, 159
 scoping, 52, 140
 storage area, 331

Eager evaluation, 250
`EATS`, 307
`ECASE` (cl macro), 174–175, 264
`ED` (cl function), 46
Edges in a graph or tree, 222
`ELEMENT-21`, 187
`:ELEMENT-TYPE` (cl keyword), argument to `MAKE-ARRAY`, 210
`ELSE`, 133
`ELT` (cl function), 201
`EMPTY-STREAM-P`, 252
`END`, 96
`ENDORA`, 290, 294
`ENGINE`, 221
`ENSURE-GENERIC`, 272, 273
`ENTRY`, 109
`ENUMERATE`, 44, 230, 231
`ENV`, 205
Environment (of a function definition), 128
`EOF`, 311
Ephemeral garbage collection, 343
`EQ` (cl function), 21–23
`EQL` (cl function), 23, 56, 61
`EQUAL` (cl function), 23, 60–61
`EQUALP` (cl function), 249
`ERROR` (cl function), 80, 106, 375
Error handling, 375
`ESCAPE`, 161
Escape character, 177
`ESCAPE-IF-FIXED-POINT`, 161
`ESCAPE-IF-FIXED-POINT-ENTRY`, 158
`*ESCAPE-PROCEDURE*`, 158, 160
`ETYPECASE` (cl macro), 264
`EVAL` (cl function), 79, 100–101, 111–113, 137–138, 310–313
`EVAL-APPLICATION`, 311, 317
`EVAL-DEFUN`, 313, 314
`EVAL-FUNCTION`, 313, 314, 333
`EVAL-IF`, 312
`EVAL-OVER-RANGE`, 113, 115, 153, 154
`EVAL-QUOTE`, 312
`EVAL-SETQ`, 312
`EVALUATE-AT-POINT`, 113, 114
`EVALUATED`, 63
Evaluation, 9, 79
`EXIT`, 314

EXIT-DO, 156
EXPONENT, 52
EXPORT (*cl function*), 373
Exporting a symbol from a package, 373
EXPR, 102, 103, 104, 109, 113, 114, 153
Expression, 9
EXPT (*cl function*), 12, 79, 80, 114
EXPT-ITERATE, 127, 130
EXTEND-ENV, 316
EXTEND-TREE, 240
Extent of an object's lifetime, 159
External symbol in a package, 373
EXTRACT-FIELDS, 212

FACT, 34–35, 45, 319, 354, 360, 361–364, 371
FACT6, 361, 363, 364
FAIL, 66, 68, 69, 290, 292
:FAIL, 248, 249
False, 22
fasl file, 326
FBOUNDP (*cl function*), 273
File, 202
:FILL-POINTER (*cl keyword*), argument to **MAKE-ARRAY**, 195
FIND (*cl function*), 19, 120, 196
FIND-FIXED-POINT, 156, 157, 158, 159
FIRST (*cl function*), 169
First class object, 130
Fixed points, 154
FIXNUM (*cl type specifier*), 259, 263, 267, 328–329, 357, 362, 364
FIXNUM-*, 263
FLAG, 63
FLAT-MATRIX, 191, 195
FLATTEN, 66, 472
FLET (*cl special form*), 134, 135, 136, 137, 183, 317
FLET-RECURSIVE, 135
Flipping during garbage collection, 338
FLOAT (*cl type specifier*), 260, 264, 267
FLOAT-FLOAT-*/2, 267
Font, 199
FOO, 351
FOOBAR, 30
FOR, 143
Forcing evaluation, 133, 255
FORCE-EVALUATION, 255
Foreign function, 375
FORM, 9, 311, 312
FORM-A, 180
FORM-B, 180
Formal parameter of a function, 27

FORMAT (*cl function*), 106, 210, 248, 376
Format
  string, 106
  directives, 106
Forwarding pointer, 339
Frame walking during debugging, 149
Free list, 92, 344
Free variable, 127
FREE-CONS, 92
FREE-LIST, 344
FRESH-TABLE, 216
FRONTIER, 336, 339
Frontier of a heap, 336
FRONTIER-LIMIT, 336, 338
FTYPE (*cl declaration*), 370
funarg problem, 129
FUNC, 117, 119, 120, 128, 264
FUNC/N, 264
FUNCALL (*cl function*), 108–111, 117–119, 128, 133, 184
FUNCTION (*cl special form*), 111, 124, 125, 127, 130, 131, 136, 313, 314, 370
Function, 3, 10
  auxiliary, 50
  computed call, 111
  constructor, 76
  continuation, 298, 318
  foreign, 375
  generic, 3, 263
  hashing, 214
  helping, 50
  namespace, 110
  lexical closure, 129
  overloading, 263
  sequence, 96, 198

Game tree, 221
Garbage collection, 93, 335
  compacting, 340
  ephemeral, 342
  incremental, 341
  generation-scavenging, 342
  mark and sweep, 344
  new space, 335
  old space, 338
  reference counting, 346
  root set, 338
  semi-space, 335
  stop-and-copy, 335
GC. *See* Garbage collection
GCD (*cl function*), 59
Generalized variables, 91
Generation scavenging garbage collection, 342
Generic functions, 3, 263

GENERIC-FUNCTION-METHODS, 271
GENERIC-FUNCTION-P, 274
GENSYM (*cl function*), 173, 177, 351
GET (*cl function*), 219
GETHASH (*cl function*), 214
GET-TABLE-VALUE, 216
giant-ints, 52, 268
GLOBAL-COUNTER, 54
GM, 294
GO (*cl special form*), 170, 317, 322, 323, 351
GOAL, 301
Goal
   query in Prolog, 284
   state of a search, 242
GOALS, 298
GOAL-STATE-P, 246
goto, 170
GRANDMOTHER, 294
GRAPHIC-WINDOW, 280
GRAVITATIONAL-CONSTANT, 14, 15
GREEN, 16, 311
GROW-TREE, 234, 240
GUMBY, 311

HANDLER, 271
Hashing
   closed, 214
   collision, 214
   function, 214
   open, 214
   table, 213
HASH-TABLE, 269
HEAD, 41, 95
Head of a rule, 293
Header of an object, 329
Heap, 331
HEAP-ALLOCATE, 338
HEIGHT, 28, 29, 83, 123
Helping function, 50
Heuristics, 223
HEXIFY, 209, 210, 212
HIGH, 113, 153
Horn clauses in logic programming, 285
HUMAN-MOVE, 237
HUMUNGOUS, 30, 31
HUNT, 86, 90

IDENTITY (*cl function*), 318
IF (*cl special form*), 30–31, 49, 61–64
IGNORE (*cl declaration*), 95, 96

Imperative programs, 281, 288
Implicit **PROGN**, 96
IN-PACKAGE (*cl function*), 373
:INCLUDE (*cl keyword*), argument to **DEFSTRUCT**, 276
Incremental garbage collection, 341
Indefinite extent, 159
Index, 186
Indicator in a property list, 218
Inference in logic programming, 286, 297
Infinite
   list, 98, 332
   recursion, 35
INFINITE-ZEROS, 332
infix notation, 73
INFIX->PREFIX, 73, 198
Inheritance
   in structures, 276
   multiple, 279
   single, 277
INIT-DB, 283, 293
:INITIAL-ELEMENT (*cl keyword*), argument to **MAKE-ARRAY**, 186
Initial state of a search, 242
INLINE (*cl declaration*), 370
INNER, 353
INNER-FUNC, 160
INPUT, 208
:INPUT (*cl keyword*), possible value for the **:DIRECTION** argument to **OPEN**, 210
INPUT-NAME, 209
INSPECT (*cl function*), 378
INTEGER (*cl type specifier*), 259, 262, 276
INTEGERP (*cl function*), 258
INTERN (*cl function*), 176, 177, 373
Internal symbol, 373
Interpreter for Lisp, 9, 310
INTERSECTION (*cl function*), 74
Interrupts
   asynchronous, 376
   deferral, 377
   synchronous, 377
Invalidating a memory space, 341
ITERATE, 169, 182, 184, 232, 233, 245, 252
ITERATION-LABEL, 184
Iteration, 146. *See also* tail-recursion

JETHRO, 296
JOHN, 307
JUMP, 355
JUMP-TO-SUBROUTINE, 355
JUST-A-JUMP-TO-THE-LEFT, 13

INDEX **389**

&KEY (*cl lambda-list keyword*), 122
Key
   in an a-list, 67
   in a CASE form, 104, 105
   in a hash table, 216
   in a property list, 218
KEY-ITERATE, 182, 183
Key list, 105
KEY-LIST-1, 105
KEY-LIST-2, 105
KEY-LIST-ITERATE, 184
Key object, 105
Keyword arguments, 81, 123
Kleene closures in patterns, 70

LABEL, 183
LABELS (*cl special form*), 134–135, 151, 154, 169, 170, 184, 317, 322, 349–350
LAMBDA, 124, 167, 274, 349, 361
LAMBDA-LIST, 275
Lambda-list keyword, 119
Lap code, 358
LAST-NAME, 5
Lazy streams, 252
LAZY-PAIR, 254
LAZY-STREAM, 254, 255
LDB (*cl function*), 211, 212
Leaf in a tree, 222
Left recursion in a rule, 307
LEGAL-MOVE-P, 246
LENGTH (*cl function*), 36, 37, 41, 43, 150, 197, 308, 309
LET (*cl special form*), 53–55, 96, 114, 125–126
LET* (*cl special form*), 55
LET-RECURSIVE, 137
LEVEL, 300
Lexical
   block, 125
   closure, 129
   contour, 125
   environment, 310
   scoping, 125
Lifetime of an object, 159, 342
Linked lists, 87
LISP->CPS, 324
LIST (*cl function*), 42, 76, 101
List surgery, 91
LIST-IF-GREATER-THAN-0, 124
LIST-ROTATE, 74, 198
LISTP (*cl function*), 258
LOAD (*cl function*), 45, 46, 379
Local state in a lexical closure, 131

LOGAND (*cl function*), 211
Logic programming
   backtracking, 293
   inference, 286, 297
   left recursion, 306–307
   rule, 285
   unification, 289
LOOK-AHEAD, 228
LOOKUP-DERIV-FUNC, 109, 110, 111, 112, 131, 219
LOOKUP-DERIV-FUNCTION, 109
LOOKUP-FUNCTION-VALUE, 314
LOOKUP-METHOD, 272
LOOKUP-METHODS, 271
LOOKUP-VARIABLE-VALUE, 311, 316
LOOP (*cl macro*), 169, 375, 376
LOOP-LABEL, 350, 351
LOOP-LABEL-987, 351
LOW, 113, 153
Low tag, 329

McCarthy, John, 6, 99
MACROEXPAND (*cl function*), 165, 166, 167, 172
MACROEXPAND-1 (*cl function*), 172, 178
MACROLET (*cl special form*), 182, 183, 184
Macros, 99, 108, 158, 164
MADAM, 72
MAIN, 125, 127
MAKE, 379
MAKE-ADJACENT-STATE-STREAM, 248, 250, 251, 255
MAKE-ARRAY (*cl function*), 186, 189, 190, 195, 197
MAKE-CYLINDER, 76, 81, 122
MAKE-HASH-TABLE (*cl function*), 214
MAKE-INITIAL-STATE, 246
MAKE-MOVE, 235
MAKE-PAIR, 88, 131, 132, 133
MAKE-PATHNAME (*cl function*), 209
MAKE-STREAM, 254
MAKE-TABLE, 216
MAPCAN (*cl function*), 117, 118, 121
MAPCAR (*cl function*), 117, 118, 119, 124, 167, 168, 230, 231, 236
Mark and sweep garbage collection, 344
MARKED, 187, 188, 189
Marked registers, 338
MATCH, 66, 67, 68, 69, 70
MATH, 373, 374
MATH:MATRIX-MULTIPLY, 373
Matrix, 189
MATRIX, 263

MATRIX-ADD, 194
MATRIX-MULTIPLY, 193, 267, 369, 371, 373, 376
MAX (cl function), 65, 235
MAX-PLAYER, 228
Maximizing player, 224
MAXIMUM-HEIGHT, 65
MAYBE-EXTEND-BINDINGS, 69, 291
MEMBER (cl function), 55, 56, 63, 112, 121, 288
Memoizer, 255
Memory
  address, 84, 91, 92
  storage area, 331
MERGE-LISTS, 198
MERGE-VECTORS, 198
Message passing, 269–270
Meta-level programming, 309
METHOD, 271
MIN (cl function), 236
MIN-PLAYER, 228
MINIMAX, 235, 240
Minimax search, 221, 224
Minimizing player, 224
MOD (cl function), 215, 216
MOST-POSITIVE-FIXNUM (cl constant), 367
MOTHER, 294
MOTORCYCLE, 221, 222
MOVE, 278, 342, 358
MR-TOAD, 256
Multiple inheritance, 279
Multiple values, 161
MULTIPLE-VALUE-BIND (cl macro), 162
MULTIPLE-VALUE-PROG1 (cl macro), 207
MULTIPLICAND, 51
Multiprocessing, 377
:MUST-CONSTRAINTS, 358
Mutator process, 342

:N (next frame in debugger), 149
N-ARY, 118
N-STREAM, 251, 252, 254
NAME, 183
NAMES->SYMBOL, 176, 177
Namespaces
  function vs. value, 110
  single, 351
Native machine code, 359
NCONC (cl function), 98, 117, 168
Nested backquotes, 179

New space in garbage collection, 335
NEW-FRONTIER, 336
NEW-$X, 90
NEXT-DIGIT, 57
NEXT-STATE, 249
Nibble, 211
NIL (cl constant), 22, 251
Nodes in a tree, 221, 348
NOT (cl function), 64, 65, 261
Notation
  infix, 73
  postfix, 73
  prefix, 73
NOTINLINE (cl declaration), 370
Noun phrase, 305
NREVERSE (cl function), 92, 93, 95, 154, 188, 200
NSUBST (cl function), 98
NULL (cl function), 39, 65, 252
Null lexical environment, 137
NUMBER (cl type specifier), 259, 276
NUMBER-OF-ARGUMENTS, 218
NUMBERP (cl function), 25

Object, 21, 269
  header, 329
  reference, 21
Object-oriented programming, 3, 108
  class, 277
  generic functions, 268
  message-passing, 270
  method, 266
  multiple inheritance, 279
  single-inheritance, 277
Occurs check during unification, 292
OK, 156
OLD, 145, 149, 152
Old space in garbage collection, 338
OLD-BASE, 140
OLD-L1, 95
ONCE-ONLY, 179
OPEN (cl function), 202, 208, 210
Open hashing, 214
OPERATOR, 103, 106, 109
OPPONENT, 229
OPTIMIZE (cl declaration), 368, 369
&OPTIONAL (cl lambda-list keyword), 121, 122
Optional arguments, 121
OR (cl macro), 62, 63, 64, 155, 175, 261
ORTHONORMAL-MATRIX, 263
OTHERWISE (in a CASE form), 105
OUR-, 37

OUR-APPEND, 40, 41, 119, 281
OUR-CONS, 92
OUR-COPY-TREE, 65
OUR-DO, 169
OUR-DOTIMES, 170
OUR-EQUAL-P, 61, 64, 68, 69
OUR-EVAL, 310, 311, 312, 313, 314, 315, 317, 322
OUR-FUNCALL, 119
OUR-LENGTH, 37, 38, 39, 45
OUR-LET, 167, 168, 182
OUR-MAPCAN, 121
OUR-MAPCAR, 119, 120, 127, 128, 129, 130, 147, 152
OUR-MEMBER, 56, 121
OUR-NCONC, 98
OUR-NREVERSE, 95, 96
OUR-NREVERSE-1, 96
OUR-NREVERSE-2, 95, 96
OUR-NSUBST, 98
OUR-REVERSE, 144, 145, 146
OUR-SORT, 131
OUR-SUBST, 71, 113
OUR-WHEN, 164, 165
OUR-ZERO-P, 48, 49, 52, 53, 58
OUTER, 353
OUTER-FUNC, 160
:OUTPUT, possible value for the DIRECTION argument to OPEN, 210

:P (previous frame in debugger), 150
Package, 177, 350
    accessing symbols, 373
    qualifier, 373
    package system, 373
PACKAGE (cl variable), 373, 374
PAIR, 88
PAIR-CASTOR, 88
PAIR-POLLUX, 88
PAIRLIS (cl function), 89
Palindrome, 72
PALINDROMEP, 72
Parallel processing, 378
Parent in a tree, 221
PARSE-INTEGER (cl function), 199, 200
Parsing
    a program, 348
    natural language, 302
Path through a tree, 222
Pathname, 46, 202
PATH-SO-FAR, 249
Pattern, 66, 69

Pattern variable, 66
pdlnums, 368
Peano Arithmetic, 48
PEANUTS, 307
Peephole optimization, 360
Performance monitoring, 371
Photocopying model of function calls, 32
PI (cl constant), 13, 14, 22
PLAN-PATH, 5
Ply in a game tree, 224
POINT, 78, 83, 113, 114
Pointer to a memory location, 21, 85
POLLUX, 131, 132
POP (cl macro), 72, 195, 196
Popping off of a stack, 72
POSITION (cl function), 233
POSITIVE-P, 49
POSITIVEP, 49, 50, 134
POSITIVEP-1, 49, 50, 134, 135
POSITIVEP-2, 50
POSSIBLE-TIC-TAC-TOE-WINS, 230, 231
Postfix notation, 73
POWER, 128, 130
PREDECESSOR, 48, 50, 52, 58
Predicates, 22
Prefix notation, 73
PREFIX->INFIX, 73
Prepositional phrases, 305
Primitives, 47, 358
PRINC-TO-STRING (cl function), 176
:PRINT (cl keyword), option to DEFSTRUCT, 270
PRINT (cl function), 30, 101, 138–140
PRINT-ARRAY (cl variable), 191
PRINT-BASE (cl variable), 139, 140, 141, 333
PRINT-BOARD, 237
PRINT-CIRCLE (cl variable), 98
PRINT-GENSYM (cl variable), 173
PRINT-IMAGE, 140
PRINT-LAZY-PAIR, 254
PRINT-LINE-OF-PIXELS, 139
PRINT-SEARCH-RESULT, 301
PRINT-STATE, 248, 250
PRINT-STRUCTURE, 81
Procedural
    programming, 281
    attachment, 308
PROCLAIM (cl function), 368
PRODUCE-A-SIDE-EFFECT, 30
PROG (cl macro), 170, 171, 184, 349, 350
PROG-REVERSE, 171, 322
PROGN (cl special form), 96, 97, 134, 156, 160, 162, 170, 208

Programs equal data, 3
PROLOG, 283, 299, 300, 301
[promise-to-compute-more], 254
Proper list, 87
Properly tail-recursive, 147
Property, 218
Property lists, 218
Protected form in UNWIND-PROTECT, 207
PUNY, 30, 31
PURPLE, 76
PUSH (cl macro), 72, 195, 196, 271
Pushing onto a stack, 72

QUIEF, 30
QUIT, 300, 309
QUOTE (cl special form), 14, 16, 17, 37

RADAR, 72
RADIUS, 28, 29, 123, 175
Rank, 190
RANK-BOARD, 229, 230
RANK-POSSIBLE-WIN, 230, 231, 232
RASTER-IMAGE, 280
RASTER-PRINTER, 280
RATIO-*, 263
RATIO-ADD, 59
RATIO-TIMES, 59
RATIONAL (cl type specifier), 259
READ (cl function), 203, 205, 208, 210, 237, 348
Read time, 350, 373
READ-BYTE (cl function), 210
READ-CHAR (cl function), 203, 204
Read-eval-print loop, 10
READ-INDEX-DATA, 205
READ-INDEX-ENTRIES, 204, 205, 206, 207, 208
READ-INDEX-ENTRY, 206
READ-LINE (cl function), 203, 204
Read-only memory space, 331
Readtables, 88
record, 80. *See also* STRUCTURE
RECTANGULAR->POLAR, 161
RECTANGULAR-WINDOW, 277
RECTANGULAR-WINDOW-X-POS, 277
Recursion, 3
　base case, 35
　recursive case, 35
　tail-recursion, 147
RECURSIVE-P (argument to READ), 205
RED, 16

REFERENCE, 349
Reference
　counting, 346
　to a parameter, 29
REGISTERS, 71
Rehash, 214
REHASH-PERCENTAGE, 217
RENAME-TERM, 299, 300
REPL, 314
Representation analysis, 357
RESLT, 149
Resolution, 305
Resource allocation, 372
&REST (cl lambda-list keyword), 118, 119, 122, 156, 168, 182, 371, 372
REST (cl function), 19, 95, 120, 155, 169, 184, 254, 255
REST-DB, 299
RESULT, 145, 152, 153, 154
RETURN (cl macro), 156, 158
Return address, 355
RETURN-FROM (cl special form), 154–156, 158–160, 207, 233, 317, 320, 321, 324
REVERSE (cl function), 39, 41, 58, 93, 135, 145, 146, 154, 188, 200, 288, 349
REWRITE, 71
Rewrite rules, 70
Root set in garbage collection, 338
Root of a tree, 222
Row-major order for array storage, 192
RPLACA (cl function), 91
RPLACD (cl function), 91
Rules in a logic program, 285
Runtime vs. read time, 373
Runtime type checking, 3

SAFETY (cl declaration), 368
SAMANTHA, 289
SAME-LENGTH-P, 43
SAMPLE, 96, 97
SATISFIES (in type specifiers), 263
SBIT (cl function), 189
SCAN-NEXT, 339
Scanning during garbage collection, 339
SCHAR (cl function), 199, 357
Scope of variable references, 159
Search
　backtracking, 242, 249, 294, 296
　dependency directed backtracking, 309
　depth-first, chronological backtracking, 296
　initial state, 242
　goal state, 242
　space, 241

INDEX 393

SEARCH-FOR-SOLUTION, 248, 249, 250, 252, 255
SEAT, 221, 222
SECOND (cl function), 67, 312
Secondary tag, 329
SELECT, 172, 173, 174, 228
SELECTOR, 132, 172, 173, 174
SELF, 270
Semi-spaces in garbage collection, 335
SEND, 270
SENTENCE, 40, 41
SEPARATE, 183, 184
Sequence, 96, 198
Sequence functions, 198, 200
SET-CASTOR, 133
SET-CYLINDER-COLOR, 78
SET-POLLUX, 133
SET-VARIABLE-VALUE, 316
SETF (cl macro), 15–17, 43, 51, 52, 82, 83, 90–96
SETQ (cl special form), 312, 349
Sets of objects, 73
Setting function, 82, 344
Shadowed symbol, 126, 173
Shallow binding, 333
Short circuiting evaluation, 63
Side-effect, 30, 95
SIDE-EFFECTY, 54
SIEVE, 188, 189, 255
Sieve of Eratosthenes, 187
SIFT, 183
SIGNED-BYTE (cl type specifier), 259
SILLY, 96
simple-string, 199
SIMPLE-STRING (cl type specifier), 328, 357
SIMPLE-STRING-P, 25
SIMPLE-VECTOR (cl type specifier), 186
SIMPLIFY, 104, 106, 112
SIMPLIFY-RATIO, 58
SIN (cl function), 108
Single namespace, 351
SINGLE-FLOAT (cl type specifier), 367
Single-inheritance, 277
SINGLE-LIST-MAPCAN, 118
SINGLE-LIST-MAPCAR, 117, 120
:SIZE (cl keyword), argument to MAKE-HASH-TABLE, 214
SIZE, 183, 216
SIZE-TABLE, 183
Slots in a structure, 81
SNARK, 5, 21
SOLUTION-STREAM, 297, 299, 300
SOLVE, 243, 245, 249, 255, 297, 298, 299, 309

SOME (cl function), 120, 121
SOME-NULL-ELEMENT-P, 120, 121
SORT (cl function), 131, 136, 365
SOURCE, 357
SPACE, 368
Spaces in memory, 331
SPARK-PLUGS, 222
SPECIAL (cl declaration), 371
Special
 bindings, 140
 form, 14
 variable, 140, 245
SPEED (cl declaration), 368
Splicing lists, 167
Spy point in Prolog, 309
SQUARE, 116, 124, 179
SQUARE-ITERATE, 116, 117, 127
SQUARE-MATRIX, 263
SQUARES, 227
Stack
 allocation of objects, 372
 for bindings, 335
 for function calls, 332
 groups, 377
 as a list, 71
 overflow, 38
STACK, 196, 197
STANDARD-INPUT (cl variable), 202, 203
STANDARD-OUTPUT (cl variable), 202
State (in a search), 241
Static space in memory, 332
STEP (cl function), 43
Stop and copy garbage collection, 335
Storage area in memory, 331
STREAM (cl type specifier), 269
Stream, 106, 202, 250
STREAM-REST, 254, 282
String, 46
String character, 199
STRING-CHAR (cl type specifier), 198, 210
STRING->INTEGER, 200
Struct, 80. See also STRUCTURE
STRUCTURE (cl type specifier), 261, 276
SUBST (cl function), 71, 98, 113, 114
Substitution model of function calling, 29
SUBTRACT, 50, 364
Subtrees, 222
Subtype, 256
SUBTYPEP (cl function), 259
SUCCESSOR, 48, 50, 51, 52, 55, 56, 57, 58
SUCCESSOR-1, 57
SUMMING, 376
Supertype, 256
SVREF (cl function), 187

394 INDEX

`SXHASH` (*cl function*), 214, 215, 216
`SYMBOL-FUNCTION` (*cl function*), 333
`SYMBOL-NAME` (*cl function*), 333
`SYMBOL-PACKAGE` (*cl function*), 333
`SYMBOL-PLIST` (*cl function*), 218, 333
`SYMBOL-VALUE` (*cl function*), 141, 149, 150, 333, 335
Synchronous interrupt, 377
Syntactic sugar, 143, 158
System building, 379

`T` (*cl constant*), 22–25
`TABATHA`, 295
`TABLE`, 216, 217
Table, 213
Tag bits, 329
Tag in a `TAGBODY`, 170
`TAGBODY` (*cl special form*), 170, 323, 350, 351
`TAIL`, 41, 95
Tail call, 146
`TAIL-FACT`, 147, 152
`TAIL-LENGTH`, 151, 152
Tail-recursion removal, 147
`TAIL-REVERSE`, 145, 150, 151, 171, 322
`TAIL-REVERSE-1`, 145, 146, 147, 148, 149, 151, 152
`TEMP`, 356
`TEMP-2`, 354
`TEMP-3`, 354
Template, 106
`TENTH` (*cl function*), 20
`TERM`, 300
Term in a pattern, 289
`TERM-2`, 291
Terminal node in a game tree, 222
`TERMINAL-BOARD-P`, 232, 233
`*TERMINAL-IO*` (*cl variable*), 202
`TERMINATION-LIST`, 181
`TEST`, 122, 165
`:TEST` (*cl keyword*), argument to list and sequence functions, 112, 119, 214
`TEST-TRUE?`, 319
`TEXT-WINDOW`, 277
`TEXT-WINDOW-X-POS`, 277
`THE` (*cl special form*), 367
`THIRD` (*cl function*), 20, 312
Threads, 377
`THROW` (*cl special form*), 159, 160, 161, 207, 324
Throw tag, 160
Thunk, 253
`:TIE`, 233

Time
  compile, 365
  read, 350, 373
  run, 365
  video, 269
`TIMES`, 50, 51
`TIMES-POSITIVE`, 51
`TRACE` (*cl macro*), 31–33
`TRANSPOSE`, 194
trees, 221
true, 22
`TTT`, 236
`TWISTY`, 321
`TYPE`, 205
`:TYPE`
  argument to `MAKE-PATHNAME`, 209
  argument to `DEFSTRUCT`, 370
`TYPE-CONSTRAINTS`, 271
`:TYPE-CONSTRAINTS`, 358
`TYPECASE` (*cl macro*), 264, 266, 267
`TYPEP` (*cl function*), 258, 259, 260, 261
`TYPES`, 275

`UNAPPEND`, 281, 282, 288
Unboxing data, 357
Unifier, 289
  occurs check, 292
`UNIFY`, 289, 290, 291, 292
Uninterned symbol, 177
`UNION` (*cl function*), 74
`UNLESS` (*cl macro*), 166
`UNMARKED`, 187, 188, 189, 338
`UNTRACE` (*cl macro*), 32
`UNWIND-PROTECT` (*cl special form*), 206, 207, 208, 324, 334
`UP`, 49
Updating function, 78, 82
Upward
  continuation, 323
  funarg, 131
`USE-PACKAGE` (*cl function*), 373

`VALUE-COUNT`, 216
`VALUES` (*cl function*), 161, 162
Values of a function
  single, 21, 95
  multiple, 161–163
`VAR`, 70, 102, 103, 110, 111, 113, 153
`VARIABLE`, 291
`VARIABLEP`, 70
`VARIABLE-VALUE`, 291
`VECTOR` (*cl function*), 187

VECTOR-POP (*cl function*), 196
VECTOR-PUSH (*cl function*), 196, 197
VECTOR-PUSH-EXTEND (*cl function*), 197
VECTOR-REVERSE, 198
VECTOR-ROTATE, 198
Vectors, 186
VERB, 40
Verb phrase, 305
Video times, 269
Virtual machine, 359
VOLUME, 269

WALLY, 68
WARD, 66
WHEELS, 221
WHEN (*cl macro*), 157, 164, 166
WHILE, 143
Whitespace, 10
WINDOW, 277
WINDOW-X-POS, 277

WINNING-BOARD-P, 233
WINNING-SCORE, 232
:WISH-CONSTRAINTS, 358
WITH-OPEN-FILE (*cl macro*), 208, 210
WRITE (*cl function*), 138, 139, 140
WRITE-BYTE (*cl function*), 210
WRITE-BYTE-IN-HEX, 210, 212
WRITE-CHAR (*cl function*), 211, 212
WRITE-NIBBLE-IN-HEX, 212
WRITE-STRING (*cl function*), 212

X, 48, 55
X-POS, 277

YOW, 321

ZERBINA, 142
ZERO, 48, 52
ZEROP, 24, 25